An Integrated Psychological and Philosophical Approach to Justice

Front Cover: King Hammurabi receiving laws from a God.
By the Author based on 18th Century B.C. stele.

AN INTEGRATED PSYCHOLOGICAL AND PHILOSOPHICAL APPROACH TO JUSTICE
Equity and Desert

Graham F. Wagstaff

Problems in Contemporary Philosophy
Volume 50

The Edwin Mellen Press
Lewiston•Queenston•Lampeter

Library of Congress Cataloging-in-Publication Data

Wagstaff, Graham F., 1948-
   An integrated psychological and philosophical approach to justice : equity and desert / Graham F. Wagstaff.
      p. cm. -- (Problems in contemporary philosophy ; v. 50)
   Includes bibliographical references and indexes.
   ISBN 0-7734-7406-4
   1. Justice (Philosophy) 2. Justice (Philosophy)--Psychological aspects. 3. Equity--Psychological aspects. 4. Merit (Ethics)--Psychological aspects. I. Title. II. Series.

B105.J87 W34 2001
172'.2--dc21

00-054616

A CIP catalog record for this book is available from the British Library.

Copyright © 2001 Graham F. Wagstaff

All rights reserved. For information contact

   The Edwin Mellen Press   The Edwin Mellen Press
   Box 450   Box 67
   Lewiston, New York   Queenston, Ontario
   USA 14092-0450   CANADA L0S 1L0

The Edwin Mellen Press, Ltd.
Lampeter, Ceredigion, Wales
UNITED KINGDOM SA48 8LT

Printed in the United States of America

To Jo and Ellen

CONTENTS

Foreword	ix
Preface By Professor Elaine Hatfield	xiii
Acknowledgements	xvii

Part 1: The problem

Chapter 1: Defining justice	3

Part 2: Justice in modern philosophy

Chapter 2: Liberty, rights and equality	29
Chapter 3: The problem of punishment	39
Chapter 4: Agreement, impartiality, and equal resources	47
Chapter 5: The philosophy of desert	59

Part 3: The psychology of justice

Chapter 6: The rise of equity	77
Chapter 7: Motives and multiprinciples	95
Chapter 8: Responsibility, morality and punishment	117
Chapter 9: Bargaining, just procedures, allocation preferences, and the aftermath of equity	137
Chapter 10: Interdisciplinary chaos?	153

Part 4: The origins and nature of equity and desert

Chapter 11: The historical origins of desert: Plato and the principle of geometrical equality — 163

Chapter 12: Aristotle's justice: the mathematics of desert — 185

Chapter 13: Defining perfect equity — 205

Chapter 14: 'An eye for an eye': equity, reciprocity and just punishment — 227

Chapter 15: Equity, choice and responsibility: the foundations of 'Equity as Desert' — 235

Chapter 16: Equity, equality and need — 263

Part 5: The historical development of equity and desert

Chapter 17: Stoicism, Christianity and the Scholastics — 279

Chapter 18: The Age of Enlightenment: desert, contract and rights — 299

Chapter 19: Utilitarianism, egalitarianism and communism — 327

Part 6: Towards an integrated perspective on justice

Chapter 20: The fragmentation and survival of desert — 353

Chapter 21: Modern philosophical views reconsidered — 367

Chapter 22: The psychology of justice reconsidered — 391

Chapter 23: The evolutionary origins of justice — 435

Bibliography — 459

Author index — 483

Subject index — 489

FOREWORD

Any psychologist who has attempted to study the area of justice will know that it now seems impossible to study the subject meaningfully from the perspective of any single academic discipline. However, those who attempt to venture across disciplines in this area will soon find themselves engulfed in a mass of conceptual and terminological confusion. In this book I attempt to impose some order on this confusion.

From equity to confusion

As a social psychologist, I first became interested in the psychology of justice in the late 1960's and early 1970's. At the time the area seemed to be dominated by the theory of psychological equity. In its basic form the equity principle states that relationships between people are 'just' or 'fair' when individuals who have made large contributions receive proportionately large outcomes, and those who have made small contributions receive proportionately small outcomes. The contributions can be either assets that entitle one to rewards, or liabilities that incur penalties. So for example, if you work harder than others you should receive more positive outcomes than them, and if you commit a crime, the more serious the crime, the more you should be punished. What could be simpler?

At first, some psychologists saw the equity principle as *the* basic principle of justice; a principle that governs not only economic relationships, but also social relationships. Moreover, often equity was, and still is, referred to by its proponents as a scheme of 'deserving'; thus the terms 'justice', 'fairness', and receiving what we 'deserve' were neatly encompassed by a single principle. Also popular during this period was the idea that people will often distort reality to restore 'psychological equity', or a 'just world' in which the good are rewarded and the bad punished.

However, during the 1970's an increasing number of critics expressed discontentment with the notion that equity is the most important psychological principle of justice. There were problems finding a satisfactory way of expressing the equity principle in mathematical terms. But more important perhaps, was the growing adherence to multiprinciple perspectives on justice. Many researchers argued that when individuals are placed in a position of distributing rewards or resources, there are other allocation principles they can, and sometimes do use; particularly those of equality and need.

At first, all this was very useful to me as a lecturer in social psychology; justice seemed to possess all the ingredients for an excellent study topic for students. There was a major theory (equity), a number of searching criticisms, and a series of research papers to examine critically. But as the years went by and social psychology entered the 1980's, the task of teaching justice as a topic in psychology became considerably more difficult. The literature was growing at an alarming rate and becoming more and more interdisciplinary. Many psychologists recognized that their theories looked somewhat parochial, if not naive, when compared those found in other disciplines. Consequently, psychologists began to incorporate other perspectives into their books and articles. As a result, my students and I found ourselves wading through collections of journal articles and book chapters, each ostensibly about 'justice', but covering an utterly bewildering range of topics and controversies. We were introduced to different kinds of justice: social justice, distributive justice, legal justice, commutative justice, comparative justice, non-comparative justice, economic justice, procedural justice, Darwinian justice, Marxian justice, corrective justice, remedial justice, retributive justice, macro justice, micro justice, and so on. There were references to subjects such as social contracts, natural rights, altruistic behaviour, attributions of causality and responsibility, humanitarian norms, punishment reactions, allocation preferences, economic efficiency, legal theory, income distribution, rational bargaining, game theory, impartiality, and conflict resolution, to name but a few. There was particular confusion as to what distinction, if any, should be made between justice and morality; theories of moral reasoning and development often appeared alongside, or were included as, theories of justice. We read about Kantianism and utilitarianism, encountered inconsistencies in the use of words such as 'deserving' and 'entitlement', found disagreements about the relationship between justice and fairness, and came across definitions of equity that differed from our own in psychology.

Particularly bothersome was the tendency for some writers to decorate their papers with perfunctory references to philosophers, and especially to John Rawls and Robert Nozick; two philosophers who, during the 1970's, had written highly influential books on justice. The problem was that, not only do philosophers often disagree quite radically about the nature of justice, but a preliminary reading of their major works frequently reveals little of relevance to psychological theory and research into justice. This problem was very apparent in the cases of Rawls and Nozick. Rawls' theory is primarily a hypothetical social contract theory, whereas Nozick's is primarily a theory of historical property rights, and neither hypothetical social contracts nor historical property rights have figured in most psychological accounts of justice. Also, whilst the notion of 'deserving' has played a prominent part in most psychological approaches to justice, both Rawls and Nozick appear to reject the whole concept of 'desert'. The introduction of philosophical issues into the psychological study of justice seemed only to add to the confusion.

These trends continue today, and, if anything, the situation is getting worse. In 1992 Klaus Scherer commented, 'serious integrative work on justice has barely begun' (p. 14). I am sure that most theorists and researchers in the area would still agree with this statement; though, given the present state of affairs, some might wish to question whether integrative work is even *possible*. It was against this background that I decided to write this book.

Making sense of justice

In writing this book I have two aims; the first is to overview psychological theorizing and research on justice and identify some of the philosophical issues associated with the term justice, in the hope of making these areas comprehensible to psychologists and others who are not familiar with them. To this end the first three parts of the book give an account of the main psychological and philosophical issues in the study of justice. One could perhaps accurately describe these sections as 'an overview of the chaos'. However, more important, these opening chapters act as a preamble to the final three parts of the book, in which I attempt to develop a second aim.

I want to suggest that hidden in thousands of years in philosophical, religious, and legal theorizing and practice, is a psychological core feature of justice; a principle that is, in essence, a fusion of modern equity theory with traditional historical and philosophical conceptions of desert. In the early part of the development of Western civilization, especially in ancient Greece, this core feature dominated. Since then, because of various historical developments, it has become distorted, fragmented and disguised, but it has never gone away. In fact, it permeates the everyday lives of all of us, and can be found in some form in virtually every significant theory of justice. Moreover, so deep rooted is this idea in our psychological, and probably biological make up, that it creates enormous problems for any theory of justice or economic or political system that purports to ignore or downgrade it. In fact, I would argue that the current crisis that faces research and theory into justice stems mainly from a failure to fully acknowledge the influence of this idea.

The result is a book that contains an essentially psychological account of justice, but, of necessity, also includes a large amount of philosophy, both past and present. This balance reflects my belief that, unless placed in an appropriate multidisciplinary context, no theory of justice can really make any sense.

PREFACE

One only has to focus on any real-life dispute to be reminded how daunting are the claims of 'justice' and 'desert'. In March, 2000, Pope John Paul II made a pilgrimage to Jerusalem in the hopes of promoting world peace. The Pope acknowledged that Jerusalem is 'a part of the common patrimony of Christianity, Islam and Judaism, the Holy City par excellence'. He urged that Jerusalem be designated an international Holy City[1]. It wasn't more than a few minutes before leaders in that Holy City were squabbling. In Tel Aviv, Israeli president Ezer Weizman, acting more like a politician than a statesman, greeted the Pope by insisting that Jerusalem was 'the capital state of Israel and the heart of the Jewish world'[2]. An Israeli Rabbi added: 'Jerusalem is ours ... In ancient times, God promised Abraham, Isaac, and Jacob the land of Israel. You may not like it. You may object. But it is God's will. We are the Chosen People'.

The next day, in Jerusalem, Yasser Arafat described Jerusalem as the 'Eternal Capital' but this time he was speaking of the capital of Palestine. Grand Mufti Ekrema Sabri, Jerusalem's chief Islamic cleric, added to the chorus, warning that Jerusalem is 'eternally bonded to Islam'[1]. An Arab resident of the Old City added: 'Who lived in Palestine for centuries before the arrival of the Zionists? Who paid for these stones with their tears and blood and sweat? The Arabs. Who owns the land of Palestine? It is the Palestinians'.

Within minutes after the Pope left the Al Aska Mosque, young people, frustrated at the loss of their land, began crying, 'Jews, the army of Muhammad will come back!' and started to hurl pebbles.

In this brief visit, we see all the problems that have plagued generations of philosopher's and psychologists who have attempted to understand the nature of justice and deservingness. What counts? God's promise? But who today can testify as to what it was? What sort of inheritance counts? Christians, Arabs and Jews *all* see themselves as the descendants of the patriarch Abraham, and therefore as inheritors of the Promised Land. The Christians and the Jews, or Israelites, trace themselves to Isaac, son of Abraham and his wife, Sarah. Arabs trace their lineage to Ishmael. Which lineage counts? What is the place of tradition, documents, and deeds in all this.

In this scholarly manuscript, *Making Sense of Justice*, Graham Wagstaff tackles one of life's thorniest questions: What is the nature of justice? In Parts 1-3, he reviews the attempts of distinguished philosophers and psychologists to define justice and promulgate rules for deciding what is just and what is not. This comprehensive review tells philosophers and psychologists all they need to know about the current state of theory and research. Dr Wagstaff's scholarship would have done the old Biblical/Talmudic/Qur'anic scholars proud. As the author notes: 'New principles of justice seem to spout like weeds in a garden' (Folger, Sheppard and Blair, 1995, p. 261). The advantages and problems with each of the theories are made clear. Sometimes voluminous evidence is marshalled to devastating effect; at other times all that is needed to demolish a theory is one skewering example. As an example, in Chapter 12 – 'Aristotle's Justice: The Mathematics of Desert' – Wagstaff reviews a staggering number of Aristotle's calculations. Then the author says simply: 'If virtue is it's own reward, why should we assign "goods" according to virtue? Is this not rewarding the virtuous twice?' Ah hah! We see the problem. At the end of the first section, we are left agreeing with the author that, at present, the various definitions of 'justice and desert' leave us with 'a burgeoning terminological and conceptual confusion' (p. 151).

In Parts 4 and 5, influential theories of equity and desert are reviewed. Part 4 focuses on the views of the Greek classicists: Socrates, Plato and Aristotle.

Part 5 centres on the theorizing of the Stoics, of early Christians, of Enlightenment theorists such as Hobbes and Kant, of Utilitarians theorists such as John Stuart Mill, and Karl Marx. The author concludes, on the basis of this overview, that although philosophers and theologians may have had problems defining what they meant by 'justice', nonetheless the idea of justice as desert, in the form of equity as desert, has run through all of the commentaries.

In Part 6, the final section: 'Towards an Integrated Perspective on Justice', Graham Wagstaff attempts to bring order out of chaos. One morning Oliver Wendell Holmes Jr. was climbing the marble steps of the United States Supreme Court when he met a new law clerk. 'Do justice, Judge Holmes', the newcomer called to him. 'I don't do justice', the Chief Justice replied. 'I merely apply the law'. In the final section, the author reminds us that in different historical eras, it is not just 'law' and 'justice' that have meant very different things. 'Justice' itself has been equated with a number of very different concepts: i.e., what is 'moral, virtuous, just, fair and equal, worthy, equitable and deserving'.

In a final coda, the author comes full circle. He concludes that if what the evolutionary psychologists and biologists tell us is true, then the prevailing view of justice (in the form of 'equity as deserving') does derive from an instinct for self-preservation. It is indeed a 'natural law'. Wagstaff speculates that perhaps that is why early philosophers viewed justice as 'in accordance with the will of God'. In all historical eras, in all philosophical and religious traditions, perfect justice exists 'when all receive exactly what they deserve' (p. 457). This section is exciting and most rewarding. I suspect that Dr. Wagstaff's book will reap the attention it 'deserves'. That would only be justice.

ELAINE HATFIELD *Professor of Psychology, University of Hawaii*

[1] *New York Times*, March 27, 2000, p. A.10.
[2] *New York Times*, March 23, 2000, p. A.8.

ACKNOWLEDGEMENTS

I am most grateful to all who have personally supported me in this endeavour, but my special thanks go to Jo Brunas-Wagstaff, Tim Perfect, Stephen Clark, and Anne Halliwell. Without Tim's insights and talents in mathematics, Jo's continuing advice and patience, Stephen's initial guidance with regard to the philosophical literature, and Anne's secretarial expertise, I would probably still be trying to write this book in 20 years time. I would also like to thank all those scholars and researchers whose works I have consulted and used. However, I owe a particular debt of gratitude to Elaine Hatfield. As will be evident to any psychologist reading this book, her pioneering work on equity and justice has long been an inspiration to me.

PART 1

THE PROBLEM

CHAPTER 1

DEFINING JUSTICE

Anyone attempting to identify a core feature of justice, or even provide some kind of coherent summary of the area, will want to start with a definition of the term 'justice'. However, if we briefly look at how various philosophers and behavioural scientists have tried to define justice, we will soon realize that finding a definition is no easy matter.

Justice as law

It is commonly assumed that the word 'justice' is derived, at least in part, from the Latin word '*ius*' (or '*jus*') relating to 'law'. For example, Hospers (1961) states, 'Historically, the idea of justice is closely related to that of law and legality. The word *jus* in Latin means the same as "law", and the derived word "*Justitia*" is the word for justice' (p. 416). Over one hundred years ago, John Stuart Mill came to a similar conclusion. He says, 'In most, if not in all languages, the etymology of the word which corresponds to Just, points distinctly to an origin connected with the ordinances of law .... *Justum* is a form of *jussum*, that which has been ordered' (1861/1993, p. 48).

The idea that justice simply relates to obedience to law has a long tradition. Probably the most famous proponent of this view was Thomas Hobbes, who stated categorically, 'no law can be unjust' (1651/1960, p. 227). Also, more recently, some legal positivists have argued that, considered as anything other than the maintenance of law, justice is nothing more than an irrational ideal or expression of emotion (see Bell, 1992; Bodenheimer, 1962; Kelsen, 1973). However, most modern authorities seem to think that although the term 'justice' was originally related to law, it now functions more as a moral term than a legal term (Bell, 1992; Hospers, 1961; Raphael, 1981; Sadurski, 1985). Indeed, there are a number of seemingly obvious examples of how, in modern usage, the word 'justice' is used to refer to more than the maintainance of existing law. For example, as Dworkin (1986) points out, 'Many lawyers in both Britain and the United states believe that progressive income tax is unjust .... but none of them doubts that the law of these countries does impose tax at progressive rates' (p. 36). Different nations, at different times, sometimes have radically different laws, thus if we are to question laws in the name of 'justice', we must assume a conception of justice that is independent of existing law.

However, perhaps when we equate justice with law, we do not mean law in terms of the current laws of the land, that is 'positive law', or 'civil law', but 'natural law', or 'the law of nature'. The idea that justice coincides with 'the law of nature' has been a popular idea throughout the history of philosophy (see Bell, 1992; Bodenheimer, 1962; Finnis, 1980; Flew, 1979; Weinreb, 1987). For example, St. Thomas Aquinas (13th Cent./1925) argued that any law that is unjust, unreasonable, and repugnant to the law of nature, is not a law, but a perversion of law. But what do we mean by 'natural law'? If we adopt a Christian perspective, then natural law might be deemed equivalent to 'divine law', and might include obedience to the ten commandments, and traditional Christian virtues. If we adopt a secular perspective, however, then 'natural law' could mean virtually anything depending on one's views as to how nature functions, from mercy and benevolence, to 'survival of the fittest'. History is littered with attempts by various philosophers, theologians and politicians, to argue that their particular, sometimes contradictory, notions of justice and morality coincide with what is 'natural'. Besides, according to Thomas Hobbes (1651/1960), justice is only *one* of nature's moral laws, in which case we are still left trying to define what exactly this law, or part of law, is.

Justice as fairness

If we reject the simple equation of justice with law, as many theorists do, what is the difference between 'justice' and 'injustice'? Is the distinction perhaps one between fairness and unfairness?

The term 'fairness' is often linked to justice by lay-people as well as some philosophers and behavioural scientists (see, for example, Hochschild, 1981; Homans, 1982; Lansberg, 1984; Rawls, 1972). However, to others, the terms are by no means synonymous. For example, Furby (1986) writes, 'justice refers not only to fair treatment but also to respect for the needs and rights inherent in human nature' (p. 154); also Evans (1981) argues that, 'It is a mistake to identify justice with fairness' (p. 48). Hardin (1987) suggests that although academics tend to use fairness and justice interchangeably, 'in the vernacular, we commonly speak of fairness but almost never of justice. In the world of policy we use both terms, often with clear distinctions' (p. 104). And Dworkin (1986) concludes, 'Most political philosophers - and I think most people - take the intermediate view that fairness and justice are to some degree independent of one another, so that fair institutions sometimes produce unjust decisions and unfair institutions just ones' (p. 177).

Justice as morality

Perhaps then, justice has something to do more specifically with 'moral rightness'. An act is 'just' if it corresponds to what is morally right. In as much as justice seems to be about 'oughts' and 'rights' and 'wrongs' it does seem to be within the realm of morality. However, not all principles or rules of morality obviously coincide with conceptions of justice. At various times people have argued, on moral grounds, against activities such as masturbation, suicide, eating dead relatives, poor hygiene, and taking drugs, but it is not immediately obvious whether objections to these kinds of activities have been made on grounds of injustice. Perhaps then what distinguishes moral issues in general from those of justice is whether other people are involved; that is, justice may concern, more specifically, morality in the treatment of others.

Some writers do appear to equate acting justly with acting morally towards others, and often discussions about justice seem indistinguishable from discussions of morality in general (see, for example, Bayley, 1981; Furby, 1986; Karniol and Miller, 1981; Montada, 1980; Sher, 1981). Indeed, according to Furby (1986), 'justice involves an evaluative judgement about the moral rightness of a person's fate' (p. 153), and Kohlberg (1971, 1976) argues that all sets of moral principles used by children and adults are 'justice structures'. Kohlberg says, 'the core of the specifically moral component of moral judgement is a sense of justice' (1976, p. 50); he argues that to act morally is to act justly, and to reason in accordance with justice is to display the highest level of moral reasoning.

However, others make a clear distinction between principles of justice and other moral principles in the treatment of others. Thus Sadurski (1985) argues that acts which affect others, such as deceit, obscene language, and treason, may be morally reprehensible, but he says, 'condemnation in terms of "injustice" hardly comes to mind on such occasions' (p. 12). And Lucas (1980) says, 'I can be just yet lack many moral virtues' (p. 263). One would have thought, for instance, that acts of charity, benevolence, mercy and generosity would be regarded, in particular, as moral 'goods' in the treatment of others. Yet Frankena argues that, 'Societies can be loving, efficient, prosperous, or good, as well as just, but they may be just without being notably benevolent, efficient, prosperous or good' (1962, p. 9). Campbell (1988) also argues that, 'common humanity, or even generous beneficence, may sometimes be in conflict with, and even more important than, the claims of justice' (p. 35), and Sidgwick (1874/1907) comments, 'benevolence begins where justice ends' (p. 242). Buchanan and Mathieu (1986) even suggest that someone could show callous disregard for the suffering of a poor person without necessarily being unjust. As for mercy, Bell (1992) states that 'Mercy is usually seen as corrective to law, and is not generally considered as part of justice. Not all moral virtues are covered by justice' (p. 140).

These views draw attention to what seems to be a major contemporary source of controversy in the area of justice. To some it may be laudable act to show generosity and alleviate the plight of the poor, but it is not an obligation of justice. On the other hand, to others, it may be extremely unjust to disregard the poor, because justice demands that the worst-off in society are entitled to a share of the wealth of society (for various views see, for example, Dworkin, 1978ab, 1981; Nozick, 1980; Rawls, 1972).

Perhaps then justice involves something rather more fundamental in moral reasoning, like the pre-eminence of human life. In Kohlberg's (1976) view, justice does indeed dictate, as a moral principle, that one person's right to life is more important than another's right to property. However, Posner (1981) proposes that justice does not necessarily dictate life before property; he says, 'Only a fanatic refuses to trade off lives for property' (p. 84). Nozick (1980) also argues that, 'a right to life is not a right to whatever one needs to live; other people may have rights over these other things' (p. 179).

Justice as rights

This brings us to another possible conception of justice; justice could be about 'rights' (Dworkin, 1978ab). The preservation of rights is commonly proposed as an important element of justice. To say people have a 'right' to something, is usually to mean that they are entitled to it, and no one else can claim or deny them it. Thus Hospers says, 'A right is the reverse side, as it were, of an obligation. If one person has a certain right, then another person has an obligation not to interfere with its exercise' (1961, p. 386). But how do we establish which 'rights' are appropriate? When a woman says, 'In the name of justice I demand my rights', to what rights is she entitled; the right to equal shares, the right to have her needs satisfied, the right to hang on to what she has worked for or what has been given to her, or something else? Can one have a right to murder? Can one have an 'unjust' right, and, if so, what distinguishes a 'just' from an 'unjust' right? Opinions differ widely (see, for example, Dworkin, 1978ab; Nozick, 1980; Rawls, 1972; Silver, 1981).

These issues seem problematic enough, but some have questioned the whole status of rights as a defining feature of justice. For instance, MacIntyre (1982) argues that if the concept of 'right' is so fundamental to our ideas of justice, it is odd that it 'lacks any expression in Hebrew, Greek, Latin or Arabic, classical or medieval, before about 1400, let alone in Old English, or in Japanese even as late as the mid-nineteenth century'. He says, 'the truth is plain: there are no such rights, and belief in them is one with belief in witches and unicorns' (p. 67). Also Evans (1981) argues that 'Justice is not to be identified with that which is warranted by an appeal to rights .... A person may have a right to walk along a certain street, but it is pointless to say that it is just that he may walk that street' (p. 48).

Distributive and procedural justice.
Clearly it is difficult to come up with consensus definitions of justice based on notions of law, fairness, morality and rights, so in our search for some defining feature of justice, perhaps we should look instead at the general domain of justice. That is, to which activities can the term 'justice' meaningfully be applied?

Most philosophers and behavioural scientists seem to agree that justice has something to do with rules or principles that are used to evaluate and guide human activities. Moreover, it has become popular to narrow down the focus of these rules to two major human activities. The first concerns how we 'share-out', distribute, or allot, the things in life that people positively and negatively value; that is, the benefits and burdens of life. This aspect is commonly called *distributive justice*. The second concerns more specifically how we treat people who violate the rules of society; this area is often termed *corrective justice* (see, for example, Flew, 1979; Rawls, 1972). However, these far from exhaust the different types of justice to which justice theorists make reference. For instance, sometimes all types of justice are seen to form part of a general scheme entitled *social justice*; whilst justice in economic dealings, such as in pay settlements, and exchanges of goods and services is sometimes called *commutative justice* (Fogerty, 1961; Sadurski, 1985).

The idea that justice is about allotment or distribution pervades many definitions of justice. For example, Frankena says, 'Justice whether social or not, seems to involve at its centre the notion of an allotment of something to persons - duties, goods, offices, opportunities, penalties, punishments, privileges, roles, status, and so on' (1962, p. 9). Others emphasize the notions of 'entitlement'. For example, Buchanan and Mathieu state, 'Justice is usually said to exist when a person receives that to which he or she is entitled, namely, exactly these benefits and burdens that are due the individual because of his or her particular characteristics and circumstances' (1986, p. 11). Such definitions suggest that justice is about awarding or allotting benefits and burdens that are 'due' or 'owed' to people.

Unfortunately, however, theorists do not even seem to agree as to whether or not justice is about distributing or allotting things. For example, Nozick (1980) objects to the term distributive justice. He says that in a free society we are not entitled to some central share of benefits or burdens. Rather we should be speaking of who is entitled to 'hold' something, or what belongs to whom. Thomas Hobbes was also dismissive of the term 'distributive justice'; he argues that it is improper to call the allotment of goods to people 'distributive justice'; such allotment is of relevance only to the moral principle of 'equity', not 'justice' (1651/1960). Still others question whether justice is being 'entitled' to something. For example, Evans says, 'It is a mistake to identify justice with entitlement. Often people are entitled to have something or to be something, but this may not be a matter of justice' (1981, p. 47).

The difficulties continue when we consider a further distinction that some writers have attempted to make between justice in procedures and justice in outcomes (see, for example, Buchanan and Mathieu, 1986; Lerner and Whitehead, 1980; Lind and Tyler, 1988). The area of *procedural justice* allegedly concerns the decision making procedures involved in distributing benefits and burdens, and the procedures involved in the conviction and treatment of offenders. According to Rawls (1972), 'perfect procedural justice' exists when a fair procedure produces a just outcome; however, sometimes procedures and outcomes may not coincide. In a criminal trial, for example, an innocent man could be found guilty (an unjust outcome) even though the legal procedures were followed scrupulously (he had a fair trial). Dworkin (1986), however, argues that 'Justice is a matter of outcomes', not procedures (p. 108); and Sadurski (1985) emphatically agrees with Dworkin; he states that 'Pure procedural justice is .... no principle of justice at all' (p. 50).

But even if we were to agree that justice has something to do with the rules that determine how we are to distribute benefits and burdens, which rules should we use?

Justice, equal treatment, and need

If the object of justice is to make sure that people receive the benefits and burdens that are 'due' to them, or to which they are 'entitled', is there any general or formal rule that ought to be applied?

A popular rule is that justice is simply 'equal treatment'. However, Lucas (1980) argues that justice is not equal treatment; he says, 'if a ruler were to boil his subjects in oil, jumping in afterwards himself, it would be an injustice, although there would be no inequality of treatment' (p. 172). Another possible principle is one derived from Aristotle. The principle is, 'treat equals equally, and unequals unequally'. Sometimes this principle is interpreted to mean 'treat like as like and unlike as unlike', or 'treat similar as similar, and dissimilar as dissimilar' (Buchanan and Mathieu, 1986). However, few would argue that the application of this principle alone would give rise to 'justice'. If one allowed an electoral vote only to white males over six feet tall and excluded everyone else, this would apparently obey the principle. Consequently, various qualifications have been added. For example, Frankena (1976) argues that the principle is not simply the consistent treatment of equals as equals, and unequals as unequals, or of treating like cases or persons similarly, it also assumes that the similarities and differences are 'relevant'. According to Buchanan and Mathieu (1986), the full principle is thus, 'treat equals equally and unequals unequally - in proportion to their relevant similarities and differences' (p. 17). But what should count as relevant similarities and differences in the allotment of benefits and burdens?

Western philosophers and behavioural scientists have come up with various lists of possible distributive principles that would seem to emphasize very different relevant similarities and differences. These include distribution according to merit, works, rank, historical entitlements, rights, deserts, choices, agreements, abilities, efforts, sacrifices, productive contribution, economic utility and human worth, or the quality of being human (see, for example, Deutsch, 1975; Feinberg, 1970; Irani, 1981; Lucas, 1980; Reis, 1984; Rescher, 1972; Vlastos, 1975; Walzer, 1983). Although some of these principles or criteria may appear to overlap, there is clearly a huge problem in deciding how they are to be ordered in terms of priority, and clashes between the principles seem bound to occur.

Let us suppose, for example, we were to decide that being human is all that is necessary to qualify for a share of resources. We could then argue that everyone is entitled to an equal share of benefits (and burdens) regardless of other characteristics such as sex, age, ability, hard work, authority, accomplishment and so on, because these latter characteristics are not a legitimate basis for claiming different proportions (Sampson, 1975). But according to many modern theorists, any attempt to operate this principle will inevitably conflict with human 'rights'. For example, if people have a right to property they have legitimately earned, it would be a gross infringement of that right if, in the name of equality, others were to take such property and give it to someone else. (see, for example, Levine, 1981; Machan, 1982; Miller, 1982; Nozick, 1980; Silver, 1981).

Perhaps equality might be better defined as giving people an *equal opportunity* to achieve benefits. However, it seems inevitable that some people will use their opportunities well and others will waste or squander them; some may prosper, others may lose everything. As a result, people will end up with unequal outcomes. Thus, so the argument goes, equality of opportunity will inevitably conflict with the goal of equality in benefits or outcomes (see, for example, Flew, 1982; Levin, 1981; Williams, 1975). Moreover, if we seriously want to create a situation of 'equal opportunity' we would constantly need to redistribute resources, taking them away from people who might have legitimately acquired them, to give to others who, due to their backgrounds, physical characteristics, foolhardy actions and so on, are disadvantaged in terms of opportunity. The result again, say some, would be an unacceptable interference in people's lives that conflicts with human rights (Levin, 1981; Machan, 1982; Nozick, 1980; Silver, 1981).

In any case, others have argued that justice must consider the different *needs* that people have. According to the need principle of justice, those in need, regardless of their characteristics, whether they be positive or negative, should receive sufficient resources to maintain an equal level of opportunity and lifestyle (see, for example, Schwartz, 1975; Vlastos, 1975). However, once again, some have again argued that distribution according to need must inevitably interfere with people's 'rights' to hang on to what they have legitimately acquired, and provision for need is a matter of charity not justice (see, for example, Nozick, 1980).

Comparative and non-comparative justice

This brings us to another source of disagreement in justice considerations. Are there basic minimum living standards to which any person is entitled or due, irrespective of what others receive? In other words, are there *non-comparative* or 'absolute' standards to which we can appeal when deciding whether a certain allocation or treatment is just, or is all justice *comparative*? According to some, justice can be non-comparative as well as comparative, for example, Montague (1980) states that non-comparative cases of justice are those 'in which it is possible to determine whether someone has been justly treated with no knowledge whatever of the treatment given to others' (p. 132; see also Feinberg, 1973). According to Sadurski (1985), however, there is no such thing as 'non-comparative' justice. He says, 'Most examples of what is considered to be non-comparative justice are actually cases of comparative justice, while the rest of the examples of alleged non-comparative justice do not concern justice at all' (p. 15).

Justice, desert and merit

However, even if we could iron out or minimize these difficulties there would still be the problem that the equality-needs and 'rights' approaches to justice seem to conflict with a principle of justice that assumes that human beings should be given resources on the basis of 'merit' or 'desert'. For example, Evans (1981) seems to be in no doubt; justice is not about equality, rights, or fairness, it is 'deserved treatment' (p. 45). The principle of awarding resources according to merit or desert is another commonly attributed to Aristotle (MacIntyre, 1982), but it has its own problems, not the least of which is defining what is meant by 'merit' and 'desert'. If I 'merit' something do I necessarily 'deserve' it, and am I automatically 'entitled' to it? There seems to be some disagreement as to how we should apply these terms. For instance, whereas some treat 'entitlement' and 'deserving' as synonyms (for example, Lerner, 1977; Silver, 1981), others distinguish between 'entitlement' and 'desert' (for example, Lucas, 1980; Rawls, 1972; Sadurski, 1985). Thus in support of the latter, Rawls (1972) argues that it is possible to be justly entitled to something even if one does not deserve it (see also, Nozick, 1980).

The common good

However, even more problematical is the fact that if we were able to come to some agreement on these issues, we would still have to acknowledge that there are a number of other influential conceptions of justice, both old and new, that seem to employ principles that have nothing to do with any of the principles we have discussed so far. For instance, in the 18th century, David Hume's view was that justice should consist of a set of rules, governing property, and the rules should be chosen purely on the grounds of their usefulness or *utility* for promoting the peace and security of human society (Hume, 1777/1962).

This suggests another definition of justice: namely, 'justice is that which promotes the 'common good'. But what is 'the common good'? To those philosophers known as utilitarians, the 'common good' was originally described in terms of the 'greatest happiness principle', or 'the greatest amount of happiness altogether' (see, for example, Bentham, 1789/1996; Mill, 1861/1993). But how do we define 'happiness'?

The early utilitarians attempted to define 'happiness' in terms of maximum pleasure with minimum pain, and Jeremy Bentham even invented a 'felicific calculus' to measure pleasures and pains in terms of intensity, duration and purity. However, as people can have very different needs, tastes and experiences, finding some estimate of the relative degrees of pleasure and pain that any individual experiences in a particular situation is a problem that many feel is intractable. Hence, the idea underlying the modern economic conception of utility is that, given the variability in what actually makes particular individuals happy or satisfied, the best we can do is to assume that, given the choice, people are rational maximizers of the things they prefer, and we can judge individual utilities through the way people express their preferences. In modern economics, therefore, 'utility' takes on a meaning more akin to 'what individuals tend to maximize in making choices' (Vickrey, 1973, p. 286). And, consequently, the good or goal of utilitarianism can be described as 'maximizing the sum of individual utilities' (Le Grand, 1991). But how do we measure individual preferences?

A fairly obvious possible indicator of the strength of a person's preference for something is the amount of money he or she is willing to pay for it, or the amount of money the person is willing to forego (lose in earnings) to indulge the preference (Campbell, 1988). However, how can we know the strength of a person's preference, as measured by money, unless that person has the money to express the preference? Richard Posner (1981) has invented a neat way round this problem. In his book on economic justice, he suggests that the goal of utilitarianism should be 'wealth-maximization' or 'the aggregate satisfaction of those preferences (the only ones that have weight in a system of wealth maximization) that are backed up by money' (p. 61). The problem that some people may not be able to express their preferences is then eliminated because, in Posner's view, if you have no money, say because you are old and destitute, your preferences do not count; effectively you have no preferences. To opponents of Posner, however, this idea is an ethical absurdity (see Dworkin, 1986).

However, even if we ignore the problem of measurement, the time honoured criticism of justice defined in terms of utility or expediency in obtaining a goal such as the 'common good', is that it is *consequentialist*: i.e. it would seem to allow any kind of activity to be judged as 'just', including killing of the innocent, and slavery, so long as the activity increases whatever measure of the 'common good' one decides to choose. This is fine, of course, unless you take the view of many others that the killing of innocent people and slavery are unjust in principle, regardless of consequences.

To find a way round these problems some utilitarians have argued that acts are just only if they correspond to moral rules that promote some ultimate good; this view is known as *rule utilitarianism*. Thus, it could be argued that, the long term, society benefits more in terms of aggregate utility by denouncing malicious actions against innocent people. However, critics have argued that this argument is circular, and there is no reason, in principle, why such rules should comply with our moral intuitions (Earle, 1992; Hospers, 1961; Raphael, 1980).

To many, therefore, it is a mistake to equate justice with the attainment of some ultimate measure of the 'common good' or 'general interest' (see, for example, Raphael, 1981; Dworkin, 1978a, 1986); for instance, Dworkin (1978a) argues, 'if someone has a right to something, then it is wrong for the government to deny him it even though it would be in the general interest to do so' (p. 269). To draw our attention to this distinction, Le Grand (1981) cites two very clear statements of primacy of justice over 'the common good'. The first is from the Holy Roman Emperor, Ferdinand 1, who proposed *'Fiat justitia et pereat mundus'* (let justice be done, though the world perish). The second is from William Watson, who said, *'fiat justitia et ruant coeli'* (let justice be done though the heavens fall).

To cope with the problems of utilitarianism, theorists often turn, in preference, to the moral dictates of Immanuel Kant (1724-1804).

Justice as consent and impartiality

Kantian theory is often described as *deontological*, in that it makes morality and justice matters of absolute duty or obligation, independent of considerations of consequences (Earle, 1992). Kantianism stresses the dignity of human beings as rational creatures who are 'ends in themselves'. To Kantians it is wrong to victimize anyone for the greater good of another, for in doing so, one would be treating the victim as an object, as means to an end only.

Kant's most famous axiom, which turns up in many discussions of justice is, 'act as to treat humanity, whether in thine own person or in that of any other, in every case and as an end withal, never as a means only' (1785/1965, p. 56). We must never treat anyone as a means to an end only, no matter how worthy the end. Kant actually derives this from a more fundamental axiom, or 'categorical imperative' which states, 'Act only on the maxim whereby thou canst at the same time will it should be a universal law' (p. 46). Thus, our rules must be 'universalizable'. We must never act according to a rule that could not, in principle, be consented to by any other rational person. Kant calls this is a 'categorical imperative', because it states that you ought to do obey it its own sake, not as a means to something else.

However a classic objection to Kantianism is it could lead to what Posner calls 'moral squeamishness or fanaticism' (1981, p. 58). For instance, supposing we can only save humanity by killing one innocent man, but this man would rather die with humanity than for it. Arguably, if we take Kant's axiom literally, then presumably we must let humanity die rather than kill this man; for to kill him, without his consent, would be to treat him as a means to an end only. However, a standard Kantian riposte to this is to argue that the categorical imperative requires not that we should never do anything to individuals without their actual consent (we do not usually ask for the consent of offenders before punishing them), rather we should ask, could a rational person consent to be used in this way? Kant uses this idea to distinguish between a 'just' and an 'unjust' law. Kant says that an unjust law is one to which the people as a whole would find it impossible to agree, but he argues that, 'if it is at least *possible* that a people could agree to it, it is our duty to consider the law as just, even if the people is at present in such a position or attitude of mind that it would probably refuse its consent if it were consulted' (1797/1973, pp. 162-163).

But how do we decide how a rational person would behave in such a situation? How do we decide whether, hypothetically, a person could possibly or not possibly agree to a particular law or rule? The categorical imperative by itself will not help. This brings us to another major problem with Kantianism; it does not actually tell us what our rules should be (Earle, 1992; Flew, 1979; Hospers, 1961; MacIntyre, 1982).

For instance, Kant himself thought that the principle of benevolence to the poor could be derived from the categorical imperative. His argument was that nobody could possibly rationally will a rule of ignoring the poor as a universal law; he says, 'What would happen if you yourself wanted the love and sympathy of others? If you needed help you would have deprived yourself of any hope of gaining it' (1785/1965, p. 56). But benevolence does not of necessity follow from Kant's principles; if you leave a person in abject poverty you do not necessarily treat him as 'a means to an end', and if you believe that charity discourages the poor from working and damages their self respect, and you are convinced that you would not want charity if you were poor, you might not wish to will benevolence towards those in need as a universal law. Indeed, if you believe that your ethnic group should rule over another, and that, if they were acting rationally, the 'inferior' group would willingly accept your superiority as being in their own best interests, then racial discrimination, and even slavery, could be construed as a moral 'good'. This was, in fact, exactly how many of the apologists for slavery justified the institution of slavery; as Ryan (1970) points out, 'Slavery .... was justified - even praised - on the basis of a complex ideology that showed quite conclusively how useful slavery was to society and how uplifting it was for the slaves' (p. 19). (See also, Sampson, 1971; Walvin, 1993.) Hospers (1961) identifies the problem succinctly when he says that Kant's categorical imperative 'will not yield a set of maxims on whose universalization everyone can agree' (p. 283).

Kantian theory illustrates some of the difficulties involved in using the notion of consent, actual or hypothetical, as the basis of rules of justice. These difficulties crop up again in the writings of Thomas Hobbes. Hobbes argued emphatically that justice is nothing more than the keeping of valid agreements or covenants. Thus, he says, 'When a covenant is made, then to break it is unjust; and the definition of injustice is no other than the not performance of covenant' (1651/1960, p. 94). However, we usually consider behaviours such as child murder as acts of injustice; but in what sense can we say that murderers have broken their agreements? To get round this problem, Hobbes was forced to concede that justice was concerned not only with actual agreements, but with *tacit* agreements also. But is it really the case that child murderers have tacitly agreed to obey laws forbidding child murder behaviour? It seems that, without some independent notion of the rules to which people *should* tacitly agree, the notion of justice as an agreement becomes vacuous.

Similar problems occur with attempts to stress the related notion of *'impartiality'* as the defining feature of justice; particularly the view taken by some modern philosophers that a just decision is one that might be made by a disinterested or neutral person (for example, Ackerman, 1980; Barry, 1989). This conception of impartiality immediately invites the question of what sort of decision rule would appeal to a disinterested party? In a situation where there are conflicts of interest, would an 'impartial observer' apportion according to merit, property rights, contractual obligations, need, equality, public utility or something else? Rawls (1972) argues that justice cannot be impartiality *per se* because, 'The impartial spectator definition makes no assumptions from which the principles of right and justice may be derived' (p. 185).

Freedom and liberty

To make matters more confusing, however, although theorists often cite Kant's categorical imperative in discussions of justice, and even use it as a principle of justice, Kant's actual definition of justice is far more specific; it relates to that which is necessary to preserve individual freedom. He says, to preserve freedom, we must restrict freedom; thus justice is, 'the restriction of each individual's freedom so that it harmonizes with the freedom of everyone else' (1793/1973, pp. 155-156). The emphasis towards the idea of justice as some kind of guarantee of freedom is also evident in the thinking of those modern theorists, mentioned earlier, who argue that justice concerns the right to private property and the freedom to acquire and dispose of that property as one chooses (see, for example, Nozick, 1980). However, things brings us to the problem of how, within the context of justice, we should define the term 'freedom'.

According to some theorists, known as libertarians, justice essentially concerns the maintainance of the natural right to freedom or liberty; to them, a 'free' society is one in which one is not held captive by others; one in which one is free from the control or violence of others (see, for example, Harman, 1982; Nozick, 1980; Rasmussen, 1982). However, as a number of writers have argued, freedom from restraint is only one way of viewing freedom (see, for example, Bodenheimer, 1961; Raphael, 1981). In common parlance, when we use the term 'freedom' we often not only refer to freedom *from* restraint (sometimes called a negative freedom), but also freedom as having the power or means to *do* something (a positive freedom). For example, if I wish to buy a Rolls Royce, but the law prevents me from doing so, then my freedom to buy it is obviously restricted. However, if the law permits me to buy a Rolls Royce, but I have no money to buy one, then in another sense, my freedom to buy it is still restricted, even if no law prevents me. Nevertheless, according to the libertarian conception of freedom, the destitute person is actually perfectly 'free' or 'at liberty' to buy a Rolls Royce, a swimming pool, golf course, or anything else, providing no one actually prohibits the buying and selling of such commodities. Similarly, when libertarians refer to a 'right' (or even 'equal right') to private property, they do not mean that everyone should be given private property, but rather, no one should be restrained by others from possessing private property gained without fraud or force.

Many find the libertarian use of the concepts of freedom, liberty and right unacceptably limited and inadequate to satisfy the requirements of justice (see, for example, Bayley, 1981; Williams, 1975) Critics argue that to give everyone a right, for example, to health or a fair trial is one thing, but if health care and legal representation can only be secured by money, then for destitute people, such 'rights' are worthless because they cannot be exercised or secured.

So far, therefore, we appear to have come up with no clear consensus as to how benefits or burdens should be distributed to accord with the requirements of justice, assuming of course that justice even concerns the distribution of benefits and burdens. Is there any more agreement with regard to the treatment of wrongdoers?

Corrective justice

Technically, in English law, not all those we would class as 'wrongdoers' are 'criminals'. A criminal is usually defined as someone who commits an illegal wrong against society, and is liable to be prosecuted and punished by the state. However, many wrongs do not fall within the remit of the legal system, thus in most countires, the 'civil law' as distinct from the 'criminal law', deals with the rights and duties of individuals among themselves. Hence, though a wrongdoer may not be criminally liable, it may, nevertheless, be possible to seek redress from him or her for a wrong (either a breach of contract or a tort), through the civil courts. This creates a number of semantic difficulties, not the least of which is that the term 'civil law' has been, and still is, often used to refer to the general laws of society, including criminal law, as opposed to say, natural law.

Given that the term 'criminal justice' may be too narrow to apply to the treatment of wrongdoers, other popular terms to cover the treatment of those who infringe social rules and obligations are *corrective* or *remedial justice*; not in the sense of reforming the offender to make him or her a better member of society, but correcting the situation (see Bell, 1992; Bell and Schokkaert, 1992; Curzon, 1989). But which justice principles should used to 'correct' a situation?

Some theorists have more or less avoided the problem of deciding to do with offenders by arguing that the two areas of distributive and corrective justice are so radically different that one cannot apply similar principles of justice to them. According to Rawls (1972), for instance, the problem for distributive justice is to design a system for those who will comply with the rules; how we treat those who disobey some of the rules is a different issue. Indeed, if we want some material principles to govern how we should treat offenders we will have difficulty finding them amongst the principles offered for distributive justice. Do we give offenders equal shares with non-offenders, or punish them according to their equal worth, needs or rank? How about treatment according to property entitlement, abilities, covenants or rights?

The German philosopher, Hegel (1864/1942) argued that offenders actually have a 'right' to be punished; though, as Honderich (1976) points out, it seems odd to give people a right from which they cannot escape. Moreover, simply giving someone a right to be punished does not in itself dictate the form or severity that the punishment should take. Hegel's compatriot, Kant (1797/1970), had a different approach to rights and punishment. He argued that, by offending, criminals lose their rights against others. However, if justice is about rights, but offenders have no rights, then presumably we can commit any number of atrocities against them, even for the most minor offences, without committing injustice. Kant attempted to get round this by arguing that the only principle that makes sense is to punish such that 'punishment fits the crime'. But this brings us to one of the most long-standing debates in the area of criminal justice; that is, whether punishment should be inflicted as retribution, for deterrence, for reform, or indeed, at all (Honderich, 1976; Hospers, 1961; Lee, 1981). Some typical arguments are as follows.

Deterrence, reform or retribution?

To retributivists, the sole justification for punishment is that the offender has committed a crime and thus he or she deserves to be punished. For example, Bradley says, 'Punishment is punishment only when it is deserved .... if punishment is inflicted for any other reason whatever than because it is merited by wrong, it is a gross immorality, a crying injustice, and abominable crime' (1876/1927, p. 26). Probably the most famous proponent of the retributivist position was Kant who argued that we must not punish the innocent, but we actually have a *duty* to punish the guilty regardless of any considerations of consequences. His famous statement in this regard reads, 'Even if a civil society were to dissolve itself by common agreement of all its members .... the last murderer remaining in prison must be executed, so that everyone will duly receive what his actions are worth and so that the blood guilt will not be fixed on the people because they failed to insist on carrying out the punishment'

(1797/1970, p. 102). As mentioned previously, Kant also held the view, commonly associated with retributivism, that 'punishment must fit the crime'; the greater the wrong done, the greater the punishment deserved (see also, for example, Evans, 1961; von Hirsch, 1985; von Hirsch and Jareborg, 1989).

To others, however, the only justification for punishment is to deter future crime and/or reform the offender. For example, Kenny argues that to punish for retribution is wrong; he says, 'two wrongs don't make a right. We must not render evil for evil' (1978, p. 73). Another famous supporter of the deterrence/reform position was Hobbes (1651/1960). According to his seventh 'law of nature', it is wrong 'to inflict punishment with any other design than for the correction of the offender or direction of others' (p. 100). However, if the only justification for punishment is to deter future crime, this could lead to some decisions that many people in our culture might find disquieting; for example, if the sole purpose of punishment is to deter others, then it is not obvious why the person to be punished even needs to be guilty. One could punish the innocent for the 'greater good'. If we really want to deter shoplifters why not take an innocent woman and cut her hands off to show prospective thieves we mean business? Better still, why not round up a few thousand innocent destitute people, pretend they have shop-lifted and shoot them all as a warning to others? According to Honderich (1976), the problem with the strict deterrence position is, being utilitarian and consequentialist, it allows 'victimization', or punishment of the innocent.

Similar problems occur if we propose that the main justification for punishment is to reform the offender. As in the case of deterrence, the justification rests on the assumption that punishment does reform. What if punishment is not the best way to reform the offender? Perhaps hours of reward, sympathy, group therapy and so on would be better. Of course, some people have argued that this is precisely how offenders should be treated; such eminent figures as Robert Owen and Florence Nightingale have held the view that offenders should be 'treated' rather than punished (Mill, 1861/1962). However, if we assume that punishment can reform, what form should it take? Eysenck (1977) argued that 'punishment must fit the criminal not the crime' (p. 200); his rationale is that different criminals need different treatment regimes, not because the crimes they commit differ in their severity or evil, but because offenders may require different kinds of treatment to reform or rehabilitate them. However, the difficulty then is deciding whether the 'treatment' conflicts with 'justice'. What if some murderers and rapists are best reformed or rehabilitated by hours of care and encouragement, whilst pick-pockets and shop-lifters respond more readily to torture; should we torture shoplifters and pick-pockets, and give murderers and rapists tender loving care? What does 'justice' require?

The failure to agree on these issues has led to the adoption by some of compromise theories. For example, Honderich (1976) argues that punishment may sometimes be justified, when not deserved, though most of the time it must be deserved. However, such theories raise familar semantic problems about the connection between justice and morality. Some writers make reference to both justice and morality in the treatment of offenders; for example, according to Bradley (1876/1927), to punish people for any other reason than they deserve it is both immoral and unjust. However, if one holds a utilitarian position that punishment is morally right only if it does some future good (by, for example, maximizing the aggregate happiness of society or the wealth of society), but justice demands that it is inflicted only if it is deserved, then, in theory, one could treat an offender justly according to desert, but behave immorally in doing so if no future good ensues; a possibility that presents difficulties for those who equate justice with acting morally towards others.

All of this also also assumes that we can agree on what is meant by the term 'punishment'. In philosophy the word punishment has tended to take on an extremely restricted legalistic meaning, denoting something like 'penalties inflicted by authority figures on guilty individuals who have broken authorized rules'; as a result, it is actually not possible, by definition, to unjustly 'punish' an 'innocent' person, one can only 'telish' or 'penalize' them (see, for example,

Bradley, 1876/1927; Flew, 1979; Murphy, 1970; Raphael, 1981; Rawls, 1972). However, in everyday language we frequently talk of 'unjust punishment' and consider this meaningful; moreover, people often feel justified in 'punishing' harmdoers of all kinds, whether they be individuals, in gangs, or whole countries, and it apparently matters not a jot whether we have authority over them, or they have broken 'authorized' rules.

So what is justice?
It seems evident so far that all we can really say about 'justice' is that it has something to do with how we decide who should receive what, and how we treat people, including criminals and other wrongdoers, and it might involve in part treating people equally or unequally, though not necessarily. When one considers that wars are fought, and lives lost and ruined under the banner of justice, we might have hoped for something a little more definitive than this!

Nevertheless, there exist some very influential but very different modern philosophical theories of justice that purport to tell us exactly what our principles of justice should be. We have touched on some of them briefly in this chapter, but perhaps by looking at these in more detail we may be able to detect some common themes that might help us reach a coherent definition of justice.

PART 2

JUSTICE IN MODERN PHILOSOPHY

CHAPTER 2

LIBERTY, RIGHTS AND EQUALITY

If one reads any modern account of justice, one is very likely to find some reference to the theories of John Rawls and Robert Nozick. As the arguments that revolve round the theories of Rawls and Nozick illustrate well what many see as the main issues in modern philosophical views of justice, it is worth looking at them in some detail.

John Rawls: justice as fairness

John Rawls' theory of justice is stated most comprehensively in his book, 'A Theory of Justice' (1972). Rawls argues that the subject of justice is 'the basic structure of society' (p. 7). Rawls says that one could structure a society on the basis of utilitarian principles; that is, one would arrange matters so that the good of society would be maximized. However, he argues against utilitarianism because he says it takes no account of how the good would be distributed; it would allow the violation of the liberty of a few to be made right by the greater good shared by many. To Rawls, the principle that underlies our considered judgements of justice is not utility, but *fairness*. Therefore, we should choose our principles of justice according to 'fair' procedures. But what is a fair' way of choosing principles of justice?

Rawls argues that 'justice as fairness' should involve the evolution of principles from a situation in which people can fairly agree to such principles. To do this Rawls devises the concept of an 'original position'; a hypothetical situation that insures that the fundamental agreements reached in it are fair (p. 17).

Rawls' 'original position'
Rawls argues that, for an original position of choice to be fair, one would have to assume that all participants are motivated to agree principles of justice and that they are rational, self-interested persons capable of a sense of justice; however, they must not be able to exploit their particular social and natural circumstances. To achieve this latter end, Rawls uses another hypothetical device, 'the veil of ignorance'. All persons in this hypothetical position of choice would be situated behind a veil of ignorance; they would not know their social status, assets, abilities, levels of intelligence, strengths, psychological characteristics, conception of the good or plans of life, or the particular circumstances of their society. Rawls thus sees his concept of the original position as a sort of abstract social contract between people. Interestingly, he also thinks that his method is implicit in Kant's ethics; he assumes a situation in which free and equal rational moral agents devise laws for themselves, laws that all could generate, agree to, and abide by (see also, Rawls, 1980). But what principles of justice would be adopted by people in this hypothetical original position?

Rawls' principles of justice
According to Rawls', the job of principles of justice is to distribute primary goods; that is, things that every rational person is presumed to want. At first, Rawls argues that people in the original position would wish to advocate a general conception of justice that would prescribe equality, unless inequality was to everyone's advantage. He says, 'Injustice, then, is simply inequalities that are not of benefit to all' (1972, p. 62). However, later he becomes more specific, and

argues for a 'maximin' principle. That is, people would want a situation that would maximize the minimum share of primary goods that any individual could receive. He thus argues that the 'general conception' is that, 'All social primary goods - liberty and opportunity, income and wealth, and the bases of self-respect, are to be distributed equally unless unequal distribution of any or all of these goods is to the advantage of the least favoured' (p. 303).

Rawls proposes that his scheme would give rise to two main distributive principles. The first he calls, 'The Principle of the greatest equal Liberty'. This is defined as follows: 'Each person is to have an equal right to the most extensive total system of equal basic liberties compatible with a similar system of liberty for all' (p. 302). The basic liberties are freedom to participate in the political process (to vote, run for office etc.), freedom of speech, freedom of conscience (including religious freedom), freedom from arbitrary arrest and seizure as defined by the rule of law, and the right to hold personal property. The second principle has two parts. He states that social and economic inequalities are to be arranged so that they are both, a) attached to offices and positions open to all under conditions of fair equality of opportunity; and b) to the greatest benefit of the least advantaged; this is the 'difference principle'.

It is important to note that these arrangements are not seen as self-evidently 'just' simply because they satisfy our moral intuitions. Rawls sees them as 'just' because they would also be chosen in the original position (p. 42). He says, 'the idea of the original position is to set up a fair procedure so that any principles agreed to will be just' (p. 136).

Rawls on desert

It is also significant that Rawls has no time for the idea of merit or desert as the basis of justice. He argues that in the original position would not award goods according to desert. He says, 'The idea of rewarding of desert is impracticable'. To Rawls it is a matter of commonsense; if one bases desert on the principle of rewarding according to contribution, then in a competitive economy the extent or value of one's contribution depends on supply and demand; but surely a person's moral worth does not vary according to whether others happen to want what he or she produces. Neither can measure desert by 'effort', because effort is influenced by natural abilities and skills for which a person can claim no credit; for instance, he says 'the better endowed are more likely, other things equal, to strive conscientiously'. He argues that even to say a man deserves his superior character is problematic, for 'character depends in large part upon fortunate family and social circumstances for which he can claim no credit' (p. 104). And, in his view, 'all this is perfectly obvious and has long been agreed to' (see pp. 310-312).

The proposal that people do not deserve their natural abilities and skills is also used by Rawls to justify what he terms the 'tendency to equality' that is expressed in this theory. He argues that to treat people equally, and provide genuine equality of opportunity one must give more attention to those born with fewer native assets and born into less favourable social circumstances. To this end, for example, the less intelligent might require greater resources spent on their education. The fundamental rationale underlying Rawls position here is that, as people do not deserve their natural endowments and such as talent, character, physical advantages and the social environments into which they are born, they cannot acquire exclusive benefits from these advantages in ways that do not contribute to the welfare of others. He says that people must neither gain nor lose from their 'arbitrary place in the distribution of natural assets or their initial position in society without giving and receiving compensating advantages in return' (p. 102); and 'undeserved inequalities call for redress .... in the direction of equality' (pp. 100-101).

Criticisms of Rawls' theory.
Rawls' theory has provoked a vigorous debate (for reviews see Barry, 1973; Buchanan, 1982; Buchanan and Mathieu, 1986; Campbell, 1988 Cullen, 1992; Daniels, 1975; Gordon, 1973; Lucas, 1980; Nielsen, 1979). Some have argued

that Rawls' theory is not egalitarian enough (see Dworkin, 1978b); by allowing resources to be distributed unequally if this allows the most disadvantaged to be better off, it offends a strict egalitarian principle of justice; to maintain their self-respect, the disadvantaged might prefer a situation in which everyone is worse off, but equal. However, most criticisms of Rawls have come from those who argue that his theory is too egalitarian. These criticisms tend to take the form that egalitarian prescriptions unjustly restrict liberty and spell economic disaster. The arguments concerning restrictions on liberty are stated very clearly by Robert Nozick (1980), and will be presented shortly along with his theory. However, there is another fundamental problem with Rawls' theory to which a number of writers have drawn attention.

Even if we accept the idea of an 'original position' concept, one could question whether a rational person, in the original position, behind a 'veil of ignorance', would necessarily want a society that minimized the effects of misfortunes (Buchanan and Mathieu, 1986; Raphael, 1981). Why should a self interested person necessarily play safe? Why not choose a society in which it might be a bit more uncomfortable at the bottom, but one which gives a few a chance to gain prizes, or fortunes, without heavy taxation constantly redistributing ones gains to those worst-off? If you could be a billionaire or a pauper, you might just be a billionaire, so why not take the risk? In other words, even if we accept that the concept of an original position, or social contract, is a useful device for generating and rationalizing principles of justice, it is not at all obvious that people in this position would come up with the principles that Rawls has proposed. In fact, Rawls ends up in a similar position to Kant; both purport to have devised a mechanism for generating morally defensible rules, but the mechanism itself does not tell us what those rules should be. People in Rawls' original position might even prefer the rules of Robert Nozick.

Robert Nozick: Justice and individual rights

Robert Nozick's theory of justice is most comprehensively stated in his book 'Anarchy, State and Utopia' (1980). Nozick's views have been both motivated by, and an inspiration to, the libertarian school of thought. Nozick begins his analysis by stating that 'Individuals have rights, and there are things no person or group may do to them (without violating their rights)' (p. ix). Nozick then proceeds to argue that, given these far-reaching rights, the question is raised as to what, if anything, a political state can be empowered to do.

Nozick's theory of rights

Nozick's assumption that people have natural rights is an idea he develops from the views of the 17th century English philosopher, John Locke (1632-1704). To evolve his political theory, Locke used a device, popular during his era, known as the 'state of nature'. The 'state of nature' is a description of human existence in the absence of any political state. The central idea is that if one is to devise a rationale for the existence of a political state, one must demonstrate that a state or civilization is actually to be preferred to anarchy or a 'state of nature'.

Nozick cites Locke's basic view that in a state of nature people are free to order their actions and dispose of their possessions as they think fit without being constrained by, or needing the permission of others. They have rights to life, health, liberty and possessions, and no one can violate these rights; if they do violate these rights, then people also have the right to punish offenders to a degree proportionate with the transgression. Nozick comes to the conclusion that the only permissible state is a minimal state, limited to the narrow functions of protection against force, theft, fraud, enforcement of contracts and so on, and that any more extensive state will violate persons' rights not to be forced to do certain things, and is unjustified (p. ix).

Nozick argues that it is wrong to violate someone's rights for a utilitarian purpose such as the greater social good. Accordingly, it is a violation of a person's rights to force him or her to contribute to someone else's welfare, whereas not giving someone what he or she needs does not itself violate the rights of the needy person. Nozick argues that his position reflects 'the underlying Kantian principle that individuals are ends and not merely means; they may not be sacrificed or used for the achieving of other ends without their consent' (pp. 30-31). To fail to give a man the things he needs greatly does not treat him as a means to an end; but to force him, against his will, or without his consent, to contribute to the welfare of others, does treat him as a means to an end. By the same token, Nozick objects to the redistribution of wealth through taxation; he says, 'Taxation of earnings from labour is on a par with forced labour .... Seizing the results of someone's labour is equivalent to seizing hours from him and directing him to carry on various activities' (pp. 169-172)

Nozick's theory of justice in holdings

The chapter in Nozick's book that has excited most interest to those concerned with justice is one to which he gives the title 'distributive justice'. However, as I pointed out in the previous chapter, Nozick is not fond of this term. He argues that the term 'distributive justice' is not neutral; it assumes that there is some central source from which, or whom, resources are distributed. Nozick (1980) objects to the idea that justice involves some maxim such as, 'to each according to his –', because, he says, it treats objects 'as if they appeared from nowhere, out of nothing' (p. 161). He says this idea is misleading, for in a free society 'What each person gets, he gets from others who give to him in exchange for something, or as a gift' (p. 149).

Nozick prefers to speak of 'justice in holdings'. He says that, if the world were wholly just, the subject of justice in holdings would be exhaustively covered by the following definitions, or 'principles of entitlement'. 1) A person who acquires a holding in accordance with the principle of justice in acquisition is entitled to that holding. 2) A person who acquires a holding in accordance with the principle of justice in transfer, from someone else entitled to the holding, is entitled to the holding. 3) No one is entitled to a holding except by (repeated) applications of 1 and 2.

Nozick argues that to say a distribution is just is to say simply that all are entitled to the holdings they possess under the distribution. Basically then, people are entitled to hold whatever assets they hold so long as they gained them without fraud or force; and they entitled to transfer them to whoever they please, and to receive assets from others, as long as the others first gained them without force or fraud.

Nozick does not actually specify a principle of acquisition; that is how one can come to acquire previously unowned things. However, he argues that the crucial point here is not whether the object is free for others to acquire for themselves, but whether the appropriation of an unowned object worsens the situation of others. Nozick borrows another element of Locke's theory of property rights to cope with this issue; it is called his 'Lockean proviso'. The proviso is that one cannot simply acquire a property right over some previously unheld object or resource if doing so worsens the position of others. To determine the criterion for what worsens' someone's position, Nozick introduces the notion of a 'baseline' for comparison. The baseline is the highest level a person would be at if the property were not privately appropriated. For example, let us suppose someone appropriated a lake. If the result was that the situation of others, who otherwise would have had access to the lake, was made worse, for example, they had less water to drink or fish to feed themselves, than before the appropriation, then some kind of compensation would be in order. Moreover, Nozick allows for constraints on subsequent actions. For example, if a person 'justly' acquires title to a water hole, but then the other water holes dry up, then this person's rights to the water hole must be limited. For you to override someone's right to something, therefore, it is not enough to say you have been prevented from owning it, rather you must be able to demonstrate that you personally would have been better-off if it had not been appropriated privately. Nozick recognizes that not all existing holdings would have arisen through the steps described by him; that is, some individuals' rights may have been violated in previous acts of acquisition and transfer. He argues, therefore, that past injustices need rectification, and a principle of rectification would need to estimate what might have occurred if the injustice had not taken place.

Nozick emphasizes, however, that his approach is fundamentally against 'patterned' distributions. A patterned distribution of holdings is one that conforms to some criterion or principle imposed on it, such as equality, desert, usefulness, or need. Nozick says no distributional pattern is required or needed. Instead, people are historically entitled to things, and if there is one simple maxim which summarises the principle of historical entitlement it is, '*From each as they choose, to each as they are chosen*' (p. 160). By way of illustration, if gives the following, now famous, example. Suppose we first distribute holdings according to some pattern, for example, everyone might have an equal share. But then a famous basketball player, Wilt Chamberlain, signs a contract with a team so that twenty-five cents from the price of each ticket of admission goes to him. People then turn up and freely choose to buy tickets because they want to see Wilt Chamberlain. At the end of the season Chamberlain winds up with 250,000 dollars, a much larger income than anyone else; and the original distribution is upset. Nozick argues, 'can anyone else complain on grounds of injustice?' (p. 161); everyone was entitled to the twenty-five cents they had before they freely chose to give it to Chamberlain, so how can the new distribution be unjust?

Criticisms of Nozick's theory

Nozick's theory has also provoked a lively debate (for example, Buchanan and Mathieu, 1986; Dworkin, 1978b; MacIntyre, 1982; Miller, 1982; Paul, 1982). According to Buchanan and Mathieu (1986), one of the most striking deficiencies in Nozick's theory is that he fails to provide any systematic justification for the principles of right that he puts forward. Nozick simply states that 'people have rights' and goes on from there. Rawls tries to develop his principles from the concept of an original position, whereas Nozick simply takes it as given that 'people have rights'.

Dworkin (1978b) objects that, in any case, Nozick's theory of the rights that people have seems entirely arbitrary. Dworkin says, 'I see no reason why Nozick's right to property is exclusive of other rights, or why it is necessarily more important than others' (p. 254). Dworkin proposes that whilst the right not to be deprived of one's possessions has intuitive appeal, so does 'the idea that people in a desperate situation have a right to the concern of others' (p. 254). Part of the problem seems to stem from Nozick's insistence that 'there are only individual people, different individual people, with their own individual lives' (1980, p. 33); yet, according to Murphy (1972), individuals do not have inherent rights; rights are a social concept; thus 'whatever rights a person possesses are those which belong to him as a member of the group' (p. 154; see also, MacIntyre, 1982).

Liberty, equality and morality

Whilst neither Rawls nor Nozick claims that his theory encompasses the whole of morality, both do claim that their theories coincide with morality, and ironically, both claim their positions are commensurate with Kantian ethics. The Kantian moral maxim 'never to treat anyone as a means to an end only' seems to be a particular favourite amongst libertarians (see Flew, 1982 as well as Nozick). But as libertarians are quick to point out, you do not necessarily treat someone as a means to an end if you let him or her die in misery for want of your help.

So far we have only looked at Rawls' and Nozick's views of distributive justice and both seem to have encountered difficulties; but how do they fare with their treatment of criminal justice?

CHAPTER 3

THE PROBLEM OF PUNISHMENT

Commentators on Rawls and Nozick, usually pay little attention to their views on the treatment of those who violate their principles of justice. However, when we examine what Rawls and Nozick have to do say on the subject of the treatment of offenders, some very interesting ambiguities and contradictions emerge.

Rawls and the criminal

Rawls argues that his theory is primarily one of distributive justice, and that it is a mistake to mix up criminal justice and distributive justice. Distributive justice, says Rawls, assumes people will comply with the rules; what we do with people who disobey some of them is another matter. Nevertheless, he does argue that in any cooperative venture it will be necessary to have penal sanctions. Rawls' justification for penal sanctions is primarily utilitarian. Penal sanctions are to be applied because sanctions deter others from opting out of the arrangements. Consequently, although Rawls adds that his justification for punishment implies that those punished must have committed an offence, and be criminally responsible for their actions, nevertheless, he does allow that there may be occasions on which it might be necessary to hold people guilty for things they have not done, if greater liberty is thereby preserved. For example, in times of civil unrest, expediency may require that people be convicted for possessing weapons simply because weapons were found on their property, regardless of whether the individuals concerned actually knew the weapons were in their possession. Like all utilitarian theories, therefore, Rawls' views on criminal justice would appear to allow a degree of victimization; the conviction of the innocent for the greater good of all; the 'good' in this particular case being the preservation of liberty. Rawls concedes that such policies would not be ideal, but he says that, in such circumstances, 'All that can be done is to limit these *injustices* in the least unjust way' (p. 242, my emphasis).

However, Rawls is presented with a problem here; if justice is that to which people in the original position would agree, and they would agree that in some circumstances it may be necessary to punish (or, more strictly, 'telish') the innocent, then, so long as those in the original position would agree to it, punishing the innocent cannot be an *injustice*. Put simply, this issue is this; if people in the original position would sometimes agree that sometimes an injustice may be allowable, then *justice must be something other than that to which people would agree in an original position of fairness*.

However, even if we ignore this problem, there is another difficulty, for although Rawls seems to be committed to the idea that criminal responsibility is an important element in criminal justice, it is difficult to see how anyone in his scheme of things could actually be held responsible for his or her actions in any case. According to Rawls, 'a propensity to commit criminal acts is a mark of bad character, and in a just society legal punishments will fall only upon those who display these faults' (p. 315); but in defence of equality in distributive justice, Rawls also tells us that 'a person's character depends in large part upon fortunate family and social circumstances for which he can claim no credit' (p. 104). Apparently one is not entitled to advantages gained from good character, but one can be punished if one offends as the result of bad character; an odd position given that, in Rawls view, one is not really responsible for one's character in any case. If responsibility is so important to Rawls, it is strange that punishments should fall only on those who largely, through no fault of their own, have a bad character.

The difficulties continue when we consider what the actual penalties should be. Rawls does not specify penalties, all he says is that 'in agreeing to penalties ... the parties accept the same kind of constraint on self-interest that they acknowledge in choosing the principles of justice in the first place' (p. 576). But again, if, in the original position, behind a veil of Ignorance, you do not know whether you will be rich, poor, black, white, *murderer, rapist, or conman*, how can you possibly fix a set of penalties? If committing homicide is a mark of 'bad character', and character is something for which you are largely not responsible, it is a moot point whether you would choose to be punished at all.

The source of much of this difficulty seems to be a failure in Rawls' theory to specify what exactly is meant by the terms 'just' and justice; for whilst the theory claims that just principles are those that can be derived from an idealised social contract, Rawls nevertheless attempts to uphold a number of other criteria for justice at the same time. For example, at an intuitive level, it may seem unjust to punish the innocent if you are a retributivist and believe punishment is only just if deserved, but if people in the original position would sometimes for good reason, elect to punish the innocent, which criterion of justice do we choose? Is justice what derives from an idealized social contract or is it punishment only when it is deserved, regardless of whether people devising a social contract would necessarily agree to it? We cannot decide on the basis of Rawls' account, for he seems to blur these distinctions.

Rawls apparently wants his theory of justice to conform to our moral intuitions, to derive from a social contract, to uphold liberty, to conform to an equality/needs principle, yet deviate from this principle when it is useful to the worst-off, to prescribe punishment for utilitarian purposes, yet make punishment fall only on those who deserve it. This is a tall order and inevitably he has difficulty dealing with conflicts between these different conceptions of justice. Indeed, according to Lucas (1980), much of Rawls' approach to justice is not about justice at all; he says 'it seems to be a rational reconstruction not of justice, but of prudence' (p. 186).

Nozick and the rights of the criminal

Nozick's conception of what is 'just' is also problematical. When discussing justice, most commentators tend to concentrate on the chapter in Nozick's (1980) book entitled 'distributive justice', in which he presents his theory of 'justice in holdings': but how are we to interpret the rest of his theory of 'rights', and his idea of 'moral side constraints' that prevent one from violating the rights of others? Are these also parts of a theory of justice? What exactly is the status of justice in Nozick's theory? Is justice simply 'not violating the rights of others'? In Nozick's opinion people do not have 'welfare rights', but suppose a group of people wanted to claim welfare rights, would these rights not be real rights, would they be 'unjust' rights, immoral rights, all, some or none of these? As with Rawls, the problems associated with the failure to present clear consistent definitions of these terms are most obvious when we look at punishment.

Nozick's theory of punishment, like the rest of his theory of rights, derives much from the writings of John Locke. According to Locke, and Nozick, we have a natural right to punish those who injure us. So, along with our inalienable rights to life, liberty and property, we have a right to punish those who violate our rights. It should be noted, even at this point, however, that some dispute the possibility of a 'natural right to punish' (see, for example, Murphy, 1970). Nevertheless, Nozick proceeds along Lockean lines to argue that, in practice, people without government, might overdo things somewhat and misenforce 'their rights of retaliation, punishment, and exaction of compensation' (p. 55). He also says that, 'in a state of nature a person may lack the power to enforce his rights; he may be unable to punish or exact compensation from a stronger adversary who has violated them' (p. 12). Given these problems it might be preferable says Nozick, for people to put the punishment of offending the hand of some central protective agency. However, how should the individual or protective agency treat harmdoers?

Nozick examines both retributive and deterrence theories of punishment, and comes up with an idea -that combines self-defence with retribution. The idea is that one should be able to retaliate to defend oneself, but the degree of retaliation should be proportional to the harm done or intended; and one must not use more in self-defence than is necessary to repel an attack. However, in addition to this defensive retaliation, one is also allowed, for the purposes of deterrence, to punish the attacker further, but only to the extent that the attacker *deserves* it. The amount of 'deserved punishment' is a function of both the harm intended or done, and the offender's degree of responsibility (pp. 62-63). The more harm intended or done, and the greater the offender's responsibility for his or her actions, then the greater the punishment one is allowed to inflict. In operation, this means that if responsibility is zero, one cannot inflict more punishment than is necessary for defense. Nozick argues that all this is necessary to prevent 'wrongful and unjust retaliation' (p. 55).

At first, Nozick's idea of preventing 'wrongful and unjust retaliation' might seem reasonable, but what is meant by 'unjust retaliation'? If he sees injustice as the violation of a person's rights, what right is violated if one punishes individuals more than is necessary to repel them, and more than they deserve? Or if I argue that, by violating my rights, a man has given up his rights, why cannot I do whatever I like with him; why is it an injustice to inflict more punishment than he deserves? Like other libertarians, Nozick seems to get into trouble trying to adapt his theory of rights to the treatment of offenders. Indeed, it could reasonably be asked, if the man who harms me has rights too, rights that cannot be violated, why am I justified in harming him at all?

Recognizing this problem, Roger Lee (1981), another supporter of the view that individuals should have the right to pursue their own interests unhindered by others, thinks the solution is to send offenders off to certain confined areas where they can indulge their 'natural right to undertake actions to promote their own well-being' (p. 91). However, even this does not really seem to work. To libertarian rights theorists, the natural right to undertake actions to promote individual well-being is usually seen as part of, or deriving from, the fundamental right to liberty (see Rasmussen, 1982), and being confined to a geographical area is still an affront to liberty, regardless of whether those confined can still engage in capitalistic activities. Moreover, according to Lee, it is a violation of rights to punish offenders as retribution; one can only punish them as a) a disincentive to crime, and b) 'to purge ourselves and express our commitment to the law' (p. 96). However, by offering these solutions Lee falls foul of the Kantian accusation that offenders are being treated as 'a means to an end'. Indeed, we could presumably purge ourselves, express our commitment to the law and deter future crime by punishing innocent people as scapegoats and examples to others.

Given these problems, it is perhaps not surprising that Nozick resorts to the language of desert in the treatment of criminals. But like Rawls, Nozick seems to have devised a theory in which desert is applied somewhat selectively. To Nozick, it is not necessarily an injustice if you leave me, a limbless war hero, to suffer in poverty while you give all your unearned surplus wealth to an undeserving reprobate; but it is an injustice if you punish me more than I deserve if I steal from you.

Rawls versus Nozick

Is there any way of choosing between Rawls and Nozick? Is either theory more internally consistent or more conguent with the concept of justice than the other? Is one more 'moral' than the other? Can either help us clearly define what distinction, if any, is to be made between justice and morality, or justice as a moral principle and other moral principles? Can either offer a meaningful definition of justice? Whilst some readers may have more sympathy for one or the other positions, I doubt whether many readers would be able to answer these questions with any confidence. According to MacIntyre (1982), the two theories are actually incommensurable. He says, 'our pluralistic culture possesses no method of weighing, no rational criterion for deciding between claims based on legitimate entitlement against claims based on need' (p. 229). MacIntyre argues that each theorist derives principles from grounds that are not challenged by the other. Rawls arrives at his principles in accordance with how a rational person with no history would dictate behind a 'veil of ignorance', Nozick arrives at his principles by assuming people have inalienable rights. Consequently, there is no common standard to which we can appeal to decide between them.

Even though the theories of Rawls and Nozick have been heralded as possibly the two most important approaches to justice in recent decades, it seems somewhat disappointing that neither actually provides us with any satisfactory or consistent definitions of the terms 'justice', 'injustice', 'just', and 'unjust'. However, despite their disagreements, there does seem to be one point on which both Rawls and Nozick do seem to concur, one cannot base a theory of distributive justice on the principle of giving people what they deserve; though their reasons are somewhat different. Rawl's basic objection to the use of desert as a criterion for distributive justice is that it is impracticable, and would not be agreed to by people in the original position. Indeed, Rawls is so confident that one cannot apportion goods according to desert that he asserts, 'All this is perfectly obvious and has long been agreed to' (1972, p. 311). On the other hand, Nozick's objection is that any attempt to apportion goods according to desert would represent a patterned principle of distribution, with a subsequent, inevitable, violation of people's rights.

MacIntyre (1982) has noted Rawl's and Nozick's views on the matter and comments, 'neither of them make any reference to *desert* in their account of justice, nor could they consistently do so' (p. 232). However, as we have seen, although both Rawls and Nozick seem to have rejected desert as an overall guiding principle in justice, it is not quite the case that they entirely disregard it. Dispensing with deserts in favour of rights and entitlements is not so easy when it comes to those who violate your rights or rules of entitlement. Neither Rawls nor Nozick attempt to argue, like Hegel (1864/1942), that we have a 'right to be punished', instead they both seem to lapse into the kind of language associated with desert, with Rawls talking about 'responsibility' and 'bad character', and Nozick explicitly referring to 'responsibility' and 'deserts' in the assignment of penalties. The result is a sort of ethical pot-pourri, an unhappy mixture of rights and entitlements for the law abiding and deserts for the law breakers.

As we shall see in the next chapter, Rawls and Nozick are certainly not alone in apparently dismissing desert as a guiding principle in justice. Indeed, in 1971, Kleinig remarked that, with few exceptions, the notion of desert had been assigned to the 'philosophical scrapheap'.

CHAPTER 4

AGREEMENT, IMPARTIALITY, AND EQUAL RESOURCES

The trend to dismiss desert is exemplified in what some consider to be the most important modern theory of justice since the theories of Rawls and Nozick, that of David Gauthier (1986, 1991).

David Gauthier: morals by agreement

In his book 'Morals by Agreement', Gauthier argues that morality and justice involve rational constraints on behaviour; indeed, rationality is the key concept in Gauthier's approach. According to Gauthier, the formal aim of a rational person is to maximize his or her own personal substantive aims and objectives; to behave otherwise, such as to seek the good of others, at the expense of one's own aims and objectives, is to act irrationally. However, in our unavoidable dealings with others, the unfettered pursuit of individual interest can often be counterproductive or self-defeating. Take an extreme example; if two people wish to obtain all of a good 'x' for themselves, and end up destroying the good, or even themselves, in the process, their attempt to pursue their own ends, unconstrained, has been mutually self-defeating. To game-theorists, this type of scenario is often referred to as 'the tragedy of the commons' (Hardin, 1986). Consequently, says Gauthier, in view of the ubiquitous nature of situations in which the unconstrained pursuit of one's own aims is counterproductive, it makes more sense (is rational) to adopt a policy of mutual restraint in our interactions with others. Moreover, in as much as such restraints are mutual, they, according to Gauthier, possess the attribute of *impartiality* that identifies them with morality. Thus to Gauthier, the basic test for the moral acceptability of any principle, practice or institution, is whether the constraints they impose would be agreed upon by rational individuals pursuing their own individual good. But how do rational people decide what is a 'rational constraint' in a particular situation?

Gauthier argues that we can discern what constitutes a rational constraint by adopting the criterion of the choices that would be made by rational individuals bargaining in a hypothetical situation. Gauthier's theory, like that of Rawls, is thus 'contractarian'; it assumes one can evaluate the moral status of something by reference to the criterion of whether it conforms to what would be agreed to by people under certain specified conditions. Gauthier's hypothetical initial bargaining position is, however, different from Rawls' 'original position' in a number of respects. In Gauthier's initial bargaining position, agreements are made only by parties who can mutually benefit each other (thus, for example, children and the severely handicapped are excluded) and, significantly, the parties do not care about what happens to each other. Moreover, all the parties in this initial bargaining position have full knowledge of their natural capacities and circumstances, and there is no question of seeking redress for natural disadvantages. People in this situation are free to gain full benefits from their natural advantages, and are not obliged to cooperate with or help others if to do so would not be to their own individual advantage (in fact, to do so would be irrational). The only constraint they operate under in their non-cooperative activities is that of a 'Lockean proviso'; this specifies that no one can make him or herself better off by making someone else worse off. However, should rational people decide that a cooperative relationship would be mutually beneficial, how should they proceed to bargain?

Gauthier suggests that rational people, when bargaining, would always attempt to minimize the maximum relative concession that anyone makes; this is referred to as the 'minimax relative concession' principle, or MRC; he later reformulates this as maximizing the minimum relative benefits that anyone will receive (1991, p. 325). According to Gauthier, this affords each participant equal relative concessions or benefits. Basically the MRC principle dictates that, when distributing the benefits of cooperative endeavour, each participant who has been instrumental in producing those benefits, should receive a) what they would have received had they acted alone (without cooperation), plus b) an equal share of the remaining surplus. Gauthier argues that his scheme thus covers two basic domains of justice; first, the domain of the prohibition of gain at another's expense, and second, the cooperative provision of mutual benefits.

Gauthier's account has provoked a number of criticisms (see, for example, Barry, 1989; Vallentyne, 1991). Most have tended to question Gauthier's idea of rationality. For instance, it has been argued that, given that some people manifestly do care about others, it does not follow that an agreement made between people who do not care for others will be 'rational' for those who do care about others. Also, if rationality is to be equated with the pursuit of one's own personal aims, and rational people do not care about others, why should a rational person accept a Lockean proviso not to benefit him or herself at the expense of others? If all care about no one except themselves, is it irrational for the stronger to take advantage of the weaker, or the disadvantaged to attempt to gain benefits at the expense of the advantaged? To his critics, Gauthier has generally failed to demonstrate why a rational person, whose sole aim is to benefit him or herself, should obey moral rules. For example, the Lockean proviso would suggest that a poor person cannot make himself or herself better off at the expense of a rich person, but as Copp argues, 'The unlucky poor woman, starving at the gate of a rich man who is meanwhile feasting on caviar and champagne, would be unlikely to accept a principle, such as the proviso, that would permit him to let her starve' (1991, p. 212). And, in any case, is 'constrained maximization' necessarily the most rational disposition for a person interested only in pursuing his or her own objectives? A rational person might do better as a 'reserved maximizer', violating the rules of Gauthier's scheme to gain a jackpot, if he or she thinks it possible to do so (see Copp, 1991).

These are important criticisms; but, significantly, whether, as an issue of justice, anybody *deserves* any more or less than any one else, seems to be of no consequence to either Gauthier or many of his critics (see, for example, Vallentyne, 1991).

Brian Barry: Justice and impartiality

The rejection of desert is also illustrated in Brian Barry's (1989) important book, 'Theories of Justice'. In this book, Barry consider's two major notions of justice. The first is justice as rational prudence. According to this view, justice exists when rational, self-interested, people are able to achieve a situation that is mutually advantageous. To demonstrate this approach Barry looks at various kinds of bargaining and arbitration procedures that theorists have put forward as solutions to the problem of what is mutually beneficial to self-interested persons. Barry then compares this approach with second conception of justice, justice as *impartiality*.

Barry emphatically rejects the notion that justice is based on self-interest; he says 'Self-interest cannot be expected to bring about just institutions in general' (p. 366). According to his own approach, the motive for justice stems, not from self interest, but from the desire to be able to justify one's actions to others on grounds they could not reasonably reject. From this latter point of view, an action is unjust if it cannot be publicly defended; that is, 'that the principles of distribution it initiates could reasonably be rejected by those who do badly under it' (p. 292). Justice is thus not some kind of bargaining game, or making self-interested choices behind a veil of ignorance, rather it follows from a *debate* in which the object is to convince others that it would be reasonable to accept your view; and all must be willing to accept a good argument even if it runs against their interests to do so. Hence Barry argues that 'everybody's point of view must be taken into account', and accordingly, 'To say that a principle could not reasonably be rejected by anyone covered by it is, I suggest, a way of saying that it meets the test of impartiality' (p. 372).

However, by arguing this way, Barry is presented with the obvious problem of deciding the criteria for 'public defensibility'. For example, presumably both Nozickians and Rawlsians would consider their principles to be 'publicly defensible'. To a Rawlsian, those who do badly under an unequal distribution could reasonably reject that distribution if the inequalities fail to benefit them. But, to a Nozickian, there may be perfectly sound reasons why a person who might do better under a more equal distribution should, nevertheless, tolerate gross inequalities; reasons that, according to Nozick, such a person could not reasonably reject.

There is one issue, however, that appears to present no problems for Barry; and that is the whether justice should consider people's deserts. Although Barry's book is entitled 'Theories of Justice' the concept of desert does not even appear in the index let alone play a prominent role in the text.

Another theorist apparently uninterested in justice as desert is Bruce Ackerman.

Bruce Ackerman: justice and neutrality

In Bruce Ackerman's (1980) book 'Justice in the Liberal State', Ackerman sees justice essentially as concerning how power can be legitimised in situations of scarce resources. To do this he draws on what he calls 'the spaceship myth'. In this fantasy, an assembly of fellow space travellers come across an uninhabited planet which contains one valued but scarce resource called 'manna'. They must then decide, by a process of debate and dialogue how this resource is to be distributed amongst them. However, in debating they must abide by certain ground rules laid down by the all-powerful spaceship commander. The result, according to Ackerman will be a 'neutral dialogue' from which rules of justice can be derived.

So what rules would derive from this 'neutral dialogue'? Ackerman argues they would ensure the following. 1) No citizen genetically dominates another. 2) Each citizen receives a liberal education. 3) Each citizen begins adult life under conditions of material equality. 4) Each citizen can freely exchange his initial entitlements within a flexible transactional network. 5) Each citizen, at the moment of his death, can assert that he has fulfilled his obligations of liberal trusteeship, passing on to the next generation a power structure no less liberal than the one he himself enjoyed. Consequently, he says, all inhabitants will 'enjoy the condition of undominated equality that is required by an undeviating insistence on liberal dialogic legitimacy' (1980, p. 280).

Ackerman has been criticized too (see, for example, Campbell, 1988). Many of the arguments will by now be familiar. It has been argued that his principles of justice do not derive from a 'neutral dialogue' by *necessity*, any more than Rawls' principles derive from his 'original position', Nozick's from his theory of property rights, Gauthier's from his 'rational bargaining position', or Barry's from the criterion of 'public defensibility'. The members of the assembly on the spaceship could come up with any number of different sets of 'defensible' rules, depending on their political and moral preferences. For instance, from a Nozickian viewpoint, how can you 'begin adult life under conditions of material equality' without gross infringements of people's property rights? We would have to take material resources from the children of rich parents and distribute them amongst the poor. And from an egalitarian viewpoint, there is something odd about a system that goes to great pains to start everyone off equal but then allows free market economics to take over such that 'some will .... gain enormous wealth (whilst) others will die with nothing to their name' (Ackerman, 1980, p. 201). As Campbell remarks, 'The fact that (Ackerman) can see no grounds for correcting these inequalities in an ideal society, except in the interests of the next generation or in order to maintain neutral dialogue itself, suggests that something has gone radically wrong' (1988, p. 115).

Problems also crop up in Ronald Dworkin's egalitarian approach.

Ronald Dworkin: justice, rights and equality

Ronald Dworkin (1978ab; 1981; 1986) is best known for his commitment to an egalitarian conception of 'rights'. He rejects utilitarianism on the usual grounds that, in principle, it would allow practices that would offend our moral convictions.

The starting point for Dworkin's theory is that everyone has a fundamental moral right 'to be treated with equal concern and respect' (1978a, p. 275), and thus justice involves the right to be treated as an equal. This does not mean, however, that everyone should be treated the same, or receive exactly the same, but that everyone's views and interests will be given the same sympathetic consideration. Thus governments must not distribute resources on the grounds that some citizens are entitled to more or are 'more worthy of concern' than others, and must not constrain liberty on the grounds that 'one citizen's conception of the good life is nobler or superior to another's' (p. 273). He then develops a theory as to how this sort of equality might be realized in a political system. Dworkin argues that ultimately justice is about outcomes, not procedural fairness; thus he says, 'Justice is a matter of outcomes: a political decision causes injustice, however fair the procedures that produced it, when it denies people some resource, liberty, or opportunity that the best theories of justice entitle them to have' (1986, p. 180). But what is a 'just outcome distribution'? Dworkin rejects concepts such as equality of welfare or satisfaction because individual preferences are too varied, and such ideas unfairly pander to those who have expensive tastes and unusual objectives. Instead, he argues for the concept of 'equality of resources'.

Dworkin suggests that rules for determining a fair or equal distribution of resources could be construed as those that might arise from a situation in which a number of shipwrecked survivors were washed up on an uninhabited desert island that has abundant resources. In this situation it can be assumed that no one is antecedently entitled to any of the resources, but instead they shall be dispersed equally among them. If, after distribution, none of the survivors would prefer or 'envy' anyone else's bundle of resources, the distribution could reasonably be called fair and equal. Here Dworkin uses what is popular known to economists as the 'envy-free' criterion of equity or fairness (Le Grand, 1991; Schokkaert, 1992). Thus the idea is not that each person will end up with an identical bundle of resources, rather each person should be sufficiently satisfied or content with his or her bundle of resources that he or she will not prefer or 'envy' that held by someone else.

So what sort of system would give rise to a 'no-envy' distribution? According to Dworkin, in principle, a just outcome should ensue if, at the start, there is an equal share of resources available for each to consume or invest as he wishes. From this 'equal' starting place, people then make choices and express their preferences through market transactions. Through these market transactions Dworkin maintains that equality is preserved even though, because people make different choices about investment and consumption, they may end up with different amounts of material wealth and happiness. Dworkin's scheme is thus what he terms, 'ambition sensitive'; it allows some to end up with more material wealth than others if their 'ambition' (as expressed through choices and preferences) directs them accordingly.

If, however, people are truly to start off equally, and for this 'equality' to be maintained in the market place, then it is necessary to control for chance or luck, such as the distribution of natural endowments, such as natural talents, and the effects of accidental misfortune. One of the most important aspects of Dworkin's scheme, therefore, is that it is 'endowment insensitive'. To control for the influence of luck, Dworkin puts forward the idea of a hypothetical insurance scheme which operates as cover to provide compensations and safeguards against a variety of circumstances, such as poor opportunities and profound disabilities in skill. The scheme assumes that when people take out the insurance they know what the income distribution will look like, and what talents they have, but they do not know where they stand with regard to the distribution; that is, they do not know what income their talents can produce. In practice he suggests that this could be realized by a progressive income tax system.

Dworkin's views have been criticized on a variety of grounds (see, for example, Campbell, 1988; Roemer, 1985; Schokkaert, 1992). One of the most important difficulties concerns Dworkin's proposals that a system of justice should be 'ambition sensitive' but not 'endowment' sensitive. To Dworkin, we are entitled to the results of our ambition, in fact, the results of our ambition simply take on the status of 'choices' or 'preferences', but we are not entitled to the results that accrue from the use of 'natural talent', because we are not responsible for the latter (they are due to luck). However, as Schokkaert puts it, the difficulty here is that 'If people are no longer responsible for their innate characteristics, it is not obvious how they can be held responsible for their preferences' (1992, p. 101). 'Ambition' may also be determined by inherited biological characteristics, or environmental influences beyond our control, so as Roemer (1985) says, 'At what point do we decide the person bears responsibility?' (p. 179).

But perhaps most significantly, and it hardly needs stating by now, to many libertarians, Dworkin's scheme of compensating for natural inequalities through a progressive income tax scheme would be anathema. It would be seen as contrary to the natural rights of people to do whatever they wish with the things that they have legitimately acquired. In other words, it cannot be assumed that those shipwrecked on Dworkin's island would necessarily want the system of justice he has designed for them. It is worth noting that the 'envy-free' criterion for 'equality' is of little help in this respect. The problem is that the 'envy-free' criterion blurs the distinction between what people might actually envy in practice, and what they *should* envy, in principle. It is a fact of life that the unambitious often envy the wealth of the ambitious; the point for Dworkin, however, is that, within his scheme, they *should* not. But once we accept the idea that 'envy-test' concerns not what people *do* or *would* not envy, but what they *should* not envy, we leave the door open for accepting any 'defensible' allocation procedure as 'envy-free', including one based on Nozick's principles. (For further criticisms of the 'envy-free' notion of fairness, see Le Grand, 1991.)

Also, like many other modern conceptions of justice, Dworkin's theory is ill-equipped to deal with justice in the treatment of criminals. We are told that everyone has a fundamental moral right 'to be treated with equal concern and respect' (1978a; p. 275), and that governments must not distribute resources on the grounds that some citizens are entitled to more or are 'more worthy of concern' than others, and must not constrain liberty on the ground that 'one citizen's conception of the good life is nobler or superior to another's' (p. 273). Presumably, therefore, we cannot assume that the conceptions of 'the good life' held by minority groups such as bankrobbers, sadists, muggers, arsonists, rapists and child-molesters are any less 'worthy' than the those of anyone else; we must treat these people with as much respect and concern as we treat anyone else, and make the necessary compromises so that they too end up with 'envy-free' bundles of resources.

In Dworkin's (1986) comprehensive and influential work on the theory of law, entitled 'Law's Empire', there is no detailed consideration of how the law should treat criminals; we are simply directed towards striking some sort of balance between punishment, culpability, deterrence and expense, depending on the situation (see p. 224). But, if all people are 'equally worthy', and no one's conception of the good life is any better than anyone else's, it is questionable whether we could anyone possibly claim that anyone has done wrong in the first place, let alone sacrifice them to utilitarian ends such as cost minimization and deterrence.

These problems illustrate a feature of Dworkin's view that it is by now familiar in modern philosophical conceptions of justice; in Dworkin's approach, justice apparently has nothing to do with what people deserve. But having nothing to do with desert, it has great difficulty dealing with the treatment of offenders.

Conclusion

If the approaches of those such as Gauthier, Barry, Ackerman and Dworkin represent the next stage after Rawls and Nozick, it does indeed look as though desert has been assigned to the 'philosophical scrapheap'. Nevertheless, a few modern philosophers have been willing to give the concept of desert sympathetic consideration; so before abandoning desert altogether, let us see what they have to contribute.

CHAPTER 5

THE PHILOSOPHY OF DESERT

Those who are prepared to give desert a sympathetic hearing are at least decided on one fundamental point. Desert *is* an important principle of justice. To a few it represents the whole of justice, to others, a part of justice, and not necessarily the most important part; but a scheme of justice that ignores desert will be deficient (see, for example, Campbell, 1988; Evans, 1981; Feinberg, 1970; Franklin, 1968; Garcia, 1986; Hospers, 1961; Lucas, 1980; Miller, 1976; Sadurski, 1985; Slote, 1973; Walzer, 1983). Discussions of desert tend to focus on two well-worn themes; the assignment of punishment or blame on the one hand, and reward and praise on the other.

The nature of desert

To proponents of desert, desert usually implies punishment as retribution for wrongful acts. Thus Kleinig (1971) argues that, to say people deserve punishment is to say they should be punished simply because they have done something morally wrong, and not because it will reform them or deter others. As pointed out in Chapter 1, some have gone as far as to argue that one cannot actually use the word 'punishment' to describe harm, unless the person on whom the harm is inflicted deserves it (see, for example, Bradley, 1927; Evans, 1981). Whilst others do not seem to insist that there is no such thing as undeserved punishment, nevertheless, deserved punishment is often given a special moral status. For example, Franklin (1968) argues that one can legally punish a man if he does not deserve it, but 'a man cannot deserve punishment in any full sense unless he morally deserves blame, and he cannot even be properly punished in a moral sense unless he deserved it' (p. 173). According to Walzer (1983), punishment without desert is 'an act of tyranny' (p. 272).

The opposite notion, of deserving reward and praise, seems to relate to a set of rather miscellaneous things we can be said to deserve. We can be said to deserve prizes if we win competitions or races, deserve grades by achieving certain performance levels on tests, deserve honours for worthy actions, deserve selection or appointment if we achieve certain selection criteria, deserve income according to skill, time expended, effort, and risk, and deserve compensation for injuries done to us (for examples, see Feinberg, 1970; Evans, 1981; Hospers, 1961; Kleinig, 1971; Lucas, 1980; Sadurski, 1985; Walzer, 1983).

As the range of items that can count as desert claims is so wide, some attempts have been made to classify them. Feinberg (1970) splits desert claims or bases into five categories; prizes, grades, rewards and punishments, praise and blame, and compensation. He them makes a distinction between polar and non-polar items. He says grades and prizes are non-polar, because they have no opposites; you either receive them or you do not; whereas reward and praise are polar, because they have the opposites, punishment and blame. Kleinig (1971), on the other hand, uses only three headings; raw claims, institutionalized claims, and specific claims. He gives the following definitions and examples. Raw desert claims do not require any institutionalized set of rules, and responsibility for their fulfilment does not rest upon any particular person or authority; as when we say, 'Smith deserves a break-through. He's been working on that problem for years now'. In contrast, institutionalized claims refer to some institutionalized set of rules; as when we say, 'McKenzie deserves to go to jail for robbing that old lady'. Finally, specific desert claims, concern not so much what is deserved, but how much is deserved; as when we say, 'McKenzie deserved about five years jail for his offence'.

A significant aspect of Kleinig's treatment of desert is the inclusion of the notion that people can be said to deserve something even when no one can be held liable. Feinberg (1970) also seems to accept this idea; for example, he argues that 'the unemployed may deserve compensation for their loss, but it is not necessarily true that there is someone who deserves to be held liable for it' (p. 75).

Can we find agreement on desert claims?
I expect that most readers will find these examples of desert claims fairly familiar. However, any impression that proponents on desert largely agree as to what count as desert claims or bases would, unfortunately, be unfounded. In fact, as one delves deeper, one finds that theories of desert are plagued by contradictions and differences of opinion as to what do and do not count as desert claims. For example, Feinberg (1970) argues that the main characteristic of a desert claim is 'worthiness'; we are deserving of something if we are 'worthy of it'. Thus Feinberg says, to deserve to be president of the United States one needs to be 'worthy' in the sense of possessing qualities such as intelligence, honesty, and fair-mindedness; but one is not deserving simply because one is 'over thirty five' or 'a natural born citizen', because these are not qualities of worthiness. He also argues that in contests where prizes are to be awarded, it is usually skill that determines worthiness. However, Kleinig (1971) does not pin-point worthiness as the essence of a desert claim; instead he contends, more generally, that desert claims rest on the evaluation of characteristics possessed, or things done, by people; though he says he is unable to define the basis on which such evaluations are made. In contrast, Lucas (1980) questions whether qualities or characteristics possessed by people are relevant to desert at all. Lucas argues that desert is solely about deeds done; he says personal qualities and characteristics refer to 'merit', not 'desert'.

Another difference of opinion concerns the status of natural events. Feinberg (1970) says that his analysis does not include construing natural events as deserts; thus he excludes statements such as 'the villain crushed in the land slide got what he deserved'. On the other hand, Kleinig (1971) does include natural events under what he calls 'raw desert claims'; in his view, it is acceptable to argue, for instance, that 'Peter deserves to get good weather for his holidays'. And, in Sadurski's (1985) view of desert, natural occurrences in themselves are not just or unjust, it is how we treat people that is just or unjust.

There are other contentious issues. For example, who deserves selection for a post: the most experienced, the most productive, the most conscientious, or the most liked? And what should count as the desert basis for economic rewards: responsibility, effort, ability, risk, or the value of one's contribution in the market place? Views differ. Feinberg (1970) argues that, whilst it is reasonable to use ability as a desert basis for prizes and grades, it is 'repugnant' to distribute economic goods in this way. He says, 'it is no more self evident to me that superior intelligence or skill *per se* deserves reward than that of great height or physical strength does' (p. 92). In Feinberg's view then, it is repugnant to argue that the skilful and intelligent deserve economic rewards, but at the same time, it is acceptable to argue that intelligence is to be included as a desert base for the Presidency of the United States, and that in competitive situations, where prizes are to be won, or grades awarded, skill can be preeminent as the desert base. Unfortunately, Feinberg offers no account of how these apparent inconsistencies are to be reconciled, and to complicate matters further, Evans (1981) thinks it perfectly reasonable to distribute economic goods on the basis of intelligence and ingenuity.

Desert and entitlement
Whilst there is both disagreement and contradiction in establishing the basis for desert claims, there does seem to be some agreement concerning a possible distinction between the notions of desert and entitlement (see, for example,

Feinberg, 1970; Evans, 1981; Kleinig, 1971; Lucas, 1980; Sadurski, 1985). The general consensus seems to be that entitlement concerns established, institutionised, conventions or rules, legal or quasi-legal, whereas desert claims may, or may not, fit into an established scheme of institutionised rules. For example, according to Lucas, entitlement depends on historical conventions and awards, whereas desert depends on past deeds. He says, 'If I buy a hundred shares in ICI, then I am entitled to a hundred dividends. I may be undeserving and lacking in merit. But it would be unjust none the less to deny me them, because I am entitled to them, and that is the relevant basis of distribution' (1980, p. 167). And Feinberg (1970) argues that, 'The wife who sacrifices all to nurse her hopelessly invalid husband through endless tortuous years until death, deserves a reward, but unless she qualifies under some set of institutional rules, she may not be entitled to one; she may not even be eligible for one' (p. 72). Nevertheless, the relationship between desert and entitlement is complicated by the varying conceptions of how justice is to be defined. For instance, according to Evans (1981), if one receives something to which one is entitled, but one does not deserve it, then, necessarily, an injustice has been perpetrated. On the other hand, both Lucas (1980) and Feinberg (1970) argue that a clash between entitlement and desert is not a clash between justice and something else; it is a clash between two sorts of justice.

Another way desert theorists have sought to distinguish between desert and entitlement is by relating them to luck or chance. Most theorists assert that one cannot deserve something on the basis of a characteristic or behaviour that arose by chance, but one may, nevertheless be entitled to it. Thus, Feinberg (1970) says, one can win a game or contest by chance, and be entitled to a prize regardless of one's worthiness or deservingness; but, 'in a game of chance one cannot speak of who "deserved to win" for .... no skill is involved' (p. 65); he adds that one can even win a game of skill and not deserve it, if one's winning was by fluke. Sadurski (1985) also emphasizes that to determine what someone truly deserves, we must exclude the influence of 'dumb luck'. However, this brings us to another source of considerable difficulty in discussions of desert; the role of responsibility.

Desert and responsibility

The popular view of human responsibility, as proposed by many lay-people as well as philosophers, is usually stated in negative form; that is, we are *not* responsible for our actions if we cannot behave, or could not have behaved, otherwise. Thus, for example, Hospers states, 'we say that a person is responsible for performing a wrong act unless he has an acceptable excuse for performing it .... a person is morally excusable for an action if he *couldn't help it'* (1961, p. 488).

According to many philosophers and theologians, there is an inextricable link between desert and responsibility, for we cannot be said to be truly deserving of praise and condemnation, or reward and punishment, unless we are responsible for our actions (Franklin, 1968; Hospers, 1961). Desert and responsibility are also often linked with the notion of *intention*. Thus Franklin (1968) states that it is a 'moralists truism that desert depends upon intention'(p. 181), and 'An ethic of intentions .... implies that a man is responsible only for what in some sense is under his control' (p. 191). Also Evans (1981) says, 'Desert may be characterized as giving harm for inexcusable harm or doing good or giving restitution for having intentionally and inexcusably harmed' (p. 50), and Sadurski argues (1985) 'Intention is a necessary condition of the moral quality of an act which constitutes the basis of positive desert' (p. 138).

However, the relationship of intention to desert and responsibility is not straightforward. It is commonly assumed, for example, that one does not need to intend to do harm to be blameworthy; a point recognized in English criminal law. A careless person may be held responsible for his or her actions, even though no harm was intended. Also, one can be held innocent of blame for an act that was fully intended, and over which one exercised a degree of control, as in the case of self-defence (Curzon, 1980; Flew, 1983; Cross, Jones and Card, 1988).

Nevertheless, despite these difficulties, it seems fairly easy to find discussions of the relevance of responsibility to issues of blame and punishment. There is clearly general agreement that one cannot be said to deserve blame or punishment unless one is responsible for one's actions (see, for example, Franklin, 1968; Hospers, 1961; Honderich, 1976; Raphael, 1981; Sadurski, 1985).

In contrast, whilst desert theorists have argued that responsibility *should* relate also to positive desert claims (see, for example, Franklin, 1968; Evans, 1981; Sadurski, 1985), in practice, it is difficult to find anyone prepared to offer a comprehensive treatment of the relationship between responsibility, and positive desert claims such as praise, prizes, grades, positions, honours and economic benefits. If we look at the complexity of this issue as it relates with very common desert claims, this is perhaps not surprising.

For instance, Evans (1981) asserts that in a hunting band those who put in more time and effort, take greater risks than others, or are intelligent enough to invent ingenious devices for snaring prey, deserve a greater share of the prey caught. But suppose there is a man in the band who, through no fault of his own, is physically disabled, and is not able to hunt. It is not his fault that he cannot put in time, effort and risk to hunt; so should he be less deserving than those who do expend their time and energies in hunting? Again, suppose intelligence is an innate trait, or a product of environmental deprivation; should the more intelligent hunters, who invent labour saving traps, deserve more than those who lack the intelligence to invent traps? After all, the latter cannot help if they were born with low intelligence, or into environmental deprivation. And, by the same token, why should those of superior intelligence be said to deserve the positions and prizes for the performances that their 'unearned' intelligence enables them to manifest? Evans does not consider these problems.

Kleinig (1971), like Evans, seems to think that promotion and payment for labour should rest on desert considerations such as industry, efficiency, and initiative; but he makes no attempt to relate these to responsibility. If he had, he would soon have encountered some difficult questions; such as, is efficiency something we can help? Are not the physically stronger or more mentally agile sometimes, by virtue of these assets, more efficient than those less well endowed by nature or by circumstance? And if so, should we not accept Feinberg's view that it is 'repugnant' to reward physical strength and intelligence?

The psychological assumptions involved in relating desert and responsibility seem to be enormous, though writers differ in the degree to which they consider this to be a problem. Walzer (1983) recognizes the argument that the issue of responsibility creates a problem when desert claims are based on the 'arbitrary gift of nature or nurture', but he simply dismisses this as 'an odd argument' (p. 261). To Sadurski (1985), however, the exclusion of 'dumb luck', including gifts of nature is essential when considering desert. Moreover, he argues that the exclusion of luck is achievable, so long as one confines the desert base to 'conscientious effort which has socially beneficial effects' (p. 116). However, this assumes of course that the capacity for 'conscientious effort' is not a 'natural ability'. As we have seen, according to Rawls, one cannot measure desert by effort because effort is influenced by natural abilities and skills for which a person can claim no credit; he argues, 'the better endowed are more likely, other things equal, to strive conscientiously' (1972, p. 312).

Another of the few people willing to take on the issue of positive desert claims and responsibility is Feinberg (1970); but he too runs into difficulties. For instance, he suggests that when people are doing arduous or unpleasant jobs, through no fault of their own, they can be said to deserve compensation. Hence he says, if refuse collectors are doing a dirty unpleasant job, not through their own choice, 'but only due to bad luck, lack of skill, or want of opportunity' (p. 92), then they deserve some compensation. But if, as Feinberg claims, the refuse collector's lack of skill has the status of 'bad luck', why, as mentioned earlier, should he suggest that having an abundance of skills makes you deserving of a high grade or prize, but 'good luck' does not. Why is 'lacking skills' equivalent to 'bad luck' in the case of the refuse collector, but 'having skills' different from 'good luck' when a prize or grade is involved? Are we responsible for our skills or not? And besides, what about the other desert bases put forward by Kleinig (1971) and Evans (1981), such as initiative, industry, and efficiency? Do we compensate the unindustrious, inefficient refuse collector who is collecting refuse 'through no fault of his own', but give less payment to industrious, efficient workers who became refuse collectors through choice, because they wanted to do a useful job?

The difficulties do not end here, for included in Feinberg's (1970) idea of deserved compensation is provision for need; thus, he says, the needy are deserving of compensation, but 'only when the need is blameless' (p. 94). However, many writers see need, blameless or not, as usually something alien to the concept of desert. For example, David Miller (1976) says, 'except in special cases, a person could not deserve on the basis of need, because we do not admire .... people for their needs' (p. 89). Kleinig (1971), Sadurski (1985) and Walzer (1983) also contrast need and desert.

Desert, equality and equilibrium

Although desert and equality are often set in contrast, according to some writers, it may be possible to combine them; for example, Feinberg (1970) argues that the idea of deserving compensation for onerous and burdensome tasks fits in with the view that, 'in respect to social benefits, all men should be treated equally' (p. 94). However, to make Feinberg's scheme work, not all benefits and burdens would necessarily count; for instance, to be consistent with the rest of his analysis, because only 'blameless need is compensatable', then, presumably, 'blameworthy need' would not count as a relevant compensatable burden; and if we consider that only work that is incurred 'through no fault of one's own' is compensatable, then, presumably, work that is onerous but 'chosen', or 'one's own fault', such as nursing work done from duty, would not count as a relevant compensatable burden either. Some might argue that it is an odd form of equality that compensates only those whose needs are blameless, or who do onerous tasks 'through no fault of their own'.

The idea of using desert as a mechanism for achieving an overall state of equality or equilibrium, has been developed more extensively by Sadurski (1985). Indeed, Sadurski bases his whole notion of desert on the idea of 'justice as equilibrium' Sadurski's view is that justice exists when there is an appropriate 'balance of benefits and burdens' (p. 105). The basic idea is that when people engage in 'conscientious effort which has beneficial consequences' they incur a burden that deserves compensation; and when such compensation is given, the result is an equilibrium position regarding the balance of benefits and burdens for all participants in the scheme. However, no matter how intuitively appealing this sort of equilibrium idea may appear, once again, its operation requires the adoption of a rather limited view of what constitutes relevant benefits and burdens. In Sadurski's scheme only a certain kind of 'effort' is a burden. Thus, the criminal who undergoes all kinds of hardships, and expends huge amounts of effort trying, unsuccessfully, to rob a bank, has not, in Sadurski's view, incurred a burden. Indeed, according to Sadurski, those who engage in criminal activity *gains*, regardless of their efforts or sacrifices, because they are enjoying the extra freedom that results from breaking a rule or law that constrains the freedom of others (and is therefore a burden on the lawful); hence he argues that all those who commit criminal acts enjoy the extra benefits of 'non-self restraint' (p. 229).

Moreover, as Campbell (1988) has noted, Sadurski implies that effort which produces social benefits always counts as a burden, even if those employing the effort actually experience it as enjoyable. Thus a man who spends three hours a day helping his colleagues, and enjoys every minute of it, has, nevertheless, incurred a compensatable burden. There is also the problem of unscrambling the *efforts* to contribute to society, from the *success* of those efforts in contributing to society (see Slote, 1973); does a person who expends 10 hours of effort doing something that is mildly beneficial to two people, deserve less than a person who spends one hour's effort doing something that greatly benefits millions? And what about a person who puts in hours of 'conscientious effort' to help others, but, because of a fluke of fate, is unable to produce 'beneficial consequences'; does he deserve nothing for his pains?

In effect then, in the schemes of both Feinberg and Sadurski the idea of desert is not to maintain a 'balance of benefits and burdens' *per se*; but rather to maintain a balance of certain kinds of benefits and burdens, defined in a rather specific way.

What is desert?

There are clearly some anomalies and inconsistencies both within and between modern approaches to desert; but this situation is perhaps not surprising given that there is so little consensus as to what exactly it means to deserve something. What exactly is it that test performance, meeting selection criteria, doing disagreeable work, suffering injuries, taking risks, being intelligent, and putting in conscientious effort, are supposed to have in common? We do not usually praise skilful criminals who show initiative, or compensate murderers whose crimes were disagreeable, arduous, risky or time consuming for them. Furthermore, why are all these things linked, if somewhat inconsistently, with issues of chance, intentions and responsibility?

The question of why all these items should be classed together is intriguing, especially when one notes other assumptions that often enter into desert considerations; such as the idea that punishment should fit the crime. For instance, Evans (1981) says, 'pickpocketing is a relatively minor sin, and those who practice it do not deserve the extreme punishment of being hung' (p. 46). This idea is usually taken for granted; it is simply assumed that desert implies some principle of proportionality. But why? Why does deserving punishment imply the use of some rule of proportionality? Having dispensed with the consequentialist notions such as of deterrence, why not hang or give life imprisonment to pickpockets and murderers alike?

In the absence of any satisfactory answers to these questions, desert remains a vague, heterogeneous concept, and it is perhaps not difficult to see why so many theorists have rejected it. Nevertheless, even if we could sort out these problems, perhaps the main difficulty is not so much that desert is entirely irrelevant to justice, but it may be only one of many justice principles, applicable to a rather restricted set of circumstances. For instance, David Miller (1976) argues that what we call 'Social Justice' is actually made up of three separate conflicting principles, those of rights, desert and need, and that these operate in different situations. Thus rights operate when we need to defend ourselves against the 'destructive possibilities' of human nature; deserts operate in 'competitive market' situations, and needs operate when community solidarity is the goal. However, probably the most famous and radical exponent of this 'multiprinciple' view of justice is Michael Walzer.

Walzer's spheres of justice

In his book, Spheres of Justice (1983), Michael Walzer asserts that distributive justice relates to 'the entire world of goods within the reach of philosophical reflection', and that 'this multiplicity of goods is matched by a multiplicity of distributive procedures, agents and criteria .... there has never been a single criterion, or a single set of interconnected criteria for all distributions' (pp. 3-4).

Walzer's basic idea is that there are, and should be, different principles for each 'distributive sphere', because different social goods have different social meanings, which, in turn, determine the reasons and procedures for different distributions. Thus, for example, public honour should be distributed according to desert, and offenders should be punished according to desert. However, the principle of 'membership rights' is most appropriate for establishing associations or communities of men and women; the provision of relief, work, and training is appropriate in relation to the needy; free exchange, or 'the right to give and the right to receive', is the principle that should govern money and commodities; being 'open to talents' is a principle that, in the main, should apply to public office; and hard work should be shared as equally as possible. The only overriding principle that, according to Walzer, should limit these principles, is that none should generalize to any other sphere of justice. For example, people who attain political power should not be able to gain goods from other spheres, such as money, or superior medical care; neither should someone who has amassed a fortune through free exchange be able to 'buy' public office.

Walzer calls this idea, and his general system, one of 'complex equality', which he summarizes as follows, 'No good "x" should be distributed to men and women who possess some other good "y" merely because they possess "y" and without regard to the meaning of "x" ' (p. 20). The 'social meaning' of each set of goods is, according to Walzer, 'the inevitable product of historical and cultural particularism' (p. 6). Thus Walzer's scheme is historical in orientation rather than intuitive; he argues that conceptions of what is a just distribution for a particular set of social goods may change over time. Nevertheless, he admits of some continuity; he states, 'No one would deny there is a range of morally permissible alternatives' (p. 6).

Unfortunately, however, Walzer does not distinguish between the principles that, he claims, can vary according to historical and cultural circumstances, and those that are limited by more universal conceptions of what is 'morally permissible'; in fact he provides no analysis of the alleged historical and cultural origins of the principles, or the circumstances that allegedly affect them. One commentator, Campbell (1988), is actually doubtful whether some of the distributive principles put forward by Walzer are issues of justice at all. Arguing that different distributive principles should apply to different circumstances is one thing, but coming up with convincing reasons, on grounds of *justice*, for why any particular principles should be relevant to different circumstances or distributive spheres, and not others, is another. Walzer seems to get into difficulties because, once again, he provides us with no obvious definition of 'justice', and no analysis of how, or even if, it differs from other moral principles. For example, it might seem 'inappropriate' for a variety of practical reasons to award wages and salaries, positions of public office, and sexual love on the basis of desert, but why should such awards necessarily be considered 'unjust'? And, if there is no single distributive principle that characterises justice, why bother with the overriding notion of 'complex *equality*'?

So what is justice?

The outcome of this overview of some of the most important modern philosophical theories of justice seems quite clear. There is no obvious consensus definition of justice, and no overriding principle, or set of principles against which to judge whether an act is 'just' or 'unjust'; and there is no consensus about whether justice and morality coincide, or even whether they should.

We are left with the concept of 'justice' merely as a sort of vague umbrella term to cover the numerous values, rules and social arrangements that humans invent and use to promote social cooperation and individual well-being; rules, values and arrangements that change according to social and historical circumstance. So, not surprisingly, when philosophers and others attempt to define the central concerns of justice, the definitions are so vague and wide-ranging that they verge on the vacuous. For instance, Barry (1989) says that 'a theory or justice is a theory about the kinds of social arrangement that can be defended' (p. 177); and Bodenheimer (1962) suggests that, 'justice is concerned with the fitness of a group order or social system for the task of accomplishing its essential objectives' (p. 177). Whereas to Bayley (1981) justice 'would be that order or arrangement of state and society that takes as its consummate ideal the principle that all human beings are equally objects of moral respect' (p. 16).

Others seem to have gone further and have more or less given up trying to define justice. Thus Markovsky (1991) states that 'there is no true or essential justice beyond its socially constructed meanings' (p. 33). MacIntyre (1988) also argues that what conception of justice one adopts depends on a variety of historical and cultural factors. He particularly rejects the idea that one can derive principles of justice from some notion of an agreement between 'rational' people. According to MacIntyre the whole exercise of attempting to derive rules of justice from conceptions of 'rational behaviour' is doomed, because there is no single standard of 'rationality'; there is 'no such neutral ground' (p. 346).

One of the most famous statements expressing the more negative view is that of Ross (1974) who says, 'to invoke justice is the same thing as banging on the table: an emotional expression which turns one's demand into an absolute postulate. There is no proper way to mutual understanding. It is impossible to have a rational discussion with a man who materializes "justice" because he says nothing that can be argued for or against. His words are persuasions not arguments .... This explains why all wars and social conflicts have been fought in the name of the exalted idea of justice' (pp. 274-275). Hayek is similarly negative; he states, 'I have come to feel strongly that the greatest service I can still render to my fellow men would be that I could make the speakers and writers among them thoroughly ashamed ever again to employ the terms "social justice" ' (1976b, p. 97).

This attitude, however, is not new. Although one might equate Marxian ideas with justice as 'equality and need' there is considerable debate amongst philosophers as to whether Karl Marx accepted any notion of justice at all (Buchanan, 1982; Cullen, 1992). Marx was obviously not too enamoured with ideas such as 'equal right' and 'just distribution'; he described these terms as 'a load of obsolete verbal rubbish' (1875/1986, p. 166).

Have we reached a dead end?

But is it really true that there is no agreement between people as to the basic principles of a theory of justice? Is there really no principle, or set of principles, that in people's minds possesses a quality to which the term 'justice' seems especially or uniquely appropriate? Is it ultimately all a 'load of verbal rubbish'?

If there really is some central core feature of justice to be identified, perhaps it may help to change discipline. Most modern philosophical works on justice seem fundamentally to be in the business of prescribing what principles of justice we ought to adopt, and are rather less interested in actually measuring what people are actually doing, or might even want to do. Hence, the methodology of moral philosophy is not one of scientifically testing hypotheses by systematically collecting and analyzing data about what people actually do, and what they think and feel. Psychology, however, purports to do exactly this; in fact, to psychologists, the views of philosophers can be used as pieces of data. So have psychologists anything substantive tell us about justice?

PART 3

THE PSYCHOLOGY OF JUSTICE

CHAPTER 6

THE RISE OF EQUITY

Psychological research into the nature of justice grew largely out of work on social exchange (for example, Blau, 1964; Homans, 1961, Thibaut and Kelley, 1959). Up until the late 1960's, social psychologists had displayed little interest in the notion of what constitutes a just distribution of resources. However, when psychologists did eventually turn their thoughts to the concept of justice, the dominating theory was that of *equity*.

It is worth noting at this point that the meaning of the term 'equity' can differ according to discipline, and sometimes within disciplines. For instance, in economics, 'equity' is often used simply as a synonym for fairness (Le Grand, 1991); whereas, in law, it is often used to refer to a body of rules that supersedes the civil law, or a set of rules that can be used to correct defects in common law (Curzon, 1988). Some psychologists have also used the term in this legal sense (see, for example, Austin and Tobiasen, 1984); however, in general, when psychologists use the term 'equity', they are usually referring to the particular scheme originally described by J. Stacey Adams, or variations of this scheme (Adams, 1963, 1965; Adams and Freedman, 1976; Adams and Jacobsen, 1964).

Adam's equity principle

The thoroughness of Adam's analysis, and his anticipation of many of the issues that other theorists have considered problematical for, or missing from, equity theory, have often gone unnoticed. It is, therefore, worth looking at his classic 1965 book chapter, entitled 'Inequity in Social Exchange', in some detail.

Adams based his ideas particularly on the exchange theory of George Homans. Homans describes justice as 'a curious mixture of equality within equality' (1961, p. 244). Schematically, Homans proposes that a relationship between two individuals, A and B, will be considered just when the profits of each (that is rewards minus costs) are equally proportional to their investments or contributions. Hence, justice exists when:

$$\frac{A\text{'s rewards less } A\text{'s costs}}{A\text{'s investments}} = \frac{B\text{'s rewards less } B\text{'s costs}}{B\text{'s investments}}$$

Thus the general rule is that, relative to others, the greater one's investments, the greater one's profits should be.

Within this formulation, costs can be psychological as well as material (for example, risk and discomfort), and the investments in the exchange can be a variety of 'relevant attributes' including, skill, effort, education, training, age, sex, and ethnic background. Homans also proposes that injustices will be felt in different ways. Thus those receiving less than justice demands will feel anger, whilst those receiving more will feel guilt; moreover, other things being equal, advantageous injustice, or excessive profit, will be experienced as less unpleasant to the person receiving it than disadvantageous injustice, or insufficient profit.

Developing this general idea, Adams decided to use the term 'inequity' rather than 'injustice', and set about investigating 'the causes and consequences of the absence of equity in human exchange relationships' (p. 276). According to Adams, equity exists between two people, or schematically represented as P

(Person) and A (another), when their contributions, or *inputs*, exist in equal proportion to their receipts, or *outcomes*, such that:

$$\frac{\text{Outcomes for P}}{\text{Inputs of P}} = \frac{\text{Outcomes for A}}{\text{Inputs of A}}$$

The terms P and A can also refer to groups, but the general rule still applies: relative to others, *the greater one's inputs, the greater the outcomes one should receive*. It also follows, of course, that *equal inputs should receive equal outcomes*. So, for example, according to the formula, if I work for 5 hours and receive £10, and you work for 1 hour at the same job, you should receive £2, for then our input/outcome ratios will be equal (10/5 = 2/1). But if you work for 5 hours, you should receive £10 also.

Adams argues that the inputs vary in type and relationship with each other and include education, intelligence, experience, training, skill, seniority, age, sex, ethnic back ground, social status, and effort expended on the job; they can even include 'personal appearance, attractiveness, health, possession of certain tools and characteristics of one's spouse' (p. 277). Positive outcomes can include pay, rewards intrinsic to the job, seniority benefits, fringe benefits, job status, status symbols, and the privileges of status. They can also include affection, love, formal courtesies, expressions of friendship, fair value (as in merchandise), and reliability. However, outcomes can also be *negative*; such as, poor working conditions, monotony, fate uncertainty, insult, rudeness and rejection. If we add the positive outcomes to the negative outcomes to produce 'net outcomes', then the result is essentially analogous to Homans' idea of profits, or rewards minus costs. Adams also notes that his scheme encompasses the notion of 'reciprocity' or 'equality of exchange' that involves reestablishing a parity in outcomes between people (p. 278).

The consequences of inequity

Having developed a formula for equity, Adams goes on to consider the consequences of inequity. Like Homans, Adams argues that it may be easier to tolerate overreward than underrreward, but, nevertheless, both will be experienced as unpleasant (overreward and underreward, or what Gergen (1969) calls *benign* and *malignant* inequity, respectively, were to become an interesting feature in work on equity).

Adams uses Festinger's (1957) theory of cognitive dissonance to derive some ideas about how people might respond to inequity. According to Festinger, people have a need for 'cognitive consistency'; thus when their thoughts feelings and actions are perceived to be discrepant or dissonant, the result is an unpleasant state of tension that motivates them to reduce the dissonance. Moreover, the greater the dissonance, the greater the motivation to reduce it. Adams, therefore, further proposes that a) inequity will be experienced as an unpleasant state of tension that is proportional to the magnitude of inequity present, and b) the tension will motivate the person possessing it to reduce the inequity. Moreover, the greater the inequity, the greater the motivation to reduce it. So how is this unpleasant 'tension' reduced?

1) *Alter the inputs*. Adams argues that one obvious method is to alter the inputs. So, if one feels one has been overpaid or underpaid, one can increase or reduce the magnitude of one's inputs respectively. Adams found support for this in a number of studies (Adams, 1963, 1965; Adams and Jacobsen, 1964; Adams and Rosenbaum, 1962). For instance, on a proofreading task, subjects who were led to believe that their pay was excessive for their qualifications produced higher quality work (increased their outcomes) relative to other groups who were led to believe that their pay was commensurate with their qualifications. Similarly, Adams cites an unpublished study by Arrowood who found that subjects worked for longer than that for which they had officially been paid

2) *Alter the outcomes*. If one is overrewarded or underrewarded another way of reducing equity 'tension' is to reduce or increase one's outcomes,

respectively. Adams (1965) reports no evidence for the former, but in support of the latter he cites a study by Homans (1953) in which workers who felt that their pay did not match their work, expressed dissatisfaction with the inequity, and voted to join another union (presumably in the hope of putting themselves in a better position to bargain for a more equitable set of outcomes).

3) *Distort inputs and outcomes cognitively.* Sometimes people in a situation of inequity may be unable, or unwilling to actually alter their inputs; consequently, says Adams, they may distort the inputs cognitively, or psychologically. Techniques for distortion include altering the importance or relevance of the inputs and outcomes. As evidence for this, Adams refers to a study by Weick (1964) in which subjects who were induced to work for no credit evaluated their task more favourably than subjects who worked for normal course credits. This could be interpreted as showing that subjects who thought they were receiving less than equity demands reevaluated or distorted their outcomes upwards.

4) *Leave the field.* Another way of minimizing inequity is to sever social contact; one could, for instance, quit a job or obtain a transfer. In support of this idea, Adams cites a study by Patchen (1959) who showed that men who said that their pay should be higher, had higher rates of absenteeism (though presumably this could also be construed as evidence that they had reduced their inputs).

5) *Act on others.* Adams also argues they inequity can be reduced by 'acting on the other' person or group with whom one is interacting. For instance, one can attempt to alter the other person's inputs and outcomes, or even try to force him or her out of the relationship. So, for example, one could try to make the other person work harder, or give you some of his or her outcomes.

6) *Change object of comparison.* Finally, Adams suggests that one can change the object of one's comparison. For example, one could decide to compare oneself with other whose input/outcome ratios are more similar to one's own ratio.

Adams further suggests a number of principles to cover how these principles might be prioritized. Thus individuals will tend to try to maximize the importance of their outcomes, and iminimize increasing effortful inputs that are costly to change. They will also resist real and cognitive changes to inputs and outcomes that are central to their self-concept and self-esteem, leave the field only as a last resort, and be resistant to changing their objects of comparison when such comparisons have become stabilized over time, and, in effect, have become an anchor. Adams concludes his chapter with the plea that 'More research is required' (p. 297). He was certainly not to be disappointed.

Elaine Hatfield and Equity Theory

Whilst Adams and Homans are often cited as the founders of equity theory, there is little doubt that it was the incisive and prolific work of Elaine Hatfield (previously Walster) in the 1970's that really brought equity to the forefront of psychological theorizing about, and research into, justice.

Hatfield and her associates set out to put the concept of psychological equity on a firm theoretical and empirical basis (see, for example, Austin and Walster, 1974; Austin and Hatfield, 1980; Walster, Berscheid and Walster, 1973; Walster and Walster, 1975; Walster, Walster and Berscheid, 1978). Hatfield et al. start from the fundamental assumption that *'man is selfish'* (see Walster et al., 1973, p. 151, and Walster et al., 1978, p. 7), and then go on to formulate four key theoretical propositions. These propositions are as follows.

1) Individuals will try to maximize their outcomes (where outcomes equal rewards minus costs).

2) Groups will maximize collective reward by evolving accepted systems for equitably apportioning resources among members. Therefore, groups will evolve systems of equity and will attempt to induce members to accept and adhere to them; hence they will reward members who treat others equitably, and punish, or increase the costs for, those who treat others inequitably.

3) When individuals find themselves in inequitable relationships they feel distress, and the greater the inequity, the greater the distress felt.

4) Individuals in inequitable relationships will attempt to eliminate the accompanying distress by restoring equity. Moreover, the greater the inequity, the greater the resultant distress, and the harder they will try to restore equity.

During the 1970's Hatfield et al. developed their own version of the equity formula. They started with a formula that resembles that devised by Homans (see Walster et al., 1973), but later changed it to cope with some mathematical problems (see Walster et al., 1975, 1978). We will consider the problems with equity formulae shortly, but for the moment, suffice it to say that their aim was to maintain the basic principle that, the greater one's inputs, the greater one's outcomes should be, and those with equal inputs should receive equal outcomes. However, they wished to allow this to happen for *negative inputs* as well as positive inputs. For example, Hatfield et al. argue that in an industrial setting, assets such as 'capital' and 'manual labour' may entitle one to rewards, because they are positive inputs; however, negative inputs, such as 'incompetence' and 'disloyalty' may entitle one to costs. Hatfield et al. also propose a similar distinction between inputs in social settings. Thus, social assets such as beauty and kindness may entitle one to reward, whereas social liabilities, such as drunkenness or cruelty, entitle one to costs.

Like Adams, Hatfield et al., suggest that those in a situation of inequity will experience tension or distress that will motivate them to reduce the inequity. Hatfield et al. categorise the distress in two ways. First, there is *retaliation distress*; this occurs when 'exploiters' (those on the advantageous side of inequity) fear that their victims, their victims' sympathizers, legal agencies, or even God, may retaliate against them because of the injustice. This may not necessarily reflect a real threat of harm, it can be conditioned also. For instance, children are often punished if they are caught injuring others, so they may come to experience conditioned anxiety at the thought of harming another. 'Victims' (those on the disadvantageous end of inequity) may also feel retaliation distress, for fear that they will be ridiculed or considered a 'pushover'. The second form of distress is *self-concept distress*; this occurs when people feel that they have violated their own moral code or standards. Austin and Walster (1974) briefly refer to the fact that when people are undercompensated 'they may describe their distress as resentment or anger' (p. 208), however, the motivating force of being 'angered' by 'exploitation' is given less consideration at this point in the theory.

Nevertheless, no matter how it is caused, the distress motivates the person experiencing it to restore equity, and again, following on from Adams, Hatfield et al. suggest that the restoration of equity is accomplished in two main ways. First, people can restore *actual equity* by altering their own, or their partners' inputs and outcomes. Thus, for example, they can work less hard (decrease their own inputs), steal equipment from work (raise their own outcomes), and so on. Second, alternatively, or additionally, they can distort reality so that equity is restored *psychologically*. For instance, a male worker who feels that he is being underrewarded may attempt to convince himself that he is uneducated or unmotivated (reduce his inputs), or the job has special advantages (increase his outcomes), or his boss is doing a lot for him (increase his boss's inputs), or that his boss is suffering from stress (minimize his boss's outcomes). (See Walster et al., 1978, pp. 18-19).

Another important feature of Hatfield et al.'s theory of equity concerns the use of power to legitimize particular inputs and outcomes. Given that, according to the theory, 'society can define anything - bravery or cowardice, humility or arrogance, beauty or ugliness - as valuable input', we need some ideas to explain 'who gets to decide whether such inputs as good breeding, skin colour, sex, or tap dancing ability, prevail' (Walster and Walster, 1975, pp. 29-30). Hatfield et al.'s answer is clear, those in power determine who decides what counts. They argue that those in power will not only capture the lion's share of goods but also be successful in persuading those of the equitableness of using the inputs those in power favour. Moreover, over time, those in power will evolve a social philosophy to support their position, and the community will come to accept this justification of the status quo. That is, unless there are marked shifts in the balance of power, in which case the process will start again (Austin and Hatfield, 1980; Walster and Walster, 1975; Walster, Walster and Berscheid, 1978).

Finally, Hatfield and her associates draw attention, as did Adams, to the fact that equity does not simply refer to interactions between pairs of participants (Walster et al., 1978). The standard of comparison for equity judgements may be another person, another group of people, an organization, or even a 'generalized other' (that is, a general grouping such as 'other workers', 'men', 'women', or even 'the World'). Hence comparisons can be *local* (aimed at particular individuals), or *referential* (aimed at some generalized grouping). Here Hatfield et al. echo what is known as the 'status-value' approach to equity, which looks at the status of various inputs and outcomes and emphasizes that a 'just' state in local comparison may be viewed as 'unjust' in a referential comparison (see Berger, Zelditch, Anderson and Cohen, 1972).

The evidence for equity: the early work

Hatfield and her colleagues were able to point to a large number of empirical studies conducted in the 1960's and 1970's that could be interpreted as supportive with the general predictions of equity. Only a very small portion of the voluminous literature will be mentioned here (for more comprehensive reviews see, Austin and Walster, 1980; Lawler, 1968; Opsahl and Dunnette, 1966; Pritchard, 1969; Walster, Berscheid and Walster, 1973; Walster, Walster and Berscheid, 1978).

For instance, in a laboratory decision making task, Austin and Walster (1974) found that subjects who felt that they had been equitably rewarded expressed greater satisfaction and emotional contentment than subjects who had been overrewarded, as well as those who had been underrewarded. Though, interestingly, as both Homans and Adams had predicted, overrewarded subjects expressed greater contentment than underrewarded subjects. A number of studies have shown that individuals who feel overbenefitted produce better quality work

(Adams, 1963; Adams and Jacobsen, 1964); whereas those who feel they have been paid inequitably decrease the quality of each unit of their work for which they are paid (Lawler and O'Gara, 1967). Also people who have been overbenefitted often voluntarily surrender part of their benefits to their deprived partners (Leventhal, Allen and Kemelgor, 1969; Marwell, Ratcliffe and Schmitt, 1969). Other studies that are interpreted as supportive of Adams' basic predictions about equity in the work place include those by Andrews (1967), Moore and Baron (1973), and Pritchard, Dunnette and Jorgenson (1972). Although a few studies seemed to show that subjects did not alter their quantity and quality of work to cope with inequitable pay (for example, Gergen, Morse and Bode, 1974; Kessler and Wiener, 1972; Valenzi and Andrews, 1971), Walster et al. (1978) argue that, in these studies, workers responded to inequity in ways that were perfectly compatible with equity. For instance, they quit their jobs, changed their perceptions of what constituted a fair wage, or considered other factors, such as praise, as a suitable compensatory outcome.

One of the predictions of equity as developed by Hatfield et al., is that subjects who have caused harm to others, or made them incur costs, can restore equity through *compensation*. In support of this general idea, Buss and Brock (1966) found that, compared to other students, students who had been led to believe that they had seriously damaged university property (by blowing it up in an experiment) were more likely to sign a petition agreeing to a raise in student tuition fees.

As support for the idea of the psychological restoration of equity, Hatfield et al. were able to refer to a number of studies on a topic very popular at the time, known as *victim derogation*, or 'blaming the victim'. In a typical laboratory set up, subjects would be induced to administer, or be party to the administration of, electric shocks, or some other aversive stimulus, to a 'victim'. In general, these studies indicate that when subjects are given no opportunity to compensate the victim, and perceive that the victim has no opportunity to retaliate back, there is a tendency for the 'harmdoers' to denigrate their victims, and make negative evaluations of them (see, for example, Berscheid, Boye and Walster, 1968; Glass, 1964; Legant and Mettee, 1973; Lerner, 1965, 1971; Lerner and Matthews, 1967; Lerner and Simmons, 1966).

For example, in a classic study by Lerner and Simmons (1966), subjects participated in an experiment allegedly on the perception of emotion. In two of the conditions, subjects were required to view a television monitor that showed an 'innocent victim', on 'live' television, writhing in pain as she allegedly received electric shocks. When subjects were given the opportunity of helping the victim, by assigning her to another condition in which she would receive a reward (compensation), all but one voted to do so. However, for other subjects this alternative was not available, and the victim continued to suffer. The results showed that when the victim was doomed to suffer, subjects were significantly more likely to devalue her, by rating her as less intelligent, less mature, 'cold', and so on. In equity terms, this kind of derogation could be construed as adding negative inputs to the victim's input/outcome ratio to justify the negative outcomes (harm or costs) that the victim has incurred. However, giving the victim an opportunity to retaliate would, according to equity, tend to equalize the input/outcome ratios of the harmdoer and victim, by adding negative outcomes to the harmdoer's input/outcome ratio; and, indeed, it seems that giving victims an opportunity for retaliate back reduces the derogation effect (Berscheid, Boye and Walster, 1968; Glass, 1964; Legant and Mettee, 1973).

Within equity, if you are an 'exploiter' or 'harmdoer', another way of restoring equity psychologically is to minimize your perceptions of the victim's suffering (that is, reduce the victim's costs or negative outcomes); and in support of this, Brock and Buss (1962) found that students who administered electric shocks came to underestimate the painfulness of the shocks they were delivering. On the other hand, when one is on the disadvantageous end of inequity, as a 'victim', equity predicts that, psychologically, one way of restoring equity would be to convince oneself that the 'exploiter' is justified in reaping excessive benefits. And, indeed, Jecker and Landy (1969) and Walster and Prestholdt

(1966) found that subjects pressured into performing a favour for an unworthy recipient tended to justify their behaviour by convincing themselves that the recipient was worthy after all.

More recent research

Although the 1960's and early 1970's probably saw equity theory at its peak, since then we have seen some important collections of papers devoted to equity (for instance, Greenberg and Cohen, 1982; Messick and Cook, 1983) and a steady stream of empirical studies has emerged that could be interpreted as supportive of some of the basic predictions of equity theory.

A number of studies endorse the general point that, in a work situation, most subjects prefer a distribution in which increases in inputs or contributions are met with increases in outcomes; thus the more work a person does, the more he or she should receive (see, for example, Farkus and Anderson, 1976; Harris, 1980; Lansberg, 1984; Mellers and Hartka, 1989; Wagstaff, Bowles, Hughes, Rogers, Turner and Perfect, 1994; Wagstaff and Perfect, 1992; Wagstaff, Huggins and Perfect, 1996). Other investigators have looked at responses to inequity. For instance, in real life work settings, Griffith (1989) found that subjects will alter the quantity and quality of their work in response to overpayment and underpayment, and Greenberg (1988, 1989) found that employees will alter their performance, or cognitively reevaluate their outcomes, in response to relative changes in status value and pay (all in the directions predicted by equity).

Other studies have shown that job and pay satisfaction are significantly related to perceptions of pay equity in comparison with others (Berkowitz, Fraser, Treasure, and Cochran, 1987; Orpen and Bonnici, 1990; Summers and DeNisi, 1990), and both overpayment and underpayment lead to less satisfaction, though again, workers seem to be more sensitive to underpayment (Sweeney, 1990). Interestingly, with regard to the latter, Hassebrauck (1986) found support for Homans' and Adams' predictions that a) the greater the perceived inequity, the greater the distress felt, and b) overpayment would be associated with feelings of guilt, whilst underpayment would be associated with feelings of anger.

Greenberg (1990) also found that employee theft rates increased during a period in which employee pay was temporarily reduced. As Hatfield et al. suggest, theft could be interpreted as a way of restoring equity through increasing the employees' outcomes, and decreasing the outcomes of their employer. Another prediction of Hatfield et al. is that those who feel underbenefitted or unjustifiably harmed, may seek to restore equity by harming, or destroying the property of those whom they feel are responsible, or who have benefitted at their expense. Accordingly, Clarkson (1989) found that, in an aggressive encounter, subjects who had inequitably treated retaliated with increased levels of aggression; also, Demore, Fisher and Baron (1988) found that students who felt they had been inequitably treated, and had no control over their outcomes, were more likely to report engaging in vandalistic acts.

With a growing interests in the psychology of sport, some researchers have even looked out how equity considerations may influence the performance of athletes. Thus, for example, Lord and Hohenfield (1979) found that baseball players showed decrements in batting performance, when, relative to others, they received pay cuts; when their income was restored, however, their batting performance improved. More recently, in a study of baseball and basket ball players, Harder (1992) found that players who considered themselves underrewarded behaved less cooperatively and more selfishly (presumably depriving others of positive outcomes), whilst overrewarded players behaved more cooperatively (for other examples of the alleged operation equity in sport, see Mark and Greenberg, 1987). Research has also continued to support equity's predictions regarding victim derogation. For instance, Craig, O'Neal, Taylor, Levi and Yost (1993), showed that harmdoers were less likely to negatively evaluate a victim if they were given an opportunity to do the victim a favour. More of the literature on victim derogation will be mentioned in the next chapter.

Equity in intimate situations

Although Adams (1965) suggests that equity is not limited to workplace situations, the idea that equity that may operate in intimate personal relationships has played an important part in Hatfield's work on equity, and has had a considerable influence on theory and research into the psychology of interpersonal attraction. In fact, it is difficult to find any psychological publication in the area of interpersonal attraction that does not refer to Hatfield.

Hatfield and her associates argue that, as in the workplace, people in personal relationships want their relationships to be equitable; relative to their partner, they expect a return commensurate with their contributions to the relationship. Consequently, when they perceive themselves to be inequitably treated this can have detrimental effects on the relationship. In couples, for example, one partner may feel angry and cheated, the other feel guilty (Berscheid and Walster, 1978; Hatfield, Utne, and Traupman, 1979).

A number of studies indicate support for the view that equity can have a profound influence on personal relationships. For instance, married and dating couples who see their relationships as equitable in terms of the balance between their contributions to, and their receipts from, the relationship, are more likely to express satisfaction with the relationship, stay together and have more optimistic estimates of their future. In contrast, couples who perceive that their relationship is inequitable in terms of the balance of contributions and benefits are less likely to engage in sexual activity with each other, and the underbenefitted members are more likely to be dissatisfied, depressed, and report engaging in extramarital affairs (Berscheid and Walster, 1978; Hatfield, Traupman and Walster, 1979; Houlihan, Jackson and Rogers, 1990; Schafer and Keith, 1980; Walster, Walster and Traupman, 1978). Women, in particular, seem to be especially unhappy when the division of household labour is deemed to be inequitable (Robinson and Spitze, 1992). Importantly also, equity does not only apply to younger couples, it strongly influence satisfaction amongst older couples and friends (Reynolds, Remer and Johnson, 1995; Rook, 1987).

The decline of equity

Although it may be possible to find alternative explanations for individual studies, taken as a whole, these studies would seem to provide a fairly impressive and convincing case for the idea that equity is perhaps *the* guiding principle of justice in human relationships. Indeed, it seems to encapsulate and make sense of the popular philosophical view that justice involves 'treating equals equally, and unequals unequally' (Buchanan and Mathieu, 1986). Nevertheless, despite this wealth of evidence, and the apparent parsimony of the equity concept in describing the 'essence' of justice, equity is no longer the force it once was. For although at first the proponents of equity seemed tried hard to ward off the critics, eventually the critics gained the ascendant and managed to relegate equity to its present rather impoverished and precarious position in the psychological literature on justice. So what went wrong?

Finding a formula

Even during equity's hey day, a number of theorists and researchers expressed concern at the limitations of equity as a general explanatory and descriptive justice principle. It did not help that none of the formulae put forward to describe equity actually 'worked' in a way that made psychological sense.

As originally conceived, equity was supposed to concern *equal* ratios of outcomes and inputs between individuals. Hence Walster et al. (1973) define an equitable relationship as existing when 'all participants are receiving equal relative outcomes from the relationship' (p. 152). However, one does not need to be an expert in mathematics to realize that Adams' (1965) formula does not work with various combinations of negative and zero inputs and outcomes. To reiterate, according to Adams, equity exists between two people, P (Person) and A (another), when their contributions, or *inputs*, exist in equal proportion to their receipts, or *outcomes*, such that:

$$\frac{\text{Outcomes for P}}{\text{Inputs of P}} = \frac{\text{Outcomes for A}}{\text{Inputs of A}}$$

This works fine when all the inputs and outcomes are greater than zero and positive. But what if P contributes 5 'good' or positive inputs (such as hours of work), and receives 5 negative outcomes, such as punishments, whereas A contributes 5 'bad' or negative inputs (such as theft) and receives 5 positive units of reward? In this case, the good person will have been punished and the bad person rewarded, but, according to Adam's formula, such an arrangement would be perfectly equitable, because $-5/5 = 5/-5$ (the equation works out at -1 in each case). Also, if both these participants received nothing at all for these rather different activities, the relationship would still be perfectly equitable, because $0/-5 = 0/5$ (the result is zero in each case). Such distributions would obviously offend what, according to Harris (1976), is the fundamental assumption of equity, namely that 'when equity holds, outcomes are an increasing function of inputs' (p. 196); that is, the more one contributes, the more one should receive.

Because of this problem various researchers in the 1970's attempted to come up with a formula to describe equity in mathematical terms (see, for example, Anderson, 1976; Farkas and Anderson, 1979; Jasso, 1978, 1983; Walster and Walster, 1975; Walster et al., 1978), but none of them was able to solve the problem of dealing with negative and zero inputs and outcomes within an equal ratio framework that makes psychological sense. A variety of solutions have, therefore, been suggested, such as abandoning the whole idea that equity concerns negative inputs (Anderson, 1976; Huppertz, 1978); thus Anderson says, 'it might not overstate the case too far to say that equity theory does not apply to negative input' (p. 296). Other suggestions include converting the negative inputs to positive inputs (Samuel, 1978), and defining equity purely in *ordinal* terms (for example, Moschetti, 1979). In the latter case, if the inputs of one partner exceed the inputs of the other partner(s), then any values of the outcomes to be assigned would be equitable, so long as the outcomes assigned to the first partner exceed those assigned to the others. However, again there seems to be something intuitively adrift with this idea. It would mean, for example, that if I input 100 negative units (say, for armed robbery) and you input 100 positive units (say, a year working to help the sick), justice would be done if I received ten pennies, and you received eleven pennies. Alternatively if I put in two hours of work, and you put in one and a half hours of work, justice would be done if I received a million pounds or dollars, and you received 20 years imprisonment followed by the electric chair.

The issue of the most appropriate way of expressing equity in mathematical has resulted in a lively and continuing debate (see, for example, Harris, 1983, 1993; Harris, Messick and Sentis, 1981; Romer, 1977; Mellers, 1982, 1986; Wagstaff and Perfect, 1992)[1]. However, it does not bode well for equity theory that theorists and researchers cannot actually agree, except in the most vague ordinal terms, what the 'equity formulation' actually is or should be. For equity's critics, however, the failure to come up with an adequate formula is the least of its problems.

---

[1] Probably the most cited equity formula after that of Adams is that of Walster et al.'s (1978). This is a revision of an earlier formula (Walster and Walster, 1975) and states that equity exists between two persons, A and B, when:

$$\frac{O_A - I_A}{|I_A|^K} = \frac{O_B - I_B}{|I_B|^K}$$

where the K's are +1 or -1 according to whether $O - I$ and I have the same or opposite signs. The vertical lines around the inputs indicate that the sign of the input should be ignored. This formula deals with both positive and negative inputs but as Farkas and Anderson (1979) and Harris (1983) point out, it makes some counterintuitive predictions. For example, if the inputs for A are 10, and for B, 5, and there are 18 outcome units to be divided between A and B, then the division would be 12 outcome units for A, and 6 units for B. This seems perfectly reasonable; A inputs twice as much as B and receives twice as many outcomes. However, if there are only 9 outcome units to divide the formula would give 8 to A and only 1 to B; in other words, A still only inputs twice as much as B but now receives eight times as many outcomes. This difference becomes even more difficult to reconcile when we consider that the outcome units could have been different measures of the same amount, such as 18 fifty pence pieces in the first instance, and one pound coins in the second.

A similar problem arises with Harris's (1980) 'linear equity formula' that states that equity exists when, $O_i = aI_i + r_a$, where O are the outcomes, and I are the inputs for individuals i in a relationship, a is a constant >0 for a particular situation, and r_a is a constant for all contributors. (Expressed in graphical form, this means that if we assign a given set of inputs or contributions from various individuals to the x axis, then a fair distribution of outcomes, represented on the y axis, is one that assigns outcomes according to a straight line sloping upwards from left to right).

In a dyadic or two person relationships Harris' formula would again allow any combination of inputs and outcomes, obeying the ordinal rule, to be equitable. And even in situations where there are more than two people the situation is hardly better. For example, of I do nothing, you do 10 hours of work, and our partner does 20 hours of work, and we produce 300 units of reward between us, it would be as equitable to distribute the rewards such that I receive 90, you receive 100, and our partner receives 110, as it would such that I receive a fine of -200, you receive 100 and our partner receives 400. Apart from appearing somewhat counterintuitive, both distributions would offend the original assumption of those such as Homans, Adams, Walster et al., and Anderson, that equity involves some kind of *equal* proportion.

The problem of offending the notion of equal ratios is also evident in was has been termed the 'equal excess norm' (see Harris, 1983; Komorita and Kravitz, 1979) that defines a relationship as equitable when the difference between the inputs and the outcomes of all participants is equal; that is when, $O_i - I_i = r_i$. Thus, for example, if I do no work and receive £10, our partner works for one hour and receives £11, and you work for two hours and receive £12, this is equitable (our inputs minus our outcomes are the same, 10 in each case). You may think it unfair to work that much harder than me yet receive only £2 more in pay. But, once again, to turn things round all we need to do is alter the units. If I do no work, our partner works for 60 minutes (rather than one hour) and you work for 120 minutes (rather than two hours), then these outcomes become inequitable (my difference score is still 10, but our partner's is -49, and yours is -108).

CHAPTER 7

MOTIVES AND MULTIPRINCIPLES

Almost from the start, one of equity theory's most vociferous opponents has been another outstanding justice theorist and researcher, Melvyn Lerner; though, on first consideration, part of Lerner's theorizing and research seems to fit quite nicely with the concept of equity.

Lerner's 'Just World'
During the 1960's and 1970's Lerner and his associates developed a theory that is frequently referred to as 'The Just World Hypothesis', or 'The Belief in a Just World' (Lerner, 1980; Lerner and Miller, 1978). According to Lerner, 'A Just World is one in which people "get what they deserve" '(1980. p. 11). Lerner (1980) argues that there are two bases for 'deserving', or 'entitlement' (like equity theorists, Lerner uses the two terms synonymously); these are 'behaviours' and 'attributes'. Some acts and attributes, such as failing to take care, not working hard enough, being ugly, inconsiderate or stupid, entitle one to, or are deserving of, negative consequences or punishment. Others, such as generosity, conscientiousness, and handsomeness entitle one to desirable or positive consequences. Put simply, good or desirable acts or attributes deserve positive outcomes, and bad or undesirable acts or attributes deserve negative outcomes.

The basic idea behind Lerner's 'Just World' hypothesis is that we all to some extent have a fundamental psychological need to believe that the world operates in this way; that is, 'Individuals have a need to believe that they live in a world where people generally get what they deserve' (Lerner and Miller, 1978, p. 1030). Consequently, whenever we see examples of people suffering, or being rewarded by chance (that is, without possessing the appropriate attributes or showing the appropriate behaviours), this threatens our belief that the world is just, so we engage in various techniques to restore justice. These can involve actual prevention and restitution, or psychological distortion techniques such as denial and withdrawal, and reinterpretation of the event. In the case of the latter, one can reinterpret the outcome, the cause, or the character of the person who has undeservedly benefitted or suffered. Lerner has been particularly interested in these methods of psychological distortion, that he calls 'psychological defences' (1980, p. 20).

For example, in one study subjects witnessed two workers doing a task. When, quite arbitrarily, one of the workers was given a fortuitous or chance reward, the worker receiving the reward was deemed by subjects to have worked harder (Lerner, 1965). Lerner concludes, 'The observers in this experiment construed a social event to fit a rather simple and understandable process. One of these can be paraphrased as "people deserve what happens to them" or "once I know what has happened to someone I will be more comfortable if I can believe that he has earned it" '(1965, p. 360). Lerner and his associates are probably most well known, however, for their victim derogation studies (see, for example, Lerner, 1965, 1971, 1980; Lerner and Matthews, 1967; Lerner and Simmons, 1966). As mentioned briefly in the last chapter, these studies demonstrate that when observers are confronted with a situation in which an innocent victim is suffering, and they are powerless to help, there is a significant tendency for observers to derogate or downgrade the characteristics of the victim.

The concept of the Just World has generated a huge volume of research, and it has obvious relevance to research on social issues such as blaming the victims of crime and poverty for their plight (Ryan, 1971; Symonds, 1975; Wagstaff, 1982, 1984). There is even a 'Just World Scale' (JWS) designed to tap the extent to which individuals share this belief (Rubin and Peplau, 1975; Furnham and Procter, 1989). On the JWS, some of the items refer to a just world in which good deeds are rewarded and bad punished (for instance, 'People who get "lucky breaks" have usually earned their good fortune', and 'By and large people deserve what they get'); whereas other items refer to a world in which good deeds are no more likely to be rewarded than bad deeds (for instance, 'Good deeds often go unnoticed and unrewarded', and 'Careful drivers are just as likely to get hurt in traffic accidents as careless ones'). As predicted, studies have shown that high JWS scorers (people who believe the world is just), are more likely to condemn individuals who lost a national draft lottery (the lottery was for drafting to Vietnam), derogate victims in victim derogation experiments, uphold the Protestant Work Ethic (that is, the belief that hard work will be rewarded), have negative attitudes towards the poor and minority ethnic groups, be less in favour of social security benefits, support the traditional role of women and generally show political conservatism (that is, support the status quo) (see, for example, Furnham and Procter, 1989; Rubin and Peplau, 1975; Wagstaff, 1984; Wagstaff and Quirk, 1983).

The concept of a Belief in a Just World has not gone uncriticized, however. For instance, some researchers have argued that victim derogation only occurs when the observer feels, in some sense, personally responsible for the plight of the victim (for a review and reply see, Lerner, 1980). Others (including Lerner, 1980, in fact) have argued that Just World Scale measures more than one dimension (see also Furnham and Procter, 1989; Harper and Wagstaff, 1992). Nevertheless, the evidence that in many circumstances people appear to distort reality such that situations approximate more to ones in which the good are rewarded and the bad are punished, and that individuals differ in the extent to which they do this, seems fairly impressive.

Thus far, the overlap between the Just World belief and equity would appear to be considerable. Indeed, noting the overlap, authors of social psychology textbooks have often tied them together (for example, Samuel, 1975; Sabini, 1995). If a just world is one in which the desirable acts and attributes (positive inputs) are rewarded (given positive outcomes), and undesirable acts and attributes (negative inputs) are punished (given negative outcomes), then the 'Just World' is remarkably like a 'equitable' world. Moreover, on first consideration, the tactics to which people resort in an attempt to maintain a 'Just World' look little different from those proposed by equity theorists as methods individuals use to restore psychological equity. Lerner, however, rather than being a firm advocate of equity theory, is one of its most ardent critics. To understand why, we first need to look very briefly at Lerner's views regarding how our interest in justice comes about.

The 'Justice Motive'

According to Lerner, underlying the belief in a Just World is the 'justice motive'. The justice motive is basically a commitment to seeing that both oneself and others receive appropriate deserts or entitlements. Hence, Lerner (1975, 1977) argues that, 'People have wants but they design their lives so that they deserve, are entitled to, what they want or modify their desires to fit what they can deserve' (p. 5). Lerner suggests that the roots of this motive are to be found in childhood as children learn to control or regulate their behaviour by delaying gratification. Children learn, for example, that if they want an expensive toy they must learn to save up, and not buy a less attractive toy immediately. However, learning to delay gratification assumes a stable environment; that is, an environment in which one can anticipate consequences. There must be a meaningful and predictable relationship between what the child does and what happens to him or her. It is no use putting off immediate gratification, unless the child knows that know that the consequences of doing so are stable and predictable.

Lerner proposes that through such learning the child develops a *personal contract*; a contract to give up things that feel good immediately on the assumption that a certain good will come about. This contract then becomes the basis of personal deserving or entitlement, and the child will become concerned when the contract is threatened or violated. This has important implications for the perception and treatment of others. If anyone else suffers by chance, this threatens the child's own personal contract; it upsets the meaningful relationship between what people do and what happens to them, and the child perceives that the same could happen to him or her. Thus, if possible, the child will attempt to restore this relationship by, for example, helping the blameless person who has suffered, but not the person who is responsible for his or her suffering. Lerner (1977) reviews a variety of evidence in support of this view. For instance, a number of studies have shown that children are more likely to help another child when the child in need of help is an innocent victim of fate, rather than someone who has done something foolish. Importantly also, the tendency to distinguish between the innocent and foolish victims of fate is most pronounced in those children who have learned to delay gratification (Brabant and Lerner, 1975; Lerner, 1977; Long and Lerner, 1974).

So far again, one might think that there still is not much discrepancy between Lerner's views and those of the equity theorists. The idea of that people will sense injustice when their 'personal contracts' are threatened does not seem markedly different to the idea from equity theory that people will experience 'self-concept' distress when their internal moral code or standards are threatened. Lerner is adamant, however, equity theory and justice motive theory are very different.

His first objection to equity theory concerns the assumption made by equity theorists that justice is motivated by a selfish desire to maximize one's pay-offs. Lerner argues that justice related behaviour is motivated by considerations of what people deserve, not selfishness. People do not wish to restore justice simply to maximize pay-offs, whether these be in terms of rewards or reducing distress, rather they are motivated to restore justice because injustice threatens their personal contracts and the whole stability of the environment on which the contracts are based. To illustrate this, Lerner refers to some experimental studies that demonstrate that children who show a capacity for delayed gratification will help 'deserving others' quite anonymously, so they do not do it 'selfishly', simply to gain respect and admiration. Some of the most interesting findings indicate that personal deserving seems to predominate over the deserving of others; thus both older children and adults will only donate to a 'deserving other' when they feel that they themselves have received an appropriate 'deserved' outcome for their actions. However, when, but only when, they have received what they think they deserve, are they willing to work to help a deserving other, than to earn extra for themselves (Lerner, 1977, 1980; Miller, 1977). Lerner's colleague, Dale Miller, argues that if subjects were motivated to help simply to maximize their pay-offs, such as to gain extra money, to gain social approval, or alleviate the pain of guilt, one would not predict this pattern of results. Subjects would either work to gain maximum pay, or to benefit others, but not to give themselves what they deserve, no more no less, and *then* benefit others.

However, ultimately it is not this aspect of Lerner's theorizing and research that has proved most damaging to equity theory. Far more damaging has been the view held by Lerner and many others, that equity is only *one* of many justice principles, and not necessarily the most important.

Lerner's multiprinciple approach

Lerner has come up with a number of variations on a central scheme for classifying rules of justice (Desmarais and Lerner, 1994; Lerner, 1974, 1975, 1977; Lerner, 1981; Lerner and Whitehead, 1980). Lerner started with four principles, the 'Marxian justice of need', the 'justice of equity', the 'justice of parity', and the 'justice of laws'; this was subsequently expanded to nine, but in recent papers there are eighteen. The eighteen rules are classified along two dimensions, depending on one's relation to someone, and the kind of interaction.

Relations with others can vary depending on whether one feels exactly the same as them (identity), similar to them (unit), or dissimilar to them (nonunit), and interactions can varying according to whether the goals of the interaction are perceived to be the same, similar (convergent) or dissimilar (divergent). The result is nine cells or combinations, and within each cell there are two rules depending on which dimension dominates (relation or interaction). Hence there are eighteen rules or forms of justice. The scheme can be summarized as follows.

When 'identity' or 'sameness' is the relation, the rules for the three types of interaction goals are, needs (same goals, relation dominant), nuturant welfare concern (same goals, interaction dominant), individual oriented commune (convergent goals, relation dominant), collective orientation (convergent goals, interaction dominant), heroics and self-sacrifice (divergent goals, relation dominant), and utilitarian decisions (divergent goals, interaction dominant).

When the relation is 'unit' or 'similar', the rules for the three types of interaction goals are, reciprocity (same goals, relation dominant), mutual responsiveness (same goals, interaction dominant), team effort, parity or equality (convergent goals, relation dominant), cooperation, contribution or equity (convergent goals, interaction dominant), formal contest (divergent goals, relation dominant), and justified self interest or parallel competition (divergent goals, interaction dominant).

And finally, when the relation is 'different', or 'non-unit', the rules for the three types of interaction goals are, judging others' personal worth in terms of one's values (same goals, relation dominant), evaluating others' acts in terms of one's goals (same goals, interaction dominant), status consistent division of labour (convergent goals, relation dominant), contractual relations or 'mock equity' (convergent goals, interaction dominant), 'fight' to maximize differential outcomes (divergent goals, relation dominant), and regulated conflict, to maximize legal outcomes (divergent goals, interaction dominant).

As Lerner now postulates eighteen different kinds of justice, he has adapted his justice motive theory such that each person's 'personal contract' now involves an implicit recognition of all these 'rules of entitlement'; that is, we all carry round with us, in memory, a set of prototypes, scripts and schemata, informing us which rule of entitlement to use with a particular person or group of people in a given situation (Desmarais and Lerner, 1994).

However, reconciling these various forms of justice with Lerner's original concept of the 'justice motive' is problematical. Lerner still argues that 'Entitlements capture the full range of perceptions of one's own as well as others' *deserving*' (Desmarais and Lerner, 1994, p. 43, my emphasis). The guiding principle that 'people want what they deserve' thus clearly remains, and all of these forms of justice presumably represent 'desert claims'. But some of Lerner's justice rules seem to fit rather uncomfortably with the notion of 'desert' as it functions within the 'justice motive'. Consider an illustration of what Lerner calls the rule of 'justified self-interest'; that is, a rule that allegedly operates in some situations when we feel similar to people but have different goals. As a demonstration of this, Lerner (1977) cites a study by Lerner and Lichtman (1968) in which women students had to choose whether to let themselves, or their partner, take a dose of electric shock. Only one member of each pair was given the opportunity to choose, and the decision as to which student would be allowed to choose was determined by random number tables. The results showed that about 90 percent of the students chose to assign their partner to receive the shocks. Moreover, there were few signs of guilt or regret, common responses being "Anyone would have taken the control (harmless) condition", and "I would have been a fool to take the shock". Lerner argues that these results illustrate that people consider it legitimate to act selfishly under conditions of 'parallel competition', where there is 'equal investment, risk, opportunity' (1977, p. 21). Perhaps so, but there seems a conflict here with the idea, fundamental to the basis of the justice motive, that it is contrary to the idea of desert *to see innocent people suffer*.

As Lerner (1977) puts it, 'Undeserved suffering elicits compassion and help; but people react with indifference or satisfaction to deserved suffering, depending upon whether the suffering was caused by the victim's blameworthy act or was the "deserved" fate meted out to a villain by the agents of goodness and truth' (p. 1). It seems an odd theory of desert that argues that a person who ends up taking electric shocks because of the whims of a random number table and the selfish impulses of her partner *deserves* to suffer. If a 'Just World' is a world in which each receives what she deserves, and good acts or attributes deserve reward, and bad acts and attributes deserve punishment, then unless there was some reward to be gained from receiving the shocks, in terms of 'justice motive theory', arguably no subject in this particular study *deserved* anything.

There are also problems with the notions such as 'need' and 'parity', as desert bases, and justice motive theory. Lerner argues that there is an important distinction to be made between the innocent victim of fate, and the blameworthy victim, and that recognition of this is related to the development of delayed gratification, and forms an integral part of the 'personal contract' in children. But how is it then that one can have a whole categories of justice, like need and equality (as well 'welfare', 'self-sacrifice' and 'fighting' to maximize one's differential outcomes) that seem to ignore totally the responsibility of the people in the various interactions for the situations they find themselves in? As we shall see, one of the fundamental assumptions underlying the principles of need and equality is that, unlike equity, they are supposed to ignore the inputs or actions of the individuals to whom they apply. In fact, within Lerner's theoretical approach, although concepts such responsibility, blame and culpability are seen as important elements in determining 'entitlement and deserving', they are not mentioned as a principle of justice by themselves, and are not especially related to any other principle.

Other multiprinciple approaches

Lerner's model is unusual in attempting to account for as many as eighteen principles of justice. Reis (1984) postulated seventeen principles, but his aim was to see if these could be collapsed and described in terms of a few basic themes. In an empirical study, Reis (1984) asked subjects to rate the seventeen principles of justice in terms of their similarity. The principles were derived from the literature in various disciplines and can be summarized as follows: it is all right to choose to let someone else be harmed rather than yourself; you are justified in meeting your own needs first; you should help regardless of whether you receive benefits in return; you should consider your own welfare first only when resources are scarce; group welfare is more important than individual welfare; outcomes should be based on actions but not intentions; you should expect favours to be returned; rewards and benefits should be distributed strictly according to the laws and rules of the situation; resources should be divided equally regardless of contribution; you must conform to the moral principles of groups you volunteer to join; you should do favours without expecting favours in return; as long as you obey the rules you are justified in maximizing your own self interest; you should live up to your own moral principles; those in power are justified in using their power to further their own interests; people should receive rewards proportional to contributions; rewards should be distributed according to need regardless of contribution; and people ought to fulfil their obligations through duty, contract or promise

When Reis looked statistically at how the principles were grouped in terms of similarity three dimensions emerged; these he describes as favouring rules that provide long-term gratification versus immediate reward; favouring rules that assert one's status versus rules that neutralize it; and favouring rules that focus on oneself rather than the group. Given their emphasis in other models, it is interesting to note (as Reis does) how the principles of need, equality, and proportionality (equity) related to the dimensions. Proportionality was more associated with delayed gratification, status assertion, and a personal orientation, whereas need and equality were more associated with immediate gratification, status neutralization, and a group orientation. Also, notably, need and equality were always closely related. If this is the case, however, it would again seem to create problems for Lerner's hypothesis that the understanding of justice principles is related to the development of delayed gratification. Reis's results would suggest that some of Lerner's justice principles, particularly equality and need, are actually associated with immediate gratification.

Another champion of the multiprinciple approach to justice is Morton Deutsch (1975, 1985). Indeed, he was one of the first theorists to devise a system for categorizing the conditions underlying multiple rules of justice. In a key article in 1975, Deutsch lists eleven ways in which justice has been described; thus people can be treated so that they receive outcomes proportional to their inputs, as equals, according to their needs, ability, efforts, accomplishments, the supply and demand of the market place, requirements of the common good, the principle of reciprocity, so that they have equal opportunity to compete, and so that none falls below a specified minimum. However, in this 1975 paper, Deutsch, like most other multiprinciple theorists, then goes on to look in detail at only three principles, equity, equality and need. His basic hypothesis is that equity, equality and need are three separate principles that operate in three different kinds of situation. Hence equity, or proportionality, dominates in cooperative situations in which economic productivity is a primary goal. Equality dominates in cooperative relations in which enjoyable social relations is the common goal, and need predominates in cooperative relations in which the fostering of personal development and personal welfare is the common goal. Later Deutsch (1985) summarizes his position as follows. 'The preference for sociocentric principles of distributive justice (such as egalitarianism and generosity) is associated with positive social-emotional, solidarity-oriented social relations, whereas the preference for individual-centred principles (such as proportionality or equity) is associated with impersonal task directed, economic social relations' (p. 202).

These ideas have been elaborated also by Sampson (1975) and Schwartz (1975). Sampson argues that 'By nature man is not an equity theorist' (pp. 49). In a society that fosters collectivism, communion and cooperation, equality will be the dominant principle of justice; the basic assumption of equality being that 'differential investments do not provide a legitimate basis for making claims to differential outcomes' (p. 49). Sampson argues that equity simply reflects the particular cultural pattern that dominates Western capitalist civilization; that is, a system that stresses agency, individualism, and competition. Sampson thus seems to differ slightly from Deutsch in emphasizing the more competitive nature of equity relations. Schwartz (1975) suggests that the justice of need is motivated by 'humanitarian norms' or the norms of 'social responsibility'. According to Schwartz, need also ignores inputs; he says, 'Need-based norms differ in that they do not prescribe a relative balance of inputs and outcomes between claimants .... Further, these norms are unique in that the person called on to forgo resources has performed no act justifying either a reduction in his own claims or an increase in others claims' (p. 112). Thus when humanitarian need norms are evoked, *the acts and attributes of the person in need are presumed to be irrelevant.*

In Greenberg and Cohen's (1982b) model there are four main rules of justice, mutual need, equality, self-interest, and own desires. Which of these rules is applied depends on the levels of interdependence, levels of intimacy and potential conflict over resources, the latter ultimately determining which rule applies. For example, mutual need dominates when interdependence and intimacy are high resulting in little conflict over resources (as in married couples); equality dominates when interdependence is low, intimacy is high, resulting in some conflict over resources (as between friends); self-interested justice dominates when interdependence is high, and intimacy is low, resulting in some conflict over resources (as between bargainers), and one's own desires predominate in situations where there is low intimacy and interdependence, and conflict over resources is very high (as between strangers).

In yet another variation, Kayser, Schwinger and Cohen (1984) have suggested that, in the mind of a layperson, the five principles of need, equality, contribution (equity), maximal difference, and maximal harm are differentially applied according to variations in four characteristics; 1) cognitive motivational intentions (partner's welfare, relationship welfare, own welfare, relative advantage competition, and other's harm); 2) affective relationship (from very positive to very negative); 3) the class of resource (particularistic, such as love or service, or universalistic, such as money), and 4) the direction of the transaction (giving, taking, or both). Thus, for instance, need is used when the partner's welfare is prominent; the affective climate in the relationship is very positive; the resource classes are particularistic and the transaction is directed to giving. The contribution principle is applied when one's own contribution is prominent; the affective climate is neutral; the resources are both particularistic and universalistic, and the direction of the transaction is both giving and taking. At the other extreme, however, maximal harm is applied when aggression towards the other in the relationship is prominent; the affective climate is very negative; the resources are particularistic, and the direction of the transaction is taking.

Can equity accommodate the other principles?

Thus far then, we have a number of schemes that describe a variety of rules of justice, of which 'equity' is only one rule. At first the equity theorists made an attempt to incorporate some aspects of the various multiprinciple perspective theories within equity theory. For instance, Hatfield et al. argued that equality and need can be incorporated into the equity principle (Walster and Walster, 1975; Walster, Berscheid and Walster, 1978). To incoporate need into the equity principle, 'need' simply takes on the value of an input. And to account for equality, 'humanity' becomes the relevant input; the rationale being 'since all men possess equal humanity, all men are entitled to equal outcomes' (Walster and Walster, 1975, p. 29).

However, critics of Hatfield's view remain unconvinced by the kind of account. Multiprinciple theorists argue that this view is imprecise, makes equity theory unfalsifiable, and obscures more than it clarifies (see, for example, Schwartz, 1975; Schwinger, 1980; Utne and Kidd, 1980). Indeed, Schwartz comments, 'This extension of equity theory seems essentially sleight of hand'

(1975, p. 132). Citing the work of Topitsch (1972), Schwinger (1980) also points out that, as an historical analysis shows, 'different groups posit and use justice principles that are at odds with proportionality' (p. 106). According to Schwinger, in the ancient world of the Middle East, for example, the allocation system was such that the members of an elite received the Lion's share of resources. Slavery was justified by regarding slaves as not human and thus possessing no rights. However, although these particular 'justice concepts' were enshrined in law by the powerful governing classes they were not unanimously shared by the lower classes who sought 'to acquire larger shares of the goods they themselves produced'. Also demands for equality have appeared throughout history since the beginning of Christianity. And even in modern industrial societies, in connection with the declaration of human rights, one usually finds 'a system designed to prevent persons from falling below an existence minimum'; thus 'alongside the performance principle, there is a norm whereby citizens have an a priori right to a certain amount of material wealth (variable from society to society) to satisfy their needs'. And with regard to educational opportunities, some political movements prefer allocations to be based on 'equal chance rather than on performance'. Schwinger thus concludes, 'The assumption of the equity theorists that the proportionality principle is the one and only, always effective concept of justice would seem to have more of an ideological than a scientific explanatory function' (pp. 104-106).

The empirical evidence for the multiprinciple approach

But what is the empirical evidence for the various alternative multiprinciple schemes? Empirical evidence relating to details of the more elaborate multiprincipled schemes is scant. Instead, with a few exceptions, researchers have tended to confine their empirical studies to a few basic rules, the most popular being equity, equality and need. To summarize, despite some inconsistencies and disagreements, if one looks at the various multiprinciple schemes the standard hypothesized pattern that emerges might be described as follows (see also, for example, Mikula, 1980; Schwinger, 1980; Leventhal Karuza and Fry, 1980; Folger, Sheppard and Buttram, 1995).

Equity, or the contributions rule, operates when there is little or no intimacy or affection (these are neutral), and although the relationship possesses a degree of cooperation, it is impersonal, and there is a sense of conflict and competition; also, the goal of the interaction is to maximize economic productivity.

Equality operates where there is more intimacy, slightly less potential for conflict, and an affective bond and attraction are present; the relationship is cooperative, and the group goal is one of group solidarity, harmony, and enjoyable social relations.

Need, or what was originally termed by Lerner, 'Marxian justice', operates in situations where there is high intimacy, affection, empathy, and attraction, an absence of conflict, and welfare is the shared goal.

To these we could also perhaps add another rule, though this has received comparatively little attention in the literature.

Winner takes all (Maximal difference) operates when there is no affective bond and no desire for cooperation. Instead, conflict and competition abound, and the goal is maximize one's own individual outcomes. This could be considered the same as Lerner's (1977) notion of 'Darwinian justice' (p. 43).

A number of researchers have reported support for some of these ideas. For instance, in a study reported by Deutsch (1985), some subjects were told that the goal of the research was to determine how productive people were under various conditions, whereas the other half were told that the research was concerned with friendship formation. The results showed a significant tendency for the 'productivity' group to follow an equity distribution, and the 'friendship formation' group to follow an equality distribution, though the difference was small (see also Stake, 1983). Subjects also appeared to enjoy tasks more when an equality rule was in operation, and subjects in the equality and needs conditions reported having cooperative feelings towards each other, whereas subjects in the contributions (equity) condition reported having competitive feelings towards one another. It can be noted that Lerner (1974) also showed that an equality rule was preferred over a contributions rule when the relationship between participants was defined as a 'team'. General support for Deutsch's proposals has also been reported by Assmar and Rodriques (1994). Using a questionnaire method, they found that equity was rated fairest when economic productivity was the primary goal, whereas equality and need were rated fairer when the goal was to foster friendly social relations or personal development.

One of the most obvious predictions from the general multiprinciple schema is that people in close, intimate relationships will prefer need and equality distribution rules to an equity or proportionality rule, and a number of studies indicate support for this idea (Clark and Chrisman, 1994). For instance, there is some evidence to suggest that in friendships and romantic relationships, partners can react negatively to receiving requests for repayments for benefits received, and they do not 'book keep' or keep track of individual inputs and outcomes; in fact, individuals interpret a strong inclination of the other to reciprocate favours as a sign that the other person is not interested in a romantic relationship (Clark, 1984; Clark and Mills, 1979; Clark, Mills and Corcoran, 1989). These results seem to fit with others that show that people infer more liking, closeness, friendship amongst people who using a need or equality rather than a contributions rule (Greenberg, 1983; Peterson, 1987). Desmarais and Lerner (1994) have also reported that people who define their relationship as extremely close are more satisfied when they have contributed effectively to their partner's welfare.

Problems for the multiprinciple perspective
However, apart from problems of defining exactly how many rules we should be considering, there are a number of difficulties with the multiprinciple approaches. The most obvious problem is that people clearly do not always operate the rules in the ways suggested. As pointed out in the previous chapter, a large volume of evidence suggests that equity, or proportionality between

contributions and outcomes, can be very important, if not dominant, in intimate relationships, and Soltan (1982) has commented that there are many close knit communities that are designed to foster enjoyable social relations that are highly inegalitarian in nature.

Some of these discrepant findings could possibly be explained in terms of differences in attitudes towards relationships both between individuals and within a relationship over time. For instance, there is some evidence that equity, or a contributions rule, is considered important in close relationships only by people who are judged to be high on *exchange orientation*; that is, individuals who favour reciprocity, expect immediate and comparable rewards when they have provided rewards for others, and feel uncomfortable when they receive favours they cannot reciprocate. In contrast, people low on exchange orientation seem relatively unconcerned about whether they are disadvantaged, advantaged or treated equally in terms of these factors, and generally feel more satisfied with their relationships (Buunk and VanYperen, 1991). Possibly, therefore, different findings may emerge with different subject samples. Subjects high on exchange orientation might be more likely to follow an equity rule, regardless of the nature of the relationship, than those who are high on what Clark and Mills (1979) have called *communal orientation*, that is primarily need responsive. However, as studies of close relationships rarely consider this dimension, it is impossible to assess the extent to which it may help to reconcile conflicting findings.

Desmarais and Lerner (1994) have also proposed that, within close or intimate relationships, variations over time in the elements relating to the various rules (like conflict and an emphasis on dissimilarities) may influence which rule is applied on a particular occasion. Sometimes couples or friends may feel very close (in an 'identity' relationship) whilst, at other times they may feel very far apart and at odds with each other (in a 'non-unit' relationship), resulting in the application of different rules. However, whilst finding a degree of support for this view, Desmarais and Lerner (1994) also found that a conflict-resolution strategy based on reciprocity in respecting needs, and equal contributions to decisions, was the most preferred strategy in dating partners, regardless of how they described their relationship in terms of Lerner's 'identity', 'unit' and 'non-unit' constructs.

Perhaps more troublesome, however, for both the equity and multiprinciple approaches to justice in close relationships, are some findings that indicate that, overall, the main determinant of whether dating and married couples are satisfied with their relationships is not whether equity, equality or need rules are followed, but the overall level of rewards they receive (Cate, Lloyd, Henton and Larson, 1982; Clark and Chrisman, 1994; Desmarais and Lerner, 1994; Martin, 1985; Reynolds, Remer and Johnson, 1995).

It is not the case, either, that an equity rule is followed exclusively in economic productivity situations. For instance, a number of studies have indicated that individuals who have made most contribution to a particular task tend to distribute outcomes more equally than those who have contributed little (Schwinger, 1980; Törnblöm, 1992). Also Hoffman and Maier (1959) found that in small work groups, students distributed additional grade points (that is grade points in addition to those currently held) on the basis of need. And Elliott and Meeker (1986) found that subjects took into account both contributions and need when allocating money on a productivity task. Elliott and Meeker's results fit with other evidence that suggests that distribution according to need is not confined to situations in which participants are intimate with, or attracted to, each other (Lamm and Schwinger, 1983). Also, Harris (1980) has pointed out, 'Every equity study that has explicitly checked for adoption of equality has reported a sizeable percentage of equality adoptions' (p. 112; see also, Harris and Joyce, 1980).

A standard way of attempting to account for these findings is to invoke the view that individuals may sometimes combine or attempt to balance principles (Leventhal, 1976; Lerner, 1991; Schwinger, 1980). For instance, Leventhal (1976) suggests that the various justice rules, and in particular, equity, equality and need, might be used in combination to determine what he calls the 'deservingness' of any particular person. When this happens, each rule will have a weighting that indicates its relative importance. Equity, or the contributions rule, will be most heavily weighted in work situations in which productivity is the goal; the equality rule will be weighted most heavily when the maintenance of harmony and solidarity amongst receivers is important, and the needs rule will be most heavily weighted when there is a close friendly relationship between people and welfare is the group goal. Thus, for instance, in a productivity situation, if subjects want to maintain a cooperative spirit, they might temper equity with equality. This idea seems feasible, though there seems to be a little if any empirical research on it (see Tornblöm, 1992). However, as an interpretation of some of the aforementioned findings, it begins to look somewhat question begging. If the various principles of justice operate in the way most of the multiprinciple theorists suggest, then the most obvious prediction should be that when information relevant to one justice 'sphere', such as information about need, is introduced into a situation that would normally be associated with another justice rule, such as an 'equity' situation in which unrelated individuals are involved in an economic productivity task, the former information should be deemed irrelevant and *ignored*. Hence, the fact that participants fail to ignore 'irrelevant' information suggests that something has gone seriously wrong with the model.

There are a number of other findings that do not really sit happily with any of the major multiprinciple perspectives on justice. For example, according to the basic multiprinciple model, if the goal of a group interaction is harmony, an equality rule should be preferred. However, Leventhal, Karuza and Fry (1980) found that in situations where there were sizeable differences in performance an equal distribution may generate conflict; therefore subjects considered that harmony would be best preserved by using an unequal distribution that takes contributions into account. Also, according to the multiprinciple model, one might expect friends (with affectional ties) to follow an equality rule, and nonfriends or acquaintances (with neutral ties) to follow an equity rule; but

Lamm and Kayser (1978) found that, whereas acquaintances allocated benefits equally, friends preferred unequal allocations when unequal inputs resulted from unequal amounts of effort.

In addition, a number of studies also suggest that individuals tend to allocate rewards more equally when they want to present themselves favourably to recipients, as in situations in which the allocators will be aware of their allocation decisions, or they expect to meet them, or their impressions are valued (Austin, 1980; Leventhal, Michaels and Sanford, 1972; Reis and Gruzen, 1976; Von Grumbkow, Deen, Steensma and Wilke, 1976). However, other results suggest that if subjects think that equity would create the most favourable impression, they prefer an equity distribution (Leung and Bond, 1984; Reis and Gruzen, 1976). Also, in cooperative situations, those who have contributed most are likely to follow a 'politeness ritual' and distribute rewards more equally than those who have contributed little. In a competitive situation, however, the reverse seems to be the case; it is the higher contributors that prefer unequal allocations (Schwinger, 1980). Other findings suggest that individuals may apply more equal allocations when they are unable or unwilling to perform the calculations necessary to operate a proportionality rule (Harris and Joyce, 1980).

To complicate matters further, many of these effects also interact with sex differences. An obvious prediction with regard to sex differences would be that, according to stereotype, females, being more care oriented and interested in social harmony, would prefer to allocate equally, whereas males, being less empathic and more competitive, would prefer to follow an equity rule. However, the evidence on this has been complex and conflicting (see, for example, Benton, 1971; Kahn, Nelson and Gaeddert, 1980; Kidder, Bellettirie and Cohn, 1977; Asdigan, Cohn and Blum, 1994). In a review of the relevant literature, Major and Deaux (1982) conclude that, by and large, sex differences in the application of allocation rules appear only occur when the allocator is a co-recipient of the resource to be allocated. When the allocator is a co-recipient women take less for themselves than men, and if their performance is superior to the other participants, women will tend to distribute resources more equally than men. When their performance is inferior to others in the relationship, however, both men and women follow an equity rule.

It is perhaps not surprising, therefore, that reviewers of various aspects of the literature on the operation of the multiprinciple schemes have described parts of the literature as 'confusing' (Clark and Chrisman, 1994) and 'inconclusive' (Tornblöm, 1992).

CHAPTER 8

RESPONSIBILITY, MORALITY, AND PUNISHMENT

By now the reader may feel that psychological theorizing and research on justice is somewhat confused and disjointed. Unfortunately it gets worse. There are a number of other topics that psychologists have attached to the term 'justice' that are frequently invoked in criticisms of equity. However, whilst these topics do indeed seem to contain elements that are ignored by equity theory, it is arguable whether they bear much relationship to any of the alternative theoretical approaches either, and in any case, their relevance to conceptions of justice *per se* is not at all clear. For instance, although the idea of 'denial of responsibility' is briefly mentioned by Hatfield et al. as a possible way of dealing with inequity (see Walster et al., 1973), a common criticism of equity theory is that it pays insufficient attention to causal attributions or 'locus of responsibility' for behaviour (Deutsch, 1983; Utne and Kidd, 1980).

The problem of attributions

As previously noted, an important part of Lerner's original conception of the justice motive is the idea that people help the 'innocent' but not the 'blameworthy'. Cohen (1982) also comments, 'Perceptions of justice are tied fundamentally to beliefs about the causes of, and responsibility for, important human characteristics' (p. 128). Taking up this point to criticize equity theory, Utne and Kidd (1980) argue that people need not, and do not, always distort their view of reality or objectively adjust outcomes and inputs to restore equity. Instead they may use attributions in the form of additional information about the intentions and abilities of the participants to 'keep the perception of inequity intact, while at the same time reducing or eliminating the unpleasant feelings resulting from *perceived injustice*' (p. 67, my emphasis). The basic idea here is that attributions are not used to *eliminate* inequity or injustice, or restore equity and justice, as Walster et al. imply, rather they are used as a means to make inequity or injustice *tolerable*.

Certainly research suggests that attributions may have an important influence on equity judgements. For instance, if an observer perceives an underbenefitted woman to be responsible for her situation, she will be less likely to receive help than when she is a victim because of the actions of someone else (Berkowitz, 1969). Also, people are more likely to allocate higher outcomes to those whose superior contributions are based on effort, rather than ability or chance factors (see, for example, Cohen, 1974; Greenberg, 1980; Lamm, Kayser and Schanz, 1983; Leventhal, 1976; Leventhal and Michaels, 1971). Utne and Kidd (1980) suggest that, if we accept Heider's (1958) view that 'people are held responsible for their intentions and exertions but not strictly for their ability' (p. 112), then we may be able to explain the preference for effort. Perhaps people prefer to award higher proportional outcomes to those who can be held responsible for their greater contributions. In fact, according to Schwinger, some studies show that 'contribution differences that are clearly caused by factors outside a person's control are hardly considered in the allocation' (1980, p. 109).

However, Utne and Kidd's position that attributions of responsibility are used to make *injustice* tolerable, rather than eliminate injustice, makes the interpretation of these findings somewhat difficult. If Utne and Kidd are correct, then it is not our conceptions of what is unjust and unjust that are, in Cohen's (1982) words, 'tied fundamentally to beliefs about the causes of, and responsibility for, important human characteristics'. Instead it is our 'feelings' about our perceptions of justice that are affected by attributions of responsibility; in other words, attributions of responsibility do not affect our conceptions of what is just and unjust at all, they simply make injustice easier to tolerate. This seems to be very much at odds with Lerner's 'justice motive' position that attributions of responsibility directly affect what is actually considered just and unjust. Significantly also, one implication of Utne and Kidd's position is that if equity is construed specifically as a theory of *justice*, rather than a general attitudinal theory describing when justice and injustice will be tolerated, then, as a theory of justice, equity remains unaffected by the criticism that it ignores attributions of responsibility.

But what about the other multiprinciple theories of justice? With the exception of the earlier work of Lerner, perhaps, there is little evidence that they pay much attention to responsibility either, at least not in any systematic or consistent manner. Indeed, the failure of theories of justice to consider responsibility has given rise to considerable confusion. For example, as has been already been noted, the prevailing view on rules such as need and equality is that they are applied regardless of the actions or characteristics of the recipients. Hence, referring to equality, Sampson (1975) states, 'differential investments do not provide a legitimate basis for making claims to differential outcomes' (p. 49). And referring to need, Schwartz (1975) remarks, 'these norms are unique in that the person called on to forgo resources has performed no act justifying either a reduction in his own claims or an increase in others claims' (p. 112). But if this is the case, how is it then that people apparently take responsibility into account in deciding whether to help someone in need? There is a body of research that appears to support the general principle that people are significantly less likely to offer help to someone in need of help, when they consider that the 'cause of need was internal to the actor and was controllable' (Weiner, 1980, p. 186). This includes situations such as needing class notes, requiring assistance after collapsing in a public place, and requiring financial help to pay rent (Weiner,

1980; Meyer and Mulherin, 1980). (See also, Berkowitz, 1969; Lerner, 1977; Utne and Kidd, 1980.) So what exactly is the 'justice' rule that governs 'responsibility for actions'? It is not to be found in equity theory, but is does not appear to exist in any of the main multiprinciple approaches either.

The matter does not end here. For whilst there is wide agreement that at some level theories of justice *should* take attributions of responsibility into account, there appears to considerable disagreement over exactly what it means to be 'responsible' for one's actions in the first place. Concepts such as causality, foreseeability, intention, blame and justification often turn up in psychological models of the attribution of responsibility (see, for example, Heider, 1958: Fincham and Jaspers, 1980), but the relationship between these concepts is more complex than it might first appear. For example, as we have already noted, in English law, in cases of negligence, a person can be held criminally liable for the death of another even though there was no deliberate intention to kill the deceased (Cross, Jones and Card, 1988; Curzon, 1980).

According to Shaver (Shaver, 1985; Shaver and Drown, 1986), these problems arise because theorists and researchers often fail to recognize the theoretical and empirical distinctions between the concepts we associate with responsibility. In Shaver's analysis, a person may have been instrumental in *causing* a set of outcomes or consequences, but be neither responsible nor blameworthy for these consequences. *Responsibility*, however, is a more complex and varies not only depending on the extent to which the person a) caused the effect, but also whether the person, b) was aware that these effects might ensue from an action, c) intended to bring about the effect, c) had volition or choice, and e) appreciated the moral wrongfulness of an action. *Blameworthiness* is then a different judgement that is based on whether one accepts someone's *justification* or *excuse* for what happened. Thus a person can bear some responsibility for what happened, but not necessarily be blamed for it, so long as the person has an acceptable excuse (Shaver, 1985; Shaver and Drown, 1986).

Nevertheless, the idea that one can be responsible for an action, but not be held blameworthy, still necessitates some kind of theory to explain what counts, and what does not count, as an acceptable 'excuse' or justification. Moreover, Shaver's analysis only considers blame. Do the same or similar processes operate in ascribing responsibility for actions that can have positive consequences, like job performance? Although there is a philosophical literature on this subject, within the social sciences most justice theorists and researchers do not appear to have considered such issues in any detail, if at all. As Cohen (1982) has remarked, 'None of the major theoretical statements on justice makes attributions a central, explicit concern' (p. 124).

The development of justice

As well as including some references to causal attributions, most collections of works on justice also include some account of how children acquire a sense of justice, or justice norms.

Some theories of the development of justice do appear to have a degree of overlap with other psychological approaches to justice. I have already referred to Lerner's (1977) account of the development of the justice motive, but Lerner does not go into detail about the developmental ordering of the eighteen principles he identifies with justice. Hook and Cook (1979), however, make specific predictions about how various rules develop. They suggest that the development of justice can be understood from the perspective of equity theory. According to their view, at a young age (4-5 years), children ignore the amount of work or contribution; they make allocations on the basis of self-interest or equality. The reason for this is that the equity or proportionality rule is too cognitively complex for them to apply. But, as they grow older, children adopt a simple ordinal approach to equity (more contribution, more reward); and finally, children are able to perform the calculations necessary to award according to proportion, and ratio equity is followed.

There seems to be some parallel here with Jean Piaget's (1932/1965) often cited views on the development of distributive justice. According to Piaget, children progress through three stages. In the first, there exist only 'germs' of 'equalitarianism'; in the second 'equalitarianism grows in strength and comes to outweigh any other consideration', and in the third, (in early adolescence) 'mere equalitarianism makes way for a more subtle conception of justice we may call "equity" '. Piaget defines equity as 'never defining equality without taking account of the way each individual is situated' (pp. 284-285).

Expanding on Piaget's work, William Damon (1977, 1981), has proposed a more extensive set of six stages. At the first stage, level O-A (age 4), children confuse justice with desire. They assert choices without attempting to justify them; thus a typical justification would be, 'I should get it because I want to have it'. At the second stage, O-B (ages 4-5), the desired choices are justified in terms of rather arbitrary external characteristics such as, 'We should get the most because we're girls'. At the third stage, 1-A (ages 5-7), justice choices derive from notions of strict equality; so a typical response would be, 'Everyone should get the same'. At the forth, 1-B (ages 6-9), justice is based on reciprocity in actions. Damon says at this stage 'notions of merit and deserving emerge'; hence a typical justification would be, 'she should get most because she works hardest'. At the fifth stage, 2-A (ages 7-10) the child starts to realize that different people may have different claims, though the claims of persons with special needs, such as the poor, are weighed heavily. Damon calls this a 'benevolent' mode. Finally, at the sixth stage, 2-B (ages 8-12), the child recognizes that there are many competing justice claims (need, equality, contributions, compromise, utility) that need to be balanced; yet justifications reflect the recognition 'that all persons should receive their due' (1981, p. 61).

The idea that there are unidimensional and sequential stages in the development of justice principles has been a source of considerable controversy (see, for example, Damon, 1977, 1981; Moore, Hembree and Enright, 1993). Some have even questioned whether there are detectable age differences at all, and/or point out that children can be influenced by situational factors (see Moore, Hembree and Enright, 1993; Tornblöm, 1992). Nevertheless, in a comprehensive review, Keil and McClintock (1983) argue that empirical data generally support the developmental trend as proposed by Hook and Cook, Piaget and Damon; that is, first, self-interest, then equality, and then equity. It should be emphasized, however, that the view of these theorists is not that equity is used *exclusively* by older children, but rather it only really becomes a force in older children.

So far so good, we might say; regardless of whether we accept the idea of sequential, unidimensional developmental trends, at least the subject matter of the developmental theories overlaps with some of the main themes in other psychological work on justice. However, this is only part of the picture. Much of what is considered developmental work on justice by other psychologists seems to concern theories of *moral development* in general (see, for example, Eisenberg and Mussen, 1975). Indeed, the terms morality and justice are sometimes treated as though they are synonyms. (A look back at some of Reis's alleged 'rules of justice' in the last chapter illustrates well the difficulty psychologists have found in attempting to divorce rules of justice from moral rules in general.) This is not to say that such a view is incorrect, perhaps moral rules and rules of justice *are* best considered as the same thing, but it does open up another large and complex literature that often appears somewhat tangential to the kinds of things that the equity and multiprinciple theorists usually associate with justice. Consider for example the two theories that turn up most often in psychological works on justice; those of Jean Piaget and Laurence Kohlberg.

Moral development: Piaget and Kohlberg

Piaget's (1932/1965) general theory of moral development, as distinct from his more specific ideas about distributive justice, assumes that moral reasoning proceeds in two main stages. The first is called *heteronomous morality*. According to Piaget, very young children start off with no rules at all, but from about the ages of five to seven, they tend to defer to authority in judging the rightness of a rule, and any disobedience must be severely punished. Rules are seen as real and unalterable, like objects, and there is no attempt to relate the 'badness' of the act to the degree of punishment warranted; the rule is simply 'the greater the punishment the better'. Piaget terms this *expiatory punishment*. Young children are apparently unanimous in defending severe punishment as both legitimate and useful. Younger children also tend to think that a misdeed will automatically be punished. Thus they judge a misfortune as punishment for a misdeed regardless of whether the two are connected. Piaget calls this phenomenon 'immanent justice', which is a belief that 'a fault will automatically bring about its own punishment' (p. 256). Not only do younger children apparently believe that a misdeed will automatically be punished, they also think that any punishment decreed by authority is automatically acceptable (regardless of its severity) simply because it comes from authority; indeed, punishment by adults, and other authorities is, in itself, proof of wrongdoing. One of the central characteristics of this stage is that children show *egocentrism*. They are unable to place themselves in another's position and judge what intentions and feelings have accompanied an action, and even when they eventually do, they fail to consider intentions when judging the moral quality of an action. Hence an act is judged right or wrong depending on its consequences, regardless of whether the action was intended or accidental.

The second main stage in Piaget's scheme of moral development is that of *autonomous* morality (ages 7-11). By this stage the child can take intentions into account, rules are seen to be socially determined and alterable, and there is an understanding of reciprocity and cooperation. Hence, older children (11-12 onwards) will be more likely to take into account moral responsibility when deciding whether punishment is justified, and reject expiatory punishment in favour of reciprocity; that is, punishment should relate to the crime. Older children also consider other forms of punishment such as *restitutive* punishment (for instance, paying to replace a window one has broken), and *exclusion*, or ostracism ('I won't play with you any more').

Whilst Piaget's method was to use interviews and observation, Laurence Kohlberg's main approach has been to give children 'moral dilemmas' and ask them to justify their responses. It is not at all surprising that Kohlberg's theory of moral development is linked to psychological concepts of justice, for to Kohlberg (1971, 1975, 1976), justice is 'the central principle in the development of moral judgement'. He says, 'Justice, the primary regard for the value and equality of all human beings and for reciprocity in human relations, is a basic universal standard' (1971, p. 4). Kohlberg argues that moral reasoning progresses through three levels, with two stages in each. Each of the six stages he calls a 'justice structure', and the higher the stage the more mature and comprehensive the justice structure becomes.

The first level is the *preconventional* level (up to and around 10 years of age). In stage one, the child is egocentric, and self-interested, and the physical consequences of actions determine their goodness or badness rather than intentionality. In stage two, there is evidence of fairness, equal sharing and reciprocity, but it is motivated purely by self interest ('You scratch my back and I'll scratch yours').

Level 2 (13-16 years) is that of *conventional morality*. At stage three, good behaviour is that which is socially desirable according to the conventions of society. One does what is 'right' in the eyes of society, such as showing concern for others, so one appears to 'be good'. At stage 4, children believe one should obey authority and fixed rules, not just to do what is socially desirable, but because such rules must be maintained to avoid a breakdown in the social system.

The final level is *post conventional (principled) morality* (16-20 years). At stage 5, the young person becomes aware that one can have a variety of values and opinions, and rules are relevant to one's group. There is recognition that morality and the law may conflict, but the person has difficulty integrating them. Impartiality in the application of rules is important, and there is a feeling of contractual obligation, a consideration of utilitarian values like 'the greatest good for the greatest number', but also a recognition that rights like life and liberty must be upheld regardless of majority opinion. Stage 6 is the highest stage of moral development. At this stage the individual follows self-chosen ethical principles. There is a realization that most laws and social agreements are valid because they rest on such principles. When laws violate these principles, however, the principles guide one's actions. These principles are 'universal principles of justice: the equality of human rights and respect for the dignity of human beings as individual persons'. The stage 6 person recognizes that 'persons are ends in themselves and must be treated as such' (Kohlberg, 1976, p. 35). The Kantian origin of Kohlberg's definition of justice is clearly evident here.

Morality, justice or neither?
The theories of moral development of Kohlberg and Piaget have produced a vast amount of research and critical comment. For instance, there is some evidence to suggest that younger children may have a greater capacity to distinguish between deliberate and accidental actions than the theories would suggest, however, the distinction seems to be more apparent for actions that have positive consequences (that is, actions that warrant praise or reward), than actions that have negative consequences (warrant punishment). (See Costanzo, Coie, Grumet and Farnill, 1973.) However, many reseachers have indicated support for both Piaget's and Kohlberg's conceptions of developmental stages across a number of cultures (see, for example, Colby and Kohlberg, 1987; Eisenberg and Mussen, 1975; Lickona, 1976; Snarey, 1985).

But how relevant is all this to other psychological conceptions of justice? Piaget's theory of moral development places considerable emphasis on the development of moral responsibility, particularly as it relates to conceptions of punishment. But, as we have seen, attributions of responsibility, and conceptions of punishment have played little part in most psychological theorizing on justice. In fact, if we adopt Utne and Kidd's position, ideas about the developmental of moral responsibility are actually irrelevant to justice *per se*; they concern only our 'feelings' about justice and injustice. Kohlberg's theory also has an element of responsibility in it too, but he ends up equating 'justice' with 'equality in human rights' and Kant's categorical imperative. Hence Kohlberg actually defines justice as acting according to the part of Kant's categorical imperative that states, 'act so as to treat each person as an end (as having unconditional value), rather than as a means' (see Kohlberg, 1971, p. 210). Given that Kant considered his categorical imperative to be *the* fundamental guiding principle for our moral judgements in general, then, if accept Kohlberg's position, there is no distinction to be made between morality and justice; indeed, Kohlberg says, 'A person's sense of justice is what is most distinctively and fundamentally moral' (p. 40).

However, as we have already noted, any attempt to base a conception of justice on Kant's categorical imperative is fraught with difficulties. For example, according to Kohlberg, one of the criteria for determining post conventional morality is whether the child places 'the right to life before the right to property' (1976, p. 44). But, as we saw in earlier chapters, to some libertarians, the insistence on a rule that puts property before life could result in a gross violation of basic human rights, and a violation of Kant's categorical imperative. As philosophers and social commentators have obviously demonstrated, with a bit of ingenuity, one can derive almost any rule from Kant's categorical imperative from a Rawlsian difference principle, or a Nozickian property rights principle, to a slaveowners' racial superiority principle. And the principle of 'equality of human rights' can cover anything from the equal right to have as much as anyone else has (or more if you think you 'need' it), to the equal right to ignore the starving if one chooses.

Indeed, Gilligan (1982) has criticized Kohlberg for failing to differentiate between morality as justice. Gilligan argues that justice involves using rules and making judgements of fairness (more of a male orientation), whereas morality is also about the ethic of care (more of a female orientation). If we accept Gilligan's position, then there is more to morality than justice (a general point with which many philosophers would whole-heartedly agree); but more specifically, there is 'caring' as well as justice. However, according to those who argue that 'need' is a rule of justice, if 'caring' is seen as a humanitarian norm, then caring too is a part, or a requirement, of justice. Thus, for example, referring to a need orientated justice scheme, Furby (1986) notes, 'There is also a certain similarity between Gilligan's "ethic of care" and the humanitarian standard of justice outlined here' (p. 187).

Given all this, it would seem something of an understatement to say that the links between Piaget and Kohlberg's developmental theories of morality and the other psychological theories of justice, are not at all obvious.

Justice and punishment

Piaget's views in particular, draw our attention to another area that is potentially problematic for psychological theories of justice; that of the punishment of offenders. The difficulty stems from the fact that, although there is a fairly large literature on criminal liability and punishment within the criminal justice system (see, for example, Stephenson, 1992), very little attempt has been made to relate research in this area to any of the major psychological theories of justice. Hence, Tornblöm, Muhlhausen and Jonsson (1991) have commented that the major theoretical perspectives on justice 'either seem to assume that their component positions are equally relevant and valid for positive and negative outcome allocation, or else they simply avoid facing the issue squarely' (p. 64).

The tendency 'to avoid facing the issue squarely' is perhaps not surprising given the modern preoccupation with equality and needs principles. As the popular view seems to be that equality and need principles are supposedly motivated by factors such as 'caring' and 'cooperation', and operate in the absence of any consideration of how a person has acted or performed, ideas such as punishing according to needs, or according to equality, regardless of how a person has acted, do not seem to make much sense. Neither does a 'winner takes all' rule obviously give rise to a punishment principle, despite the fact that the 'punishment situation' is presumably the prototypical situation in which this rule of so-called 'Darwinian Justice' should apply; that is, it is a situation in which the goals of the criminal and the punisher are very different, and there is great antipathy and conflict. 'Just punishment' cannot sensibly be linked to the idea of contests or 'fights' with offenders according to rules that allow the 'winner' to take everything. As a result, most psychologists, like many philosophers, have attempted to escape the problem by drawing a fairly rigid demarcation line between what they call 'distributive justice' and punishment.

But how about equity? On first consideration, equity looks rather promising as a theory of 'just punishment'. As we have seen, according to Walster et al. (1978) equity encompasses the idea of *negative* outcomes and inputs, as well as positive outcomes and inputs. In principle at least, the theory prescribes that those whose inputs are negative or undesirable, should receive negative outcomes, or punishments in proportion. In other words, 'punishment should fit the crime'. Unfortunately, however, as we have seen, in practice, it has proved difficulty to come up with a satisfactory formula to express this idea.

As I have pointed out, one response to the 'negative input' problem has been to attempt to divorce equity from the idea of punishment. Hence, Anderson (1976) has argued that, whereas equity involves comparisons between people, punishment is non-comparative, in that 'it exhibits no interpersonal comparison structure' (p. 296). This rationale seems highly questionable; when we decide on what is 'just' outcome for a negative input do we really ignore comparative considerations? Consider the following example. Suppose a worker, Jim, deliberately damages one item of equipment (-1 input), and another worker, George, damages two items of the same equipment (-2). As a result, their colleagues, who are on a productivity bonus scheme, lose £60 of pay. In terms of compensation to the colleagues who have lost out, how much should Jim and George be penalized or fined? It is not immediately obvious that this situation should be considered any less 'comparative' than a standard equity situation in which the task is to distribute £60 in pay between two workers, one who has input 1 unit of work, and the other 2 units. Indeed, if we apply Adams equity formula, it is possible to come up with an 'equitable' distribution for both (-20/-1 = -40/-2, in the former case, and 20/1 = 40/2 in the latter). Moreover, in English law, when deciding whether a person is criminally liable, one can find numerous references to the idea that the conduct of the offender must be compared to that of a 'reasonable person' in the same situation (Cross, Jones and Card, 1988).

Hogan and Emler (1981), however, seem to have rather more fundamental reasons for rejecting equity as a theory of punishment. They propose an alternative approach that they call 'retribution theory'. Hogan and Emler argue that 'the notion of retribution does not occur in equity theory', and 'someone who takes the reality of retributional processes seriously has problems understanding equity theory'. They then identify what they believe to be a number of critical differences between equity theory and retribution theory, and argue that 'The two views reflect widely different assumptions about society and its governance that cannot easily be reconciled' (p. 125). The main differences are allegedly as follows. First, equity theory is about 'distributive justice' and the reward of virtue and accomplishments, whereas the justice of punishment, or 'retributive' justice is nothing to do with this. Retributive justice is concerned 'that everyone share equally in the burdens, privations, taxes, and renunciations that are the concomitants of civilized living' (pp. 34-35). Second, equity theory and retribution theory differ in terms of the motivation for restoring justice. According to Hogan and Emler, equity, like Lerner's justice motive, is motivated by self-interest, whereas retributive justice is not. Instead, retributive justice is motivated by 'aggressive actions' that follow from the perceptions that others are 'getting more than their fair share, or not getting their just deserts after misbehaving'. These aggressive actions are not prompted by self-interest, but are more 'akin to a reflex following perceptions of injustice' (p. 36). A third difference between retribution theory and equity rests on the assumption that the desire to maintain status and reputation is generally more important to people than the maintenance of equity; thus retribution exists to punish those who take unfair advantage in the competition for status. In other words, the sphere of influence of retributive justice goes outside of that of equity, and considers the conflicts that arise through variations in status.

Equity theorists could reasonably object to some of these ideas. For instance, although Donnerstein and Hatfield (1982) have argued that intense anger may eliminate equity considerations, equity does not deny that aggressive feelings may motivate the punishment of offenders; indeed, Adams (1965) and Walster et al. (1978), like Hogan and Emler, propose that the reactions to being 'underbenefitted' can include resentment and anger. Moreover, it is difficult to see why the desire to 'vent one's anger' should be deemed any less 'selfish' than reducing other forms of inequity distress, such as guilt or fear. Neither does equity ignore status. According to Walster et al., positive outcomes be many other things besides pay; they include satisfying supervision, seniority benefits, job status and status symbols, and the privileges of status. Status can thus be a very important issue in equity; if someone usurps the 'deserved' status of another negative outcomes, or punishments should ensue. But, perhaps most important, equity theorists could seriously question the charge that equity is irrelevant because it is a theory of 'distributive' justice. Hogan and Emler tell us that retributive justice, as distinct from distributive justice, is concerned 'that everyone share equally in the burdens, privations, taxes, and renunciations that are the concomitants of civilized living' (1981, pp. 34-35). But arguably this is in itself part of a principle of distributive justice. According to Lucas (1980), 'Distributive justice is traditionally characterized as being concerned with sharing good and bad things, benefits and burdens, among members of society' (p. 163). It seems a somewhat odd to reject a theory because it applies only to distributive justice, and then substitute another that also gains its force principally from an appeal to a principle of distributive justice. Indeed, according to Sadurski (1985), if one construes punishment as a way of restoring equilibrium in the balance of benefits and burdens in society, there is no meaningful distinction to be made between distributive and retributive justice.

In another psychological approach, Miller and Vidmar (1981), argue that, in any case, retribution is only one of the social functions of punishment; within the sphere of justice can also operate as a mechanism for *behaviour control*. According to the idea of behaviour control, punishment exists to deter or prevent future violations, but it can also include reeducation of the offender and restitution of the victim. Punishment as retribution, on the other hand, refers to 'punishment reactions involved in the moral rather than the behavioural implications of the offence' (p. 155). (If we accept this definition, it presumably leads to the rather disturbing conclusion that deterrence, reeducation, and providing compensation to the victim are behavioural rather than moral issues.) One of the main purposes of retribution, according to Miller and Vidmar, is 'to reestablish the psychological equilibrium by redressing the sense of inferiority that the act of harm has ensexed' (p. 155). The basic idea seems to be that intentional harm makes people feel inferior, so they punish harmdoers to make them feel inferior and make themselves feel as they did before the harm. They also suggest that retribution is motivated by threats to the value system of one's group, and deeply held beliefs of 'justice' or 'oughtness' (p. 156). Miller and Vidmar make no attempt to relate their approach to other psychological theories, though they note Hogan and Emler's views on the possible differences between equity and retributive motives.

All this seems to leave psychological theories of justice and punishment in a rather difficult situation. Empirical evidence suggests that two of the most enduring features of the public conceptions of 'just punishment' are a) that punishment should fit the crime'; such that the more serious the crime, the more severe the punishment should be (see, for example, Gebotys and Roberts, 1987; Hamilton and Rytina, 1980; von Hirsch, 1985; von Hirsch and Jareborg, 1989); and b), people are punishable to the extent that they can be held responsible and blameworthy for their actions. With regard to the latter, Miller and Vidmar (1981) themselves point out that offenders who are perceived as having done something accidentally are punished less severely than those who are perceived has having committed the same act intentionally. Further research suggests that the two elements interact. For instance, people who feel that criminals may be the 'accidental' victims of societal and economic pressures are more likely to favour rehabilitation than punishment (Carroll, Berkowitz, Lurigio, and Weaver, 1987). Also, although 'harm done' seems to be more important than culpability in determining crime seriousness (Hoffman and Hardyman, 1986; Rossi, Simpson and Miller, 1985; Stephenson, 1992), the more harm done (that is, severe the consequences), the more likely responsibility will be attributed to the offender (Miller and Vidmar, 1981).

In the literature from most disciplines, it is this 'proportionality/culpability' combination that has traditionally been referred to as punishment as 'retribution', as distinct from punishment for deterrence or rehabilitation (see, for example, Honderich, 1976; Raphael, 1981; Sadurski, 1985; Stephenson, 1992). As philosophers have been keen to point out, strict deterrence and rehabilitation apparently require neither proportionality nor culpability. Moreover, some empirical research suggests that retributive concerns dominate over others, such as deterrence, particularly in the case of serious crime (see, for example, Baron, 1993; Miller and Vidmar, 1981). Given this, equity theorists could reasonably argue that the general concept of equity does a fairly good job of dealing with the idea of retribution. Certainly equity theory is deficient as regards the responsibility or culpability component of retribution, but, notwithstanding the problem of finding a suitable formula, it does make some sense of the proportionality component.

But if we reject equity, where does this leave us? Hogan and Emler tell us that retributive justice is concerned with the principle 'that everyone share equally in the burdens, privations, taxes, and renunciations that are the concomitants of civilized living' (1981, pp. 34-35). But as we noted earlier, extracting a principle of proportional retribution from this idea is not easy. We rarely see taxation as a punishment for wrongdoing, and we do not usually compensate offenders for their time, effort, and privations incurred whilst planning their crimes. Neither do the rules relating to criminal liability follow obviously from this 'equality of benefits and burdens' principle, and indeed, Hogan and Emler do not attempt to derive any. And if the prime motivation for retribution is an undeliberated 'reflex aggressive action', this is hardly likely to evoke a measured response in which punishment is proportional to crime severity and culpability; as Donnerstein and Hatfield (1982) comment, 'when people are angry, considerations of logic go out of the window' (p. 329).

As we have seen, Miller and Vidmar (1981) have a different view, they tell us that one of the main purposes of retribution is 'to reestablish the psychological equilibrium by redressing the sense of inferiority that the act of harm has ensexed' (p. 155). Unfortunately, however, Miller and Vidmar provide no systematic research evidence to back up their view that retribution is motivated primarily by the distress that comes from feeling inferior, or losing one's status. Is it really the case that the public outcry, and calls for the death penalty that follow when an innocent child is murdered, stem from feelings of inferiority and a loss of self-esteem suffered by the general public? And what exactly is the 'psychological equilibrium position' for feelings of superiority and inferiority? Does justice demand that we should always want to punish those to whom we feel inferior? What if we feel inferior and lose self-esteem because we have been lazy and done nothing; we may be unhappy, but will we feel justified in punishing those who feel 'superior' because they have worked hard? The ideas that retribution is motivated by threats to the value system of one's group, and 'deeply held beliefs of justice or oughtness', do not obviously give rise to the proportionality and culpability combination either. We could deal with threats to the group by uniformly killing all those who threaten our values, and deter others from threatening our values by murdering innocent people as an example to would-be threateners. And to propose that the beliefs or principles of 'justice' or 'oughtness' themselves dictate the proportionality/culpability principle does nothing to explain why, psychologically, such principles should be adopted in the first place.

In sum, none of these alternative theories really presents much, if anything of an advance on equity theory as a way of explaining why, when and how we feel justified in punishing people. They do, however, draw our attention to the fact that most psychological theories of justice simply do not, and perhaps cannot, deal adequately with these issues.

CHAPTER 9

BARGAINING, JUST PROCEDURES, ALLOCATION PREFERENCES, AND THE AFTERMATH OF EQUITY

In this chapter we will look briefly at three further psychological approaches to justice that are also commonly assumed to indicate the limitations of equity theory. The first is that of bargaining and 'game theory'.

Bargaining and game theory

Although the subjects of bargaining and game theory have a long and distinguished history in psychology (see Sabini, 1995; Sampson, 1971), only occasionally do they actually appear in the psychological literature on justice (see, for example, Komorita and Kravitz, 1979; Camerer and Lowenstein, 1993; Mellers and Baron, 1993).

The idea behind game theory is that it is possible to devise situations or games, with certain rules, for which certain strategies and agreements are more 'rational' or 'efficient' than others (Luce and Raiffa, 1957). For instance, in a zero-sum game (so-called because the losses of one party plus the gains of the other equal zero), the winner takes all, so it makes sense to compete in the hope of winning. However, in certain 'nonzero-sum' games (in which the sum of one person's losses and another's gains need not equal zero) it might actually benefit participants to cooperate. Although the term 'efficiency' has been interpreted in a number of ways (Le Grand, 1991), within the context of game theory, a rational or efficient bargaining agreement is usually considered to be one that maximizes in some way the joint benefits for each party in a negotiation. Suppose, for example, two people play a bargaining game in which they have to reach agreement on how to share a sum 'X' of a good; but the rule of the game is that, if no agreement is reached within a certain amount of time, both receive nothing (this could be called an 'ultimatum game'). In such a situation, the most obvious example of an 'inefficient' agreement would be to compete to such an extent that no agreement is reached at all; as neither party would benefit at all from the resource. The overlap between this approach and the views of philosophers such as Gauthier on 'rational behaviour' amongst egoists is obvious; justice is assumed to be some kind of rationally derived agreement between individuals trying to do the best for themselves.

But again, equity theory seems to ignore all this; hence Deutsch (1983) has remarked that equity theory 'ignores the bargaining process involved in the participants arriving at a mutually acceptable definition of equity' (p. 308). However, most other psychological perspectives on justice seems to ignore it too.

Macrojustice and microjustice
Another apparent problem for equity is that it ignores a distinction that some have made between 'macrojustice' and 'microjustice' (Brickman, Folger, Goode and Schul, 1981). The argument is that although people may follow a basic rule when allocating between small groups of individuals, and judge this to be fair at a micro level; they may, nevertheless, disagree with the overall distribution that the consistent application of such a rule would create. For example, Brickman (1975) found that although people tended to follow a contributions or performance principle in allocating rewards, they rejected a distribution that followed this rule, but eventually left one person considerably worse off than all the rest. Brickman et al. (1981) thus conclude that 'people have preferences for the overall shape of the outcome distribution *per se*, and not only for the microlevel principles by

which such outcome distributions may be produced' (p. 174). Judgements about macrojustice are particularly evident when people look at the overall shape of the distributions of various benefits and burdens for society as a whole, and between societies. In such circumstances, Brickman et al. argue 'preferences appear to be strongly egalitarian' (p. 181). Other survey research from a variety of Western countries, however, indicates that 'macrojustice' preferences are far from uniformly egalitarian (see, for example, Himmelweit, Humphries, Jaeger and Katz 1981; Robinson and Bell, 1978; Swift, Marshall, Burgoyne and Routh, 1992).

But once again, it cannot be claimed that many of the other psychological approaches have considered this problem either. Nevertheless, there does appear to be one approach to justice that may reflect this distinction more closely. Brickman et al. draw attention to a possible distinction between 'procedural justice' as a microjustice principle, and 'distributive justice' as a macrojustice principle. Which brings us to the final topic in this brief overview of psychological approaches to justice, *procedural justice.*

The principles of procedural justice

Some psychologists do not agree with Sadurski (1985) who claims that 'Pure procedural justice is .... no principle of justice at all' (p. 50), or Dworkin (1986) who suggests that 'Justice is a matter of outcomes' not procedures (p. 180). Within psychology, we can find a number of writers who argue that there is a meaningful distinction to be made between justice in the distribution of outcomes, and justice in the procedures by which those outcomes are determined. The main impetus for psychological research on procedural justice came Thibaut and Walker's (1975) book on this topic, though other psychologists in the 1970's had also drawn attention to the idea of 'fairness' or 'justice' in procedures (see, for example, Leventhal, 1976).

Thibaut and Walker were particularly concerned with procedural differences between American and European courts, and the fact that Americans used an *adversarial* procedure in which the two sides in a dispute have the primary responsibility for finding and presenting evidence in support of their cases. In contrast, in much of Western Europe, it is the judge (with the assistance of investigators) who is primarily responsible for investigating the matter and presenting the evidence. A number of studies have shown that in Western cultures, adversarial procedures are generally preferred to inquisitorial procedures (Lind, Kurtz, Musante, Walker and Thibaut, 1980; Walker, Latour, Lind and Thibaut, 1974). Thibaut and Walker (1975) suggest that the preference for the adversarial procedure reflects a desire for people to control the process of decision making, by 'voicing' their case, as a means of affecting the outcomes of the decision. In other words, 'process control' or 'voicing' is instrumental in affecting 'decision control'. The idea that 'procedural justice' exists basically as a means to influence outcomes has also been advanced by Lerner and Whitehead (1980). In support of this idea, Tyler (1987b) found that simply providing people with an opportunity to speak was not sufficient for a procedure to be judged fair; for a procedure to be judged fair it was necessary for the subjects to infer that what they were saying was actually being considered by the decision maker.

Nevertheless, Tyler and his associates (see, for example, Lind and Tyler, 1988; Tyler, 1987ab; Tyler and Dawes, 1993), have argued that procedures that allow voicing of one's case can be preferred for their own sake, for 'process control' alone, independently of any real or imagined effect on decisions concerning outcomes. As an example of this, Tyler and Dawes (1993) refer to a study by Lind, Kanfer and Early (1990) that showed that people felt more fairly treated if they were given an opportunity to present their arguments, even if the presentation of arguments occurred *after* the relevant decision had been made. Tyler believes that the 'voice effects' allowed in adversarial procedures are 'value expressive', and are valued in their own right.

Leventhal (1980) has come up with a larger range of procedural justice rules. Leventhal suggests that six criteria might be applied when judging the fairness of a procedure; these are, consistency across time and person, suppression of biases, accuracy of information, correctability of a decision, representation in the decision making body, and the maintenance of ethical and moral standards. Arguably 'representation in the decision making body' corresponds to 'voice control' and 'decision control' processes, but otherwise, there seems to be little overlap between Leventhal's procedural factors and those of Thibaut and Walker. Research on allocation decisions using Leventhal's criteria has shown that in evaluating the fairness of a procedure, consistency across people, or 'the similar treatment of equals', is the most important criterion when judging the fairness of a procedure, together with accuracy of information, the maintenance of ethical and moral standards, and bias suppression. Interestingly, 'voice control' or 'representativeness' figure as relatively unimportant in comparison (Barrett-Howard and Tyler, 1986). Barrett-Howard and Tyler (1986) also found, using Leventhal's criteria, that the importance of procedural justice varies across situations. Thus procedural justice was judged most important in rule-directed social settings (such as fraternity meetings), and in informal productivity task settings, especially when the participants had unequal power to make decisions. Procedural justice was judged less important in informal social situations, formal productivity task settings, and where power sharing was equal. Barrett-Howard and Tyler argue that these findings reflect the facts that whereas in the first category of situations the participants 'depend on fair procedures to yield just distributions', in the latter category the relationships are 'not threatened by injustice' (p. 302).

According to Tyler's own more recent categorisation (see Tyler, 1994; Tyler and Belliveau, 1995; Tyler and Dawes, 1993) procedural rules are best viewed in the context of two distinct justice motives: one resource based, the other relational based. Tyler suggests that procedural concerns are purely relational in character, and hence can be distinguished from resource issues that are central to models of distributive justice; though he says distributive justice may involve a relational component also. His view is that people are interested in having a 'favourable self-identity' that is related to their status within a social group. Hence Tyler and Dawes (1993) argue that, 'it is evidence about status, rather than information about control over resources, which shapes people's reactions to their experiences in social groups' (p. 96). Because they care about their status or standing in the group, people focus on relational issues when dealing with others. Three relational issues are important, the belief that procedures are neutral, the belief that others are trustworthy, and the recognition of the personal standing of others through respectful, dignified treatment. Tyler argues that these 'relational issues' have been empirically linked directly to evaluations of procedural fairness, and account for more of the variance in procedural justice judgements than 'outcome variables', such as 'control' and 'outcome favourability'. Thus procedural justice is basically about affirming one's 'self-worth', and creating and maintaining 'a positive self image' in one's interactions with others (see Tyler and Belliveau, 1995, pp. 300-305). Tyler and Belliveau (1995) thus conclude that, 'social justice systems arise not just as a way to regulate and mediate people's social exchanges of resources; they also convey important messages about self-worth and self-esteem (p. 310).

However, Folger and Konovsky (1989) have produced yet another set of procedural justice criteria. They derived these by statistically factor analyzing a larger set of criteria derived from the procedural justice literature; the criteria are, feedback, planning, recourse and observation. In a study of pay rises awarded to employees at a manufacturing plant, they found that, 'distributive justice', as measured by questions such as 'To what extent did your raise give you the full amount you deserved', was more important in satisfaction with pay than procedural concerns about feedback, planning and so on. Nevertheless, procedural concerns were more important in determining employees' trust in their supervisors and commitment to the organization.

Procedural justice and equity
Despite apparent differences in the range and types of procedural criteria proposed by these various researchers, on one point most theorists seem agreed;

the concept of procedural justice creates problems for equity theory. For example, in one study by Greenberg (1987) subjects were led to be believe that they had been given a share of an $8 reward on the basis of one of two kinds of procedure; an 'fair' procedure that involved assigning the reward on the basis of the subject's inputs or work performance, or an 'unfair' procedure in which the reward was assigned on the basis of a random allocation to one of three small rooms. Greenberg found that subjects who were awarded high or medium shares of the reward ($8 or $4), were not influenced by the type of procedure when judging the fairness of their reward; however, subjects who received a low share of the reward ($1), judged this share or outcome as significantly less fair when the procedure was 'unfair'(that is, based on room allocation rather than work performance). Greenberg concludes that these results are incompatible with equity theory, because equity theory is not equipped to interpret the observed differences in the perceived fairness of low-level rewards derived from fair and unfair procedures.

In another study, Cropanzano and Folger (1989) found that subjects considered themselves more fairly treated when they could choose which of two tasks to perform to gain a reward, regardless of the actual reward obtained. Subjects whose task had been chosen for them, but at the same time would have won if another task had been selected, felt particularly unfairly treated. Cropanzano and Folger suggest that equity theory cannot explain these findings because equity theory does not take account of *procedural choice* when judging the fairness of an outcome distribution.

But again, whilst it seems reasonable to criticize equity on the grounds that it ignores these procedural factors, it is also apparent that there is as yet no theoretical basis for integrating procedural issues with the other schemes proposed by the various multiprinciple theorists.. The findings of Greenberg and Cropanzano and Folger are certainly not readily explicable in terms of the standard rationales proffered to explain the equality, needs, or 'winner takes all' principles. Also, whilst one senses that there ought to be some overlap between concepts such as 'procedural choice', attributions of responsibility, praise and blame, and moral development, the links have yet to be made.

Perhaps the most important difficulty for the concept of procedural justice itself, however, is that if one takes the view that procedural justice can stand on its own, divorced from or in some degree independent of outcomes, then we need to explain exactly what it is that the various procedural rules share in common that relates them to the concepts of justice and/or fairness, as distinct from other concerns. This brings us to a fundamental problem for psychological theories of justice in general; when is a decision rule a rule of justice and when is it not?

Rules of justice versus other rules

Although a number of researchers have pointed out that there are distinctions to be drawn between allocation principles motivated by justice and/or fairness, and those motivated by other concerns (see, for example, Cohen and Greenberg, 1982; Leventhal, Karuza and Fry, 1980; Lissak and Sheppard, 1983; Tornblöm, 1992; Tyler, 1987a), psychologists have yet to come up with an adequate theory to explain and make predictions regarding this distinction. This has serious implications for the various multiprinciple approaches.

Consider the finding referred to earlier, that in some situations high contributors to a task tend to distribute outcomes more equally than low contributors, who tend to follow an equity or contributions principle (Schwinger, 1980; Tornblöm, 1992). Some researchers have suggested this occurs because participants are following a 'politeness' ritual or procedure (Mikula, 1972; Schwinger, 1980). Yet according to Tornblöm (1992), 'the explanation for this effect apparently has to be sought in motives other than justice'. Tornblöm argues that motives that may influence allocation procedures, but are not concerned with justice, include 'the desire to maintain a positive self-image', and other 'self-presentational concerns' (p. 208). If we accept this view then presumably 'politeness' is just one of many motives that may influence allocation rules *but are not concerned with justice*.

The idea that allocations and procedures may be influenced by non-justice considerations such as the desire to create a good impression with, or obtain a positive evaluation from other people, fits with a number of findings cited earlier. Thus individuals will usually distribute more equally when they want to present themselves more favourably to recipients, as in situations in which the allocators believe recipients will be aware of their allocations, or they expect to meet them, or their impressions are valued (Austin, 1980; Greenberg, 1983; Leventhal, Michaels and Sanford, 1972; Reis and Gruzen, 1976; Von Grumbkow, Deen, Steensma and Wilke, 1976); however, in situations in which equity would appear to create the most favourable impression, equity may be preferred (Leung and Bond, 1984; Reis and Gruzen, 1976). Tornblöm also notes, like others, that an equality rule may be followed, not because it is 'just', but because it is easier to calculate (see also, Harris and Joyce, 1980; Leventhal, 1976).

On first consideration, some distinction between justice and other motives for choosing allocation rules seems very helpful; we now appear to be able to explain how people can apparently swop these rules around so readily in different situations. They do so for reasons unrelated to justice. But if rules can be adopted for motives other than justice or fairness, what exactly is it that distinguishes 'nonfairness' or 'nonjustice' motives from those guiding conceptions of justice and fairness? Once we embark on this kind of argument some the main psychological theories of justice become under severe threat. For a start, Tyler's ideas about the 'relational' aspect of procedural justice look a bit precarious, as according to Tornblöm, social behaviours designed to promote a 'positive self-image' or enhance one's status by seeking positive evaluations from others, are unrelated to justice. Perhaps 'pure procedural justice' is after all, no principle of justice.

The problem this poses for psychological perspectives on 'distributive justice' is well illustrated in a book chapter appropriately entitled 'Beyond fairness: A theory of allocation preferences', by Leventhal, Karuza and Fry (1980). In this, the authors argue that concerns of fairness relate to only part of a theory of allocation preferences; in other words, there are many reasons why people might want to use a certain kind of procedure or rule when allocating outcomes besides considerations of what is 'fair'. The basic idea is that individuals use different allocation rules to achieve different goals; for instance, in line with the standard multiprinciple view, Leventhal et al. argue that if the goal is productivity, an equity or contributions rule will be used, and if the goal is group harmony, and the reduction of conflict, equality may be used, and if group welfare is the goal, a needs rule will be used. If the goals are mixed, people may mix rules and weight them appropriately. But, according to Leventhal et al. people can do this independently of fairness considerations. They argue that fairness is not simply about expediency in achieving these aims, rather it involves some kind of moral judgement of the 'rightness' of an allocation according to some sort of ideal standard. Hence when fairness comes into play there has to be some kind of balance or tradeoff between the concerns of fairness and the other goals that are guiding the selection of rules and procedures.

Logically this may look perfectly reasonable, but if motives such as conflict reduction and expediency in achieving various group goals are also not the concerns of justice (along with politeness, modesty, self-presentation, status enhancement and so on), we could start to ask some very awkward questions.

For instance, according to the main multiprinciple models, the need rule supposedly operates in situations where there is intimacy, affection, empathy, attraction, an absence of conflict, and welfare is the shared goal. But does justice require us to allocate according to the needs of individuals simply because we like, or feel sorry for them, and want to maximize group welfare? Equality allegedly operates when an affective bond and attraction are still present, the relationship is cooperative, and the group goal is one of group solidarity, harmony, and enjoyable social relations. But does justice require equal shares simply because we like people and want to create and maintain harmony, cooperation and enjoy ourselves? Equity is supposed to operate when there is little or neutral intimacy or affection, there is a greater sense of conflict and competition, and the goal of the interaction is to maximize economic productivity. But does justice require that we give to people according to their contributions simply because we are not sure what we feel about them, sense a possibility of conflict, and want to maximize group productivity? Many of these motives seem to be based on 'expediency', which, according to Leventhal et al., is not a concern of justice.

But if justice does not concern these things, then it is arguable whether the basic 'equity, equality, needs' type multiprinciple theories of justice, even concern 'justice'. And if justice sometimes concerns these issues, and sometimes it does not, we need to how, when, and why this happens. It may very well be the case, as Leventhal et al. claim, that what uniquely identifies a rule or procedure as 'fair' is an appeal to a particular set of standards, but we still need a theory to describe the nature of these standards, and how they come about. It is no use appealing to the same explanations used for 'allocation preferences', as then the reasoning becomes circular. Suppose, for example, that a group chooses an equity or contributions rule, not because of reasons of fairness, but because they want to maximize group productivity. On what grounds could the group, at the same time, consider this rule to be unfair? We could say, perhaps, because they think that 'fairness' requires that equality should be applied in this situation, because it is morally 'right'. But why does fairness, or 'moral rightness' require equality here? If we say, because the group members like each other and want to promote harmony and reduce conflict, and equality does this best, then there is simply a conflict between two types of 'allocation preference' or 'allocation goal'; not a conflict between an allocation preference and something else called 'justice' or 'fairness'.

Unfortunately simply asking people to think up examples of what they consider to be 'fair' and 'unfair' behaviours does not seem to be particularly helpful in sorting out the problem of what distinguishes considerations of 'fairness' from other concerns. When Messick, Bloom, Boldizar and Samuelson (1985) asked undergraduate students to list as many things they could in 5 minutes that people do that would be described as 'fair' and 'unfair' a vast range of over 1000 behaviours emerged. Messick et al. categorised a random pool of 80 of these behaviours in various ways. For instance, unfair behaviours included categories of behaviour that were illegal (such as shoplifting), counternormative (such as mistreating animals), economic (such as charging too high prices), involved interpersonal comparisons (such as making everything for right-handed people), and not showing consideration for others (such as parking in handicapped zones); fair behaviours included working hard or making an effort to help others (such as always offering to clean up), and routine politeness (such as saying 'excuse me' when bumping into someone). Other behaviours were less easy to categorise and included things such as 'depending on no one' (this was unfair), 'having good study habits' and 'listening to parent's advice' (both fair). On first consideration arguably the only meaningful distinction that can made between the 'fair' and 'unfair' behavioural categories is simply one between socially 'desirable' and 'undesirable' behaviours. Messick et al. also comment that when given this task, people 'do not think of allocative behaviours of the sort that are common in social psychological experiments'; they add, 'None of the 80 behaviours that we sampled had to do with payment for work accomplished, the prototypical task used to study equity and fairness' (p. 499).

Having said this, there some evidence to suggest that when subjects are asked to allocate 'justly' or 'fairly' rather than according to other preferences, their allocations can be different. For example, Lamm and Schwinger (1983) found that the level of attractiveness of the recipient affected allocations according to need, but when the allocators were specifically asked to allocate 'justly', the level of attractiveness had no effect. Also Messick and Sentis (1979) found that people gave less to themselves when asked to allocate fairly, compared to when asked to allocate how they wished. Stake (1983) found that, when asked to award bonus and raises fairly, subjects awarded according to actual output or contribution; when asked to maximize productivity, they awarded according to capability, and when asked to maintain positive personal relationships, they tended to award equally. And, perhaps most interestingly, Ordonez and Mellers (1993) found that when asked to judge what was a fair society, most people selected a society in which salaries were awarded in proportion to work or contribution; nevertheless, when asked what sort of society they preferred, they chose one with high minimum salaries.

All this puts psychological theorising about justice in a real dilemma. There does indeed seem to be some evidence for an *empirical* distinction to be made between the concepts of fairness and preference, however, as yet we lack an adequate theory to describe what actually distinguishes between them.

Justifications and rationalizations

Also problematical is also a considerable amount of evidence to indicate that when subjects appear to be making an allocation choice for one reason, their *justifications* for this choice are rather different; interestingly, these justifications frequently concern references to attributions of responsibility.

For instance, Harris and Joyce (1980) noted that some subjects may use an equality rule in allocating outcomes to individuals who have made unequal contributions, simply because an equitable allocation may be too difficult to calculate. They nevertheless found that many subjects would attempt to justify giving equal shares on grounds that the recipients put in equal effort, or the unequal contributions 'weren't their fault' (p. 179). Similarly, Mikula (1972) found that, although apparently in the interests of politeness, high contributors divided rewards equally between themselves and their lower input partners, they attempted to justify the equal distribution by saying that their greater contribution was accidental. Lower input partners, however, who used an equity or contributions rule, justified this by reference to differential effort and /or ability. Similar results have been reported by Feather and Simon (1971); performance differences were attributed to external factors, like chance, by the higher contributors, and internal factors, like effort, by the lower contributors. However, as Schwinger (1980) points out, this finding seems to be limited to cooperative situations. When the task is competitive, the opposite seems to occur; thus lower contributors attribute performance differences to chance, and higher contributors attribute them to effort (Snyder, Stephan and Rosenfield, 1976). Hence Schwinger argues that 'causal interpretations of this type act in the politeness ritual as *rationalizations* for the allocation behaviour' (1980, p. 112, my emphasis). Reis and Gruzen (1976) also found that subjects will tend to invoke effort factors to justify unequal as well as equal outcomes, even when these outcomes are clearly motivated by other concerns.

But if subjects were applying the allocation rules as the multiprinciple theorists claim, why should want to rationalize allocations in this way? If you want to use an equality rule, why not say you are using it in the interests of friendship, cooperation and harmony? If these are interests of 'justice' surely people would understand, and even applaud, such a justification. Why attempt instead to justify your allocation by arguing that the inputs were due to equal 'effort' or 'chance' factors? Such evidence presents the possibility that, although allocation preferences may vary for a number of reasons of psychological interest, some subjects may be appealing to a common concept or principle to *rationalize* their decisions. But what is this principle? It looks like attributions of responsibility weigh heavily in it, but again, as Cohen (1982) has commented, 'None of the major theoretical statements on justice makes attributions a central, explicit concern' (p. 124).

The aftermath of equity

It seems that, despite promising beginnings, equity theory clearly seems to be inadequate as a comprehensive psychological theory of justice. Consequently, it has been displaced or appended by a whole host of principles and concepts allegedly associated, at one time or another, with the idea of justice. But where does this leave us? In 1983, Deutsch concluded the following: 'The dethroning of equity theory as the sovereign theory of justice has led to a proliferation of many alternate perspectives. There is a feeling of intellectual disorganization: the various theoretical strands within the area are not yet well-knit together' (p. 312). I doubt whether any psychologist today would want to disagree with Deutsch's observation. Indeed, Folger, Sheppard and Blair (1995) have recently made the following cogent comment, 'New principles of justice seem to spout like weeds in a garden', and they refer to Greenberg's (1990a) survey of the justice literature that notes 'a burgeoning terminological and conceptual confusion' in the area (p. 261).

CHAPTER 10

INTERDISCIPLINARY CHAOS?

It seems that psychologists are no more in agreement about the nature of justice than philosophers; and certainly neither are able to turn up an acceptable organizing core principle that can be uniquely identified with justice. This situation might appear bad enough, but if we then try to map psychological perspectives on justice onto philosophical perspectives, including those from economic philosophy, then we are surely left with something bordering on a disaster area. Let us briefly survey some of the chaos.

An unfruitful alliance
Despite the efforts of some psychologists to draw the names of modern philosophers into their papers and make comments about them, on the surface at least, there appears to be nothing really meaningful such an alliance can contribute. As Bell and Schokkaert (1992) have noted, with regard to justice, 'interdisciplinary contacts have been rather rare and seldom fruitful' (p. 252). Apart from an occasional brief reference, most psychological theories of justice have little if anything to do with social contracts, let alone hypothetical contracts drawn up behind a 'veils of ignorance', or on spaceships and beaches. And rules based on historical property rights, or any other sorts of rights for that matter, are not in the forefront of psychological theorizing. Ideas such as 'impartiality' and

'neutrality' although the essence of justice to some philosophers, occur only as part of some psychological schemes of procedural justice, and, according to some philosophers procedural justice is a misnomer, as there is no such thing. Considerations of concepts such as 'equal opportunity' are also virtually non-existent in the psychological literature.

As for a 'justice motive', between them psychologists and philosophers seem to have invoked just about every human motive and emotion one could possibly imagine to explain our concern for justice; including empathic concern, respect for oneself and others, the promotion of a positive self-image, guilt, fear, resentment, envy, anger, self-interest, outcome maximization, rationality, status anxiety, dissonance reduction, control, conflict reduction, conformity with social values, and desire for an orderly environment.

Odd bits and pieces of moral philosophy crop up now again in the various fragments that psychologists associate with justice, but they frequently serve more to confuse than clarify. For instance, Kant's categorical imperative appears in Kohlberg's theory, but as we have noted, Kohlberg's theory is not a typical psychological theory of justice. In fact, philosophers and psychologists seem incapable of helping each other define the distinction between morality and justice, assuming it is meaningful to make one. Thus whilst many philosophers claim that justice is not the whole of morality, we are left trying to fathom exactly how a morally right decision can be unjust, and a morally wrong decision just; this is particularly difficult when principles such as Kant's categorical imperative, and similar ideals, such as 'equal respect and consideration' are often held up to be the basis of both morality and justice.

Utilitarianism also creates difficulties for both philosophy and psychology, for whilst it is undoubtedly considered to be a theory of morality, its relationship with justice is extremely unclear. This problem is becoming more salient as ideas from economic philosophy infiltrate into psychology.

Utility, efficiency and fairness

Utilitarianism, and economic concepts such as 'efficiency' are becoming more popular in psychological accounts of justice (see, for example, Mellers and Baron, 1993), but there seems to be no consensus at all between disciplines as to how to define the relationships between utilitarianism, efficiency, equity, fairness and justice.

Traditionally psychologists have equated fairness with justice, and equity with the Adams/Hatfield type formulation. To multiprinciple theorists, this means that sometimes equity may be judged to be unfair. However, there is now a tendency amongst some psychologists to use 'equity' in the sense used by economic and political philosophers to refer to the global concept of 'fairness'; that is as concept to be distinguished from 'utility' and 'efficiency'. The distinction between equity (as 'fairness') and efficiency is important here because much of economic theorizing on justice concerns the latter; indeed, Cooter (1987) argues that, 'when economists argue about justice they are usually arguing about how broadly to interpret efficiency' (p. 71). 'Efficiency' has been defined by economists in a number of ways, including 'economic growth', though perhaps the most popular definition is that of *'Pareto-optimality'*.

The principle of 'Pareto-optimality' is named after the Italian sociologist and economist, Vilfredo Pareto (1848-1923). Put very succinctly, the idea is that a situation is optimal or efficient, when it is impossible to make one person better-off without making someone else worse off. Thus, for example, a situation would be non-optimal, or inefficient, if everyone could be made better off by allocating resources in a different way, or if one or more persons could be made better off by a different allocation, and no one would be made worse off. The similarity between this idea and the ubiquitous 'Lockean proviso' is particularly notable. However, it is quite easy to see how this concept of 'efficiency' might be deemed inconsistent with some notions of 'fairness'. For example, Schokkaert comments that 'some Pareto-optima may be really horrible .... it is impossible to justify on its basis any redistribution of utility. Indeed, even a redistribution from

A, who is very wealthy, to B, who is starving, will make A worse off, and therefore cannot be a Pareto-improvement' (1992, p. 69). Accordingly, many economists perceive the job of balancing fairness and efficiency to be an important goal for economic theory (Le Grand, 1991). However, as a result of all this is we now not only have a confusion between different definitions of equity, but we have an economic conception of justice in terms of efficiency that is distinguishable from 'fairness'.

The problems are compounded when we consider the status of utilitarianism as a theory of justice. Some seem to include utilitarian considerations as an integral part of justice (see, for example, Baron, 1993; Hardin, 1987; Posner, 1981). However, according to many philosophers, utilitarianism is not a theory of justice. Thus Raphael says, 'utility is not justice; utility often comes into conflict with justice' (1981, p. 76). As we have seen, the basic objection seems is that utilitarianism aims to maximize the good, however it is conceptualised, but ignores how the good should be distributed; and to many, justice very much concerns the latter (see, Hospers, 1961; Raphael, 1981; Rawls, 1973). According to this latter view, therefore, within a theory of utilitarianism, justice is only a means of obtaining a goal, it is not the goal itself. Hence Rawls (1973) argues, 'The striking feature of the principle of utility is that it does not matter, except indirectly, how this sum of satisfactions is distributed among individuals .... From the standpoint of utility the strictness of commonsense notions of justice has a certain usefulness, but as a philosophical doctrine it is irrational' (p. 320). So we now have some arguing as though utilitarianism were a theory of justice, and others more or less stating that one of the basic objections to utilitarianism is that it does not take justice into account.

To further complicate matters, whilst 'efficiency' might be considered an end state, or goal for utilitarianism (see Campbell, 1988; Posner, 1981), there has been a tendency for some theorists to distinguish between 'utilitarianism' and 'efficiency' (see, Baron, 1993; Schokkaert, 1993). Those who differentiate between the two point to the fact that the utilitarian goal of 'maximizing aggregate utilities' does not have to be 'Pareto-efficient'. If by taking something from person A and giving it to B, the utility gain to A outweighs the utility loss to B, then utilitarianism demands this reallocation even though it is not Pareto-optimal. Because some utilitarian allocations using this principle might be considered grotesque, it is perhaps reasonable to argue that Pareto-optimal allocations capture more the essence of justice because they prevent us exploiting and harming people (by making them worse off). However, sometimes utilitarianism seems to fit more readily with egalitarian ideals. For instance, utilitarianism can oblige us to transfer of money from the rich to the poor in a situation in Pareto-optimality would not necessarily require it. Assuming there is declining marginal value for money (£10 means more to a pauper than a billionaire), then if the 'utility functions' of the rich and poor are the same (they value wealth, or being rich and poor, in the same way), utilitarianism demands that wealth is redistributed to the poor, even though the rich would be made worse off by the transfer. Given all this, it seems somewhat arbitrary to claim that 'efficiency' is a principle of justice but 'utility maximization' is not; and if neither is a principle of justice, then presumably much what is commonly called 'economic justice', has nothing to do with justice at all.

The spread of ideas from economics also highlights the fact that psychologists and philosophers seem incapable of helping each other distinguish between the general principles underlying procedural and allocation 'preferences' as opposed to those specifically concerned with 'just' procedures and allocations; assuming, again, there is a distinction to be made.

The problem of punishment
Another striking feature of most modern theories of justice is the failure to provide a consistent and coherent account of the notion of 'just punishment'. In fact, despite the importance of criminal liability and punishment in our everyday notions of justice, in both psychology and philosophy these issues now tend to be fudged or hived off into some separate pigeon hole and ignored; and, once again,

economic concepts are of little help here. We have already noted the problems associated with utilitarian/deterrence approaches to the treatment of criminals; and how can one derive a meaningful theory of punishment from the concept of 'Pareto-optimality'? It might seem reasonable to punish criminals for the benefit of society, but how can this be done in such a way that the criminal is no-worse off?

This draws attention to a general problem that has sent philosophers going round in circles for centuries; and that is, if the wrong that criminals do is to harm others, how can we be justified in harming them in return? As well as the argument that punishment makes criminals better off, creative answers to this problem have included the views that criminals should not be punished at all, have a right to be punished, or have 'consented' to be punished. But as Kemp (1968) points out, even if offenders do consent to be punished, it does not follow that they ought to be punished or that punishment should fit the crime. Also if punishment makes offenders 'better-off', even if they do not consent to it, perhaps we should punish non-criminals alike so that everyone will be 'better-off' (see Berger, 1984). Unfortunately, psychology has been unable to come up with little useful theoretical contribution to this debate other than to reject or ignore the only psychological theory that purported to systematically predict and explain the relationship between crime severity and punishment, namely, equity theory.

Other problems

There are many other problems when one attempts to assess the philosophical and psychological literature as a whole. There is potential for confusion with regard to the historical and ideological bases of concepts such as equality and psychological equity. Many psychologists see psychological equity as ideologically conservative or right wing in nature (Tornblöm, 1992) and a feature of 'the marketplace economic system of Western capitalism' (Sampson, 1975, p. 51). According to Sampson, within this context, equity stresses 'agency, individualism and competition', and contrasts with equality, that is more ideologically left wing and rests on 'communion, collectivism and cooperation' (1975, p. 61). However, according to the philosophical perspective of MacIntyre (1988), the modern emphasis on individualism leads to *egalitarianism* not a contribution based scheme. MacIntyre's basic idea is that because in a modern individualist culture there is no common agreement about what is good for everybody, then 'Justice is *prima facie* egalitarian' (p. 344), and founded on the idea that individuals should be equally free to express their own personal preferences. On the other hand, says MacIntyre, a scheme of justice, that seeks to reward people on the basis of their contribution to the good of society, assumes a communal orientation, as in the ancient Greek notion of the 'polis'.

On one issue, in particular, philosophy and psychology seem to be on different planets. Psychologists like to treat the terms 'entitlement' and 'deservingness' as equivalent; the terms are semantically interchangeable. Moreover, to psychologists who use the term 'deservingness' encompasses the whole of the area of justice, regardless of what rule, or selection of rules, is applied. Philosophers, however, although far from unanimous about the exact nature of the concept of 'desert' or 'deservingness', seem to apply the term in a far more restricted sense, and frequently distinguish between 'desert' and 'entitlement'. The result is extremely confusing to those who wish to sample ideas from both disciplines. Thus, for instance, we find writers such as David Miller and Michael Walzer distinguishing between 'desert' and 'need' as principles of justice, when to many, if not most psychologists, 'need' is a principle of 'deservingness'. The situation becomes even more chaotic when one considers that so many modern philosophers, including Rawls and Nozick, have apparently more or less rejected 'desert' as the basis of justice. It seems rather strange for psychologists to attempt to illuminate their arguments on 'deservingness', as they often do, by cursory references to philosophers who have supposedly rejected the idea.

Is there a way forward?

At this point the reader may think that this is perhaps an appropriate time to give up any attempt to find a central unifying principle for justice. However, I believe that may still be hope. In the rest of this book I aim to present, with supporting rationale, a prototypical psychological model or scheme for justice that I hope may act as a central unifying focus and help to make sense of the confusion surrounding philosophical and psychological conceptions of justice. If my analysis has any merit, then the scheme I have in mind may represent what, throughout the history of civilization, most people have meant by, and expected from, a system of justice; hence most of the theories of justice I have described in this book either explicitly or implicitly make reference to this scheme, and derive their main force from it. It is, therefore, particularly ironic that at the core of this scheme are the two conceptions of justice that so many psychologists and philosophers have been so keen to abandon or downgrade; namely, the psychological concept of equity, and the philosophical concept of desert.

PART 4

THE ORIGINS AND NATURE OF EQUITY AND DESERT

CHAPTER 11

THE HISTORICAL ORIGINS OF DESERT: PLATO AND THE PRINCIPLE OF GEOMETRICAL EQUALITY

The thesis I intend to examine in the rest of this book is that at the heart of concept usually associated with the term 'justice' is the idea that people should receive what they 'deserve'; and that the psychological theory closest to the concept of 'desert', is equity theory. A major problem has been, however, that this conception of justice has become confused with the idea of justice as 'obedience to law', and more particularly, with the general idea of what 'the law *ought* to be'. To begin this analysis, therefore, we need to tie down and qualify the term 'desert', so let us start with some etymology and some history.

The etymology of justice and desert

Although there seems to be agreement that the word 'justice' derives from the Latin word *ius*, historically, the term *ius* referred to much more than the 'law' and its ordinances. Included in its meanings were also, that which is good and right, an unwritten convention or code of behaviour, the obligations, bonds, or claims arising out of a given relationship, that to which one is entitled, and one's right or due. However, the Latin word closest to our word 'justice' is, in fact, *iustitia*, which had a more limited meaning. Although *iustitia* was used in relation to the validity and adequacy of reasons, it was used mainly to refer to 'fairness and equity', particularly in the areas defined by the term *ius*. The term 'equity' here derives from the Latin *aequitas*, referring to even, equal, balanced, or impartial. The word *iustitia* itself derives from *iustus*, meaning lawful, fair, impartial equitable, to which one is due or entitled, and also, what is *deserved* or *merited* in terms of rewards and punishments. Historically, these definitions reflect a distinction that was made in ancient times between what is 'right' as determined by law in its most general sense, including civil law, social convention and authority, and what is 'fair and equal'. Importantly, the notion of desert seems particularly connected to the latter; that is, the concept of 'fair and equal'.

The term 'deserve' itself derives from the Latin *deservio*; the term *servio* meant 'to serve', and the word *deservio* meant 'to serve zealously', or to devote oneself to the service of (for instance, an employer). It is also interesting to note that, in Latin, our word 'merit', as well as meaning general worthiness to receive good and bad treatment, also related to 'service'. Thus *merito* meant to draw pay or serve as a soldier, and a *meritum* was something, such as a service, that entitled one to gratitude or a reward. This all seems to suggest the terms 'deserving' and 'merit' have an important historical connection with the concept of 'service', and in particular, the idea of rewarding positive services or contributions to the welfare of others, and punishing negative services, or disservices and demerits, that harm the welfare of others. Considered in this way, some of the actions and attributes that philosophers have associated with 'desert' start to make sense; working hard to qualify for jobs, using intelligence and conscientious effort to produce socially desirable consequences, taking risks on behalf of others, using one's talents and initiative to good purpose, and sacrificing oneself for others, could all be construed as contributions or services to the general good, or welfare of others. Whereas wrongdoing, in all its forms, can be construed as a disservice to the general good.

Thus far then, we can historically link the concept of desert to those social conventions that concern what is fair and equal, as distinct from laws and social conventions in general. And the guiding principle for what is fair and equal, in terms of desert, is that those who contribute in some way to the good of others should receive praise and reward, and that those who harm or contribute negatively to the good of others should receive blame and punishment. However, if one looks at the historical background to the division between the 'lawful' and the 'fair and equal', it becomes apparent that the distinction was not always as straightforward as this. In fact, if we really are to make sense of notion of desert, and its place in the idea of justice, we need to examine in some detail the ancient origins of the concept we now term justice.

The beginnings: Mesopotamia and Egypt
In his widely acclaimed work, 'A History of Western Philosophy', Bertrand Russell (1979) argues that philosophy, as a discipline distinct from theology, began in Greece in the sixth century B.C. Correspondingly, it is in the writings of the philosophers of Classical Greece that we find the first extensive discussion of the various concepts we now associate with the term justice. However, as a background to Greek views of justice, it is useful to look briefly at certain features of the belief systems of the two major civilizations that preceded and influenced the Greeks; those of Mesopotamia and Egypt.

Ancient Mesopotamia, the land between the rivers Tigris and Euphrates, covered the area now, more or less, occupied by modern Iraq. According to some historians, the Sumerian people of Mesopotamia developed the world's first true civilization some five and a half thousand years ago (Kramer, 1969). In Mesopotamia law and religion were closely entwined, and one very prominent belief was the Sumerian concept of the *Me*. The *Me* was a set of universal laws devised by Enhil, the father of the gods. The *Me* ensured a kind of cosmic order; every person and thing, the heavens, the underworld, the land, sea, gods and humans, were governed by the *Me*. It was the *Me* that preserved the changeless stability of the universe, and any violation of the *Me* would threaten this stability. Violations of the *Me* by humans were thus punishable, either in this life or the next, so that the cosmic stability could be restored. Allied to the *Me* were two further beliefs. First, the Sumerians believed that, after death, the souls of the dead departed to an underworld, or nether world, in which they are judged by the sun god Utu, according to their life on earth, and second, the souls of the dead could reenter the world of the living under a different guise. This enabled the Sumerians to justify some of the deprivations and sufferings in this world by reference to good and bad deeds performed in earlier lives; indeed, as one Sumerian sage put it, 'never was a sinless child born to his mother' (Kramer, 1969, p. 105).

The intimate connection between religion and law in Mesopotamia is very evident in the legacy of King Hammurabi, who ascended the Babylonian throne in 1750 B.C. Hammurabi is famous for his code of laws, believed to be one of the oldest in the world. The code describes laws relating to numerous subjects. For example, it states that doctors should charge less to the poor than to the rich. Many of the punishments prescribed tend to be based on the proportional principle of *lex talionis*, or 'an eye for an eye'; thus, for instance, the code says that a builder who builds a house so badly that it collapses and kills its occupant, shall be put to death, and a person who knocks out the tooth of another shall lose one of his own teeth (Hertz, 1956). Hammurabi asserted that the laws had been delivered to him by Marduk, son of Enki, the god who had been given charge of the *Me*. The Mesopotamians thus possessed a belief system in which religion, kingship, and law were inextricably linked, all playing an essential part in the maintenance of a grand cosmic order or equilibrium.

Whilst the culture of Mesopotamia is said to have had a profound impact on the development of Ancient Greek culture, and indeed, Western civilization as a whole (Kramer, 1969; Russell, 1984), the impact of Egyptian culture is less certain; nevertheless, certain beliefs of the ancient Egyptians are also worthy of note. Ancient Egypt reached its zenith in the era of the new kingdom that began about 1600 B.C. However, the first dynasty of Egyptian pharaohs has been dated as far back as 3000 B.C. The Egyptians possessed a concept similar in some respects to the Sumerian *Me*, that the Egyptians called *Maat*. *Maat*, like *Me*, has no precise modern translation, but corresponds to a kind of cosmic order, built into the world by the gods at the moment of creation, and its purpose was to maintain the changeless perfection of the world and society. Also, like the Sumerians, the Egyptians believed that the souls of the dead descended into an underworld where they were judged according to their lives on earth; for the Egyptians, the divine judge was Osiris. Moreover, the Egyptians too believed that the laws issued by the kings to maintain *Maat* were divine; though the Egyptian pharaohs saw themselves as gods, not simply mortals chosen by the gods to enforce divine laws. Even decisions in civil and criminal trials took on a divine dimension, in that the magistrates spoke for the vizier, who, in turn, spoke for the pharaoh (Casson, 1969).

Justice in Classical Greece
Authorities are unclear as to how the Mesopotamian and Egyptian cultures reached classical Greece. Some elements of Egyptian culture may have come to Greece through the Minoans of Crete; the Cretans traded much with Egypt. Nevertheless, regardless of the ways the ideas actually spread, there are some important commonalities between the belief systems of the early Greeks, the Egyptians, and the peoples of Mesopotamia. For example, according to works by the Greek poets Homer and Hesiod (11th to 7th Centuries B.C.), it is apparent that the early Greeks believed that law was issued by the gods, and that violations of law incurred divine curse and punishment. The oracle of Delphi was frequently consulted on matters of law, and the king who pronounced laws considered himself invested with his office by the king of the gods, Zeus (Bodenheimer, 1962). The early Greeks also believed in an underworld, The 'House of Hades', and some apparently believed that, in the after-life one would be rewarded or punished according to one's life on earth; those most noted for this belief were the followers of Orpheus, and Pythagoras (Lee, 1987; Russell,

1984). But, most significantly, the Greeks also had a concept similar to the Sumerian *Me*, and the Egyptian *Maat*.

The Greek word most often used in conjunction with this idea is *dike*, which most literally translates as, 'what is marked out'; thus to be *dikaios* is to act in such a way as to accord with 'what is marked out'. The assumption underlying the use of the term *dike* was that the universe had a certain preordained order, a state of harmony, equilibrium or rest, in which everything had a particular status; or, as Russell puts it, 'every person and everything has his or its appointed place and appointed function' (1984, p. 130). To violate this cosmic order was to overstep externally fixed bounds, and violations of *dike* required redress to restore the basic harmony or balance. As Russell emphasizes, this was one of the most profound Greek beliefs. The idea of *dike* is very important to our present discussion, because it is this term and its derivatives, *dikaos*, *dikaiosune*, *adikia* and *adikein*, that are most often, in English translation, connected with the terms 'justice' and 'injustice'; hence, one of most often cited quotes expressing this idea is that of the Greek astronomer Anaximander (610-c.547 B.C.), who said, 'Into that from which things take their rise they pass away once more, as is ordained, for they make reparation and satisfaction to one another for their *injustice* according to the ordering of time' (Russell, 1984, p. 46, my emphasis).

In the Homeric poems Zeus had entrusted certain kings with the enforcement of *dike* by punishing violators. Thus, to the early Greeks, as well as the peoples of Mesopotamia and Egypt before them, cosmic order, divinity, law and kingship were closely related, and those who offended against this cosmic order, by violating the laws handed down by the gods to mortals, were liable to punishment, in this life or the next, so that the balance could be restored. In the 5th century B.C., however, Greek law and religion became split, and philosophy was born. One possible reason for the split was political. In the area called Attica, of which Athens was capital, government had changed from monarchy that existed in the Homeric age, through aristocracy, to democracy; it was a feature of

Greek democracy that laws were created and changed by ordinary mortals; they were not all ordained by a divine being, or king. This led some Greeks to adopt a distinction between the god-given laws of nature, that were unchangeable, and the man made laws of convention, that were artificial and subject to the whims of men (Bodenheimer, 1962). It was from this background that Greece's two most famous philosophers emerged, Plato and Aristotle.

Both Plato and Aristotle offer us very extensive discussions of the sorts of topics we now associate with justice and it is well worth looking at them in some detail. To a modern psychologist it might seem strange to spend any time at all on the writings of philosophers who lived more than two thousand years ago, however, these writers give us a fascinating insight into ancient custom and reasoning about justice, and their impact on Western civilization has been enormous. Their writings have influenced and guided kings, church leaders, politicians, lawyers and philosophers for centuries, and though we may not realize it, they influence us still. Most important from the point of view of the present discussion, however, is they tell us much about the origins of our present conceptions of desert.

Plato's Republic

Plato (c.427-347 B.C.) was born to aristocratic parents who lived in Athens. He studied under Socrates (c.469-399 B.C.) and he travelled and lived abroad for a number of years before returning to set up a school at his house in Athens, known as the Academy. Certain events then occurred that were to have a profound influence on Plato's political thinking. When Plato was in his early twenties, Athens was defeated by Sparta in the Peloponnesian war. Supported by arms from Sparta, a group of wealthy individuals then overthrew the Athenian democracy and set up an oligarchy. Their reign was savage and brutal, and after only eight months they, in turn, were overthrown, and democracy was restored. These events shook the confidence of many Athenians, including Plato, and subsequently Aristotle, in the viability of both democracy and oligarchy. Plato was particularly affected because in 399 B.C. the new democratic order put to death his friend and mentor, Socrates. Plato concluded that democracy and oligarchy, like tyranny, were imperfect forms of government. Instead, he argued that government should be by philosopher rulers, who would be selected and trained to rule with wisdom and justice.

The work of Plato most often associated with the subject of justice is 'The Republic' (R), which was probably written about 375 B.C. (Lee, 1987). The main theme of The Republic is *dikaiosune*; which, literally, is the disposition to act according to *dike*, that is, what is 'marked out' in terms of the order of the cosmos. *Dikaiosune* has variously been translated as 'the disposition to act rightly', 'righteousness' and even 'morality'; however, it is most commonly translated as 'justice', and it is to this later translation I shall adhere.

Plato's writings usually take the form of discussions between characters, with Plato's own opinions expressed through the mouth of one of the characters; in the Republic it is Socrates. The first part of the Republic deals with defining 'justice'. The debate starts when a character named Cephalus describes the advantages that wealth can provide in acting justly; for example, wealth enables one to avoid lying and cheating; it enables one to avoid leaving a sacrifice to God unmade, or leaving a man unpaid before he dies (in ancient Greek culture all these behaviours were traditionally associated with acting 'justly'). But Socrates argues that justice cannot consist solely in truthtelling and returning what we have borrowed, because a just person would not return a borrowed weapon to a madman. In response, another character, Polemarchus, asserts that to act justly is, more generally, and again very much in line with Greek tradition, 'to give everyman his due' (R, p. 331e); a famous saying he attributes to Simonides, a lyric poet of Ceos, (c. 556-468 B.C.). In the discussion that follows, 'giving each his due' is further defined as 'benefitting one's friends and harming one's enemies', and then, 'to do good to one's friend if he is good, and harm to one's enemy if he is evil' (R, p. 335b). However, Socrates objects that no just person would try to make people worse, yet harming one's enemies surely makes them worse.

At this point Thrasymachus bursts in, claiming all this is nonsense: he says what is just 'is simply what is in the interest of the stronger party' (R, p. 338c). He argues that governments enact laws that are in their own interests, and whatever those in power decree as a law will be just (R, pp. 338-339). However, what Thrasymachus ultimately gives us, is not an argument for why justice is to be defined as that which is in the interests of the powerful, but a catalogue of acts he considers to be unjust, regardless of whether they are decreed or condoned by those in power; thus 'unjust' acts include the inadequate payment of taxes, appropriating public funds, showing partiality, and performing acts of tyranny. In fact, his argument is not so much that justice is doing what is in one's self-interest, but rather that, in one's everyday dealings it actually pays better to pursue one's own self interests and act unjustly.

In reply, Socrates asserts that not all the decrees of those in power would necessarily be in their own interests; indeed, he argues that rulers do not, by definition, rule for their own benefit; a ruler is someone who exercises his skill for the benefit of others. But, in any case, argues Socrates, a just life is happier than an unjust life. Plato's rationale for a just life a being happier life was to influence many who followed him, particularly Aristotle. Socrates, argues that everything that is good (*agathon*) has attached to it a particular excellence (*arete*) that enables it to perform its function well; for example, the excellence of a knife is sharpness or ability to cut. Now justice, says Socrates, (the disposition to act justly) is 'the peculiar excellence of the mind' (R, p. 353e); so justice is that which enables the mind to perform its function well. But what is the function of the mind? It is the activity of life itself says Socrates, that is, 'paying attention, controlling, deliberating and so on' (R, p. 353d). Thus the just man will always have a happier life than the unjust man, because only through the possession of justice can the mind function to the full.

Other characters are, however, unconvinced by Socrates' argument. Glaucon adopts a 'contractarian' view; he argues that people do not act justly because justice itself makes one happier, but because the disadvantages of unfettered self-interest are such that it is necessary for people to make a compact to refrain from injuring each other; and it is the laws and agreements so made that determine what is just. Adeimantus then adds that justice itself has no intrinsic value, rather people act justly because of the reputation, honours and rewards justice brings in this life and the next. In other words, the motives of the just and the unjust man are no different; they both seek their personal interest: take away the promise of reward or the threat of punishment, and the 'just man' would be unjust too. Adeimantus challenges Socrates to show him that a just life is superior to an unjust life, and produces good effects to its possessor, regardless of external contingencies.

At this point Socrates himself attempts both to define justice, and explain the intrinsic benefits it brings to its possessor. He suggests that the best way to approach the problem is to imagine, or to construct, an ideal state, a utopia, and then consider how justice and injustice might arise in it. In the political state he describes, there are three classes of citizens; the guardians, who have all the political power; the auxiliaries, a military class whose job it is to support and protect the guardians, and the common people, the producing class, whose job it is to support the other two groups. His basic idea is that justice will exist in such a state when every member of each class is performing his or her proper function, and not usurping the roles or functions of others. Correspondingly, according to standard translation, he defines justice as, 'minding your own business and not interfering with other people' (R, p. 443b). However, the translation, 'minding your own business', is somewhat misleading; a more literal translation is, 'doing the things which belong to oneself' (Lee, 1987). The whole definition thus means something more like, 'performing the function that is designated to you, and not usurping the role or function of another'.

Socrates then goes on to discuss the notion of 'justice in the individual'; which is basically to ask the question, 'what psychological state of affairs will dispose a person to be just?' Socrates says, 'each of us will be just and perform his proper function only if each part of him is performing its proper function' (R, p.441e). What he then describes is a simple theory of personality. He says that the human personality is made up of three parts; reason, 'spirit' (which seems to correspond to something like 'vigour or 'enthusiasm'), and desire or appetite. His idea is that for justice (a just disposition) to exist within the individual, the faculty of reason must be trained in rational argument to control and soothe the spirit; then reason and spirit must be put in charge of the appetite so that the latter will 'mind its own business' (R, p. 442b). When a man's reason, spirit and appetite are functioning in their correct order, he will act justly; he will, for example, show honesty, loyalty and trustworthiness. He will not commit adultery, steal, be irreligious, or dishonour his parents. But more than this, he will 'attain self-mastery and order, and live on good terms with himself' (R, p. 443d). Therefore justice not only produces harmony between individuals, it is a disposition of mind that is intrinsically beneficial to its possessor and worth cultivating for its own sake.

Plato's justice in context

On first consideration it would appear that the Greeks had as many problems defining 'justice' as we do; moreover, it is perhaps not surprising that Plato's conception of *dikaiosune* is thought by some to be far removed from modern conceptions of justice. One would be very unlikely to be taken seriously in a modern conversation about justice if one attempted to argue that justice is 'minding one's own business', or even more absurd, 'having the components of one's psyche mind their own business'. However, if we examine some of Plato's ideas about justice in their historical and religious context, they are perhaps less bizarre than at first they may seem.

An obvious observation to make is that Plato's ideas about justice seem to go far beyond, and be only tenuously based on, the idea that justice is 'minding one's own business'. His concept of a just society is one that is rigidly stratified with a select ruling class. Moreover, the 'just' person is one who possesses a range of traditional Greek aristocratic virtues. Indeed, whilst Socrates' opponents may argue over the motives, there is actually little disagreement over what actually constitutes 'just' behaviour: the just man is loyal and trustworthy; he does not lie, cheat, steal, betray his country, break his promises, or commit adultery; he does not leave a sacrifice to the gods unmade, or a man unpaid. These notions of justice obviously reflect a mixture of the prevailing cultural norms, and Plato's own social and political prejudices; however, perhaps more important is the way they can be seen to reflect the influence of the traditional Greek concept of *dike*.

As has been mentioned, the origins of the term *dikaiosune* lie in the notions of *dike* and *dikaios*, pertaining to the ancient theory of cosmic order, harmony or balance. This is important, because Plato's discussion of justice only really makes sense when set in this historical context; indeed, as Russell (1984) argues, the ancient idea of everything performing its function, and not overstepping its boundaries, is fundamental to Plato's conception of justice. The idea of linking 'justice' to the whole of the cosmos, including inanimate objects such as planets and stars, may seem odd to us; but to the Greeks, even inanimate objects could be endowed with vigour, intention, and purpose (see Trusted, 1984). Everything in the universe was subject to the same cosmic order. Plato's conception of justice thus derived from the idea that there is a cosmic order in the universe, and for this order to be maintained, everyone, and everything must perform according to its designated function; nothing must overstep its bounds, and this applies to heavenly bodies, gods, social classes, individuals within classes, and parts of the human personality. Hence, in Plato's theory, everyone and everything has a defined role or purpose that must be exercised rigidly. However, as MacIntyre (1988) has emphasized, there was more to the traditional Greek notion of *dike* than the idea that everyone has a fixed role that must not be usurped or overstepped; it was also a violation of *dike* to deprive a person of what is owed, or 'due', to that person as an occupant of that role. But if the latter applies, why does Plato appear to dismiss the notion of justice as 'giving each his due'?

The answer to the this question seems to be that, contrary to the impression he gives at first, Plato never actually dispenses Polemarchus' view that justice is 'giving each his due'. What Socrates actually says is, 'it wasn't a wise man who said that justice is to give everyman his due, if what he meant by it was that the just man should harm his enemies and help his friends' (R, p. 335e). His objection, therefore, is not to the principle of 'giving each his due', but to the particular example given by Polemarchus. Socrates' objection to the notion of 'harming one's enemies' is based on the assumption that harming people makes them worse; however, he certainly has no objection to the idea of punishment; on the contrary, on other occasions in the Republic (pp. 380b and 389d) as well as in the earlier work, Gorgias (pp. 471-480), he emphasizes not only that justice requires the punishment of those who have done wrong, but the offender who pays the penalty that justice demands, by suffering punishment in this world and the next, will be, on balance, happier than the person who is not justly punished for criminal acts. Socrates' logic is that, to be punished for one's crimes is to be treated justly, and to be treated justly is a fine and good thing; it frees the soul of badness and cures excess and wickedness; thus punishment benefits the offender who is punished. On the other hand, the offender who is left unpunished does not receive the benefits of being justly treated, and will continue to suffer from a 'badness of soul' that will prevent the achievement of happiness. 'Giving each his due' in the form of punishment for wrongdoing, therefore, makes matters better, and is an essential feature of justice (economists might wish to note this solution to the problem of finding a way of punishing criminals that is Pareto-optimal!).

The fact that Plato does not dispense with the idea of justice as 'giving each his due' is also evidenced in that, shortly after claiming that justice is nothing more than 'minding one's own business', Socrates says that it is unjust to 'take other people's belongings or to be deprived of one's own and thus justice is keeping what is properly one's own and doing one's job'(R., p. 433e). The obvious point here is that to take someone's property, that is 'properly' their own, constitutes depriving them of their due. As Russell (1984) has remarked, Plato never actually abandons the idea that one of the main concerns of justice is the repayment of debts. Plato seems to refine the concept rather than dismiss it.

Viewed from this wider historical and religious perspective, Plato's account of justice seems to assume a more coherent form. This can be summarized as follows. At the most universal level, there exists a predetermined cosmic order; an ideal state of balance, equilibrium, or rest, that is achieved when everything its functioning properly in its proper place. Within this order, and as a fundamental part of it, all people are involved in a set of interactive, and mutually dependent role relationships. By performing the reciprocal obligations attached to their respective roles correctly or 'rightly', as *dike* dictates, all role performers contribute to and serve to maintain the order and stability of the whole set of role relationships, and consequently, contribute to the grand cosmic order itself. Importantly also, as part of the same scheme, if all perform their roles correctly, each participant will receive a 'due', a social, psychological, or material reward, or 'positive return', commensurate with and appropriate to his or her respective role; thus, in return for their services, rulers receive food, clothing and housing, as well as the obedience and respect of their subjects; soldiers too receive their keep and honours for bravery, labourers receive wages, friends receive loyalty, parents receive respect, and so on.

Also, by simply taking on the role of good citizens, people can expect to be treated in certain ways; for example, they can normally expect to be treated impartially, and not to be victims of betrayal, theft, assault or adultery. If one were a victim on any of these counts, one would, in effect, be in receipt of less than one's due as a citizen. Moreover, in this scheme, the performance of one's role, and the receipt of what is due as a consequence of the performance of one's role, are very much interdependent; for example, part of the role of a son is to honour his parents, and parents, in turn, are due honour or respect in return for performing their roles as parents. As a result, the son who does not honour his parents, gives his parents less than what is due to them. Part of the role of a friend is to be loyal, and in return, friends are 'due' loyalty; thus the man who is disloyal to a friend, not only fails to perform his own role as a friend, but fails to give his friend his due. Each must perform an appropriate religious role too. The man who insults the gods, both fails in his role obligations, and does not give the gods their dues. Also, the person who usurps the role of another (or does not 'mind his own business'), automatically deprives that other person of what is due to him as an occupant of the role concerned.

Another important part of Plato's scheme requires the punishment of those who offend against a properly structured society. Thus those who assault, steal from, or lie to others, not only deprive others of their dues, but, by offending, also fail to perform their roles as good citizens. Such offenders are therefore due punishment (that is, a 'negative' due); so that the grand order is restored. In his later work, the Laws, Plato, (1960) points out that those who injure others must not only pay compensation to their victims, but also incur a penalty, not to cancel the crime, but 'by way of correction' (p. 933); that is, to restore the balance of the cosmos. Seen in this general context, it is more obvious why Plato should insist that just behaviour, including punishment, must do some good. A punishment that makes matters worse would do nothing to restore the order and harmony that offences disturb. Plato does not take up an issue that has plagued philosophers for centuries; namely what is to be done with offenders if the punishment called for by their offences actually makes them worse; he simply assumes that 'just punishment' is always beneficial. Similarly, a mad man who lends you his weapon may be 'due' his weapon in a strict sense, but if giving him back his weapon enables him to do harm to others (who, incidentally, by being harmed, will receive less than their dues as innocent citizens), then the effects on the cosmic order may be worse than the continuance of the debt.

Plato also acknowledges that truthtelling may not always be appropriate (R, p. 331c); he thus seems adopt the position that, whilst in most situations it is appropriate to display truthfulness, be honest, repay our debts, and so on, the ultimate criterion of what is just behaviour is determined, not by these behaviours *per se*, by the amount of good that follows in maintaining the cosmic order. Within the cosmic order, he thus seems to end up with a sort of 'utilitarianism of dues', in which the criterion of the greatest good could be described as, 'the closest approximation to the ideal where everyone receives his or her due'. However, according to Plato, no such approximation could ever, in itself, count as perfectly just. In fact, Plato thought that justice as a perfect ideal was actually unobtainable in the sensible world; though there does exist, independently of our minds, an ideal form or idea of justice that we can intuitively recognize and to which we can aspire.

Plato on responsibility and choice

Whilst the general scheme implicit in Plato's account gains some coherence when placed in its historical context, it is particularly noticeable that the rigid hierarchical structure of his 'just' society seems to lack any appeal to the ideals of 'freedom of choice', of 'equality of opportunity'; ideals that, according to some modern writers, are fundamental to the idea of justice. In Plato's class, almost caste, ridden society, role positions seem rigidly predetermined; there is no question of choosing one's place in life. Indeed, Plato advocates that, in his ideal society, people should be made to believe that all are fashioned by god out of different metals, gold, silver, and bronze, and the guardians should ensure that each child is put at the level dictated by his or her metallic make up; gold at the top for the rulers, then silver for the auxiliaries, and bronze at the bottom for the workers (R, p. 414-415). In fact, Plato seems to deny any place for personal responsibility at all; he argues that, as good behaviour is ultimately more beneficial than bad behaviour, no one would voluntarily act badly, except out of ignorance, hence all wrong doing must be involuntary or against one's will, and, as such, is not wrong doing at all.

Thus in his desperate attempt to convince people that 'goodness is good for you', he ends up denying that it is possible to do wrong at all. Plato recognizes in 'the Laws', that this view creates problems when assigning criminal responsibility and sentencing offenders. He attempts to get round the problem by asserting, somewhat unconvincingly, that the distinction for treating criminals is that of intentional versus unintentional acts, not voluntary versus involuntary acts (R, pp. 861-862); thus those who intend evil must be punished more severely than those who have no such intention (for their own good, as well as the good of others, of course), even though both act 'involuntarily'. But there are obvious difficulties with this view, as, ultimately, Plato still seems to end up punishing those who have offended 'involuntarily'; a position that some might consider akin to victimizing the innocent.

Nevertheless, a closer look at Plato's writings reveals that, despite appearances, he was actually very committed to the notion of choice. Plato's ideas on choice and 'equal opportunity' are to be found in an often neglected part of the Republic that concerns 'The immortality of the soul and the rewards of goodness' (Part 2, p. 608c). Plato was an ardent believer in the Orphic idea of the transmigration of souls, and he describes his ideas about the after-life in the form of a story, the 'myth of Er'. In this story, Plato asserts that the soul of each individual not only survives mortal death, but returns again to occupy a new body after a period in the after-life. Significantly, however, each soul is able to choose the mortal life it will enter. In a 'neutral place' in the immortal world, each soul is first given a turn to choose a mortal life from a selection of various lives. The order in which each chooses is determined by lot, but there is no necessary disadvantage to having the last choice, because there is plenty of choice for everyone; Plato says, 'Even for the last comer, if he chooses wisely and lives strenuously, there is left a life with which he may be well content' (R, p. 619b). Thus, ultimately, one's role in life, and the performance of that role, are one's own responsibility; Plato says, 'Excellence knows no master; a man shall have more or less of her according to the value he sets on her. *The fault lies not with God, but with the soul that makes the choice'*(R, p.617e, my emphasis).

Plato also argues that the results of our choices have important repercussions, both in this mortal life, and in the after-life. In mortal life, a just life brings both extrinsic and intrinsic rewards, whilst an unjust life brings suffering and punishment. However, these rewards and punishments are as nothing compared to those that follow in the after-life. In the after-life, says Plato (R, p. 615, my emphasis),

For every wrong one has done to anyone a man must pay the penalty in turn, ten times for each .... He pays therefore tenfold retribution for each crime, and so for instance those who have been responsible for many deaths, or have cast others into slavery, or had a hand in any other crime, must pay tenfold suffering for each offence. And correspondingly those who have done good and been just and god-fearing are rewarded *in the same proportion.*

The terms of reward and punishment are served in heaven, or in 'earthly chasms', respectively. Then, each soul returns to choose another life. Plato also points out that only those who have lived justly by means of philosophical reasoning, rather than habit, will be guaranteed to make good choices. The result is a dynamic, cyclical process that can be summarized thus. In the immortal life, one chooses a mortal role. One is then born again and receives intrinsic and extrinsic reward and punishment for one's choices during the performance of one's mortal role, to be received both in mortal life and the after life. One then dies a mortal death and, in the after-life, one chooses another mortal role; and so the cycle continues. Moreover, all this exists as part of the continuing maintenance of *dike*, the grand dynamic cosmic order. The overlap between Plato's views on the *dike* and the after-life, the Sumarian *Me*, and the Egyptian *Maat*, are obvious.

Plato's prototype for desert

Although all this may still seem far removed from any modern conception of justice, looked at in a certain, fairly obvious way, many of the parts of Plato's scheme readily make up a sort of prototypical ideal of justice that is more recognizable. The essence of the scheme is as follows.

First, we first assume the existence of a system composed of a set of interacting participants; a collective social enterprise. Within this system there are certain specified relationships between a), the participants' social actions; that is, their contributions to the maintenance of the system, and b), what they can expect to happen to them; that is, their receipts or 'dues', as a result of these social activities. More specifically, for activities, or contributions to the system, variously classed as 'positive', 'appropriate', 'to be encouraged', or 'good', the returns, or outcomes, will tend to be, on balance, 'positive' or 'rewarding' to the persons receiving them. On the other hand, when a person fails to perform the appropriate activities, or engages in disruptive, 'negative', 'to be discouraged', or 'bad' activities, then negative returns, penalties, or costs must ensue. The basic ideal rule is thus, reward for good, or positive outcomes for positive contributions, and costs for bad, or negative outcomes for negative contributions, and, as a corollary, any activities that result in penalties, or costs, to someone who has done no wrong, or result in reward to someone who has not done good, are 'unjust' activities; they result in excessive costs or penalties for the individual in the former case, and an excess of reward, or a deficiency of costs, for the person in the latter.

A second important feature of the scheme is that, in principle at least, the returns, whether positive or negative, rewards or costs, must be proportionate in degree to the positive and negative contributive activities. Thus the amount of reward must be commensurate with the amount of positive contribution, and the amount of penalty or cost must be commensurate with the extent to which the contribution is negative, disruptive or harmful. Also implicit in this rule of proportionality is the idea that 'equals must be treated equally'; there must be equal shares for equal contributions, and equal penalties for equal wrongs.

Third, and very significantly, each participant in the scheme must be able to choose freely between those activities for which the various rewards and costs are 'due' (though, of course, there are limits to this; for instance, mere mortals cannot freely choose to be Zeus and receive dues commensurate with his status). When all these elements are functioning properly, the result is a kind of equilibrium or balance; but any discrepancy at all will upset the equilibrium, and some action to correct the excess or deficiency will be necessary. In sum, making allowances for Plato's more imaginative metaphysical speculations, these elements make up what philosophers might describe as a prototypical 'desert theory'.

Geometrical equality: sheer, absolute, perfect justice

However, it could reasonably be objected that all this is rather 'going beyond the data'. How do we know whether this conception of 'proportional desert' is actually what Plato had in mind as the 'essence' of justice? Perhaps the most convincing evidence we have comes from what was probably Plato's his last work, the 'Laws'. In the Laws he leaves us in little doubt that, in his view, the idea of awarding shares in equal proportion to one's worth or value to the good of the community is the most fundamental principle of justice.

In Book 6 of the Laws Plato distinguishes between two kinds of equality; the first is inferior and involves distribution by lot; this, he says, 'appeals to luck' (p. 758). Plato argues that, in practice, it may be necessary to introduce some of this first kind of equality 'to avoid disaffection among the masses', but it must be used a sparingly as possible. In contrast, every effort must be made to use the second, superior, kind of equality, that is, he says,'true and real equality, meted out to various unequals'. This 'assigns more to the greater than to the lesser' and 'deals proportionately with either party, ever awarding a greater share to those of greater worth'. Moreover, he claims that wherever this second principle is applied, 'it works nothing but blessings'. Most significantly, however, Plato asserts that this principle of proportionality is more than simply 'true and real equality', it is, he says, 'the very award of Zeus'; it is 'sheer justice' or *'absolute and perfect justice'* (p. 757). Plato's name for this principle of 'absolute and perfect justice' is *'geometrical equality'*. According to Finley (1977), the original idea of a mathematical formulation of justice as a form of equality was Pythagorean; it was probably introduced at the beginning of the 4th Century B.C. by Archytas of Tarentum. Plato actually refers to the authority of its Pythagorean originators in a passage in his early work the 'Gorgias': in this, Socrates says to Callicles (p. 508),

We are told on good authority, Callicles, that heaven and earth and their respective inhabitants are held together by the bonds of society and love and order and discipline and righteousness, and that is why the universe is called an ordered whole or cosmos and not a state of disorder and license. You, I think, for all your cleverness have failed to grasp the truth; you have not observed how great a part geometric equality plays in heaven and earth, and because you neglect the study of geometry you preach the doctrine of unfair shares.

This passage also illustrates well Plato's adherence to the view that justice as geometrical proportion is an integral feature of the whole ordering of the cosmos, and does not apply only to human relationships; moreover, this passage shows that the idea of 'fairness' was integral to this balance.

Plato, law and justice
In the next chapter we shall see what Aristotle had to say about desert, but before moving on to him, it is worth drawing attention to Plato's conception of the link between his scheme of justice, and the notion of law. Although there seems to be an obvious continuity of thought between the early Sumerian concept of the *Me*, the Egyptian idea of *Maat*, the early Greek notion of *dike*, and Plato's concept of *dikaiosune*; nevertheless, in the treatment of law, Plato diverged from these earlier ideas. Lawfulness, in terms of both natural and man made law, was an

important element in the traditional Greek concept of *dikaiosune*, but Plato saw a distinction between his system and man made law. In fact, at first he did not wish his system to be bound by a code of laws at all; he argued that laws could not accurately prescribe what is good and right for each member of a community at any one time. Later he came to argue that, in practice, law would be necessary (see Bodenheimer, 1962). In other words, Plato saw a distinction between justice and the notion of man made law; laws might be necessary to maintain justice, but they were not the same thing. Thus 'justice', or more specifically, geometrical equality, in accordance with the natural law of the cosmos was the ultimate standard by which laws should be judged.

Plato's ideas have had a profound influence on the general course of Western thinking; however, when looking for an account of justice in terms of desert, commentators have tended to concentrate more on the works of his pupil, Aristotle.

CHAPTER 12

ARISTOTLE'S JUSTICE: THE MATHEMATICS OF DESERT

Aristotle was born in the Chalcidic village of Stagira, in northern Greece, in 384 B.C. In 367 B.C. he went to Athens where he studied under Plato, the latter having an obvious and significant influence Aristotle's philosophy. Aristotle died in 322, on the island of Euboea.

Aristotle, like Plato, was not a supporter of democracy, and his opinions were reinforced when the anti-Macedonian democrats expelled him from Athens. Instead, he also preferred government by a ruling elite; a view that was to affect much of his thinking. One of Aristotle's most important contributions to the study of justice was to attempt to describe various aspects of Greek ideas about justice in terms of mathematics; however, his ideas about justice only really make sense within the context of his theory of human character, so it is with his theory of character or personality that we begin.

Aristotle's views on human character and justice are mainly to be found in Nichomachaen Ethics (NE), Eudemian Ethics (EE), Magna Moralia (MM), and Politics (P). (All quotations here from these, and other works of Aristotle, are from Barnes, 1984.)

Aristotle's virtues

Although some have called Aristotle's theory of character his 'moral' or 'ethical' theory, these terms can be somewhat misleading. In fact, when in translation Aristotle talks of 'moral excellence', he means 'excellence of character'; indeed, the term 'ethic' derives from the Greek *ethikos*, referring merely to 'custom' or 'character'.

Aristotle claims that all human knowledge and choice aims at some good that is good in itself (*telos*), rather than a means to a good, and the only good that is good in itself is *eudaimonia*, loosely translated as 'happiness', but, more specifically, referring to a state of 'living well and faring well' (NE1, p. 1094). Aristotle says that *eudaimonia* is to be achieved by some kind of 'excellence' (*arete*), often translated as 'virtue'; and excellence is determined by function; so we first need to determine man's function. According to Aristotle, man is distinguished from other creatures by his possession of a soul, part of which can reason or act from rational principle, and this enables him to lead a certain kind of life governed by reason. Thus a 'good' man is someone who does this well; who performs his function excellently. And in fulfilling this function well, the result is *eudaimonia*, or well-being; thus he says, 'human good turns out to be activity of the soul in conformity with excellence' (NE1, p. 1098). But what characterizes the conduct of a 'good' man; that is to say, a man governed by reason?

Aristotle's account of how we can show excellence of character rests on the assumption that we possess a number of dispositions or 'passions', that, if left in untutored form, are discrepant with our ideal way of life. Not only will they prevent us from achieving our own happiness, but they will create problems in our dealings with others. These potentially disruptive human passions, or vices, can be set in pairs or polar opposites, each representing a kind of excess and defect; for example, foolhardiness and cowardice, and lavishness and meanness. However, these passions or dispositions are not fixed; we can alter the extent to which we experience and are affected by them, and we can do this by habitually acting in a certain kind of way. We should aim for the mean between the two extremes. If, before acting, we use our reason to find the mean, and then act in such a way as to achieve the mean, after a while, by habit, we will develop a different set of dispositions; those that actually coincide with the mean. So, instead of impulsively reacting to a situation, we should use our reason to work out the best, most appropriate, the right way to act. At first this will be difficult, admits Aristotle, but after a while of repeatedly doing this we will not only learn what is the appropriate way to act, but also our dispositions actually will change and fall in line. He says, 'excellences we get by first exercising them .... we become just by doing just acts, temperate by doing temperate acts, brave by doing brave acts' (NE2, p. 1103). Importantly, when this happens something else does too. When what we ought to do is something we are able to do, and also something we automatically feel like doing, as part of our characters, the result is, of course, *eudaimonia*, or happiness.

Aristotle gives various lists of excellences or virtues; for instance in Eudemian Ethics he lists 15 by way of illustration: gentleness, bravery, modesty, temperance, righteous indignation, justice, liberality, sincerity, friendliness, dignity, endurance, greatness of spirit, magnificence, and wisdom. There are no definite rules, however, that can cover how we should behave, only practical wisdom can tell us how to behave at the right time, in the right way, in the right degree, towards the right person. It all depends on the situation. Moreover, says Aristotle, 'to seize the mean is a difficult matter .... the mean is hard, and this is the point for which we are praised (MM1, pp. 1186-1187). The fact that we have the capacity to change our characters reflects an important part of Aristotle's scheme; he insists that excellences are something for which we are personally responsible; for responsibility is linked to voluntary behaviour, and virtue and vice are voluntary characteristics.

Virtue and responsibility

Aristotle argues that the main characteristic of voluntary human acts is that they 'are in (our) power to do or not to do' (EE3, p. 1110). We are therefore not held responsible (in the sense of worthy of praise or blame) for acts 'when the cause is in the external circumstances and the agent contributes nothing' (p. 1110), for in such cases we have not the power to do otherwise. Nevertheless, he suggests that there are circumstances in which it is not clear cut whether or not an act should be classified as voluntary or involuntary. For example, suppose that a tyrant orders us to do something evil, whilst holding our parents and children as hostages, and threatening them with death if we fail to do carry out his orders. Aristotle says that, in a strict sense, compliance with the orders of the tyrant could be construed as voluntary, for we do still have a choice (we can let our children and parents be killed). However, if in such cases we assume that no one would normally have chosen to perform the evil act, then obedience would be 'in the abstract perhaps involuntary' (p. 1110).

However, according to Aristotle, outside influences or pressures are not the only extenuating circumstances we can offer to absolve someone of responsibility for an act. People can be absolved of responsibility if they act through ignorance; that is to say, if, at the time of acting they were unavoidably ignorant of certain circumstances. For example, one might give away a secret, not knowing that it is a secret, or kill a man by giving him a medicine, not knowing it would kill him. Aristotle argues that one criterion we can use to determine whether or not an act was done through ignorance of this sort, is whether the perpetrator shows pain or regret when the ignorance is revealed. People are not, however, absolved of responsibility if their ignorance is due to carelessness. If knowledge of the law is easy to obtain, and it is one's duty to know the law, then ignorance of the law is no excuse for breaking it. When we blame people for carelessness, we do so because 'we assume that it is in their power not to be ignorant, since they have the power of taking care' (p. 1114a). Neither are people absolved of responsibility if they act on impulse, or out of passion, or because they are intoxicated, because, in Aristotle's view, such acts are still voluntary.

One of the more confusing elements of Aristotle's notion of responsibility, however, is his distinction between what is 'chosen' and what is 'voluntary'. He says, 'The voluntary .... is not necessarily done by choice, but the act done by choice is voluntary' (MM1, p. 1189a). For example, a man who acts out of passion or impulse acts 'voluntarily' according to Aristotle, but his acts are not necessarily 'chosen'. The key to understanding this idea seems to lie in Aristotle's conception of 'choice' as something involving deliberation; he says 'choice involves reason and thought' (NE3, p. 1112a). But what seems to be implicit, though not stated, in Aristotle's account, is the notion of undeliberated or impulsive choice. What he seems to mean is that the man who acts out of passion, without exercising deliberation, or reason and thought, has essentially, chosen not to deliberate; he has not done what it was in his power to do. Animals also can act voluntarily in Aristotle's scheme (because if they had not the power to act in different ways, rewards and punishments would not work on them), but because animals do not possess reason, unlike men, they cannot be held responsible for failing to make a deliberated choice. Also, a man who becomes incapable of making a reasoned or deliberated choice because he is drunk, is still responsible for his actions, because he chose to get drunk in the first place.

To Aristotle, the link between using one's reason, and displaying excellence or virtue, is an important one. Finding the mean, acting in the right way for the right reason, requires a deliberated or reasoned choice. Thus, in as much as we have the power to make the necessary deliberated choices (or at least we once had it if we have lost it due to intemperance), virtue and vice are voluntary, and we are responsible for them; Aristotle says, 'it is in our power to be virtuous or vicious' (p. 1113b). Moreover, because it is possible to actually change the nature of our dispositions (by continually using our reason and acting in the right way for the right reason), are characters or dispositions are ultimately also our responsibility; we have the power to control them. Consequently, even if by habit men's characters become such that they are actually incapable of behaving virtuously, they are still responsible for their actions, for Aristotle says, 'it was open at the beginning not to become men of this kind, and so they are such voluntarily (p. 1114a). Aristotle asserts that if the capacity to be virtuous or vicious were not within our power, for example, if some were simply born virtuous, then neither virtue nor vice would be voluntary, and there would be no point in praising the virtuous and blaming the vicious. What is voluntary is praiseworthy or blameworthy; thus we do not blame those who, from birth, are ugly or blind, but we do blame those who look ugly through lack of exercise or who are blind because of alchoholism: 'Of vices of the body, then, those in our power are blamed, those not in our power are not' (p. 1114a). It also follows that we cannot hold people responsible for a failure to exercise a capacity of reason, if such a capacity is absent or undeveloped through no fault of their own. Hence, we would not blame a child or an animal, or a mad person for failing to exercise a capacity they do not possess. To be blamed for vice one must have the capacity to be virtuous, and vive versa, and this assumes a capacity to know the difference.

Hospers (1961) states that 'Aristotle's ethics has been called the biggest collection of cliches, truisms and tautologies in the history of ethics' (p. 84). However, given that Aristotle lived over two thousand years ago, it is perhaps a testament to his considerable observational and analytical powers that today his views should be regarded as cliched. And, indeed, Aristotle's views have had a great influence on modern jurisprudence (Ross, 1937). Bearing all this in mind, we can now go on to look at Aristotle's account of justice.

Aristotle's justice
It is in Nichomachaen Ethics that we find Aristotle's famous account of justice. He starts by distinguishing between two meanings of the term justice; the first is the 'lawful', or 'universal justice', and the second is the 'equal', or 'particular justice'; the latter is then subdivided into a number of different categories, the

most important of which are distributive justice, rectificatory justice, justice as reciprocity, and equity.

Because of the vagaries of the concept of 'universal justice' some writers have decided to more or less ignore it as something related to 'morality in general' or 'legality', rather than 'justice' (see, for example, Ross, 1937; Sadurski, 1985). It soon becomes clear from Aristotle's account, however, that even when discussing universal justice, or justice as the 'lawful', he includes far more than simply what is lawful according to man made law. Hence when writing of universal justice, Aristotle starts by saying all lawful acts are, in a sense, just acts (NE5, p. 1129b), but he soon abandons the strict equation of law and justice in favour of the idea that justice, in this first sense, is obedience to law as law *ought* to be, not necessarily to the law as it actually exists as part of a political constitution (see p. 1137b). He says that a 'rightly framed law' will 'promote excellence and forbid vice'. As a consequence, in Aristotle's account, universal justice ends up, not as lawfulness *per se*, but as 'complete excellence - not absolutely, but in relation to others' (p. 1129b). He says that 'justice, alone of the excellences is thought to be another's good, because it is related to others' (p. 1130). The link between 'lawfulness' in general, and complete excellence, is thus very tenuous; indeed, later Aristotle introduces the notion of 'equity', that he uses in a way similar to its modern legal sense as, 'a correction of law where it is defective owing to its universality' (p. 1137b), and in Politics he admits that some laws may actually be unjust (P3, p. 1282b). Thus it is the idea of justice as excellence in dealings with others, according to *natural law*, or *dike*, that eventually dominates Aristotle's account of universal justice; and in this idea there are clear overlaps with Plato's scheme.

Aristotle, like Plato, was a firm believer in the idea that certain social roles are superior to others, however, in Aristotle's account, the most important role is clearly that of the 'good citizen'; for, he says, man is by nature a political animal' (P1, p. 1253a). But what is the role of a good citizen? He says good citizens display political excellence, or virtue, in their dealings with others; they are, for example, truthful, they observe their agreements, and do not commit adultery or outrage. Importantly, these are all actions that, according to Greek tradition, could be considered to involve giving to others, or at least not depriving others of, their dues as interacting participants in a community. Moreover, according to Aristotle, those who do this most should receive rewards in proportion to their contributions; thus shares should be apportioned in a civil community according to political excellence such that 'they who contribute most .... have a greater share in it' (P1, p. 1281a).

Although missing from Aristotle's scheme is the Platonic idea of choosing one's role in life by means of actions in a previous existence, nevertheless, there is also an important place for choice in Aristotle's justice. According to Aristotle's theory of responsibility, we choose whether or not to display political excellence; virtue and vice are within our power; thus he says, with reference to justice, 'there is a great difference between a voluntary and an involuntary act' (NE5, p. 1132b) Only voluntary acts are praised or blamed; so, only who those who are voluntarily vicious are due punishment, and very significantly, according to his theory of the human psyche, only those who voluntarily choose virtue will receive the ultimate reward, *eudaimonia*, or happiness itself.

Thus despite his digression into the 'lawful', if we view Aristotle's concept of 'universal justice' within its historical context, and the general context of his theory of human character, the basic elements of Plato's 'prototype for desert' are still to be found. In a civil community, those who exhibit excellence in dealings with others will thereby, a) give to others, or not deprive others, of their dues as interacting participants, and b) contribute most to the good of the community; also, when justice exists, those who contribute most will be rewarded most, both intrinsically in terms of *eudaimonia*, but also extrinsically, in terms of a share of the goods in the community, and those whose contributions are negative or disruptive will be penalized with unhappiness and punishments. However, an important qualifying condition is that the positive and negative contributions must be in some sense 'chosen' or 'voluntary'. Moreover, in as much as a 'rightly framed' or 'just' law maintains this situation, so long as the law is adhered to, justice will exist, and they who obey the law will be just.

Justice as 'the equal': geometrical proportion

We can now turn to what Aristotle considers to be the main topic of Aristotle's discussion of justice, the 'equal', or 'particular justice', that is seen by him as part of universal justice.

Aristotle says that injustice in this second, particular sense, refers to the man who is 'grasping' in his affairs with others; thus, in a community, the unjust man takes more than his share or due of the good things, such as honour and money. But what is an 'equal' share of these good things? Aristotle argues that good things, such as honour and money, should be divided according to the 'worth' or 'value' (*axia*) of a person. He says all men agree on this principle, but they do not agree on the standard of value; democrats identify it with the status of freemen, supporters of oligarchy with wealth (or with noble birth), and supporters of the aristocracy with excellence (NE5, p. 1131a). However, as we have seen, Aristotle's clear preference is for 'political excellence', to be the standard of 'worth'; because those who show political excellence are 'worth' most in terms of their contribution to the good of the community. Nevertheless, says Aristotle, no matter what standard is used, the rule for distribution is the same; it involves 'equality of ratios' or the rule of *geometrical proportion* (p. 1131b).

Geometrical proportion can be represented as follows: say, for example, that A represents the number of units of goods to be given to person X, and B the units of goods for person Y, and C represents the number of units of worth of X, and D the worth of Y. A just distribution is then one where $A:B = C:D$, or equivalently, $A:C = B:D$ (NE5, p. 1131b). Thus the more worthy one is, the more one should receive, such that: Goods for X: Goods for Y = Worth of X: Worth of Y, or equivalently, Goods for X: Worth of X = Goods for Y : Worth of Y. So if person A has 4 units of worth, and person B has 2 units of worth, and there are 12 good things to distribute, A should receive 8, and B, 4.

Aristotle's rule for distributive justice is thus a detailed mathematical exposition of the Pythagorean rule of 'geometrical equality' as found in Plato; that is, a more precise formulation of the general principle that those who contribute most to the good of society should receive most. And, as equity theorists have pointed out, the principle of geometrical equality is essentially Adams' (1965) formula for psychological equity (see Walster et al., 1978). In terms of equity, the goods to be distributed are the outcomes, the 'worth' or contributions of the parties involved are the inputs, and, accordingly, the outcomes should be distributed in equal proportion to the inputs. Aristotle suggests that this rule not only applies to the distribution of common funds amongst citizens, but also the distribution of profits amongst business partners (p. 1132b). However, by arguing that the input should ideally be 'political excellence' Aristotle adds an important dimension. The 'inputs' are assumed to be something for which we can be held responsible. They are 'in our power'.

Rectificatory justice

Having described the distribution of goods that a just man would endeavour to maintain, Aristotle then describes what seems to be another form of particular justice, variously termed, in translation, 'rectificatory', 'remedial' or 'corrective' justice. Rectificatory justice concerns what Aristotle calls 'voluntary transactions', such as selling, purchasing and lending, in which both parties initially consent, and involuntary transactions involving injury such as adultery, theft, assault, murder, robbery with violence, mutilation, abuse and insult (in which the injured party does not consent). Aristotle says this form of justice operates according to the rule of *arithmetical proportion*, not geometrical proportion (p. 1132a); he asserts that in the case of rectificatory justice, 'it makes no difference whether a good man has defrauded a bad man, or a bad man a good one .... the law looks only to the distinctive character of the injury, and treats the parties as equal, if one is in the wrong and the other is being wronged, and one has inflicted injury and the other has received it' (p. 1132a). The basic idea is as follows: say A represents the amount that man A possesses, and B the amount that man B possesses; if then through, for example, theft or fraud, A gains an amount C from B, then A will have gained more than his share (A + C), and B will be left with less than his share (B - C). In such a case, therefore, the judge should take a value equivalent to C from A (A + C - C) and restore the same amount to B (B - C + C).

The principle of arithmetical proportion, says Aristotle, operates in voluntary transactions, such as buying and selling, such that no participant should either gain or lose from a transaction. However, Aristotle notes that in the case of involuntary transactions, such as assault and insult, it must be assumed that the assailant has 'gained' and the victim has 'lost', so the judge must penalize the assailant and give redress to the victim. He admits that the idea of 'gain' may seem inappropriate in this latter case, but he feels this is the way the principle should operate nevertheless.

But is Aristotle's idea of rectificatory justice really a different principle of justice from that of distributive justice? It may make more sense to view it, as its name suggests, as a mechanism to rectify certain kinds of deviations from the main distributive principle of geometrical proportion. For example, suppose that perfect distributive justice exists such that Diana, who has 4 units of worth, receives 8 units of goods, and Hector, whose worth is 2 units, receives 4 units of goods (8:4 = 4:2). If Hector then unjustly gains two units of goods by depriving Diana of 2 units of her rightful goods; the ratios would no longer be equal (6:4 and 6:2). To restore the equality of ratios as determined by geometric proportion, the judge would have to take the 2 units from Hector and give them back to Diana; the solution is thus exactly the same as if we treated Diana's and Hector's shares as initially equal. In other words, the rules of arithmetical and geometrical proportion do not necessarily apply to radically different kinds of justice; rather the former may operate, exactly as the labels imply, as a mechanism to maintain, 'correct' or 'rectify' an imbalance in the the overriding proportionate distribution.

Another obvious characteristic of rectificatory justice is that it requires that punishment should be proportionate to the crime. This happens because, in Aristotle's analysis, the 'gain' to the perpetrator is, by definition, determined by the harm inflicted. For example, according to arithmetical proportion, if Hector receives 2 units of wrongful 'gains' by hurting Diana, then Hector must incur 2 units of penalties; and if Hector receives 4 units of wrongful 'gains' by hurting Diana, then Hector must incur 4 units of penalties, and so on.

The legacy of Aristotle on this point lives on in modern conceptions of punishment, such as those of Sadurski (1985) and Hogan and Emler (1981), who argue that the aim of punishment is to restore an appropriate balance of benefits and burdens. However, whilst the principle of arithmetical proportion may make some sense for 'voluntary' transactions that involve buying and selling, the idea that criminals are punished because they have 'gained', and that crime severity and therefore punishment are determined by the relative 'gain' to the criminal, is somewhat problematic. We will return to this point shortly; all we need to note for the moment is Aristotle's commitment to the ideas that 1) punishment should fit the crime, 2) victims should be compensated, and 3) we must consider the issue of responsibility or 'voluntariness' when making such judgements.

Interestingly, Aristotle disagrees with what he calls the Pythagorean view of strict reciprocity (*lex talionis*, or 'an eye for an eye'). He admits people want justice to mean 'Should a man suffer what he did, right justice would be done' (p. 1132b) but he says this does not accord with what happens in practice; for instance, if someone wounds an official, he should not only receive a wound in return, but be punished in addition. Moreover he says that strict reciprocity ignores whether the act is voluntary or involuntary. Nevertheless, Aristotle argues that there is a sphere of justice in which strict reciprocity does and should obtain; and that is in the promotion and requital of services within a community.

Exchange and reciprocal proportion

Aristotle says that it is by the promotion and requital of services that the city holds together: 'Men seek to return either evil for evil - and if they cannot do so, think their position mere slavery - or do good for good - and if they cannot do so there is no exchange' (p. 1132b-1133a). But, says Aristotle for reciprocity in services to operate, we need some measure of the 'worth' of someone's services to the community. He says that the measure must be the 'demand' or 'need' (*chreia*) for those services; for if there were no demand or need there would be no exchange. Moreover, so we can make sure we can obtain something when we want it, all items for exchange must be measurable by money, that we can exchange for them. Accordingly, every item to be exchanged must have a price, fixed by agreement, that indicates its exact exchange value.

Aristotle's attempt to show how 'reciprocal proportion' operates in economic exchange has left a number of commentators puzzled (Finley, 1977). Aristotle says that justice in exchange involves 'reciprocity in accordance with a proportion and not on the basis of equality' (NE5, p. 1133a), and he describes this as follows: 'proportionate return is secured by cross-conjunction. Let A be a builder, B a shoemaker, C a house, D a shoe. The builder, then must get from the shoemaker the latter's work, and must himself give him in return his own. If then there is first proportionate equality of goods, and then reciprocal action takes place, the result we mention will be effected .... The number of shoes exchanged for a house must ..... correspond to the ratio of builder to shoemaker' (NE5, p. 1133ab).

One possible interpretation of this is in terms of a 'labour-cost theory of value' (Finley, 1977). That is, we first determine the relative worth or merits of say, the shoemaker and housebuilder, in terms of the labour time, level of skill etc. required to make their products. So if the labour time, and skills of the builder in making a house are judged to be one hundred times more costly than those incurred by the shoemaker in making a pair of shoes, then the price of the products in terms of money must reflect this ratio; the price of a house must be one hundred times greater than that of a pair of shoes. When this is established, 'proportionate equality' exists. Following this, if then a builder builds the shoemaker, or anyone else, a house, the latter must reciprocate with something worth the same (such as, the equivalent of one hundred pairs of shoes); in this way 'proportionate equality' will hold both before and after the transaction.

However, Aristotle seems to imply that the factor that naturally determines the monetary value of products, is not the amount of labour time, or degree of skill involved on producing them, but the demand or need for them (*chrea*). But if this is the case, then for the ratio of the relative 'worth' of the parties involved to be the same as that of the value of the items they produce, the 'worth' of the producers must be related in some way to the demand for their products also. For example, normally one pair of shoes might have an exchange value of 50 loaves of bread, in which case a shoemaker may be considered of greater 'worth' than a baker; but at times when other foodstuffs are very scarce, the demand or 'need' for bread may increase such that a single loaf of bread may be assigned a higher 'value' than a pair of shoes, and accordingly a baker must be assigned higher 'worth' than a shoemaker, regardless of the fact that both do the same amount of work as before. The issue of the most appropriate way to 'value' a person's 'worth' or contribution to others was to be a continuing source of debate in later centuries (indeed, it continues today). However, from the perspective of the present discussion, regardless of which interpretation we apply, it is significant that Aristotle's concept of 'reciprocal proportion' as the basis of exchange value looks simply like a restatement of the basic principle of geometric proportion; that is, both before and after exchanges, goods should be distributed between individuals in accordance with the 'worth' of their contributions, however, determined; and indeed, as Ross (1937) has noted, in Greek mathematics, 'reciprocal proportion' is simply a rearrangement of the terms of a 'geometrical proportion' (if $A:B = C:D$, then A and B are in geometrical proportion to C and D, and A and D are in reciprocal proportion to B and C).

If this is so, then Aristotle's notion of justice in exchange accords perfectly, once again, with Adam's formula for psychological equity; all we need to do is substitute 'inputs' for the values or 'worth' of the parties, 'outcomes' for the goods they exchange and equity will exist both before and after exchange, so long as the outcomes returned are equally proportional to the inputs. For example, in Aristotle's words, with my elaborations in brackets, 'let A be a builder (inputs or 'worth' of A), B a shoemaker (inputs or 'worth' of B), C a house, D a shoe ..... The number of shoes (outcomes to A) exchanged for a house (outcomes to B) must ..... correspond to the ratio of builder (inputs A) to shoemaker (inputs B)'. So, the greater the relative 'worth' of the builder, the more a house is worth in terms of shoes.

Justice, responsibility and equity

Aristotle continues his treatment of justice with a description of justice in the political state and in the home, which revolves mainly round a discussion of role-obligations. However, more importantly, this is followed by discussion of the role of responsibility in acting justly and unjustly. In this he reemphasizes the importance of voluntariness in determining just and unjust acts. Thus he says, 'Whether an act is or is not one of injustice (or of justice) is determined by its voluntariness or involuntariness' (NE5, p. 1135b). He briefly reiterates his views on responsibility as it applies to justice. When acting under compulsion (as when someone takes your hand to strike someone else), the act does not originate from inside you; it is involuntary, and therefore not unjust. Also, if you act without intention to do harm, and inflict an injury that could not reasonably be expected, this is an accident or misadventure; the act is not unjust because the origin of the ignorance is outside you. On the other hand, if you act without intention to harm, or impulsively without deliberation (as in anger), and inflict an injury that might reasonably have been expected, the origin of the ignorance lies inside you, and so the act is unjust, but it does not imply that you have a vicious, or unjust character; it is a *mistake*. But if you act with knowledge of the consequences, and with deliberation, the act is truly one of injustice, because it implies also that you are an unjust person. Thus, says Aristotle, the most unjust acts are those that violate 'proportion or equality' through deliberate choice (p. 1793).

Finally, Aristotle discusses the idea of 'equity' as a kind of justice superior to law. Aristotle's view is that good laws are framed to promote justice, and thus we often equate justice with the lawful; but sometimes laws may be too general, and insensitive to the details of individuals cases. Equity thus exists as a correction of law when law does not allow a just decision in a particular case; and a truly equitable man, is one who, to conform more precisely to the ideal of proportional equality, takes less than his share as allowed by law. Thus ultimately the perfectly just and the equitable are the same.

The three elements of desert
Of course, Aristotle's account of justice shows many inconsistencies and leaves many issues left unexplored. For instance, if excellence brings *eudaimonia*, then 'virtue brings its own reward', so why should we also assign 'goods' according to virtue; is this not rewarding the virtuous twice? The inegalitarian nature of Aristotle's virtue centred scheme has also provoked considerable criticism. At least in Plato's scheme everyone had a chance to choose his or her role status, even if in a previous life; whilst Aristotle's claim that 'it is in our power to be virtuous or vicious' (NE3, p. 1113b), seems to require considerable qualification. According to Wood and Wood (1978), Aristotle's prejudices are such that the excellences or virtues he proposes are those associated with aristocracy, which leaves the rest of society incapable of virtue, not worthy of reward, and unable to achieve *eudaimonia*. Certainly slaves and women do not have an equal opportunity to compete for these rewards; according to Aristotle, they are naturally inferior to the freemen and need to be ruled for their own good (see P1, p. 1254b).

This is symptomatic of a general problem with Aristotle's attempt to link justice with attributions of responsibility. Most of his discussion of responsibility centres round criminal liability, or attributions of blame; there is little consideration of the circumstances under which we might vary attributions of praise, and the implications for the award of goods. For instance, when we distribute goods should we ignore, or give fewer rewards to someone who has benefitted another out of accident, ignorance, or impulse? As Aristotle links praise to voluntariness one assumes his answer should be 'yes', but he does not provide a detailed discussion of this point. The idea that justice involves a consideration of personal choice or responsibility also fits uneasily with the notion of 'reciprocity of services'; Aristotle ignores the extent to which the choice of being say, a 'shoemaker' or 'builder' is 'within our power', or whether it requires more 'education of the passions' to be one of these rather than another. Elsewhere he also makes a case for awarding offices of state according to those of 'family and fortune' for they are best able to perform the task (see P. 1282b); but these are hardly attributes we can 'choose'.

However, for the moment, these problems should not detract us from the general conception of justice that Aristotle wished to establish. He summarizes this as follows, 'Justice is that virtue of which the just man is said to be a *doer, by choice*, of that which is just, and one who will distribute either between himself and another, or between two others, not so as to give more of what is desirable to himself or less to his neighbour (and conversely of what is harmful) but so as to give what is *equal in accordance with proportion*' (NE5, 1134a; my emphases). If we look at Aristotle's writings on justice as a whole then, we can readily identify the three basic elements of Plato's scheme of desert.

1) Those who contribute positively to the good of the community should be rewarded and those harm the good of community should be penalized.

2) Rewards and punishments must be meted out in proportion to the positive or negative contributions.

3) In principle at least, we must be able to exercise choice as to whether or not we perform the actions that are worthy of reward and punishment.

Moreover, it appears that to both Plato and Aristotle these principles, that describe the operation of the fundamental principle of proportional equality, are the standard by which laws and social behaviours are judged. To operate this principle, follow *dike*, and show excellence in our dealings with others, we must know how to behave at the right time, in the right way, in the right degree, towards the right person. Hence we can perhaps hypothesize a hierarchical ordering of justice factors that can be summarized as follows.

At the top of the hierarchy is perfect justice in accordance with geometrical proportion, that assigns rewards to individuals in exact proportion to their contributions to the good of others. Deviations from this scheme are also 'corrected' proportionately by assigning penalties to individuals in exact proportion to the extent that they have harmed innocent others (that is, harmed those who have done nothing wrong). This is also, pure, perfect fairness and equity. The person who continually maintains this system perfectly, in every situation, is truly just according to the natural law, and is thereby 'lawful', showing complete excellence in dealings with others. Thus Aristotle says, 'justice is often thought to be the greatest of excellences and neither evening nor morning star is so wonderful; and proverbially, in justice is every excellence comprehended' (NE5, 1129b). Also, if a person displays excellence in relation to others, the reward will be happiness distributed in proportion to the degree of excellence; vice on the other hand, we are told, leads to unhappiness, that will therefore be distributed also in proportion to the degree of vice shown. Again, therefore, perfect justice will always ensue.

In the subordinate category are other concepts that we relate to justice, but do not always result in perfect justice. For instance, in as much as our customs and conventions, including civil laws, are designed to promote perfect justice, we will show a greater tendency to be just if we obey them, and by obeying them, we will tend to promote the common good and 'preserve happiness and its components for the political society' (NE5, 1129b); hence obedience to law and convention are associated with justice. However, ultimately, laws and conventions themselves can be judged as relatively just or unjust by the ultimate standard to which they were subordinate; that is, proportional equality as dictated by natural law.

It is important to note, however, that the three elements that comprise this 'proportional desert' scheme do not simply represent the idiosyncratic ruminations of Plato and Aristotle, and are certainly not a recent invention by the apologists for capitalism. Although both Plato and Aristotle managed to manipulate them to suit their particular political and religious views, these elements seem to have been around in various guises since the dawn of Western civilization.

CHAPTER 13

DEFINING PERFECT EQUITY

Hopefully things may already be starting to make sense. In the ancient world the terms closest in meaning to our word 'justice' were associated with a sort of elaborate balancing act in which positive contributions or services to others (including God, or the gods) were rewarded, and negative or harmful contributions were punished, in proportion, as part of a grand state of cosmic equilibrium. As such, there was no conflict between justice and natural law, for this was natural law, and no conflict between justice and man made law, so long as man made law complied with this proportional or geometrical equality principle. Moreover, this idea formed the basis of what we now term the 'desert' approach to justice, in that it related to the treatment of individuals in terms of their services and disservices towards the good of the communities in which they lived.

Geometrical proportion, arithmetic proportion, and equity
This historical account suggests that the 'reward in proportion for good', 'punishment in proportion for bad', may be an algorithm deep rooted in our psychology; but, if it really is this basic, it is disappointing that we still do not seem to have a simple way of expressing this algorithm in mathematical terms. Despite the commitment by both Plato and Aristotle to the idea of geometrical

proportion (and reciprocal proportion which is its mathematical equivalent) as a fundamental principle of justice, when it comes to punishing criminals, Aristotle decides to adopt a different formula, that of 'arithmetical proportion'. A particular difficulty for the rule of arithmetical proportion, however, is that it works solely on the principle of maintaining equality in the distribution of benefits and burdens. The assumption is that the criminal 'gains' by committing a crime, and the victim loses; moreover the more serious the crime, the greater the 'gain' to the criminal. In modern society, however, we would normally consider attempted murder a more serious crime than petty theft, but in what sense can we claim, for example, that a man who has spent 10 years of his life, and lost £20,000 pounds in earnings, preparing for an unsuccessful murder attempt, has 'gained' more than a man who has stolen £100 from a someone's pocket and is enjoying a night out on the town with his gains?

Nevertheless, Aristotle is not alone in rejecting the equal ratio equity or 'geometrical proportion' formula in favour of 'arithmetical proportion' when discussing punishment. Sadurski (1985) does the same in his equilibrium theory of desert. Thus Sadurski initially bases his theory on an Adams' type principle of psychological equity but, then, abandons it in favour of a simple arithmetical gain-loss account of corrective justice. As we saw earlier, Sadurski's answer to the problem as to what it is exactly that the offender 'gains', is to suggest that the gain is that of 'non-self-restraint' (1985, p. 229); according to this view, other gains such as financial gains, psychological satisfaction, sexual gratification, etc. are incidental. Sadurski suggests that the criminal law imposes a constraint on freedom, thus in not breaking the law, law-abiding citizens are showing 'self-restraint'. The problem, however, is that most people do not feel especially constrained by laws that prevent them from murdering the elderly, or torturing children; indeed they actually seem to find such acts repugnant (see Pietras, 1992).

Sadurski appreciates the difficulty, but argues that the idea that the criminal 'gains' or benefits 'is purely a conceptual calculus and not an empirical fact of human dispositions' (p. 228). However, having established that the offender's gains are a 'conceptual calculus', and have nothing to do with psychological dispositions, we have no measure of the construct. What determines the amount of 'non-self-restraint' involved in a particular crime? To say that a murder involves more abstract self-restraint than a petty theft, not because of the *actual* degree of self-restraint, but because murder is a more serious crime, is obviously question begging.

It is somewhat ironical, in fact, that a better case for the balancing of benefits of burdens in terms of 'arithmetical proportion' might be made for the rewarding of positive contributions to the good of others. Given that, to both Plato and Aristotle, showing excellence in the treatment of others requires a high degree of effort, practice and self-restraint, and that presumably the delivering of services including the production of commodities such as shoes and houses also requires effort and hard work, then positive services to the good of others could be deemed burdensome on the whole. Indeed, both Feinberg (1970) and Sadurski (1985) adopt the view that positive contributions are burdensome. However, once we assume that all positive contributions are 'burdensome', it is possible to apply the principle of arithmetical proportion in exactly the same way as for so-called 'corrective justice'. Thus, if say, a good samaritan by increasing the benefits of others by 12 units, incurs a burden equivalent to losing 12 units of benefits, then for equilibrium to be restored, the others must give 12 units of benefits back to the samaritan. In fact, in principle, Sadurski (1985) seems to accept this idea when he says that *'social equilibrium means that everyone's work, effort, action and sacrifice yields a benefit equivalent to the contribution: in other words that a person's "outcomes" are equal to his "inputs"* (p. 105). However, Sadurski also notes that, 'In a complex social exchange one can hardly talk of "equality" of inputs and outcomes because they are usually incommensurate' (p. 106). Here Sadurski is using the term 'incommensurate' in the sense of 'not having a common measure' or 'incapable of being measured by the same unit'. The problem is easily identified; how many pound notes (apples, cars, televisions, compliments) 'equal' two hours of work painting a house?

Because of this difficulty, Sadurski falls back on the notion of equity simply as equal proportionality; so, he says, 'equilibrium is achieved when the overall level is equal for all people, that is, when the ratio of one person's outcomes to inputs is equal to other persons' outcome/input ratio' (p. 106). One suspects perhaps that Aristotle also found himself grappling with this problem when trying to make sense of geometrical and reciprocal proportion; thus in relation to the former he says, 'This proportion is not continuous; for we cannot get a single term standing for a person and a thing' (NE5, p. 1131b). However, it is not at all apparent that the task is any easier for the distribution of punishments for offences; for instance, how many years of punishment 'equal' one burglary, and how many units of injury to the victim equal the abstract 'gain' to the burglar when conducting the crime?

The fact is, there are major problems in attempting to define desert solely in terms of a balance of benefits and burdens that go beyond those involved in equating inputs and outcomes. Unlike geometrical proportion and psychological equity, arithmetic proportion makes no distinction between the directional quality of actions or contributions (that is, whether inputs are positive or negative). Without this distinction, the various 'cost-benefit' calculi seem so contrived as to lose any explanatory or predictive power. For example, Sadurski argues that, whereas criminals 'gain', almost by definition, regardless of the effort they may have put into attempting their crimes, any effort that produces social benefits always counts as a burden. But but this only makes any sense once we recognize that decisions about which benefits and burdens count are being dictated by assumptions about fundamental qualitative differences between inputs or contributions. Within Sadurski's model, whether 'effort' is counted as burdensome depends crucially on whether the input is directed towards the good of others or their harm. As already noted, we do not usually consider compensating criminals for the 'effort' involved in committing offences, or the years of lost earnings they have incurred whilst leading a life of crime. Indeed, one could argue that the more individuals are prepared to deliberately incur personal and financial costs to achieve their objectives, the more deliberate and blameworthy their offences.

A related problem with the arithmetic proportion principle is that it takes no account of the idea that some efforts or 'costs' may make a greater contribution to the good than others. For instance, Sadurski proposes that the appropriate 'input' in a desert model is 'conscientious effort which has socially beneficial effects' (p. 116). However, as I have also already mentioned, this input actually scrambles together two rather different components; one concerns the effort put in, the other the extent to which effort is actually beneficial to society (see also, Slote, 1973). For instance, we do not usually reward people, or compensate them in full, for years of foolishly directed effort that is of minimal benefit to anybody. Also, whereas we might argue that 'taking responsibility' for others provides a socially beneficial service, and is a burden requiring compensation, the law normally makes no attempt to compensate criminal gang leaders for the 'burden of responsibility' involved in organizing the activities of their gang members.

Similarly, according to Feinberg (1970), within a theory of desert, the suffering of people in need who have brought it on themselves is not compensatable because they can be 'blamed' for their plight; so, if we accept this, such suffering presumably does not count as a burden in the overall balance of benefits and burdens. But this only makes sense if we construe the suffering of such individuals as something that resulted from 'what they decided to do with their outcomes' (such as gamble or drink them away), or a punishment for a chosen wrongdoing (in terms of psychological equity, a negative return for a negative input). It would be catastrophic for a desert theorist to adopt the general principle that the sufferings or burdens that people have 'brought upon themselves' do not require compensation, for then it is only a short step to the conclusion that those who choose to input 'conscientious effort which produces social benefits' have also 'brought their burdens on themselves' and therefore deserve nothing in return!

So how should we proceed? To progress further, it may be useful to look again briefly at one of the most important defining characteristics of the notion of desert.

Good for good and penalties for bad

According to John Stuart Mill, at the heart of the concept of desert is the principle of 'returning good for good and repressing evil by evil' (1861/1993, p. 64); we punish people for the harm or burdens they impose, or attempt to impose, on others, and reward them for the good or benefits they give to others. Moreover, we do this proportionally. Obviously this idea does imply some mathematical weighting of the benefits and burdens that people receive, especially with regard to their outcomes, but the reduction of desert to a simple balancing of costs and benefits seems to involve so many assumptions, and such a high level of abstraction, that its psychological meaning is largely lost.

It might, therefore, be more helpful if we could come up with a single 'proportional equality' formula that would reflect this 'reward for good', and 'punishment for bad' philosophy, and thus distinguish between contributions and outcomes in a more psychologically meaningful manner. In other words, we are back to the familiar problem of finding a formula for psychological equity that will accommodate both positive and negative inputs and outcomes. More specifically, we need a formula in which a 'negative input' would be viewed as a negative or harmful contribution to the good of others (as distinct from a positive service), and a negative outcome would be viewed as something that all participants would seek to avoid. Indeed, one wonders whether Aristotle was really committed to the idea that remedial justice should follow the rule of arithmetical proportion rather than geometrical or reciprocal proportion, or whether he, like the many modern equity theorists, simply could not think of a way of combining positive and negative contributions into a single formula.

Defining perfect equity

Some years ago my colleague, Tim Perfect, and I decided on a simple algebraic formula that we hoped would do the job of encompassing both negative and positive contributions into a single algebraic formula. The formula is, in fact, a special case of a more general linear equity formula devised by Richard J. Harris (1976, 1980; 1983). Drawing on ideas from the philosophical literature on desert we also put forward a supporting rationale for the idea of *perfect equity* (Wagstaff, 1994; Wagstaff and Perfect, 1992; Wagstaff, Huggins and Perfect, 1996). If this analysis is valid, then, hopefully, the principle of 'perfect equity' should capture an important feature of what most philosophers, either explicitly or implicitly, have traditionally meant by the idea of justice as 'desert'. Although this little equity formula is very simple to operate, for those who would rather gloss over the algebra in the following sections, all one really needs to remember is that, essentially, our formula is nothing more than a mathematical description of Adams' (1965) equity rule, and Aristotle's principle of geometrical proportion, but with three fundamental constraints. Thus the four main assumptions for 'perfect equity' are as follows.

1) *Outcomes should be distributed in equal proportion to inputs, such that the more one inputs or contributes, the more one should receive.* For example, if John contributes twice as much as Harry, John should receive twice as much as Harry.

2) *Positive inputs must always be returned with positive outcomes, and negative inputs with negative outcomes.* So, from a starting point in which equity exists, it is always unjust to reward someone for a harmful act or disservice to others, or punish them for a positive contribution to the good of others.

3) *Zero inputs must always be returned with zero outcomes. If one does nothing positive or negative, one should receive nothing positive or negative. It also follows that when all inputs are zero the most equitable, or least inequitable distribution is one that distributes outcomes equally amongst the participants.* It is unjust to reward or punish people who have done nothing at all to deserve such

treatment; however, in cases in which there are rewards or punishments to be distributed amongst people who have done nothing good or bad to others to deserve them, the least unjust distribution is an equal distribution.

4) *When perfect equity exists, the outcomes that individuals receive should be commensurate with their inputs. When the outcomes exceed those commensurate with the inputs the least inequitable solution is one that distributes the commensurate outcomes between participants in equal proportion to their inputs, and the incommensurate excess equally between them.* For example, suppose that a group of workers consensually agree that £10 is an appropriate or 'commensurate' reward for one hour of work; if this is so then, other factors being equal, equity will normally demand that a person who works for one hour should receive £10, and a person who works for two hours should receive £20. However, if instead there is an excessive incommensurate amount, say a £20 million windfall to distribute, we cannot distribute it with perfect equity (because most of it is 'undeserved'); so, to distribute between the two persons, the least inequitable solution is to first give each person the commensurate outcomes that each has 'earned', £10 to one, and £20 to the other, and then divide the rest of the 'unearned' £20 million equally between them.

These are the basic ideas then, so now let us look at the details.

The perfect equity formula

According Wagstaff and Perfect's (1992) formulation, 'perfect equity' exists when, for all persons in a relationship, the outcomes each receives are equal to a constant value that is greater than zero, multiplied by the value of his or her inputs or contributions. Thus, expressed algebraically,

$O_i = aI_i$

where, O represents the value of outcomes, I represents the value of the inputs, and a is a constant number greater than zero (that is, $a > 0$) for all participants, who are denoted by the term i in a relationship.

For example, suppose person Ned inputs 10 hours of positive work, and Rod, 5 hours, then according to the formula, if there are £30 worth of rewards or benefits (outcomes) to distribute, Ned should receive £20 for 10 hours work, and Rod, £10 for 5 hours work ($a = 2$). The formula, of course, works for any number of individuals or groups; suppose, for example Rod inputs 0, Ned inputs 4, Joyce inputs 5, and Jo inputs 12 positive units; if there are 21 outcome units to be distributed, then Rod, Ned, Joyce, and Jo should receive 0, 4, 5, and 12 units respectively ($a = 1$). Importantly, however, unlike Adams' formula, we can also use the formula for negative inputs and outcomes. So for example, if Capone inputs -10 units (say 10 units of criminal activity), and Kelly inputs -5 units of criminal activity, then, if there are -30 outcome (punishment or penalty) units to distribute, Capone should receive -20 outcome units, and Kelly, -10 outcome units (that is, 20 and 10 penalty or punishment units respectively). Thus equity will exist when the punishments offenders receive (negative outcomes) are equally proportional to the gravity of their offences (negative inputs). Readers familiar with algebra will instantly recognize the perfect equity formula as the formula for a *straight line* with an intercept of zero; thus equity can be represented in graph form by an upward sloping straight line, from left to right, through the origin, with the x axis representing 'inputs' and the y axis 'outcomes'.

Estimating inequity and the least inequitable solution

A major problem for equity formulae, however, is deciding how to distribute positive outcomes amongst participants when all of them have contributed negative inputs. Suppose for example we have to distribute £100 between two individuals who have committed offences of varying severity, say Capone's inputs are -40 and, Kelly's are -60. According to Adams' formula it would be equitable to assign £40 to Capone and £60 to Kelly (40/-40 = 60/-60), which clearly makes no sense (the more serious offender is receiving the greater number of positive outcomes or benefits). The same problem arises if we have to distribute negative outcomes units (penalties) to individuals who have made positive contributions to the good of others; using Adams' formula we always end up giving greater penalties to the person who has contributed most good.

However, according to the perfect equity formula no such distribution could be perfectly equitable, because for perfect equity to operate *those whose inputs are positive must receive positive outcomes in return, and those whose inputs are negative must receive negative outcomes in return*. In the first case, the problem could be presented, for instance, as one of trying to decide a perfectly 'just' way to divide up money stolen from pensioners between two criminals, one who stole a handbag on one occasion, and the other who stole a number of handbags on different occasions. There is no perfectly 'just' solution to this problem, only one that minimizes injustice or inequity.

In psychological terms, this means that we cannot, with perfect equity, ever return a punishment or penalty for a good or positive act, or return a reward or benefit for a negative or bad act. This is hardly a novel idea; indeed, according to John Stuart Mill it is the essence of 'desert'; Mill says, 'Speaking in a general way, a person is understood to deserve good if he does right, evil if he does wrong; and in a more particular sense, to deserve good from those to whom he does or has done good, and evil from those to whom he does or has done evil. *The precept of returning good for evil has never been regarded as a case of the fulfilment of justice*, but as one in which the claims of justice are waived, in obedience to other considerations' (1861/1993, p. 46, my emphasis).

Nevertheless, although according to perfect equity it can never be totally equitable to return positive for negative or negative for positive, some distributions will presumably be seen to be 'less inequitable' than others. But how does one estimate the degree of inequity? To do this we need to be able to generate a hypothetical 'perfect equity' distribution, and assess the deviations from this distribution. Take our earlier example; Ned inputs 10 hours of work, and Rod, 5 hours; if there are £30 of 'commensurate' outcomes to distribute, equity demands that Ned should receive £20, and Rod, £10. Suppose then, however, we decide to award the outcomes equally such that Ned receives £15 and Rod receives £15. The result will deviate from the distribution (or straight line) specified by the original ideal perfect equity distribution. Ned will be receiving £5 less than equity demands (15 - 20), and Rod will be gaining £5 units more than equity demands (15 - 10). Now suppose that we decide to award the outcomes such that Ned is fined £15 (-15 input units) and Rod receives £45 (we make Ned give some of his previous earnings to Rod, and also award all the £30 in pay to Rod). The result will deviate even more from the distribution (or straight line) specified by the original ideal perfect equity distribution. Ned will be receiving £35 less than equity demands (-15 - 20), and Rod will gain £35 more than equity demands (45 - 10). To deal with such examples, Wagstaff and Perfect have come up with a deviation formula so that we can express accurately the deviations of various distributions from perfect equity; this is:

$$\bar{e} = \sqrt{(d^2)/n}$$

where $\bar{e}$ is the degree of inequity; d is the difference between a particular outcome and the outcome predicted by perfect equity, and n is the number of cases involved.

One of the implications of Wagstaff and Perfect's deviation formula is that, when it is not possible to award a set of outcomes in a way that accords with perfect equity, *the least inequitable outcome will always be one where the deviations of the outcomes from perfect equity are equal*. For instance, in the negative input scenario just mentioned, let us assume that Capone should be fined £80 outcomes for his -40 inputs, and Kelly, £120 for his -60 inputs. If we accept this, then the least inequitable way of distributing the £100 between them would be to award Capone £70 and Kelly, £30. In this way, each would deviate from perfect equity by the same amount; that is, each would end up with the equivalent of £150 more than he deserves.

Another problem arises when we have to distribute positive and negative outcomes when all inputs are zero. According to the perfect equity formula, if relative to others you do nothing positive or negative, you deserve nothing positive or negative; *zero inputs must always be returned with zero outcomes.* The question might be phrased, for example, as what is a perfectly 'just' way to distribute £100 in wages for a job of overtime between two workers, neither of whom bothered to turn up for work because they went to a football match? However, again, as the *least inequitable outcome* will always be one where the deviations of the outcomes from perfect equity, are equal; which means in this case that the £100 should be shared equally between the two workers who did nothing.

The problem of input and outcome commensurateness

According to the ideal of perfect equity, outcomes must be distributed in equal proportion to inputs. However, for perfect equity to obtain, *the sum of the outcomes to be distributed must be commensurate with the inputs of those to whom the outcomes will be given.* By 'commensurateness' here, I am using the term in the sense of 'due proportion'. In principle the idea of commensurateness is easy to understand; some degree of commensurateness between inputs and outcomes is implicit in the constraints that we must never return positive outcomes for negative inputs, negative outcomes for positive inputs, or anything other than zero outcomes for zero inputs. However, for the concept of perfect equity to make sense psychologically, we need to be able to go beyond this.

Although equal ratio equity demands that outcomes should be distributed in equal proportion to inputs, it seems to make little psychological sense to argue that equal proportionality should hold regardless of the amount or type of outcomes to be distributed (see Wagstaff and Perfect, 1992; Wagstaff, Chadwick and Brunas-Wagstaff, 1996). Consider again one of the scenarios posed earlier.

Suppose that, that in return for their inputs, two workers receive what they consider to be a fair return for their work, such that Ned receives £40 for 2 hours work, and Rod receives £80 for 4 hours work ($O_i = aI_i$ where $a = 20$). Suppose further, however, that the boss of these two workers wins £20 million on the national lottery and decides to give £6 million to the workers. There is now a sum of £6 million pounds to distribute between two workers, one who has completed 2 hours work, and the other 4 hours work. If we distribute the £6 million pounds in proportion to work then worker Ned should receive £2 million for 2 hours work, and Rod £4 million for 4 hours work. However, to the workers who consider that £120 is the appropriate award for 6 hours work, it is *impossible* to distribute the £6 million between them with perfect justice; they have only 'earned', or only 'deserve' £120 between them; anything more would be an 'undeserved' excess. As such, all that one can do is to adopt *the least inequitable distribution*; which, in this case is first to give the workers the pay that is commensurate with their work (thus Ned should receive £40 and Rod, £80), and to distribute the remaining 'unearned' amount of £5,999,880 equally between them (£2,999,940 each).

The same principle applies for accidental calamities. Suppose then an accidental calamity befalls these workers leaving them £200 in debt before they can be paid. According to perfect equity, it would be impossible to distribute £200 in accidental debts between these two workers with perfect equity; the best that can be done is to distribute the debts according to the *least inequitable distribution*. So again we should first (hypothetically) give the workers the pay that is commensurate with their work (thus Ned should receive £40 and Rod, £80); then distribute what now (hypothetically) becomes £320 in debts equally between them (£160 each). As a result Ned, who put in two hours of work pays £120 (£40 - £160), and Rod, who put in 4 hours of work pays £80 (£80 - £160). The logic here is that as Ned worked fewer hours than Rod, Ned should pay more of the debt to adjust for this; if we simply split the £200 in debts equally between the workers (£150 each), Rod would lose more relative to Ned.

One important implication of the 'commensurability effect' is that *relative to the number 'commensurate' outcomes, the greater the number of excess 'incommensurable' or 'undeserved' outcomes there are to distribute, the more equal the least inequitable distribution will look*. For example, in the above case, if we distribute the £6 million of 'undeserved' outcomes between the two workers, Ned ends up with £2,999,980 and Rod with £3,000,020. However, if we distribute only £6 of excess outcomes between them, Ned ends up with £43 and Rod, £83. In the first case Rod receives less than 1% more than Ned, whereas in the second Rod receives 48% more than Ned. This kind of analysis might also explain the finding by Komorita and Kravitz (1979), that the greater the size of a prize, the more equally subjects divided it.

All this fits theories of desert that argue that people can be said to deserve something, even when no one can be held liable. According to perfect equity, individuals should receive exactly what they deserve on the basis of their inputs, no more no less; it thus follows that, if all start from an equitable position, if a person accidently loses some outcomes, or, through accident, fails to receive a commensurate return for his or her inputs, he or she will end up with less than is deserved. The concept of perfect equity goes further than existing desert theories, however, in prescribing the least inequitable solution to this problem (all in the relationship must share the costs of the person who loses, with him or her). It also follows from this rationale that it is perfectly reasonable to include compensation for natural accidents under desert claims, as Kleinig (1971) does; and contrary to Feinberg's view, it is also reasonable to argue that natural disasters may act as 'deserved' punishments (for instance, it is perfectly sensible to say that 'the villain crushed in the land slide got what he deserved', so long as death by crushing is perceived to be a punishment commensurate with the particular villainy involved).

We have found other empirical support for some of these ideas in a series of studies conducted at Liverpool University. People did not simply distribute outcomes according to the equal ratio rule without consideration of the origin or nature of those outcomes. In particular, when they considered the outcomes to result from accidental causes, or considered them disproportionate to those normally associated with the inputs in question, the tendency was to prefer, and judge more fair, allocations that first divided the 'relevant' or 'deserved' outcomes up in equal proportion to inputs or contributions, and then split the remainder equally between the contributors. Having said this, however, we also found that, the impulse to use a simple equal proportion rule, regardless of the nature of the outcomes, was extremely strong; sometimes we really had to 'spell out' the nature of the problem before subjects could be relied upon to avoid using the simple equal proportionality rule (Wagstaff, Chadwick and Brunas-Wagstaff, 1996; Wagstaff, Huggins and Perfect, 1996).

Defining commensurability

Nevertheless, whilst there may be an intuitive logic to the idea of commensurateness between outcomes and inputs we still need some a theoretical construction for 'ideal commensurateness'. The most obvious one is that provided by Sadurski (1985); that is individuals should receive benefits equivalent to their contributions. However, this still does not resolve the problem of how one's contribution or 'input' is to be measured; is one's contribution determined by the social benefits one has produced, or by the costs or 'burdens' one has incurred in terms of the amount of effort, skill, responsibility etc. one has exercised in performing the service? In the final chapter I will suggest a possible way in which equity can be more meaningfully described in terms of a cost-benefit calculus. For the moment, however, in keeping with the notion of desert, I will simply propose that, within a model of equal ratio equity, commensurateness between inputs and outcomes exists when: *all receive outcomes equivalent to the social benefits and harms that they might reasonably expect their inputs or contributions to generate.*

It will be noted that, in keeping with the traditional Aristotelian idea of desert, according to this definition, outcomes are not awarded according to the extent to which people take responsibility, take risks, put in effort, make themselves look beautiful, incur material costs etc. etc., for their own sakes, but to the extent to which, *through* these activities, they could reasonably be expected to benefit or harm others.

For example, suppose that all in an equity relationship agree that, 10 hours of a particular type of gardening work can usually be expected to produce social benefits to the value of £100. If gardener A does 3 hours of this work, and gardener B, 7 hours of this work, A 'deserves' an outcome equivalent to £30, B deserves an outcome equivalent to £70. In contrast, if all in an equity relationship know, or can reasonably assume that, 10 hours of gardening usually produces £100 worth of benefits to others, but there are £2000 in 'windfall' outcomes to distribute; then if gardener A again does 3 hours of this work, and gardener B, 7 hours of this work, other things being equal, A only 'deserves' an outcome equivalent to £30, B only 'deserves' an outcome equivalent to £70; so 'the least inequitable solution', is to give each what he deserves (£30 to one, and £70 to the other), and to split the rest (£1900) equally between them. Similarly, if I know that one act of a particular type of vandalism normally produces £100 worth of harms (costs) to others, then if offender A does three such acts, and offender B, 7 such acts, other things being equal, A 'deserves' to be fined £300, or its equivalent in costs, and B deserves to be fined £700 or its equivalent in costs. And, if in the same situation there are £1200 in fines to be distributed, then 'the least inequitable solution', is to fine each what he or she deserves, and to split the rest of the fines equally between them (£100 each).

However, that, in practice, the distributive principles that govern the 'reward of good' and the 'punishment of bad' may sometimes operate in slightly different ways. In the case of 'rewards for good', the general rule is to divide the outcomes according to the value of each input; so if as part of a joint effort, two people produce a particular set of socially beneficial goods, the benefits they receive as a result of their activities should be shared according to the relative contribution that each has made to overall production. However, in joint ventures that result in 'punishment for bad' scenarios, especially in cases of serious crimes against the person, the courts often seem to act more on the principle of 'treat each person as though he or she had generated all of the social harm'. So, for example, if two people deliberately conspire to murder person 'X', and have contributed equally towards the act, they are punished as though each had committed a separate crime, not as though each had committed 'half' of a crime. In the final chapter I will suggest a possible explanation for this somewhat different distributive principle, but it does not detract from the basic rule that punishments should be distributed in a such a way that each offender receives harms or costs equivalent to the social harms and costs that one might reasonably have expected to have resulted from his or her actions. Indeed, in practice, the prevalence and force of this idea are well illustrated in anomalies such as the award to a single person of multiple life sentences', one for each of his or her crimes, 'to run concurrently'.

Of course, 'commensurability' is a subjective concept that will vary from person to person, situation to situation, and society to society; but this does not mean that communities are incapable of developing some kind of normative consensus as to the benefits and harms can reasonably be expected to be generated from a particular activity, and how they should respond to them. Indeed, such a consensus could be viewed as an intrinisic part of human social organization. As Roberts (1979) points out, 'order in society must depend first upon some understanding existing among members as to how the activities of everyday life shall be arranged, and as to what are the acceptable and unacceptable forms of conduct in a given context. In the absence of such shared assumptions, enabling A to predict how B should behave in familar circumstances and how A's own actions ought to be received, social life could barely exist' (p. 31).

Lerner's (1980) work also graphically illustrates how, for most people, one of the fundamental features of a 'Just World' is that it should possess enough stability to allow them to be able to make reasonable predictions about the relationship between what people do, and what will happen to them as a result of their actions. As Lerner says, the belief in a just world requires there to be an appropriate fit between what people do and what happens to them. Thus in British society, the law does not excuse firing guns at shop assistants on the grounds that 'no one can agree on the social costs of the injuries caused by gunshot wounds'. Neither do people consider it fair or just to award life imprisonment to young offenders who deface public property with graffiti (Wagstaff, Chadwick and Brunas-Wagstaff, 1996). Similarly, although pay for nurses and other medical personnel is continually a matter of debate, most people in Britain would presumably not consider justice done when one nurse who works a 40 hour week and another who works an 80 hour week, receive 4 pence and 8 pence, respectively, as a reward for the benefits they bestow on others.

But what of zero inputs and outcomes?

The problem of zero inputs and outcomes

Obviously, if all are to receive outcomes equivalent to the social benefits and harms that they might reasonably expect their inputs or contributions to generate, then if you do nothing beneficial or harmful to others, you should receive nothing beneficial or harmful. Within perfect equity, 'zero' is thus a neutral point within a family of positive and negative values; if you do nothing positive or negative, you should receive nothing positive or negative. But it would make little sense to argue that the zero must constitute doing nothing and receiving nothing in a material sense. If people who did no work received nothing in a material sense they would starve to death; something that might be construed as a very negative outcome that an equitist might want to reserve only for those who have committed heinous crimes. Consequently, to award true 'zero or neutral outcomes' it may be necessary to provide the recipient with certain minimum requirements. Also doing nothing in material sense may have extremely harmful consequences. In English law a person who neglects to look after those to whom he or she has a duty of care (such as a child or infirmed person) may be charged with criminal negligence (Cross, Jones and Card, 1988; Curzon, 1980). Consequently, 'zero or neutral inputs' can include the fulfilment of basic obligations and duties that we would require of anybody. The idea of neutral or zero inputs could thus be considered similar to Baier's idea of a position in which a person has 'neither positive nor negative moral merit' (1958, p. 205).

However, the idea of a zero outcomes entitlement may also have another important implication for how we view 'commensurateness' between inputs and outcomes. The benefits that are generated by our activities can be crucially determined by our zero outcome entitlement. For example, if water is deemed to be a community resource that is part of everyone's zero outcome entitlement, then the social benefits that a water supplier bestows on others may be construed simply as saving others the cost of providing the water for themselves. Thus, we do not reward people for the commodities they give to us if we are entitled to them anyway, we reward them only for saving us the costs involved in making them available to us.

Equity and reciprocity

If we adopt the idea that, in principle, equity demands that positive and negative outcomes should in some sense be commensurate with positive and negative inputs, then equity is obviously compatible with the concepts of *positive and negative reciprocity*. In other words, according to equity, when individuals make a contribution that benefits others they should expect others to make an equivalent contribution that will provide them, in return, with benefits equivalent to those they have given to them. In the case of negative inputs, when individuals make a contribution that harms others they presumably do not expect the contribution to be reciprocated, at least not in full. Nevertheless, if offenders fail in their bids to avoid reciprocation (they get caught), they should expect others to take action that will return to them harms equivalent to those they have inflicted on others. Perfect equity and perfect reciprocity will therefore always coincide.

However, although equity demands that 'one good (or harmful) turn demands an equivalent other', this does not mean that when all exchanges are exactly reciprocal all will end up with equivalent outcomes. In a community in which people engage in vast numbers of reciprocal exchanges, almost inevitably, some will end up with more outcomes than others. For example, suppose two men, Andy and Barry, decide to pool their resources to do a favour for others in their community; but Andy contributes more to the welfare of the community than Barry. When others in the community return the favour, strict reciprocity demands that Andy and Barry should distribute the outcomes between them according to their relative contributions; thus Andy should receive more than Barry. Also, reciprocity demands that those who do favours for others should receive more in return according to the size of the favours and their frequency. Big favours deserve big favours in return, and the more you do of them, the more you should receive in return. In this way the basic structure of equal ratio equity will emerge such that, the greater one's inputs, the greater one's outcomes, in equal proportion. (For a discussion of the historical links between desert and reciprocity, see MacIntyre, 1982, 1988.)

To summarize, the principle of perfect equity makes psychological sense if construed as part of a cooperative arrangement in which people work for their common good; that is, it is a principle of desert in which each receives rewards commensurate with his or her contributions or services towards the good of others, and is punished with penalties commensurate with the harms inflicted on others who have done nothing to deserve such treatment. As such, it is a sort of implicit or covert pact or understanding that seems to have the following components.

Individuals should only accept benefits and costs equivalent to those they might reasonably expect their contributions to bestow on others. Any benefits or costs that individuals receive that could not reasonably have been expected to result from their actions must be distributed equally between participants in the interaction.

One of the most important implications of this scheme, therefore, is that, in principle, a man who labours for hours and hours 'feathering his own nest', adding value to his outcomes, but with no intention whatsoever of ever using his gains to contribute to the welfare of others, is no more 'deserving' of the rewards of his labours than a perfectly able man who has the opportunity to work, but decides to sit on his bottom and do nothing. To the rest of society, these two individuals are no more 'worthy' than (indeed they are both as 'worthless' as) each other. Another implication is that, from a position in which equity exists, if someone suffers by accident, others are obliged to help or provide compensation to achieve a position of the least inequity

However, the idea of equity as a principle that encompasses both positive and negative outcomes and inputs has other important implications for how we view reciprocity, and these we will now consider.

CHAPTER 14

AN 'EYE FOR AN EYE': EQUITY, RECIPROCITY AND JUST PUNISHMENT

We know from sources such as the code of Hammurabi and the Old Testament of the Christian Bible, that *lex talionis*, the simple reciprocity of the 'eye for an eye' variety was very popular in the ancient world. Aristotle also acknowledges this; he says 'Some think that reciprocity is without qualification justice, as the Pythagoreans said; for they defined justice without qualification as reciprocity .... people *want* the justice of Rhadamanthus to mean this: should a man suffer what he did, right justice would be done' (NE5, p. 1132a)'. Also with regard to *lex talionis* John Stuart Mill (1861/1993) writes, 'Though this principle of Jewish and Mahomedan law has been generally abandoned in Europe as a practical maxim, there is, I suspect, in most minds a secret hankering after it' (p. 58). However, Aristotle considers it to be a mistake to equate justice with simple reciprocity; he states 'reciprocity fits neither distributive nor rectificatory justice' (NE5, p. 1132a).

Equity as 'sophisticated reciprocity'

Considered from the perspective of equity, one can perhaps see the problem. The simple principle of 'eye for an eye tooth for a tooth' does not necessarily restore perfect equity. Suppose there are three men A, B and C, who start off neutrally in a particular context; their outcomes and inputs are zero. If A, the aggressor, then deliberately blinds B in one eye, out of jealousy, then the aggressor has input a negative contribution (stabbed B in the eye) and the victim has received a negative outcome (he is blind, and distressed etc.). Other things being equal, to restore equity, the aggressor must receive a negative outcome equivalent to the negative outcome he has inflicted on the victim, and the victim must receive a positive outcome sufficient to compensate for his 'undeserved' negative outcome. If the victim blinds the aggressor in return, the result will indeed be a closer approximation to equity than before. The victim will be justified in harming the aggressor because the aggressor's harmful act was directed against someone whose inputs were neutral (the victim did not deserve to be harmed), and by returning harm to the aggressor, the aggressor will receive some negative outcomes for his negative inputs.

The problem will remain, however, that although the aggressor will have received some of his 'just deserts', it is the case that, relative to person C, who was not involved, *the undeserving victim still ends up without his eye*, and, other than the satisfaction of seeing the aggressor punished, the victim will have received no compensation for the loss of his eyesight and the distress caused. Moreover, in the interests of justice, the victim will have been put to the inconvenience, and possibly danger, of punishing the aggressor. In other words, relative to the neutral person C, the victim will still end up with 'less than he deserves'; a net outcome deficit. A more appropriate outcome, therefore, would be one in which the punishment for the aggressor also results in full compensation for the victim, not only for the loss of his eye, but for the fact that he has been obliged to punish the aggressor.

Put in everyday terms, if a man deliberately damages my car, assuming I initially did nothing to warrant his actions, there will be a closer approximation to equity if I, in retaliation, damage his car; he will have received some punishment or negative outcomes to partially balance his negative input. But not only have I had to suffer the distress of having my car damaged, waste valuable time and effort, and possibly risk danger, damaging his car, *I am still left without my car;* it would be far more equitable if the punishment given to the offender included, at the same time, compensation to me for the loss of my car and other costs I have incurred.

Given this, we can see why, especially in ancient hierarchically ordered societies, it might make more sense not to retaliate against a person on a 'wound for wound' basis'. It is notable, for instance, that in the famous Biblical passage from Exodus 21 which quotes extensively the *lex talionis* rule, it is evident that high ranking figures were not to be punished according to a literal 'eye for eye' policy. Hence we are told that 'if a man smite the eye of his servant, or the eye of his maid, that it perish, he shall let him go free for his eye's sake' (v.27). In many respects this idea makes more sense, and, superficially at least, could be considered more equitable, than literal 'eye for eye' reciprocity. According to this solution, the master inflicts an injury on the servant (who would usually have been a slave), but in return the master loses his servant, and the servant gains some compensation by being freed. Indeed, a number of the laws and ordinances stated in Exodus seem to follow this general principle of 'punish the offender and compensate the victim'. For instance, we are told, 'If a man shall steal an ox, or a sheep, and kill it, or sell it; he shall restore five oxen for an ox, and four sheep for a sheep' (Exodus, 22, v.1). In doing so the offender would not simply be 'returning a sheep that he does not deserve to someone who has lost a sheep that he does deserve'; the thief would be *punished in addition* for the distress and inconvenience caused; at the same time the victim would not only receive his 'lost' sheep back but compensation for the inconvenience and distress caused, and the costs involved in seeking reparation. Thus another popular rule in Exodus is for the thief to pay back double that he has stolen; and if the thief has nothing left to pay with 'then he shall be sold for his theft' (22, v.3). The idea that punishment involves more than a simple 'eye for an eye' return is also evident in the fact that, in modern English law, it is not considered 'just punishment' simply to take stolen goods from the thief and return them to their owner.

Importantly, Baron (1993) has found some empirical support for these ideas; thus, on the whole, people seem to want more compensation or restitution when a person has been deliberately harmed by another, than when the harm was due to an accident of nature. Moreover, they also want more compensation when the harmdoer is the one providing the compensation. These data fit a direct prediction from perfect equity; if the harmdoer provides the compensation, then the debt, or outcome deficit, can, in principle, be repaid 'in full' by the harmdoer. But, if no one is to blame, or the harmdoer is not the one providing the compensation, then the least inequitable solution is to distribute the 'undeserved' negative outcomes equally across those in the relationship, *including the victim*. As a result the victim should receive most when compensated by the harmdoer, but less when compensated by others who are not to blame, or when the harm was an accident of nature; because in the latter cases, the victim must bear an equal share of the burden along with those who are compensating him or her.

It is not the case, therefore, that the 'justice of Rhadamanthus' or *lex talionis* is actually contrary to perfect equity; rather it results in an incomplete approximation to equity, because it does not fully compensate the victim. Having said this, it does not follow that, given the choice, victims will prefer monetary compensation to punishment or retaliation. In Viking societies, for example, individuals often showed a mark preference for vengeance over 'blood money' (Dunbar, Clark and Hurst, 1995). The main point is, however, is that true equity requires *both* punishment for the offender *and* compensation for the victim, a point made forcefully by this account of the practice of Northumbrian law in the 14th Century (Coulton, 1908/1993, p. 283-284):

Seman the hermit was robbed, beaten, and left for dead by Gilbert of Niddesdale .... Gilbert unluckily fell next day into the hands of the King's serjent, and the hermit had still strength enough to behead his adversary in due form of law, the Northumberland custom being that a victim could redeem his stolen goods only by doing the executioner's dirty work.

In this example, the victim received both the goods stolen from him and the 'satisfaction' of punishing his assailant.

Equity, harm and punishment

Once we conceptualize 'just punishment' in this way, many of the problems that have confronted philosophers over the ages already look somewhat less daunting. For example, consider the time-honoured philosophical problem of when or even whether it is morally justifiable to 'harm' someone. This problem goes back a lot further than libertarianism and Pareto-optimality. In Plato's Republic, Socrates attempts to argue that it is never permissible to 'harm' someone; however, by doing this, he ends up in the position of claiming that punishment is not 'harmful' to the person who is punished (not a very convincing argument to an atheist on death row).

The word 'harm' in English is problematical in that it can be used as a synonym for 'moral wrong'; however, if we adopt its more neutral meaning of 'injury', then, within a system of perfect equity, the problem of whether harm is unjust or unjust does not arise; 'harm' or 'injury' *per se* is neither good nor evil, just or unjust, rather it becomes just or unjust depending upon whether it serves to create inequity or restore equity. Thus to inflict 'unjust' harm is a) to inflict negative outcomes upon a person who has neutral or positive inputs; that is, to harm someone who is innocent in the sense of having done nothing to deserve being harmed, or b) to inflict negative outcomes that exceed those warranted on the basis of the negative inputs; that is to harm to someone who deserves to be harmed to some degree, but more than the person deserves. 'Just harm', on the other hand is that which inflicts negative outcomes upon a person who has contributed negative inputs, such that the negative outcomes inflicted are commensurate with the negative inputs; that is, it is to harm someone who deserves to be harmed, and in exact proportion with their desert. Moreover, in principle, the activity involved in inflicting 'unjust' harm is of itself a negative input or disservice to the good of the community (it is in fact, the basis of an offence), and the activity involved in inflicting 'just harm' can be considered a positive input or good. Thus those involved in harming wrongdoers can actually make a positive contribution to the good of others, and deserve a commensurate reward.

Another advantage of construing justice in these terms is that provides a way of avoiding the semantic problems now associated with the word 'punishment'. As I noted in Chapter 1, in philosophy, the term 'punishment' has tended to take on an extremely restricted legalistic meaning, denoting something like 'penalties inflicted by authority figures on guilty individuals who have broken authorized rules'; as a result, it is actually not possible, by definition, to 'punish' an 'innocent' person, one can only 'telish' or 'penalize' them (see, for example, Bradley, 1876/1927; Flew, 1979; Murphy, 1970; Raphael, 1981; Rawls, 1972). However, this is clearly not how we apply the word punishment in everyday language; we frequently talk of the 'unjust punishment' of the innocent and consider this meaningful. Moreover, In Jewish biblical law, it was not necessary for retaliation to be carried out by an authority figure for it to be considered 'just punishment'; for example, in Exodus 22 it says 'If a thief be found breaking up, and be smitten that he die, there shall be no blood shed for him' (v.2). In other words justice has been done, even if it was not exacted by the authorities. Within a traditional desert framework as described by 'perfect equity' this latter use of the term makes more sense, and we can use the term punishment in a manner more similar to that of the Dutch jurist Hugo Grotius (1583-1645), who defined it as 'the infliction of an ill suffered for an ill done'.

Within the framework of perfect equity, a punishment is a penalty of some kind (a negative outcome) returned for a real or imagined harm or disservice to a person or group of people (a negative input). Correspondingly, 'just punishment' is the return of a penalty in exact proportion to the negative input or offence, and 'unjust punishment' is the return of a penalty that is insufficient, or excessive in relation to that warranted by the negative input. Moreover, a negative outcome returned in error for an 'imagined' negative input (such as the punishment of a person wrongly convicted who may have zero or even unrewarded positive inputs) will be judged particularly unjust in terms of its deviation from perfect equity. There is thus no necessity to invent a new term 'telishment'; the inappropriate punishment of an innocent person for an imagined negative input is simply 'unjust punishment'.

The problem of responsibility

According to Aristotle, there is another characteristic lacking in the notion of simple 'eye for an eye' reciprocity as opposed to distributive and rectificatory justice; it takes no notice of the 'great difference between a voluntary and an involuntary act' (NE5, 1132b). Unfortunately, however, Aristotle seems to avoid this issue when discussing the other types of justice. He gives us no systematic account of how 'voluntariness' affects distributive justice, or how one is supposed to transpose degrees of voluntariness into the relative 'gains and loses' that allegedly form the basis of rectificatory justice. Nevertheless, it seems that Aristotle is not alone in this; although concepts such as 'voluntariness', 'moral responsibility', and 'choice' have formed an integral part of the desert tradition in philosophy (see, for example, Evans, 1981; Franklin, 1968; Hospers, 1961; Raphael, 1981; Sadurski, 1985), little consideration, if any, has been given to exactly how these concepts are supposed to map onto the 'proportionality' component of desert.

CHAPTER 15

EQUITY, CHOICE AND RESPONSIBILITY: THE FOUNDATIONS OF 'EQUITY AS DESERT'

One of the most important characteristics of Aristotle's ideal system of geometrical proportion is that the inputs or personal characteristics that form the bases for the distribution of goods are fundamentally *activities*, or measures of activities, not fixed attributes or commodities. To Aristotle, the highest form of justice is one that rewards excellence, and excellence is both an activity and the result of activity. Aristotle's analysis in this respect may provide a significant historical insight into why some modern philosophers have included personal characteristics or qualities such as intelligence, honesty, and fair-mindedness, as desert bases their schemes (see, for example, Feinberg, 1970). According to Aristotle, characteristics such as wisdom, honesty, and fairness are ongoing activities; excellences are dynamic, we are wise by practising wisdom, honest by practising honesty, and fair by practising fairness. In fact, how could one possibly make an informed judgement about someone's character without evidence of his or her actions?

The idea that desert bases or inputs primarily concern activities, or the results of activities remains implicit in most modern conceptions of desert; we are told, for instance, that we deserve prizes if we win competitions or races, deserve grades by achieving certain performance levels on tests, deserve honours for worthy actions, and deserve income according to skill, ingenuity, time expended, effort, conscientiousness and risk (see, for example, Feinberg, 1970; Evans, 1981; Hospers, 1961; Kleinig, 1971; Lucas, 1980; Sadurski, 1985; Walzer, 1983). Even ideas such as awarding more pay to those whose jobs are boring or unpleasant could be based on the activity, that of 'endurance'. In contrast, characteristics of people that might be more accurately described as 'states' rather than activities, such as being 'over thirty five' or 'a natural born citizen', are usually excluded from modern desert theories as desert bases (just as Aristotle excluded attributes such as hereditary blindness or ugliness from his scheme). However, as I shall discuss shortly, in the Greek scheme, certain characteristics such as being born a female, or a slave, and being a child, had clear desert implications when adjustments were made for need.

Put in historical context, it is not difficult to see why there should be an emphasis on activities as the basis for desert claims. It is an important feature of both Plato's and Aristotle's ideal schemes that rewards and punishments should be distributed according characteristics, attributes or inputs that can be controlled or influenced by those to whom they apply. The virtues and vices that form the 'inputs' in Aristotle's ideal model are under our control; 'it is in our power to be virtuous or vicious' he says (NE3, p 1113b). Traditionally then, activities, or the direct results of activities, are favoured by desert theorists because we can be held accountable for them; that is, they enable desert theorists to relate desert claims to *moral responsibility*; but what exactly is 'moral responsibility'?

Moral responsibility and the self

In everyday speech, the terms 'moral responsibility' and 'personal responsibility' are often used interchangeably; this is not surprising, however, as originally they meant more or less the same thing. As MacIntyre (1982) has pointed out, our notion of 'morality' is very new. There is no word in Latin or ancient Greek that is correctly translated by our word 'moral'. Like the Greek word *ethikos*, the Latin word *moralis* means 'pertaining to character or custom', and the concept of 'character' refers to nothing more than a person's personality or dispositions to behave in one way or another. From this historical perspective, therefore, when we say that a person is 'morally responsible', we simply mean that what characterizes that person as an individual is responsible for what happened rather than something else.

In doing so, however, we usually assume a psychological model of human functioning that is found not only in the works of Plato and Aristotle, but is evident in most religious teachings, both ancient and modern, and continues to influence religious, legal and political theory and practice today. Until around the 16th Century, most people conceived of 'cause' in a rather different way to how it is conceived by scientists today; in fact, the notion of causality in prescientific society was based on the idea of 'natural agency'; that is, the ultimate or final cause of anything involved some purpose or intention (see Trusted, 1984). In a world of natural agents, behind every event or series of events there is someone, or something, engaging in purposive activity. Thus in Aristotle's universe, objects as well as animals were natural agents, able to influence other objects by virtue of the powers they possessed. For example, Aristotle asks, why are wicked people often wealthy? He suggests that the explanation could lie in the fact that, as wealth is blind 'it cannot choose men's hearts and choose the best' (Problems, 1984, p. 1494). It has long been a moot point whether animals possess a 'soul' like humans; thus in France and Switzerland records of animals on trial for criminal offences can be found as early as the 12th Century, and as late as the time of the French Revolution (Laurence and Perry, 1988). The concept of an animistic world still pervades prescientific cultures. For example, some of the Mbuti people of Africa conceive of the forest in which they live as their father, mother and friend. When there is death, illness or poor hunting they believe that the forest is sleeping and not guarding its children, so they hold a festival to awaken and cheer up the forest (Ayensu, 1980; Roberts, 1979).

The idea that objects and animals possess agency is obviously modelled on the phenomenological experiences of human beings, and it this idea of 'agency' that is the core feature of the model of human causality that underpins our notion of 'moral responsibility'. The psychological model that still dominates our thinking in this respect assumes that each of us has a unique persona, character or 'self' that is the essence of our individuality. In religious terms this is our 'soul', or our essential spirit. It is what characterizes us as a 'person', a self-conscious being. According to this model, normally, our soul or essential 'self' has control over our actions such that, if by behaving in a certain way we directly produce certain predictable outcomes, we are literally 'personally responsible' for them. If, however, the outcomes are caused by influences that are not subject to the control of our essential self, including involuntary movements of our own bodies, then we are not held *personally* responsible, even though our bodies may have been instrumental in causing what happened. According to this tradition, therefore, to be 'morally responsible' literally means to be 'personally responsible'. It is the implicit acceptance of this idea that enables us to distinguish between simply being the cause of something, and being held *responsible* for it in a moral and legal sense.

However, as we have seen, the issue of personal or moral responsibility as it relates to justice concepts has turned out to be something of a conceptual and semantic jungle (Shaver, 1985; Shaver and Drown, 1986). Moreover, although most desert theorists assume moral responsibility is related to the distribution of rewards as well as punishments, most accounts have concentrated on the latter, and it is not at all clear how these concepts are supposed to impact on the proportionality aspect of desert. Nevertheless, if we try to extrapolate a little from Aristotle's observations and analysis with regard to this issue, relate them to more modern legal conceptions of responsibility, and marry them with the concept of perfect equity, some further clarification may be possible.

Responsibility and personal choice

To reiterate, according to Aristotle, the main characteristic of voluntary human acts is that they 'are in (our) power to do or not to do' (EE3, p. 1110); in other words we have a positive choice whether or not to perform them. Although when Aristotle talks about 'choice' he means 'deliberated choice', here I am using choice in its wider sense; thus to not do what it is in our power to do, is to choose not to do it. In fact, our word 'voluntary' comes from the Latin *voluntas* meaning 'choice'. What is voluntary is chosen; what is involuntary is not chosen; and the term 'our' here refers to our soul or essential self.

Consequently, although our bodies may be *causally* responsible for an outcome, we cannot be held *morally* or *personally* responsible or accountable for the results of actions that were not within the power or control of our essential self, and therefore were not subject to our powers of choice. Hence, as Aristotle says, we are not worthy of praise or blame for acts 'when the cause is in the external circumstances and the agent contributes nothing' (NE3, p. 1110a), for in such cases we have not the power to do otherwise. But neither do we blame or praise people for acts that originate from within their own bodies but over which they (their 'essential selves' or souls) have no control or choice; so for example, Aristotle says, 'Of vices of the body, then, those in our power are blamed, those not in our power are not' (NE3 p. 1114a). It also follows from Aristotle's account that we cannot hold people personally accountable for a failure to exercise a capacity they do not possess or have lost as a result of circumstances beyond their control or powers of choice, or when their actions produce outcomes that they could not have reasonably expected. In essence, then, a theory of justice based on personal or moral responsibility, necessarily seeks to exclude the influence of chance or luck in determining outcomes (see Sadurski, 1985).

This account of the idea of responsibility, and its relationship to choice reflects very closely the reasoning applied in modern English criminal law to establish defences against criminal charges. For instance, if you make a genuine mistake of fact, not law (such as marrying someone in the mistaken belief that your previous spouse is dead), or are compelled by another to commit a criminal act (someone puts a gun in your hand and makes you shoot), or display automatism (you injure someone whilst concussed, sleepwalking or having a fit), or are judged insane (you have a defect of reason or suffer an insane delusion), then, in certain cases, defences on these grounds are possible (Curzon, 1980; Cross, Jones and Card, 1988; Norrie, 1993). In other words, when the choices of your 'essential self' are non-existent or restricted, you are deemed less blameworthy, even though your physical body may have directly or indirectly caused the offending outcomes.

Notably, however, this creates problems for supporters of the standard 'arithmetic proportion' view of punishment. If an offender is judged not responsible for harming his victim, then a 'balance of benefits and burdens' is not possible; the victim ends up with a deficit, and apparently no one is responsible for doing anything about it. Perfect equity, however, makes a definite prediction with regard to this situation; because of this 'accident', perfect equity is impossible. By being harmed, the victim has an outcome deficit (that is a surplus of negative outcomes), but, being not responsible, the offender is not obliged by equity to bear the sole burden of cancelling the victim's outcome deficit. In these circumstances, therefore, the best we can do is impose the *least inequitable solution*. As there is an 'undeserved' outcome deficit, this should be equally distributed amongst all those involved in the relationship (which may involve society at large). Hence, the victim should receive some compensation from all those involved in the relationship even though none of them is actually responsible for what happened. In other words, there is a basis in equity here for a victim compensation scheme.

If we follow the same arguments with regard to positive desert claims, the logic suggests that we should not praise or reward people for services to others that result from actions that are not deliberately chosen by them; instead we should put these down to 'luck' or 'chance'. Also, we should not praise or reward people when their actions produce positive outcomes that they could not reasonably have predicted; for, once again, such outcomes would be put down to 'luck' or 'chance' rather than personal choice. On first consideration, the general principle has a certain intuitive appeal; for instance, according to this account, if my neighbour whilst watering her garden, accidentally and unbeknown to her, scares away a dangerous intruder from my house, I might be pleased, but would be under no obligation to reward her for the 'services'. And, if she accidentally provides me with material benefits (such as leaves some goods in my car), this is not a 'contribution' to my welfare, for which the accidental donor deserves a reward. In fact, if I keep the goods I may be accused of theft, and if I return them, it is I who may be entitled to a reward. If, of course, having realized her mistake, my neighbour decides to let me keep the goods, and I accept, then her action is no longer 'accidental', and she does deserve a commensurate return.

Maximum choice

At the other extreme, Aristotle, like English law, considers the offences for which the perpetrator is to be held most responsible and blameworthy are those committed with intention and deliberation, and with full knowledge of the possible results of the action. Thus, for example, in English law someone may be found guilty of murder, rather than the lesser charge of manslaughter if 'malice aforethought' is established; that is, there was 'an intention on the part of the accused person kill or to cause grievous bodily harm to another person' (Curzon, 1980. p. 83). Here the offender may be said to have exercised Aristotle's notion of *deliberate* or *reasoned* choice. Thus, knowing the outcome that might ensue from his or her actions, the offender deliberately *chose* to bring that outcome about (that is, literally 'chose with deliberation').

If we apply the same logic to the positive inputs, or actions, then those actions that are most worthy of reward are those that are deliberately chosen with the aim of benefitting others. If my next door neighbour sees an armed intruder in my house, and deliberately raises the alarm, scaring away the intruder, then I might be feel an obligation to reward her, or express my gratitude for her 'services'. Similarly, if someone deliberately provides me with goods for my consumption, that I accept, then, I will usually feel obliged to return the favour.

Intermediate choice

In between these two extremes of choice, however, are a number of circumstances that may resulting intermediate degrees of responsibility and worthiness of praise or blame. For instance, according to Aristotle, people can act without deliberate intention to do harm but still be blamed for harm if their actions were careless and did not consider the consequences; he says that in such cases 'we assume that it is in their power not to be ignorant, since they have the power of taking care' (NE3, p. 1114a). In other words, by not exercising a positive choice to take care, they effectively 'chose' to be careless in a situation in which they could reasonably have predicted certain negative outcomes. Similarly, says Aristotle, one may be blamed for acting impulsively, without deliberation (as in anger), and inflicting an injury that might reasonably have been expected; for again one has effectively chosen not to deliberate and consider the consequences. These sorts of actions Aristotle categorizes as 'mistakes' for which one must bear some blame. In such circumstances, therefore, the general principle seems to be that a person is personally accountable for outcome that was not deliberately intended, if he or she could have anticipated the outcome and influenced it, but chose not to do so. This also acknowledges the difference between what the scholastics term 'fully voluntary acts', that are fully consented to by the actor, but because of impulse or provocation, there is a failure to fully deliberate, as distinct from 'perfectly voluntary acts', that are performed after deliberation and forethought.

The same idea seems to underlie the concepts of recklessness and negligence in English law (Cross, Jones and Card, 1988; Curzon, 1980). Thus a person may be accused of recklessness if he or she injures someone whilst driving too fast, even if there was no deliberate intention to injure. And a person can be accused of criminal negligence if, as a result of a failure to exercise a duty of care, someone dies. To Aristotle as well as modern English law then, we can be held blameworthy for failure to exercise a choice, even though we may have 'deliberately' intended no harm ('deliberately' being the operative word here). Interestingly, if we apply a similar analysis to worthiness of praise or reward, then it would follow that we should be worthy of praise or reward to some extent for our beneficial actions towards others, even if not deliberately intended, so long as we were capable of realizing at the time that beneficial consequences might result from the actions. This sort of idea could apply to a whole range of human activities, especially those of scientists and inventors who pursue knowledge allegedly for its own sake, yet remain aware that the results may be socially beneficial in some way.

If accept this analysis, then the key element that determines personal or moral responsibility is the nature of the *choices* made by the agent. The concept of moral or personal responsibility assumes that responsibility exists when one has performed an action, or not performed an action that produces certain consequences, and *one could have chosen to have acted otherwise*. Thus a person who cannot exercise personal choice, that is, someone who as not the power to behave otherwise, is not held responsible for his or her actions; conversely, the more control one has over the selection of alternatives, the more responsible one may be held.

The Equity as Desert principle

Once we relate the idea of moral responsibility to choice this has fundamental implications for how we view comparative desert. To reiterate, the traditional view is that one cannot be held truly *deserving* of blame or approbation unless one could have *chosen* to have behaved otherwise; thus, as Hospers states, 'a person is morally excusable for an action if he *couldn't help it'* (1961, p. 488).

It will be noted, however, that implicit in this argument is the idea that *to be considered more or less deserving than others, one has to be given the same choices*. So, for example, if Jenny, as a result of an accidental disability, is unable to perform services to the level of Mary, then given that Jenny did not choose, or could not help her disability, it could be argued that she cannot be deemed less deserving of a reward for her performance than Mary. It is not Jenny's fault that she could not perform as well as Mary, she could not have chosen otherwise. In the same way, if Bob puts in a day's work and receives £100, and Arthur cannot work because of unavoidable illness, we cannot claim that Arthur 'deserves' less than Bob, because Arthur had no choice; he 'couldn't help' the fact that he worked less than Bob. Comparative desert thus assumes *equal choice or opportunity* to perform those activities that form the basis of desert claims. If we link this to the idea of 'perfect equity' identified in the previous chapters, the result is a compound principle that I have termed *Equity as Desert* or *EAD* (Wagstaff, 1994; 1998). If we assume commensurateness between outcomes and inputs, then this principle states that:

A just distribution is one in which the outcomes of participants are equally proportional to their inputs, but under conditions in which each participant has an equal choice or opportunity, either real or hypothetical, to provide the relevant inputs.

It must be emphasized that, within this principle, true or perfect equal choice or opportunity to perform inputs does not refer to equal 'chance'. Equal opportunity exists when two or more individuals are given the same selection of inputs to choose between; not when they are given an equal chance to perform inputs on the basis of a lottery or the throw of a die. However, as the principle states, it is not necessary for the participants to be given the same choices in a literal sense; the choices may be equivalent, or may even be hypothetical. In the latter case, we might judge someone's desert to be based on *what we might reasonably have expected of them and of others given the same choices.*

The idea of 'equal choice' in relation to the performance of inputs for which reward is 'deserved' is of course familiar in both ancient and modern thought; it is to be found in Plato's theory of justice, in which the principle of geometrical proportion in this life is merged with a system in which beforehand each human soul chooses a mortal life. It corresponds, in part, with Sampson's (1975) view of the principle that, in his opinion, actually dominates Western meritorian ideology; namely, 'inequality of outcomes within a society is justified on the basis of inequality of merit (inputs) among persons who, however, have had equal opportunity to compete individually to achieve these outcomes' (p. 50).

And the idea of 'equal opportunity' to pursue one's deserts also plays an important role in Sadurski's (1985) equilibrium theory of desert.

Equal Choice, Duress and necessity

The idea of equal choice in relation to the performance of inputs for which punishment is deserved is, however, less familiar, but it is very much implicit in the way that English law assigns blame to offenders. In fact, Hart (1968) has argued that criminal liability can be founded on the simple idea that unless a man has the capacity and a fair opportunity or chance to adjust his behaviour to the law its penalties ought not to be applied to him' (p. 181). If a 'fair opportunity' is construed as an *equal* opportunity, and a 'chance' is a real choice, then Hart's statement captures the idea well.

The most obvious illustrations of the 'equal choice' principle in criminal law concern the legal defences of duress and necessity. As Aristotle suggests, there may be circumstances in which we fully intend to perform an evil action, know full well the consequences, and have a choice not to perform it, but still be excused blame. For instance, a tyrant may order us to do something evil, whilst holding our parents and children as hostages, and threatening them with death if we fail to carry out his orders. Aristotle says that, in a strict sense, compliance with the orders of the tyrant could be construed as voluntary, for we do still have a choice (we can let our children and parents be killed). However, in such cases we may forgive the person because he 'does what he ought not under pressure which overstrains human nature and which no one could withstand' (NE3, p. 1110a). In other words, the standard we apply is to assume that if any one else were to be placed in the same situation, that is, given the same choice of inputs, they would have done the same. Modern English law takes a strikingly similar view. Thus, Cross Jones and Card (1988) note that 'the law requires an accused to have the steadfastness reasonably to be expected of an ordinary citizen in this situation, but a person may be excused certain offences in the face of duress or "Threats of immediate death or serious personal violence so great as to overbear the ordinary powers of human resistance" '; and, in principle, this uncludes threats directed towards a third party.

Aristotle comments, however, that it is debatable whether such acts are to be classed as voluntary or involuntary; his own conclusion is that they are 'voluntary, but in the abstract perhaps involuntary'. Long debates about the exact status of this kind of defence have also occurred in English Law (see Cross, Jones and Card, 1988; Norrie, 1993). Suppose, for example, that a person commits an offence, such as stealing, but under duress (say, because the accused's life was under threat). In such a case the action would still have been voluntary, and the offender would be said to be personally responsible for the theft; the offender would have caused the stealing, been aware of the consequences of stealing, intended to steal, and had a degree of choice (in principle, could still have chosen not to steal). In English law such an act would still be regarded as unlawful; however, in principle at least, the accused could be excused liability (Cross, Jones and Card, 1988; Curzon, 1980). If we adopt Shaver's terminology and definitions (Shaver, 1985; Shaver and Drown, 1986), the underlying principle here seems to be that certain acts may be regarded as wrong, the offender is, at least in some degree, responsible, but we absolve or excuse the person of blame when we consider that any reasonable person, placed in the same situation, given the same restricted choice of inputs, would have behaved in the same way. In fact, English law specifically requires as an 'objective test', that to reject a plea of duress the prosecution must prove that 'a sober person of reasonable firmness, sharing the same characteristics of the accused' would not have responded in the same way (Cross, Jones and Card, 1988, p. 567).

On first consideration, the psychological reasoning behind this defence would appear to concur with psychological theories of attribution. According to Kelley's (1967) *consensus principle*, an action is more likely to be attributed to an external or situational cause, rather than a dispositional cause, if, in the same situation, it would be performed by people other than the target actor. In other words, we are less likely to say that someone meant to do something by virtue of the kind of person he or she is, if we know that anyone else would have done the same in the same situation. If everyone reacts in the same way in a particular situation we would tend to locate the cause in the situation. According to this viewpoint, therefore, a person acting under duress or necessity, could be considered to be operating under a situation of such restricted choice, that his or her behaviour is more or less to be considered involuntary; and the criterion or cut off point for the decision about whether a behaviour is to be classed as involuntary is whether most other people would have behaved in the same way in the same situation.

However, this does not seem to be how English law actually operates in cases of duress. The main thrust of the legal defence of duress is not that it diminishes the *mens rea* or responsibility for the act; but rather it acts as an *excuse* for the act (Cross, Jones and Card, 1988). The implication seems to be that, so long as some real choice actually exists, individuals are still to be held personally responsible for their behaviour, whether positive or negative. In fact Norrie (1993) has commented that, on the whole, the English criminal law seems remarkably unsympathetic to the defence of duress; duress is not allowed, for instance, as a defence against murder. It is still an offence to kill an innocent person even if the choice is between that person's life and one's own or that of one's family. So what is the nature of the excuse and how does it operate? From the perspective of Equity as Desert, there is perhaps a another piece of logic implicit in this view.

There may be situations in which we might consider a person to be personally responsible for an offence, and in principle punishable; however, if the offender was only behaving like most other people would given the same situation or choices, then *we have no grounds for arguing that the offender is any more deserving of punishment than most other people*. Thus short of rounding up most of the population and punishing them for a crime that they would likely have committed had they been put in the same situation, it makes sense to let the offender escape at least some punishment! But, perhaps more significantly, the offender could reasonably claim that being threatened and pressured by another to perform a criminal act is in itself a negative outcome. In other words, the offender has to a certain extent already been penalized, so this would act as a factor mitigating punishment. It is notable in this respect that, even if the accused is found guilty and convicted of murder, English law allows the duress defence to be taken into consideration by 'discretionary executive action' after conviction; thus a reduction of punishment by means of early release may be considered (Cross, Jones and Card, 1988).

English law also recommends that what we could term a 'hypothetical equal opportunity' standard should be used to cover acts of recklessness and negligence where criminal intent is only indirectly involved, if at all, yet criminal guilt is still inferred; thus a person may be found guilty of negligence 'if his conduct in relation to a reasonably intelligible task falls below the standard which would be expected of a reasonable person in the light of that risk' (Cross, Jones and Card, 1988, p. 91). In theory, therefore, a man who is found guilty of recklessness and/or negligence cannot complain that no one else was given the opportunity to commit the offence of which he has been convicted, because the law has ruled that if any other reasonable person had been put in the same situation, or given the same choices, he or she would not have acted in the same way. In other words, to be deemed worthy of condemnation in relation to others, it is not necessary for there to be *actual* opportunities for all to perform or not perform an activity; instead desert can be determined by reference to a sort of 'average standard' of behaviour that represents, hypothetically, how most 'reasonable' people would have behaved, given the same opportunities.

It seems, therefore, that we may have here the basis for a theory of 'excuses' that has been missing from psychological attribution theories (Shaver, 1985; Shaver and Drown, 1986); thus, whereas *responsibility* rests on the absolute degree of choice or control available, the decision about whether the conduct is to be *blamed* or *excused* includes a relative comparison with how others might have behaved in a comparable situation. If, hypothetically, any other reasonable law-abiding person would have behaved in the same way, in the same situation, then the offender is no more deserving of punishment than most other reasonable people. Moreover, the concept of 'excuse' may even include within it a recognition of penalties already incurred.

If we apply the logic behind the operation of the defence of duress in criminal law to positive outcome claims, then being forced to make a positive contribution to the good of others under some pressure or duress might be considered worthy of reward depending on how we would expect equivalent others to behave in the same situation. So, for example, if we assume it is the duty of every working citizen to contribute taxes to maintain basic services, we would not expect to compensate a reluctant tax-payer for being forced to do likewise. If, however, a person is forced to work in circumstances that others would not normally accept, such as when individuals are pressed into slavery (circumstances that would viewed as a extreme negative outcomes), additional compensation would be necessary to cancel out the outcome deficit. This latter idea would seem to provide a rationale for Feinberg's (1970) view that when people are being made to endure arduous or unpleasant jobs, through 'no fault of their own', they can be said to deserve compensation (though, put this way, this view is no longer inconsistent with the idea that people who deliberately choose to do the same jobs deserve compensation also!).

The effects of responsibility on the inputs
From the perspective the Equity as Desert model then, the idea of moral responsibility has two main implications. We do not hold people responsible, or worthy of reward or punishment for the results of their activities, unless they have some choice as to whether or not to perform the activities, and some choice over the outcomes of the activities. But also, to argue that one person is more or less deserving of outcomes than another it is necessary for all participants to have an equal opportunity, or the same choices, either real or hypothetical, to perform the activities for which the various outcomes are appropriate or 'commensurate'.

But how exactly does all this actually affect the equity equation? For instance, if person A has fewer or no opportunities or choices to perform as person B, what exactly is A's input? In such a situation, effectively person A's input is an 'unknown'. We simply do not know whether person A is more or less deserving than person B, because person A was not given the opportunity to perform as B. Under these circumstances, the simplest way to proceed would be to follow an equality rule along the lines that, if we cannot show whether one person is more or less deserving than another, we should treat them as equally deserving; that is, assume that their inputs are equal in some way and distribute outcomes accordingly. However, another way to proceed in such situations, might be to make some kind of estimate of how A might have performed, had A been given the same opportunities as B, and use this 'estimated input' in the perfect equity equation.

Suppose, for example, that Group X have performed a valuable service to their community, and have been deemed in some degree 'responsible' for their behaviour. Equity demands that they should be rewarded accordingly. Suppose, Group Y, however, have done no such service; in fact, they are unemployed. According to the above logic, the unemployed Group Y could base a defence (claim an equivalent outcome), on the grounds that, because of high unemployment, they had no choice but to be idle, and would have worked the same as group Y if they had found themselves in Y's situation. We could, in principle, therefore, assign the same level of input to both groups.

In the case of criminal acts, this same logic applies. Suppose a man is accused of a robbery, in terms of Equity as Desert, if he is deemed responsible for his behaviour, he is technically punishable. One defence, however, could be that he had no choice, and had he been given the opportunity, he would have behaved like most other people, and *not committed the crime*. In this case, if the man is deemed not responsible, his input becomes what he 'might have done', given the same opportunities or 'free choices' as others, which is zero, and release him without punishment (and in theory, the costs that resulted from his behaviour would be equally distributed across the community as 'the least inequitable solution').

But does it also follow that we should punish people for what they 'might have done', had they been given the opportunity? This seems a rather bizarre notion. But, on reflection it is not necessarily so; in fact, it is not unusual for the courts to punish people for what they 'might have done' providing there is clear evidence to support their intention. For instance, in English law, one does not have to have fully carried out a particular act in order to be held criminally liable for it; it can be an offence to *attempt* a particular crime so long as there is evidence that one intended to do so; moreover, predictably, the more serious the harm intended, the more negative the input will be considered. On the whole, also, in terms of the punishments assigned, *attempts* are treated as though the offender had succeeded in his or her aims; thus, in English law, the maximum punishment for attempted murder is life imprisonment, and the law states that, with a few exceptions, 'in the case of any other attempt, the maximum punishment is the same as is available to the court for the offence attempted' (see Cross, Jones and Card, 1988, p. 562). However, as most people appear to have no desire to claim a right to be punished for what they might have done, and we have a special aversion to punishing the innocent, we do not have large numbers of people claiming they should be punished for what they might have done had the opportunity arisen, and attempting to provide evidence of their intentions. In contrast, many people clearly do wish to claim a right to be rewarded for what they might have done, and to a certain extent this is recognized in unemployment benefit systems; though again some evidence that one is seeking work is held to be an important criterion for claiming unemployment benefit.

At Liverpool we have even found some experimental evidence for this general idea in relation to the award of positive outcomes. In one study we gave a sample of the general public some scenarios in which one worker's input was 10 hours, another's was 5 hours, and a third worker's input was nothing. We then varied information about the zero input worker's opportunity to work, and her previous work history. Our results showed that when the zero input worker had clearly chosen not to work, she was awarded nothing, as EAD demands (none of the workers was in undeserved need). However, when the zero worker was prevented from working through no fault of her own (she was stuck in a lift), there was a tendency to award her a payment according to her previous work record. Thus if her previous work record was bad - she usually did nothing - the most common (median and modal) response was to award her nothing. However, if her previous work record was good, the most common response was to award her either exactly what she would have received had she been given the opportunity to work as usual, or a sort of 'average' compensatory payment equivalent to that she would have earned had she done 5 hours of work. And if her previous work record was not available, the most common response was, again, to award her a sort of 'average' compensatory payment equivalent to that she would have earned had she done 5 hours of work (Wagstaff, Bowles, Hughes, Rogers, Turner, and Perfect, 1994).

Another of implication of this scheme is that when conditions are such that all or individuals have an equivalent degree of 'free' choice to choose between alternative inputs, they should receive outcomes commensurate with the actual results of the input activities (or lack of them). In other words, inputs should be measured in terms of actual *results* or *output*. However, when, there is no choice at all, or the choices are very restricted or unequal, all should, in principle, be awarded outcomes based on the level of input that they realistically might have achieved had they been given a free and equal choice. So for example, in the case of criminal justice, if I have free choice, and I offend in a situation in which most others in my position of free choice would not have offended, I must accept the outcomes commensurate with the results of my offence (such as, severe punishment for an offence that causes serious harm). And, even if I do not succeed in my attempt to harm, I must still accept the outcomes commensurate with the *intended* or expected results of my offence (such as, severe punishment for an attempt to commit an offence that would be expected to cause serious harm). On the other hand, if for some reason I have minimal or no control over the consequences of my actions, and I commit an offence, I should receive commensurate with the input value that I would have achieved had I been given the same opportunities as others who can freely choose not to offend; and given that I, like most people, would wish to claim that, under conditions of free choice, I would not have offended, the tendency should be to assume my input is zero, and release me without punishment (or, at least, assign everyone else an input the same as mine and decide to give up on the idea of punishing us all).

The same general idea would then operate for positive inputs and outcomes. So, for example, if I have a free choice, and I refuse to work (and work is the relevant input), even though most others in my position of free choice have chosen to work, I must accept the zero outcomes commensurate with zero work performance. Conversely, if I have minimal or no choice, and I cannot work (say because there are no jobs, or because the jobs available are so unpleasant and badly paid that no one else would do them), I should receive outcomes commensurate with the value of the work that I would have done had I been given an opportunity to do the same kinds of work offered to those who have a free choice. On the other hand, if I have free choice, and I work, and others have an equal opportunity to do similar work, I am entitled to outcomes commensurate with my actual work performance. (Moreover, even if others do not have an equal opportunity to work, I am still entitled to more than them if I can convince them that they would not have done as much as me had they been given the same opportunities.) But if I have minimal or no choice, and I am forced to work, I should receive outcomes commensurate with the value of the work that I would have done had I been given an opportunity to do the same kinds of work offered to others who had a wider and freer choice. I may also be due extra compensation for the discomforts imposed on me.

In certain cases of recklessness and negligence, however, where offenders are not deliberately selecting between activities in order to produce harmful consequences, it seems that English law treats the offender as though he or she has to a more limited degree intended the results to come about, and/or has failed to keep to the 'zero inputs baseline' in equity; that is, has failed to engage in those activities (that is the use of care, control and restraint) that would be expected of anyone in similar circumstances); and, of course, the more harmful the possible consequences of an action the more care one is expected to exercise. In such cases, the inputs would seem to be based again on the outcomes that, on average, one could reasonably have been expected to arise from one's actions and/or the extent to which one has undeservedly gained positive outcomes by failing to keep to the zero inputs baseline. And as reckless actions might be considered, on average, to produce fewer negative consequences than equivalent deliberately intended actions, the former are considered less serious (have lower inputs values) than the latter.

There may even be a positive input equivalent of recklessness and negligence, where contributors are not deliberately selecting between activities in order to produce beneficial consequences, but are approaching their jobs and the social duties expected of everyone with such extraordinary care and diligence, that they will inevitably produce benefits beyond those they deliberately intended. In which cases, again, the inputs will be based on the effects that might reasonably have been expected to result from the contributor's actions, and/or the extent to which the contributor is due positive outcomes by exceeding the zero inputs baseline. Honours bestowed on scientists, war heroes and model citizens might serve as illustrations of this principle. In fact, in relation to awards for bravery, one is reminded here of Spinoza's definition of 'daring' as 'the desire whereby any one is incited to do anything with a danger which his equals dare not encounter'; and 'cowardice' as belonging 'to him whose desire is hindered by the fear or dread of a danger which his equals dare to undergo' (1677/1986, p. 137).

In addition, however, a consideration of the role of responsibility and equal opportunity as elements in positive desert may also be able to provide us with a significant insight into the popularity of 'effort' as an input or desert base for positive outcomes.

The relationship between effort and equal opportunity

Clearly one of the most appealing features of 'effort' (often used synonymously with terms such as 'work' and 'labour') as a positive input is that, compared to other characteristics such as strength, intelligence or skill, it is often assumed to be something that we can all have a more or less equal opportunity to provide. In other words, we like to base inputs on effort because we can be held personally responsible for our 'efforts', in a way that may not be possible for other characteristics (see, Cohen, 1974; Greenberg, 1980; Lamm, Kayser and Schanz, 1983; Leventhal, 1976; Leventhal and Michaels, 1971; Schwinger, 1988; Utne and Kidd, 1980). Indeed, according to Sadurski (1985), 'conscientious effort which has socially beneficial effects' is the only legitimate input that can be used in a theory of desert, because only effort excludes the influence of 'dumb luck' (p. 116). However, as I have noted, it makes little sense to argue that 'effort' *per se* must always be counted as an input, regardless of the degree to which it might be expected to produce socially beneficial outcomes. The man who spends 10 years of his life, and enormous effort and social resources, digging holes in an attempt to find manna from heaven to donate to others, would probably be considered a social liability rather than someone especially worthy of reward. To understand exactly how and when 'effort' will be employed as an input measure, therefore, we need to consider again how equal opportunity operates in desert.

Suppose, for example, that two women, Kit and Doris, produce 30 pairs of shoes that they sell for £90 (thus providing social benefits for others); and that each has produced 15 pairs of shoes. If we share out the money they receive for the shoes in proportion to the number of shoes each has actually produced, then each should receive an equal amount of outcomes, £45. But further suppose that, in order to produce the same number of shoes, Kit had to work for 2 hours, whereas Doris had to work for only 1 hour. If the number of hours worked is used as a measure of effort, then if we share out the £90 according to effort, the split will not be £45 each, but £60 to Kit and £30 to Doris. The latter might look fairer if the reason why Doris was able to produce the same number of shoes as Kit in less time was because she had been given a tool to which Kit had no access, or possessed a skill that Kit could never acquire.

But what if Kit *did* have full and equal access to this tool or skill that Doris used, but chose not to learn how to use it. Would we still want to reward 'effort'? To a follower of desert, it could be argued that it was Kit's fault she was not as efficient as Doris; thus Kit cannot claim she is more deserving than Doris, simply because she put in more hours of work. The opportunities were equal. In other words, in this situation, it might be deemed inappropriate to choose effort as measured by 'work time' as the input. Instead, as each had an equal opportunity to produce the goods that are to be exchanged for rewards, one might assume that the more appropriate input is 'raw output' (in this case the number of shoes produced).

Of course, in the long term, very often 'effort' may correlate with 'raw output'; especially if we invent some calculus that weights intellectual or creative work as more 'effortful' than manual work (in the above example, perhaps it involves huge 'intellectual effort' to learn how to use the tool; or months of training to acquire the skill used by Doris). But there seems to be no necessity, in principle, to measure inputs solely in terms of 'effort'; indeed, to do so would seem to penalize the more efficient contributor. According to the Equity as Desert model, so long as there is an equal opportunity to perform those acts that generate socially beneficial outputs, it makes more sense to argue that individuals should receive outcomes in proportion to the extent to which they actually generated the socially beneficial outputs, not the amount of 'effort' they expended in attempting to do this.

But if there is not equal opportunity, and all we have to go on as a measure of contribution is 'effort', how does this fit in with the idea of 'commensurateness' between inputs and outcomes? According to our previous definition, 'commensurateness' requires that all should receive outcomes 'equivalent to the value of the social benefits and harms that they might reasonably expect their inputs or contributions to generate', not the award of outcomes equivalent, or proportional to their 'efforts'. Consider again, however, the previous example. If we assume that effort is the only productive activity for which we can actually be held responsible, then, if, on the same task, Kit has input twice as much effort as Doris, but has only generated the same number of goods, then presumably Doris must have at her disposal some unchosen, 'undeserved', set of characteristics that gave her an unfair productive advantage over Kit. To control for inequalities in opportunity, therefore, we need to determine what would have happened if Kit had been given the same opportunities as Doris. In other words, what proportion of the £90 worth of goods that they actually produced would Doris have produced, if the opportunities had been equal?

Well, if Doris managed to produce £45 worth of goods with only 1 hour's worth of effort, whereas it took Kit 2 hours of the same kind of effort to produce £45 worth of goods, then Doris must have had at her disposal undeserved characteristics that enabled her to double her productive capacity. Presumably if Kit had had an equal opportunity to use these same characteristics, she would have produced twice as many goods as Doris. It follows, therefore, that if the £90 of goods had been produced *under conditions of equal opportunity*, Doris would have been responsible for producing twice as many of them as Kit. Thus, controlling for inequalities in opportunity, if the £90 is to be distributed equitably, Doris should receive £30, and Kit, £60!

In other words, under conditions of clear unequal opportunity, in which virtually all differences in productive capacity are determined by factors beyond the control of the individual's concerned, if we award the outcomes equivalent to the benefits generated by the collective activity according to 'effort', we will be closer to distributing outcomes commensurate with the input values that the workers *would have achieved under conditions of equal opportunity*. Thus, all will end up with outcomes more equivalent to the value of the social benefits that they might reasonably have expected their inputs or contributions to have generated under conditions of equal opportunity.

The prediction from all this is that in deciding how much of a contribution someone has made to an exchange relationship (that is, the value of their input activity), individuals will tend to concentrate on the actual *outputs they have generated* when they feel there were plenty of opportunities to produce these outcomes, and on the *effort they have expended* when they feel that the opportunities to do the things necessary to generate these outcomes were very unequal. And, if we accept this analysis, we can construct a hierarchy of decisions about the types of input to be considered and the choices and opportunities available.

1) If individuals perceive that there is full and equal choice between alternative types of inputs, the input measure chosen will be the actual or expected 'socially beneficial output'.

2) If individuals perceive that there is limited or unequal choice over producing certain outputs, then the inputs will be based on what each might have behaved under conditions of full choice and equal opportunity; and, in practice, the input measure most commonly chosen to reflect this, will be the relative 'effort' involved in producing the socially beneficial outputs.

3) And when individuals perceive that there is little or no choice over one's capacities, including efforts, to produce socially beneficial outputs, the inputs will either be based on an estimate of a) how each might have behaved under the other conditions, or, in the absence of such information, b) an 'equal inputs' rule for all those involved (resulting, in the latter case, in equal shares of outcomes between participants).

Given that most people likely consider that opportunities for various kinds of work are neither entirely equal nor absent, the modern popularity of the concept of 'effort' as an input measure is perhaps very understandable; especially if we couple this idea with the popular view that, on the whole, those who work hardest at honest employment contribute most to the good of others.

However, all this also draws attention to the fact that, although within traditional conceptions of desert, human activity forms the primary input or service, there is no reason why material commodities should not be used as substitutes for human activity, so long as commodities, some where along the line, can be assumed to arise from the productive activities, occurring under conditions of equal opportunity, of those who possess them. Also, we can quite legitimately use our 'outcomes' (including our zero baseline entitlements) as 'inputs' in a new exchange, so long as we fully 'deserved' these outcomes in the first place. It is important, nevertheless, that if people do wish to claim outcomes commensurate with the input values they would have achieved under conditions of equal opportunity, then 'equals must still be treated equally'. For instance, if Rod and Ned both contribute £10 of their 'deserved' funds to a mutual enterprise that produces £100 worth of commensurate outcomes, then equity demands that each should receive £50. If, however, a third person, John, wishes to claim a portion of the £100 on the basis that he was denied the opportunity to make an equal contribution to the endeavour, he may do so, but he must not undeservedly 'gain' outcomes relative to Rod and Ned; in other words, he must also be prepared incur any outcome costs (including the initial £10 outlay) that those who provided the 'real' inputs incurred in providing their contributions.

Personal, collective and implied responsibility

So far, I have been examining responsibility on an individual basis; that is, the idea that a single person is accountable for his or her behaviour. It can be noted, however, that throughout history we can find examples of extended responsibility, whereby any person in a group may be treated 'as if' he or she is accountable for the inputs of someone else. The most extreme examples of collective responsibility involve tribal revenge killings between families and groups, in which an offender may be punished by having another member of his or her family killed. One feature of Hammurabi's code of laws, for example, was that if a man causes the death of the son or daughter of another man, then it is not the offender him or herself who must die, but the offender's own son or daughter (Hertz, 1956). Family revenge killings have been common in many societies (see, for example, Dunbar et al., 1995; Roberts, 1979), and, though illegal, still survive in Western societies as in sectarian and gangland murders. In such cases, therefore, a person's inputs may be crucially determined by the behaviour of others.

Other similar examples of this 'as if', or 'implied desert' reasoning, are ideas such as 'original sin' whereby all humans are held responsible and punishable for the sins of Adam, and the 'Divine Right of Kings'; that is, the idea popular amongst the Pharaohs of Egypt, various Roman Emperors, and English Kings, amongst others, that somehow they and their bloodline have been 'chosen' by some divine power 'as if' they had done something somewhere at some time to merit their choice (see Russell, 1979).

From a psychological viewpoint, collective and implied responsibility might be construed as 'primitive attribution processes' of the variety described by Heider (1958) and Lerner (1980). In other words, they do not conflict with the idea of EAD, rather they reflect cognitively simplistic versions of it. However, it is important not to underestimate the sophistication of some of these cultural devices. They can be very elaborate, and may have served, and continue to serve, many functions. On the positive side, they perhaps contribute to psychological health, and maintain order and stability in society; whilst on the negative side, they can be used to maintain the status quo, and justify existing exploitative power structures.

For example, in his famous 'Romanes Lecture' of 1893, the celebrated biologist, Thomas Huxley (1825-1895), argued that much of this latter type of 'implied desert' reasoning is symptomatic of attempts by philosophers and theologians from all cultures, throughout history, to come to terms with the fact that the universe is patently unjust. Thus in Brahminical and Buddhist thought, we find the argument that, 'Every sentient being is reaping as it has sown; if not in this life, then in one or other of the infinite series of antecedent existences of which it is the latest term'. According to Huxley, this belief is an attempt to justify an unjust situation by claiming that, 'The present distribution of good and evil is, therefore, the algebraical sum of accumulated positive and negative deserts' (1911, p. 60). It is notable, for instance, how often reincarnation beliefs go side by side with caste systems. They did so for both the Sumerians and Plato, and were fundamental to the cultures of ancient Persia and Vedic India. In Vedic India, for example, the strict caste system was imposed by Aryan invaders who sanctioned it through the belief that one's position in the system was determined by actions in previous existences, and that actions in this life could determine one's position in the next. Having established this basic belief it was then possible for those at the top of the hierarchy to enforce it with subsidiary beliefs, such as the idea that one's entry into the next life may be jeopardized by overseas travel. This provided a very effective way of ensuring that not only did the exploited lower caste members accept full responsibility for their fate, but they did not migrate either!

Whatever their function, however, all such ideas are testament to the fundamental role that the concepts of personal responsibility and equal opportunity have always played in conceptions of justice.

CHAPTER 16

EQUITY, EQUALITY AND NEED

So far then I have described briefly a justice model that attempts to combine the idea of psychological equity with traditional philosophical conceptions of desert; the result is a sort of proportionality/responsibility model that I have labelled 'Equity as Desert', or 'EAD' for short. To repeat, the basic principle of the model can be summarized as follows.

A perfectly just or equitable distribution is one in which the outcomes of participants exist in equal proportion to their inputs, but under conditions in which each participant has an equal choice or opportunity, either real or hypothetical, to provide the relevant inputs.

The model then contains four basic assumptions in relation to this principle.

1) Outcomes should be distributed in equal proportion to inputs, such that the more one inputs or contributes, the more one should receive.

2) Positive inputs must always be returned with positive outcomes, and negative inputs with negative outcomes.

3) Zero inputs must always be returned with zero outcomes. If one does nothing positive or negative, one should receive nothing positive or negative.

4) When perfect equity exists, the outcomes that individuals receive should be commensurate with their inputs.

Nevertheless, in a world not dominated by beliefs in reincarnation and immanent justice, there seem to be some quite obvious practical difficulties with the scheme. For instance, surely this scheme implies that we must give vast sums of money to people who have various genetic and other 'accidental' disadvantages, so that they can achieve the life style that they would have achieved had they not had these disadvantages? This may seem a harrowing thought for some property rights theorists. But when faced with this difficulty, there is another concept that supporters of inequality have traditionally invoked, *need*. To assess the role of need, however, it is first useful to note how equality operates in EAD.

Equality and desert

According to the Equity as Desert principle, there are three main situations in which desert and equal outcomes would coincide. The overriding principle is that *when inputs are equal, then outcomes should be equal*. Thus all participants should receive equal outcomes under the following conditions.

1) When all inputs are equally positive or negative; that is all participants have performed either services or disservices to an equal extent.

2) When no one has any choice at all, and consequently, no one is responsible for his or her behaviour. In this case, the inputs are effectively unknown and there is no basis for arguing that one person is more or less deserving than another.

3) When, under conditions of equal opportunity, all would have provided the same inputs.

Given this, it is quite obvious that one can construct both egalitarian and inegalitarian arguments from the EAD principle to 'justify' equal or unequal shares (it can be noted here how 'justify' now takes on the literal meaning that reflects its origin; these arguments are used to make the various notions 'just'). For instance, one would expect supporters of *in*equality in outcomes to construct arguments such as, a) the positive and negative inputs of the participants are unequal (the participants are not equally 'worthy' or 'unworthy'); b) the inputs of the participants are fully known (participants are free agents who can be held fully responsible for their behaviours), and/or c) the opportunities to provide the inputs are equal, and even if they are not, given equal opportunity, all would not provide the same inputs.

On the other hand, one would expect supporters of the idea of *equality* in outcomes to construct arguments along the lines that, a) the positive and negative inputs of all participants are equal (all are equally 'worthy' or 'unworthy'); b) the inputs of all participants are unknown (none of them has any choice in the matter; they are not responsible for their behaviours), and/or c) opportunities are unequal, but given equal opportunity, all would provide the same inputs.

If equality, equity and desert derive from the same common core principle or idea, one would expect egalitarians and nonegalitarians to use these kinds of arguments to justify their respective positions. But where does need fit in?

Need and desert

If we examine the traditional concept of a desert, is not surprising that objections have been raised to the idea of need as an input or desert base. Unless considered as some sort of sacrifice, need does not readily count as a service to others or 'chosen contribution to the good of others' and many philosophers have long rejected it as a desert base (see, for example, Feinberg, 1970; Kleinig, 1971; Rawls, 1972; Sadurski, 1985; Walzer, 1983). Perhaps, however, it would make more sense if we to consider need primarily as an *outcome adjustment*, rather than as an input. Consider, for example, the link that some philosophers have made between need and equality. Vlastos (1975) has argued that 'to each according to his need' is, in fact, the most perfect form of equal distribution (p. 141); for instance, for two people to share an equal level of security (a positive outcome), it may be necessary to distribute protection resources unequally if the security of one person is threatened. Karl Marx (1875/1986) made a similar point when he argued that to equal shares to two workers who have performed equally, when one is married, or one has more children, would actually be to treat them unequally, for 'one would be richer than the other' (p. 166).

We can incorporate this logic into the perfect equity principle as follows; if two partners, A and B, are to receive exactly what equity demands such that their outcomes exist in equal ratio to their inputs, then some adjustment must be made for 'needs'. Thus, if equity exists, but then A's outcomes are diminished for some accidental reason, resulting in A being in a state of 'need' relative to B, then A will be receiving less than her 'just deserts', and must receive extra outcomes to maintain true equity. In this context, therefore it is perfectly reasonable to say that A deserves compensation for any state of need created by her accidental loss of outcomes. However, as Feinberg points out, within a theory of desert, need is only to be compensated when it is 'blameless' (p. 94). Of course, if we were to consider all need to be blameless (in the sense that our needs are determined by factors beyond our control or not subject to our choices) then this differentiation does not arise, but if we accept that need is something for which we can be held responsible, then the obvious implication is that responsibility can apply not only to how we judge inputs, but also outcomes.

It can be noted that within this context, to be in 'need' normally assumes two things; a) that the person in need has a deficiency with regard to something, and that b) the person in need is motivated to rectify this deficiency.

Responsibility and outcomes

Feinberg (1970) implies that if people fall into a state of 'need' through deliberate choice or carelessness, we are less obliged to help them, than if the loss is accidental. It is not difficult to incorporate this idea into the Equity as Desert model too. For instance, if our two friends, Kit and Doris, receive an exact equal just return or outcome for the same input, but then Kit chooses to exchange that outcome for an equivalent outcome that provides temporary pleasure, and thereby ends up destitute, the fact that Kit's outcome is expended, while Doris's is not, is not contrary to the requirements of equity; both have received exactly what they deserve. One simply chose to substitute one outcome with an equivalent outcome that afforded a more temporary outcome satisfaction. Also, if Kit's outcome loss or need arises from a negative input (such as 'voluntary' laziness that might be judged detrimental to the community, or a fine for a criminal act) then the need could be construed as an appropriate negative return for a negative action or input.

If, however, Kit's outcomes are stolen against her will, or are lost due to a freak accident she could not possibly have predicted, then she has received no benefits in return for her loss; she ends up with 'less than she deserves', and equity is not satisfied. It is interesting to note here that in both the American and German legal systems, if an offender suffers what might be construed as 'accidental' negative outcomes, such as accidental injury during the crime, lengthy pretrial detention, or brutal treatment by the police, these 'negative outcomes' may be set against the punishment that would normally be awarded, and may even be enough to convince the jury that the criminal has already been punished sufficiently before being brought to trial (see Sadurski, 1985).

The response to a loss of outcomes due to carelessness could be construed in a number of ways. It could be argued, for instance, that under normal circumstances 'taking care' involves a degree of burdensome self-monitoring and control, and that the person who loses outcomes by not taking care has essentially chosen to substitute at least part of the value of the outcomes with the temporary benefits of relinquishing this burden. Alternatively, or additionally, it could be argued that 'carelessness' is an antisocial activity; those who are 'careless' are potentially a social liability, and 'carelessness' is a negative input. In the latter case, when someone loses his or her outcomes due to carelessness, it might seem entirely appropriate for others to respond with 'that will serve you right'; meaning, 'you now have what you deserve, and justice is done'.

It is important to emphasize, therefore, that within the Equity as Desert scheme, needs can operate as genuine desert claims. The logic is that, assuming a starting point of perfect equal ratio equity, if you do nothing negative, you deserve nothing negative. Consequently, it follows that, in as much as certain needs are construed as unchosen outcome deficits, other things being equal, those in need, through no fault or choice of their own, are receiving less than they deserve. Accordingly, assuming a starting point in which a state of perfect equal ratio equity exists, it is not illogical or inconsistent to say, as Feinberg (1979) does, that 'a man who has a chronically sick wife or child *deserves* compensation since through no fault of his own he has a greater need than others' (p. 93, my emphasis). In the context of Equity as Desert, therefore, it is not the case that needs are never grounds for desert claims. It all depends on what one considers to be a 'desert claim'. For whilst traditional conceptions of desert have rejected need as in *input*, it may nevertheless function as an *outcome adjustment* in the same desert model.

Liberty, need and the zero outcome baseline
Within the Equity as Desert model, the satisfaction of basic needs may also be an important requirement for the zero outcomes baseline. As I have already emphasized, according to EAD, zero outcomes do not necessarily refer to receiving nothing in a material sense. Rather the zero outcomes position is to be conceptualized as a neutral point within a family of positive and negative values. Thus, even if one had done nothing positive or negative, to be in extreme need relative to others such that one's life is painful and impoverished (death through starvation, thirst and exposure to the elements being the obvious extremes), could be construed as a distinctly negative outcome, 'undeserved' by a zero or neutral input. The satisfaction of basic needs, however construed, could therefore be seen as fundamental to the maintenance of the zero outcomes baseline for those who by deserve to be either at, or above it.

Also, if Equity as Desert also requires an equal choice or opportunity to perform the inputs within the scheme, then the zero baseline should also include some provision for the maintenance of equal opportunity. In other words, even people whose inputs are zero deserve an opportunity to increase their inputs should they choose. This obviously requires both the financial and material means to be enable to choose between inputs, and the physical liberty to do so. Some degree of liberty and the satisfaction of basic material needs are thus fundamental to the Equity as Desert principle, and form part of the zero outcomes baseline. This idea seems to coincide in part with Sadurski's (1985) view that 'Distribution according to desert when basic needs are unmet is not genuine because some people haven't got an opportunity to deserve anything' (p. 169). The capacity to make differential contributions to society assumes that one has sufficient freedom and material resources to choose between alternative inputs.

It also follows, however, that those inputs are negative and deserve negative outcomes, such as criminals, deserve to have at least some of the benefits of the zero outcomes baseline taken from them. In most modern countries the most obvious penalty for serious offenders involves the withdrawal of liberty and the means to chose between the range of alternative inputs available to those who are not incarcerated. In extreme cases, when the death penalty is applied, there it is a permanent denial of any zero baseline resources. Nevertheless, for most offenders we do take away the provisions for sustaining life, such as food, drink and shelter, unless the offence is so serious that we wish the offender to die for it.

This does not mean, however, that only criminals can forfeit their zero outcome entitlement. According to the preceding analysis, those who freely choose to exchange part of their zero outcome entitlement for another outcome that does not satisfy their needs are not strictly due compensation. For example, if a destitute man is given money for food and shelter, but decides to spend it all on an unsuccessful gambling spree, strictly he does not 'deserve' compensation (this behaviour could be construed as an outcome substitution and/or a negative input). Nevertheless, if it is assumed that such behaviour is still insufficient to justify the negative outcome of death through starvation, it might be still be deemed equitable to provide the man with some means of feeding himself. If, of course, one concludes that the gambling spree was a uncontrollable response to frustration or depression caused by factors beyond the man's control, then the behaviour might be classed as determined by factors outside the man's control or choice, and compensation would be in order. (One is also reminded here of a judgement in 1997 in which the London Borough of Hounslow was allowed to refuse housing to a man who had served prison sentences for paedophilia. The judgement was that, because the man had knowingly committed crimes that would result in him losing his house, he had effectively 'chosen' to make himself homeless).

Need as an input moderator

This draws attention to another possible way need can operate in the Equity as Desert model. Need can also act as mitigation for liability as in the legal defence of *necessity*; for example, in English law, if a woman commits a crime (a negative input), such as stealing food, to avert a greater evil, such as the death through starvation of herself and her child, then in principle a defence of necessity is possible. As discussed earlier with respect to the duress, the defence in this case could be interpreted in a number of ways. Most important, it could be argued that in some situations, 'need' restricts choice to such a degree that it effectively renders the actor's input zero; thus, need can act as an *input moderator*.

Alternatively, it could be suggested that the offender deserves some punishment, but he or she will probably have already suffered negative outcomes in being driven to this course of action. In the case of necessity, it seems that the law actually leans toward the former; a successful defence on grounds of necessity renders conduct lawful, rather than acting as an excuse. It is very interesting to note, however, that the defence of necessity may not be available if the need to act is brought about by negligence on the accused's part (Cross, Jones and Card, 1988, p. 584). Hence, as the Equity as Desert model predicts, those who through their own choices place themselves in need are liable for any actions that may result from this.

Of course, as initimated earlier, need can also act an input moderator for positive outcomes; so, for example, a person whose choice to work is restricted by unchosen need may be deserving of compensation; for example, we may wish award outcomes on the basis of the contribution .the person might have made had he or she not been in need (see, Wagstaff et al., 1994)

Relative need and people who do nothing

All this has obvious implications for how we view the appropriate outcomes for a participant who has contributed nothing in a material sense. In a number of empirical studies we have demonstrated that, unless choice or responsibility are clearly absent or unequal, or differential need is made very salient, then quite overwhelmingly the preferred allocation is to give a zero input worker zero outcomes; when a person does nothing, he or she receives nothing (see, for example, Wagstaff, 1994; Wagstaff and Perfect, 1992; Wagstaff and Worthington, 1997; Wagstaff, Chadwick, and Brunas-Wagstaff, 1996; Wagstaff, Huggins and Perfect, 1996; Wagstaff et al., 1994). However, Wagstaff and Worthington (1997) have also shown that allocation to a zero input worker 'in need' (that is, a person who does nothing at work, but requires money for basic food and shelter), is very much dependent on the context. Thus, in the absence of comparative information, subjects tended to be unsympathetic towards a needy worker who did nothing. However, when subjects were surreptiously reminded that criminal offenders in British prisons (that is, those whose inputs are *negative*) have their basic needs for food and shelter met, subjects were far more willing to offer the zero input worker money for food and shelter.

As suggested above, this kind of comparative analysis allows an explanation as to why even the most rigid desert supporter desert might consider it perfectly 'just' to satisfy the basic needs of those who have chosen to be lazy, or have otherwise made themselves destitute. If laziness or a lack of prudence are not considered serious crimes against society, then perhaps it looks more reasonable to accord those who are responsible for their destitution at least the same basic resources we provide for serious offenders who have deliberately harmed others.

Need, opportunity and justifications for inequality

The idea of compensation for need is usually associated with more egalitarian conceptions of justice, however, this is certainly not always the case. Need adjustment can also be used to justify inegalitarian conceptions of justice. A particularly striking example of the use of need as a justification for unequal shares of resources comes from the historical literature on intelligence testing.

For most of the early part of the 20th century the psychological literature on intelligence testing was dominated by the idea that there exists a faculty of intelligence that is largely inherited (Kamin, 1974; Herrnstein, 1973). Within a conception of desert that rests on personal responsibility, however, there is clearly a conflict between the idea of a meritocracy based on intelligence, and the view that intelligence is largely inherited. If we are not responsible for (do not choose) our levels of intelligence, how can we claim that we deserve more for the exercise of this faculty? To its supporters, however, the idea of a meritocracy based on intelligence has been simple to justify; their logic is that the most intelligent *need* more to satisfy than the feeble minded. Consider the following passage from Henry Goddard's invited lectures at Princetown University in 1919 in which he attacks the opponents of meritocracy (cited by Kamin, 1974, pp. 22-23, my emphasis).

These men in their ultra altruistic and humane attitude, their desire to be fair to the workman, maintain that the great inequalities in social life are wrong and unjust. For example, here is a man who says .... "I live in a home that is artistically decorated, carpets, high-priced furniture, expensive pictures and other luxuries; there is a labourer that lives in a hovel with no carpets, no pictures, and the coarsest kind of furniture. It is not right, it is unjust" ..... As we have said, the argument is fallacious. It assumes that the labourer is on the same mental level with the man who is defending him Now the fact is, that workman may have a ten year intelligence while you have twenty. To demand for him such a home as you enjoy is as absurd as it would be to insist that every labourer should receive a graduate fellowship .... *the different levels of intelligence require different treatment to make them happy.*

The implication of this argument is clear, *true* equality (in terms of ultimate outcome satisfaction) demands that the most intelligent should receive more resources and opportunities. Consequently, there is no conflict between awarding more to the most intelligent and justice as desert, because even if the more intelligent are no more deserving in terms of their inputs, and should receive equal outcomes, to award true equal outcomes they should receive more resources according to their *needs*. But even then, Goddard cannot resist backing up this need based argument with one based on a more recognisable form of desert (cited by Kamin, p. 23).

As for an equal distribution of the wealth of the world that is equally absurd. The man of intelligence has spent his money wisely, has saved until he has enough to provide for his needs in case of sickness, while the man of low intelligence, no matter how much money he would have earned, would have spent much of it foolishly and would never have anything ahead .... These facts are appreciated. But it is not so fully appreciated that the cause is to be found in the fixed character of mental levels

Note again, how Goddard appears to be using elements from the EAD model to justify his position. According the EAD model, it is not necessary for participants to have actual equal opportunities to perform inputs, it is only necessary to establish how they would have behaved had they been given the opportunity. Hence Goddard's view here is that even if the less intellectually able had been given the opportunity to input as much as the more intelligent, they would have squandered their outcomes (that is substituted more permanent outcomes with those related to temporary pleasures), and thus ended up in a position of poverty in any case.

The idea of need as an adjustment within the EAD principle, can also perhaps help explain philosophers such as Aristotle were able to tolerate apparently gross disparities in the 'equal opportunity' or 'equal starting place' assumption of EAD. In Plato's world, and that of ancient Sumeria, Persia and India, the 'equal starting place' was displaced from this particular mortal existence. As a result, any inequalities that occurred at birth were just. On the other hand, Aristotle, whilst committed to the idea that ideally justice assumes a facility to choose between alternatives, appeared to offer no equivalent justification for inequalities at birth. Instead he attempted to justify inequalities at birth by arguing that people differed in their natural capacities to make reasoned choices; thus he says 'the slave has no deliberative faculty at all, the woman has, but is without authority, and the child has, but is without maturity' (P1, p. 1260a). In other words, slaves and women, are not capable of making responsible choices on their own, and hence (like children and animals) must be ruled for their own good. In effect, Aristotle was justifying unequal treatment in terms of adjustment for 'need'.

To Aristotle, slaves and women, like children and animals, possess different 'needs' to men in a political state, hence it would actually be unjust to treat all as though they possessed equal capacities. Because of their different capacities, women, children and slaves have what modern economists would term 'different utility functions' and must be treated differently from free men. Women, who by nature lack the capacity for authority, would be receiving less than they deserve if they were not to be ruled by men. Similarly, it would be unjust not to give slaves the benefits of authority, and as long as they fulfil their role in serving their betters, they are entitled to their appropriate outcomes (food, water, shelter etc.); but it would of course be ridiculous to award them the same things offered to their superiors, because, like Goddard's 'labourers', they would be unable to appreciate the better things in life, or use them appropriately; in fact, because they cannot deliberate, if they were given the same outcomes as free men, they might even accidentally harm themselves and end up with less than their deserved outcomes.

The idea of need as an outcome adjustment is thus not a doctrine that is necessarily to be associated to liberalism or the political left; when combined with the notion of genetically limited capacities, the idea of distribution according to need can provide, and has been used as a powerful justification for some extremely inegalitarian views. It is perhaps one of the great ironies of political history that, from the Egyptian Pharaohs to the Third Reich, those who have wished to impose their authority on others, deny equal opportunity, and reduce whole sections of society poverty and slavery, have frequently provided arguments based on 'need' to justify their actions. The rich, powerful and intelligent need more to satisfy them; the stupid and poor not only need less but thrive better with less than their superiors, and slaves, like animals, need the discipline and guidance of their superiors. The implication is clear, even if all were given equal opportunity to perform inputs, and even if all inputs were judged equal, the rich and intelligent and could still legitimately claim a greater share of resources, and do this with perfect justice. This point is well made in this classic statement by Anthony Trollope (who actually claimed to oppose slavery), published in 1859 (cited by Walvin, 1992, p. 328). The 'negro', he says,

is capable of the hardest bodily work .... .but he is idle, unambitious as to worldly position, sensual, and content with very little .... I think that he seldom understands the purpose of industry, the objects of truth, or the results of honesty. (The blacks) are a servile race, fitted by nature for the hardest physical work, and apparently at present fitted for little else.

To Trollope, natural law prescribed the needs of blacks and their white masters to be very different, such that, to experience equivalent outcome levels the former needed very little, whereas the latter needed wealth and status. In fact, as the blacks were also servile, the whites were due some compensation for the fact that they were obliged to rule over them. We can find essentially the same form of argument in Samuel Johnson's statement that 'As the mind must govern the hand, so in every society the man of intelligence must direct the man of labour'

(1775/1984, p. 96). In other words, it is not unjust that the labourer should be ruled by his intellectual betters; it is for his own benefit. And in a form more acceptable to modern democratic society, the same kind of argument enables a justification of the idea that people should have an equal opportunity to achieve those positions to which their 'talents' or 'abilities' fit them, regardless of how those talents or abilities derive (see, for example, Friedman and Friedman, 1980). If people with different talents have different utility functions or 'needs', then for equal satisfaction of their needs, they must be allowed to seek different positions.

Conclusion

To sum up, according to the EAD model, equity, equality and need, are not necessarily three different principles of justice; rather they may reflect different emphases in the interpretation of the same desert principle. Consequently, when attempting to justify or rationalize a particular allocation rule (that they may have selected for reasons unconnected with justice), we should expect people to appeal to one or more of the core arguments identified in this chapter.

PART 5

THE HISTORICAL DEVELOPMENT OF EQUITY AND DESERT

CHAPTER 17

STOICISM, CHRISTIANITY AND THE SCHOLASTICS

If the Equity as Desert principle is fundamental to our conceptions of justice, then we should find evidence of it permeating not only the ideas of the ancients, and some elements of modern psychology, philosophy and legal theory, but the whole of the history of philosophy. In the next three chapters, therefore, I will attempt to review briefly some of the other important historical figures and events that have influenced Western theorizing on justice, and show how some of the views that might at first appear at variance with the idea of desert can be readily understood in terms of the operation of the EAD model; indeed, the EAD model may provide a valuable insight into the structure of some of the most important arguments in moral philosophy. I will also attempt to draw attention to some of the historical circumstances that may have been influential in causing the conceptual muddle that confronts modern writers on justice. Of course it is impossible in a work of this length to discuss all of the most significant characters and events that have shaped modern philosophical thought on justice, however, hopefully, this analysis may act as an interpretational scheme that readers can apply more widely.

The equal shares rule in history

The most obvious objection to the idea that justice fundamentally concerns a proportional desert principle, is that throughout history we can find examples of philosophies and societies espousing the principle of equal shares, including its most sophisticated form, shares according to needs. However, although the doctrine of equal shares might appear to have ancient origins, there is little historical evidence to suggest that, in Western thought, an equality/needs principle in this form has ever played a prominent role as a justice principle in its own right. Thus Fogarty (1961) notes that societies have existed in which 'status as a consumer' is assessed separately from 'status in terms of contribution', but he states, 'they are special cases' (p. 268). In fact, Sampson (1975) argues that it was not actually until the 18th century that most of our modern conceptions of human equality were developed (see also, MacIntyre, 1982).

There is little evidence for a widespread acceptance of equal shares as the major distributive rule in the ancient world. Plato refers to equality in terms of 'distribution by lot' as a method 'to avoid disaffection among the masses'; and Aristotle notes that equality in the distribution of property can be used, 'to prevent the citizens from quarrelling'; though he suggests it is not very successful in this respect. Interestingly, these reasons would seem to reflect the same considerations of prudence noted by psychologists; that is, in some circumstances, equality in terms of lot or equal shares can be used to avoid conflict. However, philosophers such as Socrates, Plato and Aristotle considered these sorts of equality to be vastly inferior to the true and real equality of geometrical proportion.

It can also be noted that equal shares is not seen as fundamental to the Eastern religions of Confucianism, Hinduism, and Buddhism; though, all of these religions contain a very familiar pattern; that is, the ultimate reward, *telos* or *summum bonum*, whether it be union with God or nature, is accomplished ultimately through the voluntary pursuit of virtue and prohibition of vice.

However, perhaps the most obvious candidate for an ancient egalitarian philosophy would be stoicism.

Stoicism, as a school of thought, was founded by Zeno around 350-260 B.C. To the stoics, people were born naturally equal, and discriminations between people on account of sex, class and race were unjust and contrary to the law of nature. However, although many stoics preached universal love and downgraded the importance of material possessions, the stoic doctrine of 'equality of all men' meant, fundamentally, not that all should receive equal shares of everything regardless of their actions, but that all humans possess an intelligence that enables them to know the difference between virtue and vice, and to choose between them. In fact, once stoic views on justice are seen in their wider religious context, the disparity between their views and the more inegalitarian proposals of Plato and Aristotle is less obvious.

The stoics defined justice as the disposition to give each his due according to natural law (see Bodenheimer, 1962; MacIntyre, 1988; Wright, 1991). For instance, Cicero (106-43 B.C.), the Roman lawyer and follower of stoicism, argued that all natural law is right, and what is right is just and fair. But what does natural law dictate? To the stoics the only true good is virtue (*virtus* or 'nature perfected'), not health, wealth, or status. Others things may be 'preferred' (such as a degree of wealth and health), but only virtue is truly good, and only vice truly bad or evil. The stoics saw themselves as the descendants of Socrates, thus, in true Socratic fashion, Cicero (1991) argues that a virtuous action is one motivated by a virtuous disposition in accordance with 'right reason'. Virtue resides in the will; it is an activity of the soul, uninfluenced by chance or fortune. Virtue and vice thus cannot be judged solely by the external nature of actions and their consequences, that may be influenced by chance factors, but people can be held 'responsible' for their actions; they can choose between good and evil. Thus Cicero says, 'it is an essential property of virtue to exercise choice among the things that are according to nature, those who put all on a level, so as to make everything the same one way or another with no exercise of choice, actually abolish virtue' (1991, p. 33). Hence, as Russell (1979) puts it, to the stoics, 'everything really good or bad in a man's life depends only on himself .... virtue, which alone is truly good, rests entirely with the individual. Therefore every man has perfect freedom, provided he emancipates himself from mundane desires' (pp. 262-263).

Stoicism contains a number of inherent contradictions; for instance, if, as the stoics claim, it is virtuous to be benevolent with ones possessions, but material possessions are not necessary for virtue, why would anyone want to be shown such benevolence? And, if pain and suffering are not necessarily evils, why should we label those who inflict pain and suffering on others, evil doers? Also, many stoics had a very fatalistic view of the Universe that would seem to contradict the notion that people can freely choose to do good and evil (see Russell, 1979). Nevertheless, the belief in the fundamental equality of people in terms of their *capacities* to achieve virtue, and the fact that virtue can be unrelated, if not sometimes negatively related, to poverty and suffering, means something very significant in stoic philosophy; *everyone (more or less) has an opportunity to perform those actions that result in the ultimate good, virtue or harmony with nature.* Moreover, as Cicero (1991) argues, in stoic philosophy, a virtuous life is the only true *happy* (or 'blessed') life. The virtuous man is truly rich in a way that is not possible for one who possesses only material wealth, and the vicious man can never be happy.

Cicero tends to use the term justice in a way similar to the way Aristotle uses the term *'dikaiosune'*. That is, he uses it first in the particular sense, as *one* of the virtues; that which requires a person to 'give each his due'. So, for example, justice requires repaying debts, restoring to its owner that which has been given on trust, and forbidding the robbing of others to enrich oneself (all of which could be construed as maintaining equity). However, Cicero also uses it in the wider sense to refer to that all that conforms to natural law, or the ordering of the cosmos; for all natural law is just. Used in the latter sense, it is notable again how stoic scheme of ultimate justice again coincides well with the EAD principle. In the general scheme of things, everyone has an opportunity to perform those positive activities for which the ultimate reward is the experience of acting in exact harmony with nature, or happiness. As a result, happiness (outcomes) will be distributed according to one's good and bad dispositions (inputs), uninfluenced by the vagaries of fortune.

One of the most important characteristics of stoic philosophy, therefore, is that downplays the influence of material possessions in the achievement of one's ends; thus there is no obvious personal advantage to be gained by amassing material possessions. Also, pain and suffering are not necessarily to be construed evils of themselves. Given this, it is perhaps not surprising that the stoics placed little emphasis on a system that distributes material wealth to the virtuous, and inflicts pain and suffering on wrongdoers. Instead justice involves living up to reciprocal obligations, repaying one's debts, and not gaining at the expense of others; moreover, nature makes sure that justice it is ultimately done because the virtuous end up happy, and the vicious, unhappy. In other words, the stoics could be considered avid adherents to the EAD principle, but to them its ultimate expression was not to be found in the distribution of material resources, or the infliction of pain and suffering.

Early Christianity

The other most obvious candidate for a justice philosophy based on an equality/needs principle is the sort of primitive communism practised by some of the first converts to Christianity in Jerusalem (Forgarty, 1961); but again, considered in its wider religious context, it is evident the early Christians placed a strong emphasis on desert.

Certainly, many of the ideas of the early Christians seemed directly opposed to the *lex talionis* principle that was so popular in the Jewish religious law. Thus Matthew says, 'Ye have heard that it hath been said, an eye for an eye, and a tooth for a tooth. But I say unto you, that ye resist not evil; but whoever shall smite thee on thy right cheek, turn to him the other also' (5, 38-39). Also

Luke encourages you to 'love your enemies, (and) do good to them that hate you', as well as 'Give every man that asketh of thee; and of him that taketh away thy goods ask them not again' (6, 27-30). This early Christian concept of the unconditional positive regard for others thus seems totally incompatible with any 'reward for good, punishment for bad' justice principle. However, the picture looks rather different once we realize that, ultimately, justice was not something to be achieved in this world, rather it was something to be administered by God in the next.

Christian philosophy was, of course, a development of Jewish thought, and the Jews believed that there was an after-life in addition to this earthly existence, and that it was in this after-life than true divine justice would administered; the righteous would be rewarded and sinners punished. Russell (1979) argues that there were quite pragmatic reasons for proposing the notion of divine justice; he says, 'Jewish philosophy was always simple. Yahweh (God) developed from a tribal deity into the sole omnipotent God who created heaven and earth; divine justice, when it was seen not to confer earthly prosperity upon the virtuous, was transferred to heaven, which entailed belief in immortality' (p. 327). The significance of this idea of *divine justice* which turns up in the Christian approach to ethics cannot be underestimated; in fact, the early Christians doubted the capacity of anyone other than God to make an informed, unhypocritical judgement about another's merits or demerits; to them, perfect justice between individuals was actually impossible in this life.

To the early Christians this often miserable present life was seen as simple a preparation for the next life; indeed, in the language of EAD, all we can do in this life is to perform the 'inputs' in the scheme, and endure whatever might come about, in the hope that we will receive our true 'just' deserts, or 'outcomes' in the next. Thus in Luke's Gospel he points out the futility of seeking rewards in this life; instead he asserts, 'love your enemies and do good, and lend, hoping for nothing; and your reward shall be great, and ye shall be the children of the Highest: for he is kind unto the unthankful and to the evil' (6, 35). The last part of this verse seems to suggest that God cares not how you have behaved in this life, but later Luke follows the more traditional line, arguing that the person who does not follow these rules will be like a house without a foundation, and will be ruined (6, 49). He also points out how proportional requital is a fundamental part of God's scheme; thus he says, 'Judge not, and ye shall not be judged: condemn not, and ye shall not be condemned: forgive and ye shall be forgiven; give and it shall be given unto you .... For with the same measure that ye mete withal it shall be measured to you again' (6, 37-38). In other words, what you do will come back on you, in exact proportion. The essential message was God might be forgiving and merciful, but his patience is not inexhaustible, and ultimately justice will be done at the Last Judgement. As the Book of Revelation tells us, 'He that overcometh shall inherit all things; and I will be his God and he shall be my son. But the fearful, and the abominable, and murderers, and whoremongers, and sorcerers, and idolaters, and all liars, shall have their part in the lake which burneth with fire and brimstone: which is the second death' (Chap. 7-8).

The idea of a omnipotent, just God, however, posed particular problems for Christian thinkers who had to contend with problems such as how a just God could allow so much apparently undeserved suffering in this earthly life. They also had to reconcile the idea that God has planned and can foresee everything, with the notion that people possess free-will or choice, and can choose to be virtuous or vicious. The result was a set of intriguing conceptual and semantic manoeuvres.

St Augustine and original sin
St Augustine of Hippo (353-430 A.D.), for example, like his Greek and Roman predecessors, defined justice, not as equal shares, but as 'that virtue which assigns to everyone his due' (5th Cent. A.D./1976; p. 882). In one of his most famous works, the 'City of God', he attempts to argue that the concept of free-will is not incompatible with the idea that God has planned and can foresee everything. Indeed, he says that it is only because we have free-will that we can

say that 'it is with justice that rewards are appointed for good actions and punishments for sins' (p. 195). So how then can we account for what appears to be undeserved suffering in the world? Augustine's answer is to invoke the idea of 'original sin'; he argues that somehow the souls of all people (including new born infants) are tainted by the sins of Adam in the Garden of Eden. This adaptation of the ancient transmigration of souls doctrine seems to fit very uneasily with Augustine's view that justice should be based on free choice. Nevertheless, the form of the argument is clearly based on desert; our sufferings in this life are never undeserved, they are 'just' punishment for our sins (even if those sins were committed by the part of our souls that attach to Adam). Moreover, to account for the fact that not all suffer equally in this world, and that sometimes the wicked seem to prosper, Augustine argues that God leaves some suffering for the next world; if all sin were punished on earth, he suggests, there would be no need for the Last Judgement.

However, if all are sinners, how does God decide who to save? At this point Augustine's arguments about justice seem to come totally unstuck. Having decided that all men are sinners, and all must be punished, Augustine lands himself in this position of being unable to justify why some should be saved and not others. The result is something that is patently unjust in terms of Augustine's other views on the subject. He says, to be saved from the fires of Hell, Man needs salvation; but salvation is not granted on the basis of merit in this life, but it is predestined for a chosen elect, by the grace of God.

It was in recognition of this problem that, around the time of Augustine, some sought instead to espouse the view of monk called Pelagius. Pelagius denied the concept of original sin, and argued that God had endowed Man with free-will so that salvation could be *chosen*. Nevertheless, the idea of an elect, predestined by God to be saved, was to arise later, particularly in the views of Martin Luther (1483-1546) and, even more so, John Calvin (1509-1564), and was to present the same problems: as Raphael (1980) says, 'a firm acceptance of .... the Calvinist doctrine of predestination appears to produce a conflict with the further presupposition of biblical theology that God is perfectly good and just. If God has these ethical attributes, how can he predestine men to heaven and others to hell, irrespective of what they do in the course of their lives? (p. 94). Augustine recognized the problem, but his answer was basically to avoid the issue by arguing that, as mere mortals, we are incapable of understanding the ways of God.

A similar view was adopted by St Thomas Aquinas (1229-1272). In his 'Summa Theologica', Aquinas argues that the reason why God chooses some and reprobates others 'has no reason, except for the divine will' (1929, p. 330), that we cannot question. However, Aquinas comes up with an additional idea to get round the problem. He also says that justice is 'to pay what is due' (p. 297), but goes on to suggest that it is not an injustice for God to give a person more or less 'gratuitously', 'provided he deprives nobody of his due' (p. 331). This argument seems to involve turning a blind eye to the justice requirement of 'treating equals equally'; if justice is 'to pay what is due', then the award to some of a gratuity that is not 'due' must result in some receiving more than is their 'due' relative to others not treated so generously.

Another problem for the early Christians was the idea of a merciful God. If a just God rewards good and punishes evil, yet shows mercy to those who commit evil, how can God be both merciful and just? In an attempt to deal with this issue, Aquinas repeatedly refers to justice *and* mercy as two separate virtues, and treats them accordingly; hence he says, God shows *mercy* to those he has chosen for glory and dispenses *justice* by punishing reprobates (1929, p. 30). Moreover, he says, when mercy overrules justice, it punishes 'short of what is deserved' (p. 304); the implication clearly being that justice is about desert, not mercy. But does this mean that God is sometimes merciful rather than just? No, says Aquinas, for God is not only just when he rewards merit and punishes the wicked, but also when he is merciful, because by being merciful God he is giving back to himself what he is due! Aquinas apparently borrows this somewhat unconvincing logic from St Anselm (1033-1109).

The idea of awarding dues to an omnipotent deity thus presented particular problems for the early Christian philosophers, not the least of which was a possible conflict between what God deserves on the basis of his services (never disservices) to mankind, and what the rest of mankind deserve on the basis of their good and bad actions to God and each other; by forgiving sinners we serve God and give him His due for his services to us, but in doing so, we fail give the sinners their dues in terms of punishment. Aquinas saw the problem, but did not (perhaps could not) resolve it.

Nevertheless, problems and inconsistencies apart, the important point to emphasize here is that, although the doctrines of early Christianity might have appeared to espouse the virtues of mercy, humility, benevolence and sharing, these were not seen as the essence of *justice*; though they could act as *components* of justice within a wider scheme. Instead, ultimately true and perfect justice was something to be dispensed by God in the next life, and was defined fundamentally in terms of *desert*. Eventually God would give each his due, by rewarding of good and punishing bad, according to proper order and proportion.

Aquinas: Aristotle revived

Both Augustine and Aquinas found themselves grappling with the problem of how an omnipotent and just deity could create and operate in a world that was manifestly unjust, but without the more coherent reincarnationist belief systems that had served their predecessors (including Plato) so well. Ultimately, however, Aquinas was able to develop a rather more consistent and recognisable 'just deserts' philosophy, and, notably, he was able to do this by reading Aristotle. Indeed, Aquinas's views and those of his followers were to have an influence on justice theorizing and practice that survives to-day, and are worth exploring in a little more detail.

Up until the beginning of the 12th Century Aristotle's major works had been all but lost to Western philosophers, but during the lifetime of Aquinas' teacher, Albertus Magnus (1193-1280), they had come into Europe through the

Arabs via Spain. Aquinas' works thus represent a fascinating fusion of Christianity and this new-found Aristotelianism. According to Aquinas, the ultimate good to be for all rational creatures, or *summum bonum*, is eternal life and the direct contemplation of God. True happiness is thus not to be found in the satisfaction of physical pleasures, or wealth, or power. However, although Aquinas argues that this end is only achievable by divine grace, he also proposes that it is possible to increase one's chances of achieving grace by behaving virtuously, and building up merit to prepare oneself for God's forgiveness and eternal life. Thus, for those fortunate enough to be chosen, the *summum bonum* can be seen as a reward for virtue (if one is lucky enough to be chosen). Consequently, it is through the exercise of virtue (by, for example, acting with justice, fortitude, charity and temperance) and the prohibition of vice (by, for example, refraining from heresy, envy, sloth, and lust), that one builds up merit to prepare the way for the ultimate judgement.

Also, and very significantly, Aquinas argues that all creatures who possess reason have free-will and are equally endowed with the capacity to be able to work out what is 'good' and what is 'bad' conduct, and to be able to choose between the two. They can do this either through reason 'in the heart', or through consulting God's written law. Aquinas also puts forward a number of factors that influence the gravity of a sin. These include the circumstances surrounding the act, whether or not the individual was capable of knowing whether the act was sinful; whether it was done through passion or malice, and whether it was committed under the stress of great temptation. The influence of Aristotle's theory of responsibility is obvious here.

In other words, the basic scheme of 'reward for good', 'penalties for bad', and with an equal choice to choose between good and bad, was dominant in Aquinas' scheme, although as in many of the religions that preceded Christianity, ultimate justice was dispensed in the next-life. In the language of EAD, this earthly life is more about our 'inputs'. This is not to say, however, that St Thomas and his followers had no place for a system of reward and punishment on earth; 'justice' was itself deemed to be a virtue that could be practised alongside the other virtues. Indeed, Aquinas and the medieval 'schoolmen' or 'scholastics' who followed him, were to devise a highly sophisticated theory of the 'just wage' and the 'just price' that was to have a profound and lasting effect on economic and political thinking.

The scholastics

The 'schoolmen' or 'scholastics' were so called because of their work in universities, and Aquinas was one of the first to be labelled in this way. Although the scholastic doctrine shifted in emphasis over the centuries, there exists a large core of continuity that has remained intact in 20th Century Catholic teaching, as well as trades union policy (see, for example, Fogarty, 1961; Oakeshott, 1939). This can be summarized as follows.

According to the medieval schoolmen, payment for goods and services is a matter of justice. Justice is to give to each his due, and pay is a person's due, not something to be fixed arbitrarily, according to the whim of the paymaster. Underlying their philosophy is the idea that pay should be equally proportional to work. Thus in his comprehensive work on the scholastic approach to justice, 'The Just Wage', Fogarty (1961) argues that, 'The normal rule in all societies to date has been that a man's general status should be linked to his performance at work, and the scholastics approve this rule' (p. 268).

According to Fogarty, scholastic writers recognized three kinds of justice; justice between individuals (commutative justice), justice in the overall distribution of rewards and burdens amongst individuals by an authority (distributive justice), and justice in terms of the whole structure of society (social justice). In modern jargon, these conceptions could be considered equivalent to gradations from 'microjustice' to 'macrojustice'; but they do not represent radically different conceptions of justice with different rules; the same basic principles underlie each, though it may be necessary to modify one to achieve another. For instance, when isolated individuals make local bargains, or employers distribute pay amongst employees, they may not realize how their transactions fit in with justice in society as a whole (they may agree to accept or pay more or less than the appropriate and accepted societal norm). People must constantly realise, therefore, that they are participating in a collaborative venture according to the law of God, and it is up to the state or government to intervene when necessary (but only when necessary).

The first basic rule underpinning the scholastic approach to the just wage is *equal pay for equal working capacity*. Note, this rule is not just 'equal pay for equal work', it is equal pay for equal working *capacity*. Thus when a man contracts to work for another he is entitled to pay equal to the value of the work of which he is capable, given the opportunity; this means he must be free to choose or decline the contract (he must not be a slave for example), and must not suffer wage cuts or dismissals through the incompetence of employers. In EAD terms this first principle could be interpreted to mean, *equal outcomes for equal inputs under conditions of equal opportunity*. The scholastics were well aware that wages will rise and fall according to supply and demand in the market place, but they argued that, to ensure the successful operation of this principle, attempts should be made to make wages as stable as possible in the long run.

Moreover, the scholastics argued that it is the *social value* of the labour that is relevant within the general structure of society that counts as the 'input', not values determined by transactions between individuals, or small groups. In other words, the value of a person's work should be determined by the contribution it makes to the good of society as a whole; it is not something to be determined by its usefulness to isolated individuals. In this way equals can truly be treated as equals. In other words the 'inputs' in the scheme are *services to society*, and equal services deserve equal reward; thus Pope Pius XI says, 'if the social and individual character of labour be overlooked, it can neither be justly valued nor recompensed according to equivalence' (1931/1939, p. 70). It also follows that the 'just price' of a good or service is to be determined by 'what is usually costs', within the community as a whole; it would be unjust, for example, for a doctor to charge the sick in a particular area more than usual for his services just because he is the only doctor available there. This means that businesses must follow a code of practice, and not attempt to charge excessive prices or undercut each other. Thus Pope Pius XI adds, 'If .... the business does not make enough money to pay the workman a just wage, either because it is overwhelmed with unjust burdens, or because it is compelled to sell its products at an unjustly low price, those who injure it are guilty of a grievous wrong; for it is they who deprive the workers of a just wage, and force them to accept terms which are unjust' (1931/1939, p. 70).

Allied to this is the requirement that each man should receive *pay according to status*. This means that a man should be paid what is necessary to maintain himself and his family at a standard commensurate with his social and occupational class. The higher the status of the occupation, the greater the assumed value to the community, and therefore the greater the wage; moreover, those who inherit wealth must treat like a 'salary' and serve the public in ways they could not otherwise afford. There is thus no objection to some being richer than others so long as this is justified in terms of services to the common good. In terms of EAD, this principle requires that *greater the input, the greater the outcome*, and vice versa. Moreover, people should be allowed to rise in status (increase inputs) if they are willing to acquire the necessary skills. This would seem to be consistent again with the equal opportunity component of EAD. However, the baseline is also important; it is unjust for a well-behaved worker to be given less than is necessary to maintain him and his family. In the language of EAD, it would be unjust, for example, for a well-behaved worker (who contributes positive inputs) to suffer privations (negative outcomes) when he or she does not deserve them.

Pope Leo XIII presents the scholastic position as follows; in agreeing wages, 'there underlies a dictate of natural justice more imperious and ancient than any bargain between man and man, namely, that wages ought not to be insufficient to support a frugal and well-behaved wage earner' (1891/1939, p.

69); and Pope Pius XI adds, that it is wrong 'to abuse the tender years of children' or 'the weakness of women' by depriving their breadwinner of an adequate wage, hence 'Every effort must therefore be made, that fathers of families receive a wage sufficient to meet adequately normal domestic needs. If under present circumstances this is not always feasible social justice demands that such reforms be introduced without delay' (1931/1939, p. 70).

It also follows that, as an integral part of the idea of pay according to status, provision or allowance should also be made for *need* that arises through uncontrollable factors such as old age, sickness, unemployment and old age, and sufficient resources should be made available to enable a person to work at his occupation ('needs' such as tools and materials). Again within EAD this would seem to relate to the ideas of 'need as an outcome adjustment', to cover unforseen or undeserved reductions in outcomes, and need in terms of maintenance of the opportunity to provide one's inputs.

Potentially more problematic in terms of the EAD principle is the scholastic idea that people should also be allowed to rise in status if their 'natural capacities', allow them to. If 'natural capacities' are seen as the products of 'accident' then those who possess them have an unfair advantage. However, in an attempt to come to terms with this difficulty there is some indication that they attempted to apply the 'needs' argument I described in the previous chapter. That is, along with other factors, needs increase with productive capacity, so the greater one's capacities the greater one's needs (Fogarty, 1961). The scholastics also had a problem with inherited wealth; thus whilst they argued that those who inherit wealth must justify their wealth with extra service, they did not deal with the problem that those born destitute are never given the choice to justify such a reward. The problems of awarding outcomes according to natural capacities, and justifying the inheritance of private property were issues that later writers were to pursue vigorously.

Another problem for the scholastics was how to define exactly the value of someone's work or services. Pope Pius XI talks of the importance of maintaining

'A proper proportion between different wages' according to 'proper proportions between the prices charged for the products of the various economic groups, agricultural, industrial, and so forth' (1931/1939, p. 71). But how is a 'proper proportion' between wages to be determined? In fact, the scholastics found themselves in the same position as Aristotle when discussing 'reciprocal proportion' (and more recently, Sadurski, 1985, when defining what counts as an input in his desert theory); that is, should the factor that determines the monetary value of services and products be the amount of labour time, or degree of skill involved in producing or providing them, or the demand or need for them?

However, the common view amongst even the early scholastics was essentially Aristotelian; that is, ultimately the feature of services that gives a right to pay is not the labour time or work rate involved *per se*, but the *usefulness* of such labour in supplying human needs; that is, the extent to which the service is beneficial to the community. Thus, Langerstein (1340-1397) says, 'The goodness or value of anything has to be discovered by reference to the end for which it is brought about'; which in the case of commutative justice is, 'is to supply human needs' (cited by Fogarty, p. 262). The 'usefulness' of labour was based on a number of interrelated factors factors including the quantity and quality of service, the time it lasts, the skill, health and sobriety of the worker, and supply and demand in the overall market. Thus, for example, Antonio of Florence (1389-1459) wrote that 'the lawyer can charge in proportion to his eloquence and the importance of the case, and of course to what the market rate is: the architect and doctor likewise' (cited by Fogarty, p. 263). In choosing work that provides them with satisfactory remuneration, workers should therefore not only pay due attention to the time and effort involved, but the usefulness of that work in providing for the needs of the community as a whole; for on the latter depends the evaluation of the former. Hence, in the 16th century, the Professor of Louvin pointed out that 'the more learned anyone is the bigger the salary he can ask, and yet the less he works' (cited by Fogarty, 1961, p. 262); the logic here being that the learned person contributes more to the community than a person who puts in more raw effort but to a less useful end.

However, it was important also for the scholastics that workers should not unduly lose out when the demand for their services changes unexpectedly; thus workers must be paid according to their existing status and capacity for long enough to let them find new jobs, or adjust to the new situation. In other words, in accordance with the concept of 'commensurateness' I outlined earlier, workers should receive outcomes equivalent to the social benefits they would *reasonably expect* their work to generate (the social value or 'usefulness' of their work to the community). Therefore, should the demand for their work fall in an unpredictable way, workers must be given payment commensurate with the value of the work that they would have performed had they not been affected by circumstances beyond their control.

The scholastics also believed that although God is able to fix with mathematical precision the exact price that should be paid for a good or service based on all of these considerations, since the Fall of Man, people can only judge such matters imprecisely. Nevertheless, they thought that it is possible to make approximate estimates of the value of work using the above criteria, and suggested some ways in which they might be accomplished. For instance, they argued that it is better for wages to be fixed on the basis of the views of as large a number of people as possible, that is, the 'common estimate', and that employees should have maximum flexibility and freedom to seek those jobs that suit them best. We can note again here, the overlap with the EAD principle in terms of seeking agreement about what is a 'commensurate' outcome for a particular input, and providing people with the opportunity to choose between inputs. It is also important that supply and demand in the market place is not distorted by the whims of buyers and sellers, and by practises such as bribery and monopoly. The market price for goods and services must reflect the true social value of the work. And if it does not, then prices should be regulated by government. Moreover, just as those who work must receive their just reward, the idle must not expect to receive something for nothing; they must be forced to work or deported. Within the scholastic scheme, the voluntary idle are a social liability. Finally, on the whole the scholastics were not in favour of the idea that one should be able to offset one sort of positive outcome for another; for instance, they did not consider it reasonable to pay a man less because his job carries rank and prestige. Apart from some marginal cases, if a job is prestigious it should be paid a high reward accordingly; to do otherwise would be to undermine the value of the job within the general scheme.

There were obvious problems with the scholastic approach; modern economists have considered it to be naive (see, for example, Robinson, 1964), and, as I have intimated, later critics were to argue that it still does not pay sufficient attention to the effects of chance or fortune. Nevertheless, the scholastic approach to the just wage and just price clearly represents one of the most sophisticated expositions of the concept of desert ever presented, and its influences are still very apparent today. Yet, as Forgarty points out, all it does is elucidate a series of more or less timeless principles; he says, 'The essentials of a contract to work for pay are the same today as in the middle ages or the ancient world ....' (pp. 9-11). And if Fogarty's statement is accurate, then presumably the idea of EAD is 'timeless' too, for the principles governing the scholastic approach to justice bear a striking resemblance to the desert model I have identified. These are, outcomes (pay) must be awarded in equal proportion to inputs (work), such that the greater the input, the greater the outcome, under conditions in which the outcomes are commensurate with the inputs; there is equal opportunity to perform inputs, and adjustment is made for blameless or unchosen need.

Importantly also, within scholastic thought there is a recognition that although simple 'labour-cost' or 'effort' may be correlated with the value of a person's contribution to society, it is inadequate by itself as the sole measure of the value of person's contribution; for ultimately the true value of a person's contribution is measured by the *benefits it bestows on others* in terms of provision for human needs.

CHAPTER 18

THE AGE OF ENLIGHTENMENT: DESERT, CONTRACT AND RIGHT

The scholastic approach to justice clearly emphasized the idea of desert, and indeed, the historical evidence seems to suggest that desert based schemes dominated philosophical ideas about justice up until the so-called 'Age of Enlightenment' in Europe in the 16th and 17th centuries (see MacIntyre, 1982). Moreover, the scholastics maintained the ancient link between justice as desert and the natural laws of the cosmos. In their view, natural laws are created by God; God is just, and therefore all natural laws are just (even if sometimes we may not be able to fathom out exact God's plans or reasoning in this respect). The status of civil law within this scheme, however, was somewhat variable. For example, in the Summa Theologica, Aquinas argued that any civil law that is unjust and unreasonable is repugnant to the law of nature, and is not a actually a law, but a perversion of law or 'a species of violence'. Thus, whereas Aristotle was willing to accept that civil laws can be unjust, Aquinas, by circularly defining all civil laws as just (because an unjust law is no law) merged justice with obedience to civil law as well as natural law.

During the 16th and 17th centuries, however, the notion of justice as desert, operating within the laws of a grand cosmic scheme, was to change fundamentally. A number of historical factors contributed to this change. For instance, with the expansion of trade the developing middle classes were achieving economic equality with the aristocracy and were pressing for an ideology and political system that would recognize the importance of mercantilism, and eliminate the privileges of noble birth. As a result there was thus a move towards the idea that people were born equals, not only in the sense of having equal rights to material resources, but also in the sense of possessing equal capacities and needs. The new movements would thus challenge the view that some people were born to rule, and others born to follow, either by virtue of some privilege granted for deeds done by families in past times (that is, 'family desert' through the transmigration of souls doctrine) or by the dictates of nature or God, whereby the needs of both groups can only be properly, or 'justly', satisfied when such a social order is maintained (that is, some people 'need' to be ruled, others to rule, and the former require less material resources than the latter to achieve the same levels of satisfaction).

Also, there was a move to check the increasing wealth of the Catholic Church and its power over political affairs. This was manifested in a number of ways. There was a rise in Protestantism and a rejection of the idea that people could 'buy' their way into heaven by contributing fortunes to the Church. Entry into heaven became even more a feature of God's grace; we cannot know exactly how to behave to be chosen by God, the best we can do is to have faith and pray. However, there was also a rise in atheism, and a general move towards political systems that stressed individuality and did not involve religious authority. One result of this was an increasing emphasis on the idea that it is good to pursue one's own interests rather than the moral prescriptions of the Church. And with this came the notion of 'natural rights'; that is, we all have natural rights to pursue our own interests without being restricted by the actions of others, especially the dictates of Church or class (see Gay, 1966; Russell, 1979; Simon, 1966; MacIntyre, 1982). But perhaps the most significant development during this period was the rise of science.

The rise of scientific determinism

The Aristotelian notion of desert as preached by the Christian church rested on choice. With differential needs held constant, to deserve more or less than others we must be given the same choices (or at least our genetic ancestors, who somehow are judged to form part of us, must have been given the same choices). We must all be able to choose between virtue and vice; to contribute to the good, or not to contribute. In an animistic world in which people possess agency, such choice possible in principle, so long as people have the capacity to understand the difference between those actions that are deemed good and therefore deserving of reward or positive outcomes, and those that are considered bad, and deserving of punishment or negative outcomes. In a world of mechanical automata, however, in which there are no souls or agents' making free-choices, only bodies whose actions are determined or necessitated by forces outside their control, and we have no grounds for arguing that one person is any more deserving than another.

The problem of 'necessity' or 'determinism' in human affairs has troubled philosophers and theologians since ancient times; particularly those who wished to argue that the universe and everything in it, moves along an inevitable, predetermined path, and/ or that God creates and controls everything. However, this problem became particularly acute in the 16th and 17th centuries. In the 16th and 17th centuries the animistic conception of cause was challenged by a new notion of cause (Trusted, 1984). Scientists had deduced that the universe operates like a giant clock, with each movement, each event, necessitated by a previous one according to scientific laws; all physical events are determined; they occur by necessity according to fixed immutable laws. There are no ultimate or final causes, no objects or events, including 'free-will', setting off or triggering a chain of causal reactions. An obvious difficulty then was to find a place for God in all this. Some, such as Rene Descartes (1596-1650) saw God as the agent who created the machine and set it in motion. However, even if it were allowed that God created the universe and set it in motion, the notion of causal necessity or determinism, was inevitably going to conflict with the idea of moral responsibility. If humans were simply cogs in a machine, even a machine made by God, how could they be held personally responsible for their actions? As David Hume put it, if the ultimate author of all human choices is God who set the machinery of the world in motion, 'Human actions, therefore, either can have no moral turpitude at all, as proceeding from so good a cause; or if they have any turpitude, they must involve the creator in the same guilt, while he is acknowledged to be their ultimate cause and author' (1777/1962, pp. 99-100).

Descartes' answer to this problem was to argue that, although all natural phenomena are explicable in terms of mechanical and mathematical concepts mental phenomena are not subject to these causal physical laws. The result was the doctrine known as 'Cartesian Dualism'. Thus we have a mind or soul that is non-physical or immaterial and survives after death, and a material body which is subject to physical causal law. Moreover, these systems *interact such that* the mind or soul influences the body (via the pineal gland). However, those who adopted the dualist position still had the difficulty of determining just how much influence our soul or essential spirit has over our material body, let alone the external environment. Surely people must differ in the extent to which they are influenced biological appetites and capacities beyond their control. To some, however, even Descartes' theory was considered too animistic; to them, people have no free-will, there is only mechanistic causation. Scientific determinism was born, and the stage was set for the appearance of a new emphasis in justice, which I shall term, '*deterministic egalitarianism*'. To illustrate the idea of deterministic egalitarianism and the some of the problems it created, we can do no better than to consult one of history's most controversial philosophers, Thomas Hobbes.

Thomas Hobbes and deterministic egalitarianism
There is much debate as to exactly how influential Thomas Hobbes' philosophy has been on theorizing about justice; however, perhaps more than anything his views are illustrative of the conceptual tangle that philosophers found themselves in when they attempted to construct theories of justice that ostensibly rejected desert.

Hobbes (1588-1679) lived in a time of political insecurity; he fled to France in 1640 fearful of the English Civil War, and what is usually acclaimed to be his masterpiece, 'Leviathan', was published in 1651, shortly after the execution of Charles 1. Hobbes was also contemporary of Descartes, but unlike Descartes he made no functional division between mind and body; indeed, when in France he contributed to objections to Descartes' theory. Although Hobbes ostensibly accepted the idea of God, he was fundamentally a scientific determinist who rejected the notion that God had given people free-will (in fact, some have argued that Hobbes was really an atheist). Thus, in Leviathan (1960), Hobbes argues that the concept of 'free-will' described in non-mechanistic terms is an 'absurdity' (p. 27). Freedom only makes sense in terms of the idea of not being constrained by external forces. Freedom means liberty; thus a man in prison is not at liberty, just as water in a basin is not at liberty, for both have their freedom restricted. There is no free-will independent of the liberty of a whole person. Moreover, to Hobbes, the terms 'good' and 'bad' only make sense in terms of appetites and desires. What a person desires is 'good', and what a person hates is 'bad', and will is just another appetite; it is 'the last appetite in deliberating' (p. 38).

In his theory, Hobbes uses the idea of a 'state of nature'; this is a state that does or would exist before the formation of a civil or political union. The idea of a 'state of nature' was particularly popular in the 17th and 18th centuries, as political commentators tried to analyze and rationalize types of government that did not rely on religious authority; however, whether a state of nature was to supposed to refer to a hypothetical situation, or an actual situation that once existed in our own culture, and still exists in other cultures, was never really made clear. As a result of his experiences, Hobbes believed that people are fundamentally selfish, and if left in a state of nature, they would be in a perpetual state of war. They only way they can preserve peace, therefore, is to give up the natural right to do as they please; for, he says, in a state of nature, 'every man has a (natural) right to everything; even to one another's body' (p. 85). People must, therefore, form a pact, or contract together, to create a civil state or commonwealth, and give absolute power to one individual or a group of individuals (the 'sovereign'). Hobbes also argues that conflict is inevitable because people are more or less equal in their capacities to satisfy their desires; thus he says, 'Nature hath made men so equal in the faculties of the body and mind, as that though there may be found one man sometimes manifestly stronger in body, or of quicker mind than another, yet when all is reckoned together, the difference between man and man is not so considerable, to which another may not pretend, as well as he' (p. 80).

If we apply the Equity as Desert principle to Hobbes views, we might predict that Hobbes would, in principle, be an egalitarian, stressing equal shares as the guiding principle of justice. Hobbes claims that people cannot freely choose to perform good and bad acts (in fact, other than that dictated by the sovereign power, there is no common notion of good and bad); so, if we accept this, then according to EAD, there is no basis for arguing that one person is more or less deserving than another; all should receive the same. Moreover, if, as Hobbes also claims, all have equal capacities and wants, then there is no basis for unequal distribution according to differential needs that might be generated by these capacities.

There is much in Hobbes theory to support the prediction that Hobbes was a 'deterministic egalitarian'. For example, he suggests that 'reason' has prescribed 19 'laws of nature' to guide men towards the goals of 'self-preservation' and 'felicity' or prosperity. Each law, he argues, involves giving up the natural right to do what one pleases. Included in these are egalitarian/need principles such as, all should mutually agree to limit their liberty; people should accommodate themselves to others, and should not keep things that are superfluous to their needs yet necessary for others; people should not declare hatred or contempt for others; all should acknowledge the fact that, by nature, they are no better than anyone else; that, acknowledging their natural equality, people should not take more than their share of things and give themselves more liberty than they would allow others; and judges should deal with people equally and impartially.

Most significantly, perhaps, Hobbes says that things should be decided equally between people who have a right to them; otherwise, he says, 'the distribution is unequal, and contrary to equity' . In fact, 'equity' is the 11th law, which is the 'equal distribution to each man, of that which in reason belongeth to him, and (is) .... distributive justice'. He then adds that of things that cannot be divided, they should be enjoyed in common, and if this is not possible they should be divided by lot (including first seizure or possession); for, he states, *'equal distribution is the law of nature*; and others means of equal distribution cannot be imagined' (p. 101, my emphasis).

However, although there is clearly a strong egalitarian basis to these laws of nature, Hobbes obscures the issue of unequal divisions of private property with the critical caveat that things are to be equally divided between those 'who have a right to them'. 'Equal distribution' may be 'the law of nature', but it is not clear how Hobbes intends to insure this in terms of property rules. When it comes to the punishment of criminals, however, like most determinists, Hobbes comes completely unstuck. If ultimately, people are not responsible for their behaviour, and no one can be deemed more or less deserving than anyone else, what do we do with people who disobey the rules? In Hobbes' deterministic system arguably no one deserves punishment, and indeed, the seventh and eighth laws of nature assert that people should not punish others for any reason other than to reform the offender or to direct others (deter) others, and no one should declare hatred or contempt for others (presumably this includes criminals). However, as we have already seen, the idea of punishing solely to reform the offender or deter others creates a multitude of problems; not the least of which is the idea that it would not prevent the punishment of the innocent to deter others, and does not dictate that punishment should fit the crime. Nevertheless, Hobbes also asserts that punishment should fit the crime, and that one cannot punish the innocent. He argues that punishment of the innocent is, again, against the law of '*equity*' which requires an 'equal distribution of justice'.

What Hobbes ends up with then is a familiar mix of some superficially egalitarian prescriptions for the distribution of resources, based on the implicit assumption that all are fundamentally equal and no one is more or less deserving than anyone else; however, this is coupled incongruously with elements of the earlier desert scheme in the treatment of criminals, which requires not only that those who deserve punishment should be punished, but punishment should fit the crime.

Justice as a contract

But in any case, what has all this to do with justice? Hobbes actually claims to reject the scholastic idea of distributive justice, arguing that merit is not due by justice but is 'rewarded of grace only'; in fact, he says distributive justice is not justice at all, it is *equity* (p. 98). According to Hobbes justice is only *one* of the laws of nature; it is law three, that people should perform the covenants or contracts they have made. Thus he says, 'when a covenant is made, then to break it is unjust: and the definition of INJUSTICE, is no other than the not performance of covenant. And whatsoever is not unjust, is just' (p. 94, his emphasis). This definition is, however, somewhat misleading, as Hobbes goes on to qualify the statement by saying that justice is the keeping of *valid* covenants, and this requires a civil constitution with the coercive power to compel people to keep them.

In fact, his whole scheme turns into an elaborate justification for why people should obey laws laid down by the sovereign power. Hobbes attempts to argue that people in a civil community have somehow 'contracted' by tacit consent to do, more or less, whatever the sovereign instructs. And because, according to Hobbes, there are no laws unless there is a sovereign power to dictate them, then no law can be unjust, and justice neatly becomes synonymous with the idea of obedience to civil law. However, Hobbes idea of 'consent' here is somewhat liberal, and includes contracts agreed to under duress and tyranny, and contracts not formally agreed to at all. By what really amounts to a piece of semantic manoeuvring, therefore, Hobbes manages to divorce the concept of justice from desert. Justice is equated with obedience to civil law and contracts, and all the other traditional components, such as fairness, equality, merit, and even the punishment of criminals are hived off into another category, to become 'laws of nature', and particularly the law of '*equity*'; they can become 'just' again, however, if enforced by the sovereign.

Of course, the idea that justice *includes* the formation and keeping of contracts is as old as the idea of justice itself, not only as part of what Aristotle termed commutative justice in the exchange of goods and services, but also in the general idea of promise keeping and making agreements to abide by administrative decisions (see Glaucon in Plato's Republic). However, we still need to know *why* it is an injustice to break one's contracts. Hobbes attempts to tell us, and his argument is very revealing. Hobbes' basic idea is that when a man makes a covenant he transfers a right to something to another person; a contract is 'The mutual transferring of right' (p. 87). A man who breaks a covenant, therefore, receives a right, but does not transfer one in return; as a result he receives more than his due. Thus Hobbes says, 'He that performeth first in the case of a contract, is said to MERIT that which he is to receive by the performance of the other; and he hath it *due* (p. 89, his emphasis), and 'merit presupposeth a right, and that the thing *deserved* is due by promise' (p. 63, my emphasis). What Hobbes describes, therefore, is simply a piece of Aristotelian reciprocity, or scholastic 'commutative justice'. If person A contracts to do a service or deliver a good for person B, and delivers the service or good, then A deserves (merits or is due) an appropriate return; if B breaches the contract by failing to deliver whatever is agreed in return, then an injustice has occurred.

What is missing from Hobbes' approximation to the scholastic notion of commutative justice, however, is any notion of the context in which the contract is made. Hobbes is scathing of the scholastic view of the 'just price' and seems oblivious to the circumstances surrounding entry into a contract; that is, the 'starting positions'. It matters not to Hobbes *who* is making the contract, and under what conditions. Within the scholastic tradition, however, a contract was not 'just' by definition, it was a rough and ready *tool* for determining values in exchange, and for making sure that the exchange values are maintained (only God could calculate the values with precision). Later the economist Adam Smith (1776/1986) made a similar point in relation to the striking of bargains, which are essentially agreements or contracts between people. Smith argued that the true value of a good or service logic is the labour put into producing it; however, 'labour' can involve a number of different elements, such as hardship and ingenuity, and it is difficult to find an accurate measure of these various aspects. He then says, 'It is adjusted, however, not by any accurate measure, but by the higgling and bargaining of the market, according to the rough sort of equality which, though not exact, is sufficient to carrying on the business of common life' (p. 134). The idea is that if two people are contented or satisfied to exchange X number of 'A's for Y number of 'B's, then the values of the two services or commodities can be assumed to be equal for both parties; and significantly, Hobbes makes exactly this same point when he says, *'there is not ordinarily a greater sign of the equal distribution of any thing, than that every man is contented with his share'* (p. 80).

But within the scholastic tradition, being only a tool, contracts themselves can be seen as subject to the restraints of justice. When a person agrees to a contract under conditions of coercion, distress or necessity, the contract will be unjust, as the goods or services provided by the person under duress may be 'undervalued', and the person will receive less than is 'due'. The scholastic argument is emphatically made by Pope Leo XIII who points out that the dictates of natural justice 'are more imperious and ancient than any bargain between man and man', so, for example, 'if through necessity or fear of a worse evil the workman accept harder conditions because an employer or contractor will afford him no better, he is made the victim of force and injustice' (1891/1939, p. 69). It was for this reason that the scholastics recommended the setting up of local societies and boards to monitor contracts or agreements made between individuals.

It is also worth noting another sense in which breaking a contract could be construed as upsetting a system of desert; contracts or bargains usually involve some sort of restriction on the activities of the parties involved (for example, the contracting parties may temporarily or permanently be prevented from engaging in alternative inputs and/or they may give up certain outcomes); consequently, a man who breaks a contract may again be seen to gain more then he deserves relative to to the other who keeps the contract.

These ideas were not only held by the scholastics, they remain a feature of modern contract law (see, Fogarty, 1961: Sadurski, 1985). As Sadurski (1985) notes, in modern contract law, it is not even necessary for one of the contracting parties to have been pressurized; if the contract was 'freely entered into', but the bargain results in one party being severely disadvantaged relative to the other, the contract may be rendered void; thus, having reviewed a number of relevant cases, Sadurski says, 'the reasonableness of the agreement may be assessed independently of the party's consent' (p. 30). The same was also true in ancient Greece, hence Aristotle's view that rectificatory justice can apply to 'voluntary transactions', such as selling, purchasing and lending, to which both parties initially consent. In other words, a transaction can be unjust if it violates just proportion, even if 'voluntarily' entered into. It is important to note that even Hobbes admits that certain contracts would be deemed unjust; such as a contract to murder an innocent person.

From the perspective of EAD, therefore, it could be argued that contracts were first established as a rough and ready means to measure or make commensurable some of the various input and outcome elements in exchange relationships. But whether contracts are considered just or not, depends on how their outcomes fit in with an overall scheme of justice. Or as Sadurski puts it, 'commutative justice reducible to the duty to fulfil promises is not really a matter of justice because promises themselves (or rather, the structure of the distribution produced by their fulfilment) may be assessed by the standards of justice' (1985, p. 28).

The fragmentation of justice

However, in his efforts to promote scientific determinism, and at the same time, to try to show that any civil state is better than anarchy, Hobbes divorced the term 'justice' from the traditional desert framework as put forward by Aristotle and the scholastics. Instead, he identified justice solely with contractual obligations (and implied ones at that), and by circularly defining a civil law as just, he made justice as obedience to contracts synonymous with civil law.

The result was and remains a jumble of contradictory concepts. In Hobbes's view, there is no notion of good or bad beyond that which people desire, and, in a state of nature, everyone's desires have an equivalent status. People are mechanical automata but with an equal right to do as they please. So how do we treat criminals?

Hobbes' answer is that it is permissible to punish criminals because by tacitly agreeing to live by the laws of the land, they have consented to be punished (at least, in proportion to the severity of their crimes). This is, of course, nonsense, but is symptomatic of the fact that, try as he might, Hobbes could not dismiss the concept of desert from justice.

Apart from the predictable egalitarian properties of Hobbes' laws of nature, and his appeal to desert to justify the keeping of agreements, there are other obvious appeals to desert in his theory. For instance, his notion of justice as obedience to law seems to be founded on desert. If we assume, as Hobbes does, that people are basically selfish and ready to kill each other at a moments notice, then it follows that anyone who disobeys a law that prohibits such behaviour will gain an 'undeserved' advantage. The idea of 'rewarding services' actually crops up as one of the duties of the sovereign; Hobbes argues that the sovereign must not distribute rewards arbitrarily to the rich and ambitious, for, reward 'is ordained not for disservice, but for service past' (p. 229). And at one stage, Hobbes even describes an his adherence to the ancient doctrine of natural desert or immanent justice; thus he says that, in time, 'intemperance is naturally punished with diseases; rashness, with mischances; injustice, with the violence of enemies; pride, with ruin; cowardice, with oppression; and rebellion, with slaughter. For seeing punishments are consequent to the breach of laws; natural punishments must be naturally consequent to the breach of the laws of nature; and therefore follow them as their natural, not arbitrary effects' (p. 241).

Consequently, if Hobbes's sovereign actually does what 'natural law' commands, the result would be most interesting. Everyone would start in a state of relative equality, with relatively equal capacities and talents, resources would be distributed equally, but then rewards would be distributed according to services to the state, punishments would be administered to those who harm the state in proportion to their crimes, (ideally) contracts would preserve the system, and nature (if not God) would take care of the rest. The similarity to an EAD system hardly requires comment.

John Locke: Justice, desert and property rights

Although Hobbes figures prominently in the history of philosophy, he is probably mentioned less in modern writings on justice than his English compatriot, John Locke. As we saw earlier, John Locke remains one of the favourites of modern libertarian writers. Locke's main views on the political economy are laid down in his 'Two Treatises on Government' (1690/1988), though his ideas specifically on justice are to be found in a smaller work published in 1695 known as 'Venditio' (see Dunn, 1969; Vaughn, 1980).

John Locke (1632-1704) is popular amongst modern libertarian theorists mainly because of his spirited defence of private property. According to Locke, in a state of nature (that is, again, a state without government), property is created and accumulated, and it is the need to protect accumulated property that leads to the beginning of civil society. Locke argues that all men are politically equal in the sight of God, and in a 'state of nature' all have a God given natural right to this life, free from harm by other men. The right to private property derives from this right to life, free from interference by others. To this end, therefore, God has provided people, in common, with a vast pool of resources to maintain themselves. Every man then has the capacity to combine his labour with this common pool of resources and to create something new that is a part of himself and can belong to no other man. Private property is the result of this combination of labour with the common stock of resources. Locke argues that it is 'honest labour', more than anything else that gives things their value; and labour creates goods of much greater value than does nature alone.

In Locke's primitive natural state then, everyone has equal access to a common stock of goods, with which they can combine their labour to produce goods for the benefit of themselves and others. The goods so produced are private property and represent rewards for industry and labour, but it is important that each man must not exceed his 'natural share'; there must always be left a common stock for others to use. This idea gave rise to what is now popularly known as the 'Lockean proviso'; thus a man is entitled to whatever he can gain through combining his labour with the common pool of resources, but in doing this he must not make others worse off (he must leave them in the same starting place as himself).

However, Locke goes on to argue that, with the growth of population and economic development, property accumulation will centre round the most industrious and productive, and as a result, the less industrious and talented will become envious at the unequal distribution of wealth; hence people will contract to form a government to protect property, to arbitrate between competing claims, and punish transgressors. To Locke, however, government is not 'just' simply by virtue of the fact that a contract has been entered into; indeed, Locke argues that the contract is made void and the population can dispose of the government if the government fails in its purpose. Locke also acknowledges that problems will also arise because of economic scarcity; there may no more land left in common. Locke's answer to this latter problem is to assert that the living standards of everyone will increase no matter who earns the property, and men can hire themselves out as wage labour to get a share of the increased productivity.

Locke: the 'Protestant Scholastic'

Despite the emphasis on natural right and private property, the overlap between Locke's scheme and EAD is obvious. In principle, everyone has an equal opportunity to provide the inputs for which private property is the reward, even if ultimately this means hiring oneself out as wage labour. From a religious viewpoint, Locke's view coincided with the Protestant emphasis on the value of work; that is the idea that a person who labours and toils serves God. As Vaughn puts it, 'Locke was making a case for private ownership based on the virtues of industry and labour' (1980, p. 88). But Locke also maintained that by combining our labour with the common stock of resources we serve mankind, by increasing the productive value of those resources. Hence, for example, in the Second Treatise (T2) he says, 'he who appropriates land to himself by his labour, does not lessen but increase the common stock of mankind .... he that encloses land and has a greater plenty of the conveniencys of life from ten acres, than he could have from an hundred left to nature, may truly be said, *to give ninety acres to mankind*' (1988, p. 37, my emphasis). So, as Vaughn again notes, 'To Locke private property is completely moral in that it grows from men's application of natural law, operates to reward industry and punish sloth, and has the effect of benefitting the entire commonwealth' (1980, p. 107). In Locke's scheme, ultimately the accumulation of private property is our reward for our services to God and others.

In addition, however, Locke argues that there must be provision or adjustment for need; there must always be left a common stock for others to use to provide for their basic needs. Hence, in the First Treatise (T1), he says that a man cannot 'justly' deny a needy person 'a Right to the surplusage of his goods, when his pressing wants call for it' (1988, p. 42). To Locke, God has given everyone an opportunity to share in wealth, and therefore provision for basic need is a not only a matter of charity, but right or justice.

The just price and the labour theory of value

Locke's ideas were thus firmly grounded in the scholastic tradition; in fact, he has been referred to as a 'Protestant scholastic' (Vaughn, 1980). Locke even held the scholastic vision of the 'just price'. To fully understand Locke's view of the just price, however, it is necessary to look again at his views on the value of goods and services.

As mentioned previously, Locke argues that it is 'honest labour', more than anything else that gives things their value; thus he says, 'For whatever Bread is worth more than acorns, Wine than water, and Cloth or Silk than leaves, Skins, or Moss, that is wholly *owing to labour* and industry .... *labour makes far the greatest part of the value* of things we enjoy in this World' (T2, p. 42, his emphasis). Essentially here Locke is adopting the '*labour theory of value*'; the theory that can be traced back at least to the early scholastics, and which was subsequently adopted and developed by economists such as Adam Smith (1723-1790), and David Ricardo (1772-1823). Thus Smith also says 'Labour ... is the measure of the exchangeable value of all commodities. The real price of everything, what everything really costs to the man who wants to acquire it, is the toil and trouble of acquiring it' (1986, p. 133).

From a Lockean perspective, the labour theory of value has an obvious appeal as part of a system of justice as desert. According to Locke, God has given us an abundance of the natural materials we need to sustain life. Essentially, these are our 'zero outcomes' entitlement; they belong to all of us equally so long as we do nothing wrong. It therefore follows that we should not reward people for the natural raw materials they give to us, because we are entitled to them anyway. Instead, we should reward workers for the *labour costs* involved in turning the materials into other items and/or making them available to us. The social benefits we receive from others who provide us with various goods and services are, therefore, determined by finished goods, but by the labour we save by not having to provide the same services ourselves. Adam Smith makes this point explicitly when he says, 'What everything is worth to the man who has acquired it .... *is the toil and trouble which it can save to himself*' (1776/1986, p. 133, my emphasis). If this is the case, then so the theory goes, as long as goods and services always exchange at their correct social 'value' in terms of the real (labour saving) benefits they provide for others, then individuals should end up with outcomes equally proportional to the labour costs they incurred providing them. Consequently, in a correctly functioning market, controlled by God, all should receive benefits equivalent to those they have bestowed on others, and thus all should receive exactly what they deserve in just proportion to their socially beneficial labours.

To Locke the price that accurately reflects the value of labour involved in its production is then the 'just price'. However, in true scholastic fashion, Locke also argues that the true value of a good or service is its value for the whole community, not its value for isolated individuals. And for Locke, the best estimate we can provide of the social value of anything is its market price; so the just price of anything is its *market price*. There is, therefore, no question of individual price bargaining in Locke's conception of economic justice; justice requires that the price should be the same for everyone as part of a communal enterprise. Interestingly, on this point Vaughn (1980) comments, 'Obviously Locke does not understand the more modern idea that if both parties to a transaction freely agree a price, both gain from the exchange' (p. 127). Vaughn is referring here to the modern view that, being rational creatures, humans would not consent to exchange anything unless they could *gain* from the transaction (and implicit in Vaughn's comment is the idea that if a person gains from a transaction it cannot be unjust; see also Posner, 1981). However, this criticism is to misunderstand the basic logic behind the scholastic view of just price.

Suppose, for example, that, to save the life of her child, a parent 'freely' exchanges her house that would normally sell on the open market for £50,000 for a simple medicine that normally retails at £6. It is not contrary to the scholastic view to argue that she *gains* from this transaction. Presumably if she did not 'value' the medicine more than the house that she is offering in exchange, she would not engage in the exchange. What the scholastics would dispute, however, is the *justice* of such transactions within a general scheme of social justice. The woman who is so desperate to help her sick child that she will actually 'gain' from selling the roof over her head that might have has laboured for years (contributing to others) to buy, still ends up with less than her due relative to others with healthy children who still possess their houses. She has also been 'overcharged' for the medicine compared to others who would only buy the medicine at its usual market price, and the vendor of the medicine has gained more than he or she deserves relative to others. The same principles apply to the buying and selling of labour; so for example, Locke says, one cannot 'justly make use of another's necessity, to force him to become his vassal' (1988, p. 42), even if the 'vassal' does 'gain' from the contract.

Although Locke, like the scholastics, did allow for the fact that the market price, and therefore the just price may vary from one area to another, he argues, nevertheless, that *within* any particular area, it would be unjust to charge one person more or less than another. Again the principle is simple, assuming all start off in a position where they have what they deserve, if one person is allowed to buy a house at less than the market price, the buyer will unjustly gain relative to others who can only purchase at the market price. However, in any case, argues Locke, over time, fluctuations in the market will even out to give a fair and equal account. The idea that in a properly functioning free market economic system, market prices would be 'just', was self-evident to Locke, because the market operated according to natural law as laid down by God.

To summarize, the scholastic view of justice maintained by Locke and his forebears demands that individual should receive outcomes in due proportion to the social value of their labours, that equals should be treated equally such that equal contributions should receive equal outcomes, and the 'just price' was there to maintain this principle. Consequently, a transaction was not considered 'just' simply because the particular parties involved in it agreed to it, or 'gained' from it. It must also satisfy the demands of justice within the whole scheme of social justice.

Locke and desert
In Locke's ideal civil state, all should still have some access to the resources with which to combine their labour to produce results that will benefit all; and a result the most industrious and talented will accumulate most as a reward for these virtues. On the other hand, the lazy will end up with little or nothing, and transgressors will be punished. What Locke has in mind is of course a fairy-tale; in reality any desert theory of justice espousing the fundamental right to private property has to come to terms with the fact that not all people who acquire private property do so by combining their labour with it, no matter how loosely we define 'labour'. Property can be inherited, it can be given as a gift, it can accumulate or be lost through freak accidents.

Locke recognised the problem with regard to the inheritance of property, and his response was to claim that although, on death, a person's accumulated property could revert back to common ownership, there has to be some means of providing for children who, left to themselves, would not be able to survive. Thus the inheritance of property is a natural law, devised by God, so that children will have their basic needs met. However, although children may inherit material resources,

Locke argues that they cannot rightly inherit power or prestige. Locke's basic rationale for the inheritance of property, therefore, is that it is a precondition for what we might term the 'zero outcomes' baseline in EAD; for upon it, rests the maintenance of helpless children. Such a rationale does not, of course, get round the contradiction between Locke's theory of property as the just reward for honest endeavour and industry, and the gross inequalities in inherited wealth (and the privileges and freedoms attached to them), that would inevitably arise in his system, but it is a creative attempt to overcome this problem.

As we shall see, Karl Marx was later to make a stinging critique of Locke's version of events (and for a more modern critique of Locke's views on these issues, see MacPherson, 1962). Locke, however, thought that the mechanism of the free-market, directed by the hand of God, would, in the long run, sort everything out. From our point of view, however, is not the plausibility of Locke's views, but the basic structure of the argument itself that is most important. It is quite clear that, ultimately, Locke attempts to justify the accumulation of private property by a direct appeal to proportional desert, in fact, to the basic structure of EAD. In the end private property is defensible, not because of fundamental human rights, but because it is *deserved*. In Locke's scheme the God given fundamental human right to life, free from interference from others, is not justice *per se*, rather it is a *prerequisite for a principle of desert*. For how can we claim that the accumulation of private property is a deserved or due reward for the employment of industry and talent in the service of others, and punishment a deserved response to those who deprive others of their dues, unless each, initially at least, has the *freedom* to merge his or her labour with the resources that God has given? Moreover, our freedom to life assumes a basic minimum level of resources, a baseline desert, that is guaranteed by our rights to the 'surpluses' of others in times of extreme need.

It is difficult to discern from reading Locke exactly whether he intended his political theory to be a theory of 'justice'. According to Vaughn, Locke never actually defines justice, other than to say that 'justice has but one measure for all men' (1980, p. 125); nevertheless, it seems difficult to reject the view that Locke was fundamentally a desert theorist, in true scholastic tradition.

Immanuel Kant: Morality and reason

The notion of 'right' turns up again with one of the greatest moral philosophers of all time, Immanuel Kant. Born in Prussia, Immanuel Kant (1724-1804) is best known for his treatise 'Critique of Pure Reason' (1781/1929), though his views on morality and right are most clearly summarized in 'Fundamental Principles of the Metaphysic of Morals' (1785/1965) and 'Metaphysical elements of Justice' (1797/1970).

The starting point for Kant is that humans possess free-will. Kant argues that unless we assume the existence of free-will, we cannot make sense of moral principles. He thus says, 'All men attribute to themselves freedom of will. Hence come all judgements upon actions that ought to have been done, although they have not been done' (1965, p. 90). His solution to the problem of determinism, however, was not to adopt a Cartesian dualist position of a mind of uncaused mental events, and a body subject to the causal laws of nature. Instead he argues that whilst it may *appear* from experience that we are subject to external influences, we cannot conclude that we *are* actually subject to these laws. Kant is able to say this because he believes we also have what he calls 'noumenal' selves, with an existence that transcends the experience of our senses.

Kant argues that morality only applies to humans because we are rational creatures; we can derive moral principles from reason alone, independent of inclination and experience. Reason exists to help us produce a good will; and only a good will can be good without qualification. Moreover a good will will be good no matter what its consequences. Kant's most famous quote regarding the 'good will' is as follows: 'Even if it should happen that .... this will should wholly lack its power to accomplish its purpose, if with its greatest efforts should yet achieve nothing .... then like a jewel, it would shine by its own light, as a thing which has its whole value in itself .... its usefulness or fruitlessness can neither take away anything from this value' (1965, p. 11).

He then goes on to state that a good will is one that operates from duty; one should act out of duty, and for no other reason. And this means to respect the moral law for its own sake. Hence he comes up with the famous moral principle, 'Act only on the maxim whereby thou canst at the same time will that it should be a universal law' (1965, p. 46). From this formulation Kant then derives a second, 'act as to treat humanity, whether in thine own person or in that of any other, in every case as an end withal, never as a means only' (1965, p. 56). This is, is of course, his *categorical imperative*; we must act in this way not to achieve some other end, but because reason tells us this is the right way to act. Kant also suggests that all human beings should consider themselves as legislative members of an ideal 'kingdom of ends'. That is all rational creatures should recognise that each has the capacity to legislate universal laws, and to abide by them. Thus he says, 'This legislation must be capable of existing in every rational being, and of emanating from his will' (p. 62).

Kant thought that his categorical imperative would prohibit making false promises, suicide and attacks on life and property, as well as dictate benevolence to the poor. However, as we have seen, it actually does nothing of the kind; indeed, as Hospers says, Kant's categorical imperative 'will not yield a set of maxims on whose universalization everyone can agree' (1961, p. 283). Most problematical for our present discussion, however, is the question of how all this relates to justice? Well, contrary to how it is often presented in modern writings, Kant's categorical imperative, with its background rationale, was relevant to, but was *not* his theory of justice.

Kant on justice

For Kant's views on justice researchers often consult 'Metaphysical Elements of Justice', which in German is 'Meta physische Anfangsgrunde der Rechtslehre'. The German noun 'recht' has no exact English equivalent, though it means something like 'justice or right or law in the abstract' (Kemp, 1968, p. 84). Thus in translation the terms 'justice' and 'right' are often used interchangeably.

Importantly, Kant appears to make a clear distinction between justice and morality in general. Thus he says, justice does not require acts of benevolence and charity, though these are moral duties. Instead, he argues that the basic question for a theory of justice is what can people demand of others by right? That is, what can we, through *external* force, coerce people into doing, or make them refrain from doing? He says we only have *one* innate right, and that is freedom; and by freedom he means not being constrained by others from acting according to our will. Justice or right, therefore pertains to those conditions that guarantee our equal innate right to freedom; and paradoxically this requires a set of *restrictive* or *coercive* conditions that will enable the freedom of different individuals to be harmonized. Thus Kant defines 'right' as 'the restriction of each individual's freedom so that it harmonizes with the freedom of everyone else' (1973, pp. 155-156). The preservation of the right to freedom involves only external actions, yet it is a moral duty dictated by reason. Hence, he says, the moral rule or maxim of right or justice is 'act externally in such a way that the free use of your will is compatible with the freedom of everyone according to a universal law' (1970, pp. 34-35).

In familiar style for the times in which he lived, Kant further argues that for such a state of affairs to exist, people must contract to form a civil union, under a sovereign power; for, he says, a state of nature is 'a state devoid of justice' (1973, p. 178). The purpose of this civil union is then to enforce external laws that make this constant harmony of freedom possible (or 'public right'). But how do we know whether a law is appropriate or 'just'? Kant, like Hobbes, starts off with the view that citizens have the freedom to obey only laws to which they have consented, but realizing the impracticality of this assertion, he adopts the more vague idea that a law is just if it is at least *possible* that people would agree to it, as a mere idea. He then comes up with a number of laws that reason would dictate. For instance, all individuals are absolutely equal with regard to their authority to coerce others to use their freedom in a way that harmonizes with their own, so no one must hand down hereditary rank and privilege. Moreover, every member of the state must be able to reach any degree of rank which can be earned through 'talent, industry and good fortune' (1973, p. 158), thus he adds that the equality of human beings as subjects of a state is 'perfectly consistent with the utmost inequality of the mass and degree of its possessions' (1973, p. 157).

According to Kant, the civil state also has a duty to punish criminals, who forfeit their 'equal right'. This might suggest we may do as we please with criminals, but as we have noted in earlier chapters, Kant was a rigid retributivist. In his view, we must never use people as a means to an end, is it is not only wrong to punish a innocent person, it is also wrong to punish a guilty person *solely* for their own good, to reform them, or for the good of society. Hence he says that 'He (the criminal) must be found deserving of punishment before any consideration is given to the utility of this punishment for himself or his fellow citizens' (1970, p. 100). Moreover, in Kant's view, punishment should fit the crime. But as we have also noted, it is not at all clear whether the latter derives (or even can be derived) from Kant's theory of 'rights'.

Although there are some very significant anomalies that reflect Kant's prejudices and prevailing historical views, such as the denial of voting rights to women and those without property, there are clear elements of EAD in Kant's conceptions of right or justice. Everyone should, by right, be able to express their explicitly *equal* freedom to perform those inputs (involving talent and industry), that will enable them to reap the rewards that society has to offer. This also means that rank and privilege cannot be inherited, they must be earned or 'deserved'. And it is notable in this regard, that Kant adds another definition of right or justice to that concerning freedom; he says 'the theory of right will also seek an assurance that each individual receives, with mathematical precision, *what he is his due'* (1973, pp. 175-176, his emphasis). When it comes to punishment, also, Kant is an uncompromising desert theorist; punishment must be deserved and must be proportional to the crime.

Nevertheless, Kant's idea that people are entitled to *earn* what they can by 'good fortune', seems to be a contradiction in terms; and there is an obvious fudging of the problem of an unequal distribution of material possessions according to inheritance and 'good fortune' (though Kant does attempt, somewhat ingeniously, to argue that once there was communal possession of the soil, and as 'noumenal beings', that is creatures not bound by the limits of empirical experience, we can still possess things we do not actually own in the phenomenal world). However, this brings us to perhaps the most important feature of Kant's approach to morality and justice. Although what I have said so far covers the usual sort of material that modern theorists use when attempting to integrate Kant into their approaches; it is only half the story. Presented in this way, the most significant part of Kant's theory of justice, from Kant's own perspective, is still missing. For Kant clearly intended his views on morality and right, not to be taken in isolation, but to be part of a grand scheme of justice, *divine justice*.

Kant's Divine Justice

The scholastics thought that only God was capable of dispensing justice with complete accuracy and precision. We can achieve a rough approximation to justice in this life, but our lives on this earth were simply a preparation for the next life. In the next life, therefore, God would see to it that true justice was achieved; the virtuous (and only the virtuous) would be rewarded, and the vicious (and only the vicious) punished. However, if God is to reward and punish people according to their deserts, they must be personally accountable for their acts; they must have the opportunity to know the difference between good and bad, virtue and vice, and be free to practice them. This is also what Kant believed, in fact, this was the basis of his whole theory of morality and right.

In the 'Critique of Practical Reason' and 'Lectures on Ethics', Kant sets out his views on God, freedom and immortality. To Kant, an act is good if it is done from duty, out of a good will; but good will is not the complete or Supreme Good; it is not the *bonnum consummatum*, or *summum bonnum*. Instead, he summarizes his views on the Supreme Good as follows (1963, pp. 6-7):

What constitutes the Supreme Good? The supreme created good is the most perfect world, that is, a world in which all rational beings are happy and are worthy of happiness. The ancients realized that mere happiness could not be the highest good. For if all men were to obtain this happiness without distinction of just and unjust, the highest good would not be realized, because though happiness would indeed exist, worthiness in it would not. In mankind therefore we have to look for both happiness and for merit. The combination of the two will be the highest good .... Let us imagine a world inhabited by intelligent beings, all of whom behaved well, and so deserved to be happy, but were destitute and lived in the most wretched circumstances. Such beings would have no happiness, and there would be no supreme good in these conditions. If on the other hand, all beings were happy but not well-behaved and not worthy of being happy, we should again have no Supreme Good in such circumstances.

As Acton (1970) puts it, Kant's 'Supreme Good requires that happiness should be proportioned to virtue in such a way that those who deserve happiness, and only those, should have it' (p. 56). To Kant, therefore, the ultimate good was not a good will, or the right to freedom, it was a version of *Equity as Desert*, with virtue as the inputs and happiness (or blessedness) as the outcomes. And exactly as Equity as Desert requires that positive outcomes should be returned for positive inputs, never negative outcomes for positive inputs, then so does Kant's supreme good require that those who are virtuous must receive at least some degree of happiness; a distribution in which the virtuous are the least *un*happy will not do. Kant argued, however, that as this supreme good was obviously not achievable in this earthly world, impartial reason requires the acknowledgement of the existence of God. God is the ultimate judge who will see to it that the ultimate good is accomplished.

Put in this context, the various elements of Kant's theory of justice and morality now fall into place. In an Equity as Desert scheme, all must have the equal opportunity to perform good or bad actions (services or disservices) and this requires knowing the difference between the positive and negative inputs. It is very important to Kant, therefore, to establish that all rational beings are capable of devising and understanding the difference between virtue and vice. Kant says our reason serves this purpose; reason provides us with the categorical imperative, and the categorical imperative enables all of us to generate rules of appropriate conduct. Moreover, as we all have free-will, we can choose whether to act according to the categorical imperative or not. To Kant, free-will is a prerequisite to the distinction between virtue and vice. However, it is important not to aim at happiness or God's blessing directly; only by being virtuous for its own sake, will we truly reap our just reward.

Seen from this perspective, therefore, Kant's categorical imperative was intended as a device to enable all of us to generate those rules of conduct that would act as 'inputs' in Kant's supreme 'equity' scheme. In other words, it is essentially a device to guarantee an *equal opportunity to perform the inputs*. Moreover, what I have previously referred to as Kant's scheme of 'right' or 'justice' was never intended to be a complete and perfect system of 'justice'. It was a scheme to tell us what civil laws should be enacted if all are to maintain the equal freedom to pursue their own ends; for only by allowing people such freedom that we can provide them with the opportunity to carry out the dictates of the categorical imperative. It also follows, that if all individuals are to be given the equal freedom to pursue virtue, we cannot have restrictions imposed by people who break the public laws. Kant is firmly in favour of a strict retributivist penal policy towards offenders who break these laws.

In Kant's view, however, public laws cannot ensure pure and perfect justice. There are still too many factors militating against the achievement of the supreme good in this world; our environments, backgrounds, and bodies limit us. We may try to be good, and serve God and others, but be prevented from fulfilling our objectives; we may do evil but never be caught. Hence, ultimately there is only one 'input' measure that really counts, 'effort'. But not effort as measured through hours of 'work' or quantity of 'labour', but pure, unadulterated effort of *will*. And only God can know the goodness and strength of our will, and much we tried to live by the dictates of the categorical imperative. To Kant, therefore, it is the strength and direction of the *will* that motivates actions that is the ultimate 'input' in the Divine scheme of justice. True justice in the world of ethics is thus not 'civil law', or least of all 'freedom'. Indeed, Kant notes that 'all moral evil (as well as good) springs from freedom' (p. 67). Neither is it charity and benevolence. Indeed, Kant firmly states 'A benevolent judge is unthinkable'. Instead says Kant, '*Divine Justice must reward good conduct and punish bad with unerring precision*' (my emphasis). Divine justice, or holy law, therefore prescribes that happiness be apportioned exactly according to virtue, and that 'of necessity .... punishment should fit the crime' (p. 107). For this, says Kant, is *jus aequitatis*, the *'law of equity'*; and only God can dispense equity, for 'He may be regarded as one who pays men's debts' (p. 54).

Ultimately, it seems that Kant was another true desert theorist in the tradition of Aristotle and the scholastics. Indeed, not only does he adhere to the notion of geometrical proportion, but his discussion of responsibility echoes almost exactly that of Aristotle. Responsibility, says Kant, rests on freedom, and 'the degree of responsibility depends on the degree of freedom' (1963, p. 62). The more a man is restricted by external forces, or natural inclinations, the less his responsibility. Also, says Kant, 'A man who by frequent good deeds acquires the habit of doing good increases his merit. The same applies to wicked deeds and the increase of demerit. Accordingly, we should be held less responsible for habits which are innate than for those which we acquire' (pp. 64-65). There is even provision for imbalances due to need in Kant's views on justice; thus in part of a lecture entitled 'Duties dictated by Justice', he argues that poverty occurs because the rights of the poor are infringed; hence he says, 'our acts of charity to others should not be regarded as acts of generosity, but as small efforts towards restoring the balance which the social system has disturbed' (1963, p. 211).

However, although Kant was clearly a desert theorist, if his views on morality and right are taken in isolation, outside of their historical and religious context, they display a confusing, fragmented picture. Not only does the categorical imperative fail to give rise to the virtues he espouses, but divorced from the context of an after-life, the virtues themselves serve no end or purpose. They are done for no reason except 'duty'; which, arguably, to a rational person, is no reason at all. Moreover, his alleged theory of justice appears to bear little relationship to his moral theory in general.

CHAPTER 19

UTILITARIANISM, EGALITARIANISM AND COMMUNISM

According to MacIntyre (1982), the Age of Enlightenment ultimately saw the removal of the religious after-life from moral theory, and this has been a major contributor to the problems we now face with moral concepts in general. MacIntyre argues that within the Aristotelian conception of morality we practised virtues for a reason; they were to change us from what we are, to what we could be, if we achieved our true purpose or *telos*, which was *eudaimomia*. Moreover, this was achievable in this earthly world. However, the Christians transported the *telos* into the next world; to them the ultimate goal of moral action could not to be achieved in this life. So when the Age of Enlightenment arrived, and the influence of the Church declined, the telos was eventually lost, and we ended up with a set of virtues, such as honesty and benevolence, but no reason for performing them. This left philosophers trying to find a *telos* again, in the earthly world, but now without the influence of Aristotle, who both science and the religious 'predestinationists', had rejected. One result of all this was the arrival of *utilitarianism*; the idea that the ultimate criterion for judging the morality or rightness of an act is its usefulness in obtaining some earthly end, such as the greatest happiness.

If we accept MacIntyre's view, then the implications of these developments for justice theorizing would have been particularly dire. For the followers of the old religions there was no contradiction between the *telos* or *summum bonnum* and justice as proportional desert. In Aristotle's scheme, *eudaimonia* was distributed in equal proportion to virtue. The same was true for the stoics and the Christians; the supreme good was happiness distributed according to virtue with perfect justice. All would receive exactly what they deserved with mathematical precision. In contrast, although the elements of EAD clearly show in much utilitarian thought, the notion of distribution according to desert was not an integral feature of the new utilitarian *telos*. In fact, the idea of public utility could actually fly in the face of justice as desert. And try as they did, the early utilitarians were never able to deal with adequately with this problem.

However, the secularization of justice also brought forward theorists who were to lay their main emphasis on the notion of just distribution.

Hume and Bentham

Aristotle points out that 'we call those acts just that tend to produce and preserve happiness and its components in a political society' (NE5, p1129b). Hobbes also argued that the main aim of contracting to form a commonwealth, and observing the laws of nature, including justice, was to preserve 'peace and felicity'. The utilitarians, however, elevated the idea of 'usefulness' to a new status.

Although David Hume (1711-1776) is not usually classified as a 'utilitarian', as he did not actually belong to the utilitarian movement, he is notable for his argument that rules of justice should be based on their 'utility', and he clearly anticipated some of the arguments that were to be used by those such as John Stuart Mill. Hume's most famous statement on justice is that in a world abundant in conveniences, in which labour is unnecessary, and every wish can be fulfilled, 'the cautious, jealous virtue of justice would never once have been dreamed of (1777/1962; pp. 145-146). However, Hume abandons the notions of justice as merit and equality as he calls them, as impractical and counter to public utility. He also dismisses the idea of justice as a promise, or convention resulting from mutual consent, as 'absurd', because, he says, a promise or convention is only *part* of justice. In the end, however, Hume actually avoids defining 'justice'. Instead, he simply implies that it is something to do with the maintenance of 'general peace and order' and a set of rules or prescriptions for the acquisition and disposal of private property that would allow this; though he adds that to break such rules, once established, is a breach of 'equity' (1962, pp. 256-260).

Hume's linking of justice, utility and 'equity' is interesting. His approach to property rights emphasizes the idea that one should be able to keep the things one has acquired through one's 'sweat and labour'. But, by implication, for Hume it is also perfectly 'equitable' for one person to inherit enormous wealth, whilst others inherit nothing; indeed, equity is violated if the poor steal from the rich. This is not to say that services and disservices to the community are unimportant to Hume; he says, 'The characters which engage our approbation are chiefly such as contribute to the peace and security of human society; as the characters which excite blame are chiefly such as tend to public detriment and disturbance: Whence it may reasonably be presumed, that the moral sentiments arise .... from a reflection of these opposite interests' (p. 80). However, such 'moral sentiments' are apparently not the business of justice. Justice is about the enforcement of 'useful' property rights.

For Hume, therefore, justice is a vague term that concerns rules and prescriptions that are useful for preserving general peace and order (the new *telos*); it involves enforcing rights to private property (which is now the true business of justice); and somehow, at the same time, all this is supposed to be 'equitable'. Yet, according to Hume, we still supposed to praise the characters or dispositions of those people who promote peace and security, and blame or disapprove of those who do not (something nearer to the old conception of desert). It seems, therefore, whilst Hume attempted to divorce justice from desert by assigning desert to a different moral category, at the same time, he tried to hang on, somewhat precariously, to the link between justice and 'equity'.

Jeremy Bentham (1748-1832) too was keen to promote laws that would maximize utility, but this time utility was defined in terms of his 'Greatest Happiness Principle', which meant basically maximizing pleasure and minimizing pain (1789/1962). Bentham rejected the whole concept of the rights of man as 'nonsense on stilts'; and also appeared to reject justice as something independent of utility. For instance, of the terms 'Law of Reason', 'Right Reason', 'Natural Justice', and 'Natural Equity' and 'Good Order', he says (p. 51),

Any of them will do equally well .... The last three are more tolerable than the others because they do not very explicitly claim to be anything more than phrases: they insist but feebly upon the being looked upon as so many positive standards of themselves, and seem to be taken, upon occasion, for phrases expressive of the conformity of the thing in question to the proper standard, whatever that may be. On most occasions, however, it will be better to say *utility; utility* is clearer, as referring more explicitly to pleasure and pain.

Bentham's philosophy was essentially individualist; there was no question of sacrificing oneself for the good of others; in fact, he took on board the popular Lockean notion that the greatest good would be achieved if all sought their own interests; thus he says, 'Society is so constituted that, in labouring for our particular good, we also labour for the good of the whole' (1802/1972, p. 209). Nevertheless, he did appear to want to temper the idea of 'The Greatest Happiness' with a distributive rule. Bentham was a determinist, so according to the EAD principle one might expect him to be an egalitarian, and to temper the new *telos* with an egalitarian rule. Indeed, his rule did seem egalitarian; thus he said, when happiness is considered, 'everyone should count for one, and nobody for more than one'. Bentham saw equality as an important means of achieving 'The Greatest Happiness'. As Edgeworth notes, 'The purest, as being the most deductive, form of utilitarianism is that which Bentham reasoned down to equality' (1881/1973, p. 371). Many of Bentham's ideas have egalitarian overtones, including his views on punishment. For instance, Bentham argued that the aim of punishment should not be that of retribution, but reform. Indeed, he spent much time and money on a model prison called the 'Panopticon', that would fulfil this purpose. He also campaigned for the abolition of the death penalty, the ending of the transportation of criminals and imprisonment for debt (though he also wanted to outlaw begging because of the unpleasantness it caused to observers).

However, the principle that 'everyone should count for one, and nobody for more than one', if interpreted to mean 'the equal distribution of happiness' could easily contradict the principle of 'the greatest happiness'. For instance, perhaps we might make more people happy on balance, if we deprived a few of their equal share of happiness. John Stuart Mill's (1861/1993) interpretation of Bentham's principle was, therefore, that everyone should be given an equal claim to the *means* of happiness (what they do with the means is a different matter). However, giving everyone an equal means to be happy might again conflict with the idea of 'the greatest happiness'. Perhaps we could make more people happy on balance if we deprived a few of their share of means of happiness. In other words, there is a potential conflict in Bentham's philosophy between utilitarianism and the idea of what is 'fair and equal'. Mill recognized the problem, and attempted to come up with a solution.

Mill on utility and virtue

Like Plato, Aristotle and Kant, John Stuart Mill (1806-1873) was one of the most influential philosophers in history. His main views on justice are set out in his classic work 'Utilitarianism', published in 1861.

Mill revived the term 'utilitarianism' after it had been used but discarded by Bentham. The central thesis of utilitarianism is that we cannot *prove* what is good for people (as Kant thought), neither is revealed in Divine Revelation (as the early Christian scholastics thought), all we have is the evidence from experience of the things people actually desire. What is good for people, is what they desire (note again the parallel with Hobbes). And what do people desire most? 'Happiness'. Which in Mill's view, is 'an existence exempt as far as possible from pain, and as rich as possible in enjoyments, both in quantity and quality' (1861/1993, p. 12). It therefore follows that the ultimate or greatest good is the maximum happiness possible in society, aggregated across individuals, or the 'Greatest Happiness Principle'.

The idea of pleasures having different 'qualities' came about largely after a mental crisis that Mill suffered in 1826, which he said was fuelled by the 'shadow' of necessity or determinism. As a result of this crisis, Mill became discontented with the classical utilitarian idea of a moral system devised around the idea of a set of automata attempting to satisfy their desires by maximizing pleasure and minimizing pain. Instead, he adopted a dualist notion that, although our actions are partly determined or necessitated by our inherited characters and circumstances, both our conduct and character can be improved if we voluntarily exert ourselves; moreover it is our duty to do so (see Mill, 1873/1924; Semmel, 1984). He therefore modified utilitarianism to accommodate different 'qualities' of pleasure; the highest coming from the pursuit of virtue. In doing so, Mill not only accepted the doctrine of free-will, but a very Aristotelian notion of the nature of virtue and its consequences. In his view, although our genetic make-up and our environments may restrict us, it is still in our power to overcome indulgence, sloth and immediate gratification; and by doing so, we become virtuous and achieve greater happiness.

But the 'Greatest Happiness Principle' does not require that 'happiness be distributed in proportion to virtue'; in fact it would, in principle, allow the virtuous to be punished if this created more aggregate happiness overall. For Mill's solution, we look to his views on justice.

Mill on justice

In his discussion of justice, Mill identifies a number of different concepts of justice; however, whilst accepting that they are all associated with justice, he argues that none of them adequately captures the idea in its entirety. For instance, justice cannot be simply to violate the legal rights of someone, because they may have forfeited those rights through their actions, or the laws that established those rights might be unjust. Neither can justice simply be to break faith with someone, because this can be overruled by greater obligations of justice; a person might forfeit the benefit promised. Justice is also not simply impartiality, for this is 'an instrument to some other duty' (1861/1993, p. 46); favour and preference are not always censurable, as when, for example, rewards and punishments are administered. Equality is problematic, because people disagree as to what should be equal, also it conflicts with other conceptions of justice such as needs and merit.

Mill actually never comes down to a definitive statement of what principle or set of principles he prefers, arguing that people may adopt different conceptions of justice according to expediency. But in his writings there is undoubtedly a clear preference for the view that justice, in essence, involves the *moral right to what one deserves*, and it is this that sets justice aside from mere expediency. He argues that justice involves the moral right to claim from others what is due to us, and in true EAD fashion, 'equals should be treated equally'. Thus he says (p. 64, my emphasis),

If it is a duty to do to each according to his deserts, returning good for good as well as repressing evil for evil, it necessarily follows that we should treat all equally well (when no higher duty forbids) who have deserved well of us, and that society should treat all equally well who have deserved well of it, that is who have deserved equally well absolutely. *This is the highest abstract standard of social and distributive justice; towards which all institutions, and efforts of all virtuous citizens, should be made in the utmost possible degree to converge.*

And also,

The principle .... of giving to each what they deserve, that is, good for good as well as evil for evil, is not only included within the idea of justice as we have defined it, but is the proper object of that intensity of sentiment, which places the Just, in human estimation, above the simply expedient.

(The use of the phrase 'evil for evil' is unfortunate in the above quote; perhaps what Mill should really have said is 'punishment for evil'.) But what should we do when desert and utility conflict? Mill's answer is simple; they will not. It is impossible to achieve the greatest happiness for the greatest number without the moral requirements of justice, because 'justice is a name for certain moral requirements which, regarded collectively, stand higher on the scale of social utility, and are therefore of more paramount obligation, than any others' (p. 66). In other words, justice makes people so happy that happiness cannot be maximized without it. In principle, Mill's statement is empirically testable, but without such a test, of course, it simply begs the question.

However, once again, what is more important for us here is not the logic of Mill's arguments, but their form. Mill undoubtedly showed a preference for desert, which was essential given his theory of virtue (Berger, 1984; Semmell, 1984). People can chose to be virtuous and vicious, and a theory of justice and morality must acknowledge this by giving to each according to his or her deserts; good for good, punishment for evil, with equals being treated equally. In fact, the more one examines Mill's writings the clearer his picture of the operation of desert becomes. For instance, there is much to suggest that when it came to the punishment of criminals, Mill was a retributivist. Thus in a letter to Florence Nightingale in 1860, he disagreed with the view that criminals are not to be blamed for their crimes, and argued that it is natural to retaliate against those who consciously or intentionally wrong us. And, in the House of Commons he demanded the death penalty for murder, and argued that it was 'effeminate' to be horrified by the thought of executing someone (see Semmel, 1984). Mill was also very committed to the idea of merit or desert in the distribution of wealth. Essentially Mill argued that rewards are only deserved when they are produced by autonomous behaviour; you do not reward people for natural ability, disability or chance occurrences. Mill argued 'above all merit, and not birth, is the rightful claim to power and authority' (1869/1970, p. 220).

According to Berger's (1984) comprehensive analysis of Mill's political theory, a number of basic principles of justice emerge from Mill's writings that can be summarized as follows. Inequalities in wealth, education and power are *prima facie* wrong and require justification. There should be a baseline level of equality, and variations around this should only come about by desert. Economic rewards should be earned through one's labour or exertions; inherited (and therefore undeserved) wealth is wrong and should be redistributed, at least to a certain extent by taxation. In other words, Mill argues that *everyone should receive the same unless they deserve different*. A clearer statement of the Equity as Desert principle would be hard to find.

Mill thus managed to fuse utilitarianism with justice by arguing that a political system that complied with desert would make people happiest. Critics of utilitarianism, however, maintained, and continue to argue, that the theory is fundamentally flawed, and there is something wrong with a philosophy that would, in principle, allow harming the innocent, or the reward of the unworthy, even if such occasions did not arise in practice. Mill tries to argue that utilitarianism demands justice as desert, whereas his critics argue that, in principle, it would allow deviations from desert.

During Mill's lifetime, however, one philosopher in particular was to challenge almost everything that had been said about justice up to that point in history; he was Karl Marx. However, before looking at Marx, it is useful to look briefly at one of his predecessors, Jean-Jacques Rousseau. Rousseau is a significant character in the history of political philosophy as he is often presented as one of the champions of modern egalitarianism.

Rousseau: A new vision of desert

Jean-Jaques Rousseau (1712-1778) was a French writer and philosopher and inspirer of the Romantic movement. His most famous political works include

'The Social Contract', and his political discourses including 'Discourse on Equality', and 'Discourse on Political Economy'. According to Viroli (1988), Rousseau interprets 'justice' to mean 'equality before the law' (p. 129). However, taken out of context, it would be misleading to argue that such a definition in any way captures Rousseau's idea of a 'just society', because it tells us nothing of the sort of laws Rousseau has in mind. To understand Rousseau's conception of the way law should operate we need to examine his political theory.

To Rousseau man in a natural state is good, free and equal, and has 'unlimited right to everything that tempts him and to everything he can take' (1755/1988, p. 96). Rousseau admits that people obviously possess natural inequalities due to genetic influences (such as differences beauty, age and strength), but in a state of nature, equality is maintained because, in isolation, each is able to provide for his own needs. The idea that there is a natural equality in nature was later taken up by Karl Marx, who argued that, for man in a 'savage barbaric condition .... demand and supply exactly coincide' (1844/1986, p. 31). This utopian conception of man in a state of nature is, of course, flawed from the start. Living in an isolated state, even with an abundance of the necessities of life, some (such as the disabled or infirmed) might still be totally unable to satisfy their own needs. Nevertheless, for Rousseau as well as Marx, this idea serves as a useful heuristical device for establishing a baseline against which the injustices that exist in society can be measured.

According to Rousseau, the problems begin when people interact with each other. Social interaction leads people them to compare themselves with each other, and to seek esteem. There is then competition for esteem. As a result, the original equality is broken, and the natural inequalities emerge to create a social order in which inequality dominates. Wealth and power are seen as measures of esteem, and the natural inequalities are emphasized in achieving these ends; the beautiful are admired and rewarded, the stronger, more skilful and intelligent can produce more, and are rewarded more, possessions accumulate, and laws are instituted to protect private property. Rich and poor classes develop. The rich can then exert more influence, and so become more powerful, and finally, as the powerful control more and more resources, classes of masters and slaves emerge. Rousseau's answer to these problems is that men should contract to work for the common good as part of a 'general will' in a society in which virtue reigns, and the natural equality between men is reinstated. Having so contracted, the rules generated by the 'general will' of the citizens are the 'law'; and only the citizens can make laws, or change them. (Laws made by a single authority figure, says Rousseau, are not laws.)

As Russell (1979) points out, there are many ways that Rousseau could be interpreted, and his writings may have influenced many, from the leaders of the French Revolution and early socialism, to the dictators of Russia and Germany. However, it would not be surprising if Rousseau's social contract were to interpreted as an egalitarian vision, and there is much in his writings to suggest this. His vision was of a state in which all would willingly want what is good for others; the poor would be protected against the tyranny of the rich. And although Rousseau did not argue that private property should be abolished altogether, he did propose that people must be prevented from accumulating excessive wealth, no one should be impoverished, and work must always be available.

However, whilst he did indeed advocate measures that would reduce inequalities in wealth and privilege, Rousseau was actually no proponent of the doctrine of 'equal shares'. Indeed he showed a marked preference for the ancient principle of 'geometrical proportion'. Thus, of equality, Rousseau says, 'Distributive justice would be opposed to this rigorous equality of the state of nature, even if it were practicable in civil society, and since all members of the state owe it services proportionate to their talents and strengths, citizens must in their turn be distinguished and favoured *in proportion to their services*'. Rousseau goes on to argue that the appropriate criterion (input) for determining rank in society, is not the abstract 'personal merit' or moral worth of persons, which is too open to error, but 'the actual services they render to the state, which are open to a more exact assessment' (1755/1988, p. 53, my emphasis). The determination of 'moral worth' of an individual is then best left to the public who will award esteem accordingly.

Viroli (1988) summarizes Rousseau's position as follows, 'The equality which reason sees as necessary for a just political constitution is not arithmetical, ascribing the same thing to everyone, but is geometrical or proportional. If the body politic is to be sound, it is necessary for public honour and esteem to be commensurate with the degree of individual merit and the nature of services rendered to the community' (p. 5). To Rousseau gross inequalities in wealth are particularly unjust because wealth can buy power and privilege. Consequently, there should be a graduated income tax to redistribute wealth from the very rich to the poor. Rousseau says, 'It is in everyone's interest that all should have an equal chance in life, and justice is no more than an expression of this equality (see Viroli, 1988, p. 129). Everyone is entitled at least to have his her basic needs for subsistence met; otherwise this right to an 'equal chance' or 'equal opportunity' would be violated. It was also important for Rousseau that society should change its emphasis from those qualities that are disruptive and arbitrary in their distribution, like riches, birth, genius and strength, to those that are conducive to harmony and can be chosen by anyone, such as humanity, courage and moderation. If esteem were attached to virtue, rather than wealth, people would no longer pursue wealth. To encourage observance of the law, however, it is important that 'Even the citizens who deserve well of their country should be rewarded with honours but never with privileges' (1755/1988, p. 65).

Rousseau says less about punishment; he objects to the awarding of severe sentences irrespective of the crime, but argues, nevertheless that 'History affords .... no examples of leaders who fared badly merely by being equitable .... To be just, one must be severe: tolerating wickedness, when one has the right and the power to repress it, is being wicked oneself' (1755/1988, p. 68). The equation of punishment with 'equity' here is particularly notable.

In Rousseau's 'well ordered' society, therefore, EAD would be the predominant structure governing social conduct. Rewards would be distributed according to services to the community; those who do disservices will be punished, and all should have an equal chance to perform these 'inputs'; hence, those whose opportunities to perform services and achieve commensurate outcomes, are limited by need, should be compensated. According, to Rousseau, however, this can only be accomplished by the power of the law, for it only through law that men can have justice and liberty. Put in its wider context, therefore, the idea of justice as 'equality before the law', is really only a part of Rousseau's conception of justice. For although he defines law has something generated only by the citizens to whom it applies, the conception of justice as 'equality before the law' is vacuous without reference to his vision of what the rules of law should actually be.

In many respects, Rousseau was not simply advocating a utopian dream, he was making a genuine contribution to social science by questioning the assumption that inequalities in wealth and inherited natural assets are compatible with a system that claims to give all an equal choice to perform those services to society that are valued and held worthy of reward. Nevertheless, he still clung to a belief in the value of private property. This created the inevitable problem of how to deal with inherited wealth and the privilege it can bring. Unlike Locke and Kant, and most advocates of private property before them, Rousseau openly recognized the difficulty; and part of his answer was a system of progressive taxation that would redistribute wealth from the very rich to the poor. However, the other part of his answer is less convincing. He attempts to argue that unless property can be inherited, the right to property would be 'useless', and there would be 'continual changes in the rank and fortune among the citizens', that would 'disturb and confuse everything' (p. 76). To these rather conservative appeals to utility (which seem to be entirely out of step with the rest of his scheme), Rousseau adds the point that children have often contributed by their own work to the acquisition of their parent's property (in other words, they deserve it).

To Marx, however, this problem was intractable. In his view, the only way to overcome the difficulty was to abolish private property.

Karl Marx and the criticism of capitalism

Karl Heinrich Marx (1818-1883), the German political philosopher, started his university studies learning law (his father was a lawyer), but soon abandoned law in favour of history and philosophy. Marx's philosophy was developed largely against the background of 18th century industrial society in England; in fact, his most extensive work is 'The Grundrisse' of which 'Das Kapital' (Capital) is the most famous part, that was written mainly in the reading room of the British Museum (see Marx, 1965, 1976, 1978). The three volumes of Capital were published in 1867, 1885, and 1894. Marx is of, course, best known for his critique of capitalism and his influence on the Communist League and the 'Communist Manifesto', written in 1848.

Marx's views on justice have stimulated much debate amongst philosophers; the main controversy revolves round whether Marx criticized capitalism because he thought it unjust, or whether he thought capitalism was just on its own terms, but should be substituted with a different sort of justice, or whether he rejected the whole notion of justice (see Buchanan, 1982; Campbell, 1988; Cullen, 1992; Lukes, 1982, 1985). Probably Marx's most famous expression on justice is to describe the notions of 'equal right' and 'just distribution', as 'dogmas that may have made some sense at a particular time but now are only a load of obsolete verbal rubbish' (1875/1986, p. 166). By the time Marx was writing, however, the term 'justice' had already taken on many disparate meanings, so it is not surprising that modern writers on Marx disagree as to his views on the subject. Nevertheless, again, perhaps we can learn most by examining the form of Marx's arguments.

The exploitation of labour

Marx set himself the task of explaining how, from a 'savage barbaric state' in which 'demand and supply exactly coincide', we can arrive at a situation in which millions are destitute, and barely able to sustain themselves, whereas others possess wealth way beyond that necessary to sustain themselves. Marx suggests that the wealth that accumulates in a capitalist system comes about as a result of one group exploiting another. The basis of this exploitation is that, historically, a certain class or section of society, the 'bourgeoisie', have come to own the means of production; that is, all the implements, machines, raw materials, land etc., that may be used to produce the things we use and exchange. On the other hand, there is another class, the 'proletariat', who do not own any of these things; thus they have nothing to sell or exchange to buy the things they need to survive, except themselves; that is, their labour. In Marx's view, the proletariat, or labouring class, once had access (or at least more access) to the means of production; they could produce things directly for their own use, to exchange for their own use. For instance, argues Marx, in England by the 14th century, the majority of the population consisted of free peasants, working on land commonly or privately owned. However, they have since been historically deprived of the means of producing the things they need to survive; hence they now have to sell their labour to the bourgeoisie for wages, with which they can then buy back the very things that they have produced.

Marx argues that, to justify the distribution of wealth in a capitalist economy, the apologists for capitalism employ the following myth (1976, pp. 873-874): 'In times gone by there were two sorts of people; one diligent, intelligent, and above all, frugal elite; the other lazy rascals, spending their substance, and more, in riotous living ... Thus it came to pass that the former accumulated wealth, and the latter sort had at last nothing to sell but their own skins'.

He adds: 'Such insipid childishness is everyday preached to us in defence of property. In actual history it is notorious that conquest, enslavement, robbery, murder, briefly force play the great part'.

In terms of EAD, the implication of this myth is quite clear; the reason why the elite own the means of production, and the rest have nothing is that they *deserve* it. The elite have earned their wealth through their productive labour or 'positive inputs', and have held onto their outcomes by being frugal. The rest have input little or nothing, and when they have earned any outcomes they have exchanged or squandered them for temporary pleasures. According to this myth then, the situation in which the bourgeoisie own the means to production, and the proletariat own nothing is perfectly fair and equitable; in fact, it closely approximates to Locke's vision of the growth and distribution of private property in capitalist society. To Marx, however, this mythological conception of 'justice' is 'insipid childishness'.

Marx saw this myth as illustrative of the received wisdom of the time with regard to the operation of the 'labour theory' of value within a capitalist economy; that is the view that, in a capitalist system, all ultimately receive wealth in due proportion to the value of their socially productive labours. In practice, asserts Marx, this is not what happens at all. Marx begins his analysis by arguing that the value of goods and services in a capitalist economy is not determined by a measure of the actual amount of labour or work that goes into their production. The types of actual material labour required to produce different commodities vary both in quantity and quality (such as intellectual and manual labour), and cannot be equated. So, in practice, the exchange value of a commodity is a sort of abstract average measure of the labour time necessary for its production; the 'socially necessary labour time' (Robinson notes here that, 'Marx was careful to avoid the absurd argument that the products of a slow worker contain more value than the product of an efficient one', 1964, p. 45). The value of a commodity is thus the *abstract labour* required to produce the commodity (which, at the same time, is the labour saved to others by having the commodity produced for them).

In a capitalist economy, the owner of capital then buys *labour power*, like any other commodity, paying or exchanging for it exactly what is necessary to produce or maintain it; its abstract labour cost. And in the case of labour itself, this is the minimum wage necessary for workers and their families to survive. However, the capitalist (called 'Moneybags' by Marx), sets the workers to work for more time than is necessary for them to produce what is necessary to maintain themselves and their families. As a result, 'moneybags' extracts *surplus labour* or 'surplus product' from the workers. Suppose, for example, a male worker can produce enough of some commodity in six hours, that if sold directly in the market, could be exchanged for money, which in turn could provide sufficient items to feed, clothe and shelter his family. The capitalist, being sole owner of the means of production, gives the same worker the minimum wages to necessary to buy these same necessities, but sets the worker to work for 12 hours. As he owns nothing except his labour, the worker has no alternative but to accept these conditions if he and his family are to survive, and as a result, the capitalist has extracted a further six hours of surplus labour time. Thereby the capitalist makes a profit by more or less holding the worker to ransom, and selling the products of this surplus labour.

So what is wrong with the capitalist making a profit in this way? Again, if we approach Marx's analysis in terms of EAD, the implication is clear; if we adopt a labour theory of value as an ethical concept or principle of justice as desert, then socially productive labour is a fundamental 'input' value, and workers are entitled to an 'outcome' or wage that represents or is commensurate with the value of their contribution, or what some socialists at the time of Marx called the 'undiminished proceeds of labour'. By creaming off the proceeds of further surplus labour, the capitalist is both giving the worker less than his due or desert, and receiving more than he (the capitalist) deserves for minimal labour; in fact, it was Marx's conviction that the bosses and aristocrats who have acquired great wealth have 'long ceased to work'. Moreover, the claim that a contract between an employer and a worker is 'equal' (the wage is a just or equal return for the service rendered), because the employee has 'freely agreed' to a particular wage for his labour, is, according to Marx, a piece of ridiculous nonsense; for Marx says, 'The "free" labourer agrees, that is, is compelled by social conditions to sell the whole of his active life .... no matter how much it may appear to be the result of a free contractual agreement' (1965, p. 271).

Marx's objection to the capitalism in many ways echoes the general distaste that the many of the early scholastics, as well as Aristotle, had for 'usury', and the buying and selling of commodities solely to make money. Aristotle considered money making to be unnatural; the correct or natural purpose of commodity exchange is to provide for human needs, and the purpose of money is purely to facilitate this exchange, not to accumulate. Thus, in 'Politics', Aristotle says that usuary is 'most reasonably detested', and he had little time for the retail trade, both of which he considered to be unnatural (1257a-1258b). However, the scholastic objection against money making was more than the idea that money and commodities are put to unnatural use; it was that the person who uses money or commodities in this way not only often holds others to ransom, but invariably has not put in the requisite work necessary to produce or acquire the commodities that exchange for money. Hence by using money to make money, or buying commodities simply to sell them, usurers and other capitalists not only deprive the workers of their dues, but end up with a capacity to buy commodities that is disproportional to their actual contributions or inputs to society. The economic historian, Richard Tawney (1929, p. 612), summarizes this view as follows:

The essence of the argument was that payment may properly be demanded by the craftsmen who make the goods, or by the merchants who transport them, for both labour in their vocation and serve the common need. The unpardonable sin is that of the speculator or middleman who snatches private gain by the exploitation of public necessities. The true descendant of the doctrines of Aquinas is the labour theory of value. The last of the schoolmen was Karl Marx.

So just as employers 'snatch' labour hours from their workers, usurers snatch labour hours from those they extort interest, and speculators snatch labour hours from those who they overcharge for the necessities of life. Marx argues that the only way out of capitalist exploitation is, through revolution, to abolish private property and the wages system, and devise a classless, stateless, society where people produce and exchange things directly for their own shared use; that is, communism.

Thus, although Marx criticizes the received wisdom of the time with regard to the operation of the labour theory of value within a capitalist economy, his critique clearly implies that the value of one's services *ought* to be based on exactly such a theory; that, is all should receive truly outcomes in due proportion to their labours, under conditions of equal opportunity. It is very important to recognize, however, that Marx was very critical of any attempt to tie what he called 'the means of consumption' to some general measure of contribution, such as 'labour-time'. We find his most definitive views on this subject in a famous piece entitled 'Critique of the Gotha Programme', written in 1875. The Gotha Programme was a scheme advocated by the German socialist, Ferdinand Lassalle (1825-1864), who favoured 'state socialism' through intervention rather than communism. To Marx, and those he influenced such as Vladimir Lenin (1870-1924), this sort of socialism was a necessary step on the road towards communism, but it was defective in that it was still contaminated by bourgeois concepts.

Marx's critique of socialism

According to the socialist programme, private ownership of the means of production should be abolished; instead, each producer should make a contribution to the social enterprise, for which 'Society gives him a certificate stating that he has done such and such an amount of work (after the labour done for the communal fund has been deducted), and with this certificate he can withdraw from the social supply of means of consumption as much as costs an equivalent amount of labour' (1986, p. 165). The 'communal fund' here is a fund that covers administration costs, schools, health services, unemployment relief, and so on. In other words, each worker has a right to receive an outcome in equal proportion to his or her contribution, starting from a baseline in which all are provided with education, health services and compensation for when work is unavailable (obviously an EAD system).

Marx recognizes that this is an advance on the old capitalist system; for no longer can the capitalists accumulate wealth by doing no work and gaining by giving the workers less than their due. And by using the amount of labour or effort as the input it does not acknowledge class distinctions and privileges, and makes the opportunities to contribute more equal. But to Marx, the 'equal right' inherent in this programme is still a 'bourgeois right' (p. 165). The problem is that using by amount of labour as the unit of contribution, it treats people in an abstract way and ignores the real differences between them; in particular, he says, it 'gives tacit recognition to a worker's individual endowment and hence productive capacity as natural privileges'. In other words, it assumes workers have an equal capacity to provide different amounts of labour, when they do not; for he says, 'One person .... may be physically and intellectually superior to another and thus be able to do more labour in the same space of time or work for a longer period. To serve as a measure labour must therefore be determined by duration or intensity, otherwise it ceases to be a standard' (p. 165). This failure to recognise the differences between people is also shown in the way that the resulting distribution of the 'means of consumption' ignores the different values that the same outcomes may have to different producers; hence Marx' makes the statement mentioned earlier, that 'one worker is married, another is not; one has more children than another, etc., etc. Thus, with the same work performance and hence the same share of the social consumption fund, one will in fact be receiving more than another, one will be richer than another etc. (pp. 165-166)'.

In other words, in the language of EAD, for outcomes to be truly equally proportional to inputs, account must be taken of the 'undeserved' advantages that the genetically well-endowed have over the less well-endowed. Unless this is done, people do not start with an 'equal opportunity' to perform the inputs. But more than this, even when these are taken into account, the true value of the outcomes must take into account the different 'needs' of those involved. One small can of food may fully satisfy a small person, but is of less value to a large person who may require five tins of food to achieve the same level of nutritional satisfaction.

According to Marx, therefore, the only arrangement that really makes any sense is one that accords with the famous dictum, *'from each according to his abilities, to each according to his needs'* (1975/1986, p. 166). Though, as Vlastos (1975) notes, Marx did not actually invent this idea; rather it echoes, without acknowledgement a remark made by the French socialist Louis Blanc (1811-1882) that, 'true equality' is that which apportions work to ability and recompense to need' (cited by Vlastos, 1975, p. 142). But why this dictum? What is it about this idea that makes it superior to other principles? Perhaps again, EAD may be able to provide the answer.

Ability, need, effort and EAD

Imagine a situation in which all abilities are largely influenced if not totally determined by factors beyond our control. In such a situation, if we wanted an input measure that allowed all a real equal opportunity to make the same contribution as everyone else; what would the input look like? Presumably, it would look like a species of 'effort' or Kantian 'will'; something like 'the effort one is prepared to muster, given the opportunity, regardless of capacities or abilities and other factors determined by uncontrollable influences'. Consequently, if everyone put in a reasonable amount of this 'effort', to the best of, or despite the limits of their abilities, then in theory, *all inputs would be equal*. And, if all inputs are equal, under conditions of equal opportunity to perform the inputs, then according to EAD, all outcomes should be equal. However, as Marx says, for outcomes to be truly equal, we must take into account differential need.

It would thereby follow, therefore, that if we were to consistently follow the dictum 'from each according to his abilities, to each according to his needs' the result would be *perfect Equity as Desert*; equal outcomes for equal inputs under conditions of equal opportunity to perform the inputs.

The problem would remain, however, that for this principle to work, we would have to assume that all would want to put in maximum effort, no one would voluntarily do nothing, or deliberately put themselves into need, or attempt to amass more than he or she needs. Marx recognizes this problem, and indeed, in the 'Manifesto of the Communist Party' he states that will be an 'Equal obligation to work' (1848/1939, p. 100). In the end, however, Marx hoped that people would simply follow this dictum without coercion; the state would 'wither away'; and with it to compel people to follow 'laws' to guarantee 'rights'. In a communist state 'gushing' with 'cooperative wealth', with no private property, and no poverty, there would be no need to guarantee someone's 'rights'.

Lenin's vision of the transition to communism involved essentially the same logic. Hence, he argued that the first step was to create a state in which 'All that is required is that they (citizens) should work equally - do their proper share of work - and get paid equally'; with the result that, 'The whole of society will .... become a single office and a single factory with equality of work and equality of pay' (1917/1939, p. 151). At first, this arrangement would require 'swift and severe punishment' to control 'the idlers, the gentlefolk, the swindlers and similar guardians of capitalist traditions' (p. 150); but ultimately following the appropriate rules of human interaction would become a habit, and require no coercive power would be necessary.

Marx the desert theorist

Marx has been criticized on many grounds, for his naive economic theory, for his championing of revolution, and for his unworkable utopian communist society (see, for example, Buchanan, 1982; Robinson, 1964). But from our point of view, more important is the fact that, on closer examination, Marx looks very much like a desert theorist with his roots planted firmly in the desert tradition of the scholastics and the Greeks. He was obviously deeply committed to the ideals treating equals equally, and unequals unequally, according to their deserts. Indeed, his whole attack on capitalism is full of appeals to desert. The obvious implication of his arguments is that capitalism is fundamentally corrupt because the workers receive less than their true deserts, and the capitalists more. Moreover, to Marx, socialist doctrines that use only labour or work as the input unit are an improvement, but they still fail to give people exactly what they deserve. In a communist state, however, Marx implies that pure desert can be achieved; there can be *real* equal outcomes, for *real* equal contributions, under conditions in which all (including those naturally disadvantaged in mind and body) really do have an opportunity to provide the same 'inputs' on an equal footing.

Significantly, therefore, the type of 'equality' advocated by Marx and Lenin, as well as socialists like Lassalle, was not one based on the principle of 'ignoring inputs'. They were not advocating a system in which people's contributions were *irrelevant*. Thus, although Marx's analysis could be described as very deterministic, his view was not unambiguously one of 'deterministic egalitarianism'. He did not argue that all should receive equal shares (adjusted for need) because no one can ever deserve any more or less than anyone else. Indeed, the idleness of the capitalists and 'gentlefolk' was one of his main complaints about capitalism and aristocracy. The socialist doctrine on this was actually very strict; assuming all have the opportunity to work then, 'He who does not work, neither shall he eat' (see Lenin, 1917/1939, p. 150); those who deliberately place themselves in need will not be tolerated. Marx's egalitarianism rests on the premise that in an ideal communist society no one will voluntarily be idle and all will work equally within the limits of their 'natural' abilities; the communist ideal is equal outcomes (adjusted for need), for equal inputs, not that all should take, according to their needs, regardless of what they do.

Similarly, although Marx seriously questioned the deterrent effects of punishment, his view was not that those who break the law or unjustifiably harm others should necessarily be excused punishment, but rather one should concentrate on altering the system that gives rise to crimes (see Buchanan, 1982); for instance, in a state in which all can take what they need, and there is no private property, 'theft' of material goods, and crimes motivated by envy and jealousy of the possessions of others, would not exist.

In the light of all this, all the discussion about whether Marx himself considered his communist society to be 'just' or 'beyond justice', looks somewhat misdirected. For, if Marx really did not believe in 'justice', it is difficult to see on what grounds was he supposedly criticising capitalism and socialism, and what exactly he saw in communism that supposedly made it superior to these forms of political organization.

Conclusion

From this very brief overview of some of the most important characters and events in the history of the philosophy, it is obvious that philosophers and theologians have always had problems defining what is meant by 'justice'. Nevertheless, although the idea of justice as desert, in the form of Equity as Desert, may have become distorted and fragmented over the centuries, quite clearly it never actually disappeared. Indeed, as an historical analysis shows, it has remained a dominant and ubiquitous feature in moral and political theorizing even though a direct link between it and the term 'justice' has not always been made by the theorist in question.

PART 6

TOWARDS AN INTEGRATED PERSPECTIVE ON JUSTICE

CHAPTER 20

THE FRAGMENTATION AND SURVIVAL OF DESERT

We are now, perhaps, in a better position to rexamine modern philosophical theories, but first, it may be informative to go over and summarize briefly the possible origins of what now appear to be very disparate justice concepts.

At the beginning of the last chapter, I referred briefly to MacIntyre's (1982) idea that we have witnessed the collapse of virtue centred moral systems in which virtue was related to an overriding purpose or *telos*. Consequently, argues MacIntyre, modern moral theorizing in general is in a state of disarray, and one of the main reasons for this is that we are attempting to devise theories of morality using parts of various historical schemes that make no sense taken out of their historical context. In fact, MacIntyre says we are simply left with 'linguistic survivals' from older practices 'that have lost the context provided by these practices' (1982, p. 57).

. If we apply the same reasoning to theories of justice, it is evident that, historically, we may have seen the distortion and fragmentation of an ancient desert tradition of justice in which the distinctions between the various conceptions we now associate with justice were less obvious. If we accept this desert tradition as a starting point for the various conceptions of justice that followed, then, with appropriate caveats, many of the confusing and conflicting ways in which justice has subsequently been described begin to make more sense. Let us consider again, therefore, some of the critical features of the idea of justice in ancient Greece.

The ancient desert tradition

To Plato, sheer perfect justice is to give each his due according to *geometrical equality*. Everyone who plays their appropriate role in a community is entitled to a strict 'due' on the basis of the service they provide in carrying out that role, and perfect justice awards, in exact equal proportion, good those who do good for their communities, and penalties to those who harm their communities. Moreover, everyone can choose (even if the choice is made in a past life) the amount of service or good they want to contribute. Aristotle echoes Plato's view when he says that a just man is 'one who will distribute either between himself and another, or between two others, not so as to give more of what is desirable to himself or less to his neighbour (and conversely of what is harmful) but so as to give what is *equal in accordance with proportion*' (NE5, 1134a; my emphasis).

Certainly the Greeks' commitment to 'equal choice' or 'equal opportunity' to perform the services associated with particular roles, seems highly questionable by modern standards. Nevertheless, it seems undeniable that the roots of this idea can be found explicitly in Plato's ideas, and in Aristotle's theory of responsibility. In Aristotle's ideal system, punishments should be awarded in proportion to the viciousness of the act, and rewards should be awarded in proportion, not to characteristics such as inherited wealth or power, but to 'political excellence' in the form of virtue; for both virtue and vice are freely chosen. It is also evident that, when Aristotle recognized that equal opportunity or choice was incompatible with his ideas about natural hierarchies, he attempted to justify his position, in the time-honoured way, by attempting to appeal to the differential 'needs' of those on different rungs of the social and biological ladder. It would be 'unjust', or contrary to *dike*, for those such as slaves, women and children not to be ruled by their superiors, or for the aristocracy not to receive greater wealth than common men, for how else could their different needs be equally met? In doing this *natural law* is obeyed, for everything in the universe obeys the same law, maintaining the balance and equilibrium of the cosmos. This is also, pure, perfect fairness and equity. There is no question of perfect justice being 'unfair' or 'inequitable', for what is fair and equitable reflects the operation of *dike*, the law of nature or the cosmos; justice is both what is *lawful* and *equitable* according to the ordering of the cosmos.

If we assign geometrical proportion, or distribution according to desert the highest priority (it is the 'preeminent distribution'), other conceptions of justice start to fall into place. In the Greek scheme, justice in the universe is a dynamic process, and deviations from geometrical equality must be continually corrected. The deviations from geometrical proportion are corrected by what Aristotle calls '*remedial or corrective justice*'; thus anyone who violates the distribution by 'gaining' without putting in the requisite input or service, or who harms others who do not deserve it, and thereby deprives them of their dues, must be penalized. The preeminent distribution is also maintained by exact reciprocity in the exchange of commodities and social obligations between individuals, or *commutative justice*. Thus whilst remedial justice and reciprocity in the exchange of services might appear to concern different things, they are not, in principle, in conflict with each other; rather they serve to maintain the grand preeminent distribution that operates according to geometrical proportion.

Man made laws are then instituted to maintain this preeminient system dictated by natural law. Hence when a man-made law is rightly framed and does this well, we call it just, and when it does it very badly, we call it unjust; and, as a corollary, a person who violates a just law has necessarily committed an injustice, and in a world of just laws, a just person will be *law abiding*, obeying both the natural and man-made law. Moreover, to the Greeks, a well ordered society that corresponds to natural law, and in which everyone receives their due is, of course, a highly desirable state of affairs in which peace and happiness will be maximized. Hence just laws are also *useful* in attaining this end.

Measuring the value of the various services and outcomes in this distribution is difficult, though one way they can be estimated is through *mutual consent*; in other words when two or more parties agree to a reciprocal exchange of services or outcomes, this can often provide a reasonable assurance that, for each of the parties concerned, the outcomes will be equally proportional with their services. Consequently, so long as *contracts, promises or agreements* (including those enshrined in public law) to which parties *consent*, serve to maintain, and do not obviously violate the preeminent distribution, they can be considered 'just', and it will be unjust to break them, for then one person would unjustly gain more than is due or deserved, and the other would unjustly lose. However, if a contract, promise or agreement violates the preeminent distribution, it will be 'unjust', and it will be permissible to break it, even if originally it was consented to by all of the parties concerned. Also, if the preeminent distribution is to be maintained, it is essential that those who are given the job of deciding between conflicting claims that affect the distribution, should be *impartial* in their judgements. And, until the result of a judgement affecting the distribution is known, all those involved are 'due' impartiality as part of their deserts.

Within this general conception of justice, some modes of conduct are going to be more conducive to the maintenance of the system than others. Those who do evil, and harm their communities in some way by violating 'just laws', thereby deprive many 'deserving' others of their dues, and commit injustice. Those who do good, and make a positive contribution to their communities, are more likely to promote the general welfare of their communities, and give to many others their dues. But strict justice requires more than this. It requires one to regulate good actions to conform exactly to the preeminent distribution. Some excellences such as wisdom are required in all situations, but to be truly virtuous, we must be brave, temperate and good-tempered at the right time in the right way, according to the dues of those who are affected. For example, bravery in defence of one's friends and country, against a tyrant, will be just if it prevents others from receiving less than the dues. But bravery in defence of the tyrant will be unjust if we assume that the tyrant is not 'due' such a return or reward. Hence, justice is only one of the excellences or virtues that can count as 'inputs' in the scheme of geometrical proportion, but it is the most important; *it is the virtue that guides us in how to use the others in a perfect way.* In fact, only through justice can we exercise complete and perfect excellence or virtue; hence Aristotle's statement that, 'justice is often thought to be the greatest of excellences and "neither evening nor morning star is so wonderful"; and proverbially, "in justice is every excellence comprehended" ' (NE5, 1129b). For perfect excellence or virtue is that which accords with justice. It is also worth emphasizing that, within this tradition, any kind of behaviour that negatively influences others is an 'injustice', if those whom it influences are undeserving of such treatment. Hence, contrary to Sadurski's (1985) view, acts that affect others such as deceit, obscene language, and treason, can indeed be considered unjust, if those whom they influence do not deserve to be treated in these ways.

Desert and rights

Although the Greeks did not base their conception of justice on 'rights', if one likes, justice can also be seen as concerning rights, but only certain kinds of 'rights'. One has one fundamental right; *the right to what one deserves.* One should then be granted whatever subsidiary rights are necessary to secure one's deserts. Relative to others, therefore, one should have an equal positive right to choose between good and evil, or services and disservices to others (including God), and various gradations of these. This means that one *starts* with 'the equal freedom to *pursue* one's ends'. As Kant says, 'all moral evil (as well as good) springs from freedom' (p. 67).

Having been granted this right, one then has a right to benefit for the way one has decided to exercise this right. This means that those who have made positive contributions have a right to the rewards they deserve, no more and no less (though this is not a right to do anything they like with their rewards or outcomes). But at the first sign that someone is pursuing evil, this 'right to freedom' is curtailed and punishment is administered; but all still maintain the right to be punished *no more than they deserve*. Moreover, those who are receiving fewer positive outcomes than they deserve have a right to receive compensation from others until perfect equity, or the least inequitable distribution, is achieved. In other words, within a scheme of desert, everyone starts with a right to pursue his or her ends, but not necessarily the right to achieve them; one's means and ends must fit in with the overall scheme.

As for 'entitlement'; within this older desert tradition, there is no obvious distinction between 'desert' and 'just entitlement'; one is entitled to what one deserves. Moreover, in a world that in which there is transmigration of souls with cross-generation responsibility, reciprocal role obligations, and unequal genetically created needs that require some to be wealthier than others to maintain true proportional equality, it is not necessarily an injustice in terms of desert for child to be 'entitled' to inherit a fortune and to live in luxury, and for another to be 'entitled' to little or nothing and live in a state of relative poverty or slavery.

The obvious point to be emphasized here, however, is that from the perspective of this system of desert, one can only construct a theory of 'just' rights and entitlements, and laws to enforce them, when one already has a theory of justice. The 'fundamental natural right to murder children' can only be rejected once we consider that child murder is not permissible within our theory of justice. Hence one cannot derive a theory of justice from a set of rights and man-made laws or entitlements; rather justice is the standard to which those rights, laws and entitlements should conform.

Desert and the fruits of one's labour

If we view justice from the perspective of proportional desert we can also clarify some of the arguments that surround the idea of entitlement to the 'fruits of one's labours'.

The idea that we 'deserve' the products of our own labour is implicit in most of the older renditions of the labour theory of value. However, the concept of desert, as found in the views of those such as Aristotle and the scholastics, assumes a communal cooperative enterprise in which one's desert is proportional to one's contributions to the good of the community. Technically, therefore, other than that which is necessary to maintain one at a basic level of subsistence as part of the 'zero outcomes baseline', one is not simply entitled to 'the products of one's labour'; it depends on whether that labour is beneficial to the good of others and the demands of others in terms of their deserts. Indeed, the products of some people's labours may be a positive liability to the community; for example we do not normally say that graffiti artists, forgers and mutilators are entitled to the 'products of their labour'. Moreover, although a man does deserve a return equivalent or commensurate with the contribution he has made to the good of the community (assuming adjustments are made for need or 'working capacity'), if he works hard purely for his own benefit, he does not necessarily 'deserve' the 'unlimited fruits of his labour' (see Karl Marx's criticism of socialist policy on this point, 1986). Within a system of desert the only way one can legitimately gain extra outcomes for one's own consumption is to use the extra outcomes one has generated as contributions to the good of others and cycle them through the system. From this perspective, therefore, desert functions within a context of mutual cooperation and exchange; it assumes interaction between individuals. A situation in which everyone is not interested in cooperation, and simply 'does their own thing', is not a special sort of justice; it is a situation in which people have effectively given up on justice.

It is this assumption that gives rise to the argument, found in the writings of Locke and Bentham, and very common amongst modern defenders of private property and free-market economics, that working for oneself *is* a positive contribution to the community. For instance, so the argument goes, given equal resources, and an opportunity to 'combine one's labour' with those resources, people who work hard for themselves can produce a useful surplus for the community, and as they can provide for themselves and their families so when calamities befall them, they are a less of a drain on the resources of the community. Moreover, if all work for themselves, the hand of God hand or its more modern counterpart, the 'invisible hand of the market-place', will make sure that the needy are cared for.

The fragmentation of desert
Within the older desert tradition of justice the various conceptions of justice such as natural law, obedience to civil law, fairness, equality, reciprocity, choice, contract, consent, punishment, proportionality, culpability, impartiality, virtue and rights and entitlements (including those relating to the 'fruits of one's labours'), potentially make sense as parts of a coherent whole. Taken out of this context, however, they become isolated, contradictory fragments. This is particularly true in the emergence of *consent* and *utility* as major principles of justice in their own right.

Consent and contract out of context
To reiterate, the notion of 'consent' or 'agreement' in justice seems to have been borrowed from the old idea in 'commutative justice' that when two or more persons are 'content' with a situation this can be used as a rough measure of whether each receives equal 'value' from the exchange. Within the old desert tradition, the idea of a contract, or agreement, thus operated as *part* of a scheme of justice, but was subject to the dictates of the wider scheme. The notion of 'consent', however, gained particular popularity as a principle of justice in its own right during the Age of Enlightenment when political theorists were searching for a standard of justice that was independent of the authority of the Church and hierarchically ordered monarchic and oligarchic insitutions, and fitted in with increasing mercantile activity. However, divorced from its wider context, the notion of *consent* proved impossible to apply as a standard of justice.

This is not surprising; if we really think that 'mutual consent' is the basis of justice, and we take this seriously, then a pact between a wealthy landowner and a starving labourer to sell the latter into bondage, should be considered perfectly just. But even the most ardent advocates of the idea of justice as consent or agreement, such as Hobbes and Kant, seem rather squeamish about such possibilities, and end up diluting the idea of 'consent' such that justice becomes that to which people have given their 'tacit consent', or that to which people, 'should', 'would' or 'might possibly' consent. Rousseau, like Hobbes and Kant, is also very willing to give us details of the exact rules to which people *ought* to give their agreement. Thus Hobbes, Kant and Rousseau seem to use the concept of consent, not so much as a means to generate their theories of justice, but more of a way of justifying their own established preconceptions about what justice should be.

It is also notable how the attempts of the early contractarians to marry the ideas of justice as some sort of hypothetical contract and justice as legal authority (that is, an authority to which people have tacitly consented, or might possibly or ought to consent), live on in semantic curiosities such as 'punishment' is not 'punishment' unless it is administered by a legal authority against someone who has broken authorized rules (and has thereby 'tacitly consented' to be punished). As discussed earlier, within the desert tradition, punishment is simply 'the infliction of an ill suffered for a real or imagined ill done', and just punishment is the 'infliction of an ill on a person who deserves it in proportion to the ill undeservedly suffered'. Of course, whether such punishment is 'legal' will indeed depend on the laws of the land, and the law generally objects to people 'taking the law into their own hands', but in their everyday lives people do not restrict their useage of the term punishment to this legal context. Indeed, it is notable how often modern juries sometimes follow the Jewish biblical code, and look favourably on innocent, undeserving victims who have retaliated and administered 'unauthorized' punishment on those who have violated them.

Utility versus what is fair and equal

Similarly, although the idea that rules of justice should be *useful* in obtaining some objective is an old one, in the older desert tradition, there was no question of deriving a theory of justice solely from what is useful; rather it was simply assumed that what is just must be useful, because what is just reflects the operation of the cosmos. The idea with respect to morality in general is described by Pope Pius XI as follows (1939, p. 55): 'even ancient paganism recognized that the sentence ("what helps people is right") to be perfectly accurate must be inverted and read: "Never is anything useful, if it is not at the same time morally good. And not because it is useful is it morally good, but because it is morally good, it is also useful" '.

As I pointed out in the last chapter, the concept of utility was also less problematic in the older desert systems because in these, the ultimate good coincided with a principle of 'just distribution'. As Kant tells us, in the ideal ancient schemes (as well as his own scheme) ultimate rewards were distributed proportionately in accordance with virtue. However, the utilitarians scrapped the old Greek *telos*, abandoned the religious *summum bonum*, and substituted a new secular end for human endeavour, the 'Greatest Happiness Principle', that did not explicitly subsume a principle of 'just distribution'. As a result, the early utilitarians and their immediate predecessors found themselves trying to reconcile the fact that their new found standard of 'morality' could be contrary to the dictates of 'just distribution' according to what is equitable, or 'fair and equal' in terms of desert.

It was these developments that laid the seeds of modern disputes over the status of 'utility' as a principle of justice, and all the attempts to come up with compromise solutions. In terms of economic philosophy, the most obvious attempt to remarry the 'useful' with the 'fair and equal' came in the form of that most famous of 'half-way houses', 'Pareto-optimality'; that is, the idea that a situation is optimal or efficient when it is impossible to make one person better-off without making someone else worse off. Thus, for example, the political economist and utilitarian, F.Y. Edgeworth, modified the greatest happiness principle, such that it becomes, 'that arrangement to be made which conduces to the greatest sum-total of welfare, subject to the condition that neither should lose by the contract'. He did this so that, he says, 'the more delicate force of amity which even in economic men is not wanting, may become felt' (1881/1973, p. 372). However, as with the notion of consent, the concept of Pareto-optimality fails as an overreaching principle of justice because it takes no account of *who* is taking part in the arrangement, and the general context of the arrangement as part of an overall system of justice. Sometimes justice as desert may demand that someone *should* be made worse-off.

From the perspective of the older desert tradition, therefore, it is not surprising that so many philosophers have come to the conclusion that utility *per se* is *not* a principle of justice; for although utility *per se*, may be desirable, and, arguably, in some form, may even be a legitimate aim for human conduct or 'morality', it may run counter to the demands of desert.

One can see, nevertheless, how the modern connection of utility to justice might have come about; not only might it have evolved from the semantic machinations of the utilitarians, but also from the gradual divorce of the idea of justice as 'law' from that of justice as the 'fair and equal'. If we ignore justice as that which is fair and equal, and equate justice solely with 'law', not only as it exists, but law as it *ought* to be, then it is an easy step to the position that, given utility is the ultimate natural end of human action, the civil law *ought* to promote utility. As a result, what is naturally lawful, what ought to be lawful in terms of civil law, what is useful, and what is just, become the same. Similarly, if (like Hume) we try to justify a system of legally binding 'property entitlements' in terms of what is most useful to society, and equate justice with natural law and what the civil law ought to be, then again 'property entitlement' merges with justice, and 'justice as property entitlement' separates from justice as that which is 'fair and equal'.

For justice theorizing, the result of these developments was and remains, chaos. This has particularly been so in relation to systems of entitlements to gifts and inherited wealth. It may be very useful to the stability of society, as Hume (and even Rousseau) claimed, to be able to inherit wealth, but with no transmigration of souls, cross generation responsibility, unequal genetic need, and no God or other force of natural justice to ultimately sort things out, it is difficult to justify why, for example, why one 'undeserving' child should end up with a fortune whilst another is destitute. Thus we find political philosophers desperately trying to justify unequal divisions of inherited property entitlements in terms of elements of the old desert scheme. Hence we have Rousseau's claim that children have often contributed by their own work to the acquisition of their parent's property, and Hume's appeal to 'equity' as a reason for not interfering with property rights. It is as though these ideas will somehow make things 'fair and equal' again.

The 'Closest Approximation to Ideal Desert Principle'

However, perhaps this is not really the end of the story as far as clash between the 'useful' and the 'fair and equal'. Earlier, when discussing Plato's theory, I mentioned the idea of a sort of 'utilitarianism of dues', in which the criterion of the greatest good could be described as, 'the closest approximation to the ideal where everyone receives his or her due'. The basic idea here is that, within the framework of EAD, in a world in which perfect justice as desert is not possible, sometimes an apparently utilitarian solution may actually allow greater overall desert than a solution that concentrates on individual desert. This kind of analysis might help to explain why certain types of utilitarian decisions might be deemed more acceptable than others.

Consider Kant's view that it would be an injustice if, 'in a world inhabited by intelligent beings, all of whom behaved well, and so deserved to be happy, all were destitute and lived in the most wretched circumstances'. In such circumstances, it might be possible to justify policies that allow certain undeserved inequalities in wealth on the grounds that they will produce a 'less inequitable distribution' than an equal distribution. For example, it could be the case that by giving a few people more resources than the majority (when the former have no particular claim in terms of desert to them), a larger number of people might be rescued from a life of poverty and suffering. Assuming equal desert, this would technically be 'unjust'; but arguably, on Kant's reasoning, it might be considered *more just* than a situation in which the resources are distributed equally and all end up in a state of undeserved poverty and suffering. On the other hand, as Arrow (1973) points out, there may be circumstances in which policies that attempt to maximize the benefits for the worst off could have unacceptable implications; for instance, if helping a few in extreme need can only be achieved by reducing the rest of the population (including innocent young children) to (undeserved) poverty and suffering, this might seem unacceptable. In such a case the 'least inequitable solution', might be better achieved by concentrating resources elsewhere. In fact, by using Wagstaff and Perfect's (1992) deviation formula in respect to EAD, it is possible to make predictions regarding these kinds of scenarios.

Also, many people might deem it considerably less acceptable to kill one innocent person to give many others undeserved pleasure (such as slaughtering a Christian in an amphitheatre to give pleasure to thousands of Roman spectators), than to kill one innocent person to save many other innocent people from an undeserved death (such as killing someone who carries a deadly virus that could wipe out thousands of innocent people). Indeed, similar examples are often used to illustrate the classic objections to utilitarianism and the Kantianism respectively (see Posner, 1981). However, in terms of the least inequitable solution as derived from EAD, the preference for the latter is quite predictable. If we start from a situation in which perfect equity exists, then first course of action creates a greater overall deviation from perfect equity; it means that the majority of people receive undeserved positive outcomes (pleasure) for zero or negative inputs. In contrast, the second course of action minimizes the deviations from perfect equity, because a majority of innocent people will not receive extreme negative outcomes (that is, death), having done nothing the deserve it.

However, both of these scenarios might be deemed less acceptable than killing a man who is himself guilty of murder, to prevent him or her murdering other innocent people; in this case, if we accept that the harmdoer deserves to be punished in some way, then this treatment creates even less overall deviation from perfect equity. The harmdoer appropriately receives negative outcomes for negative inputs, and the majority stay in a situation in which they do not receive undeserved negative outcomes for zero inputs. Again, by using Wagstaff and Perfect's (1992) deviation formula in respect to EAD, it should be possible to make some predictions along these lines.

Such an analysis does not, of course 'solve' the desert versus utility debate. The impulse against individual victimization is undoubtedly very strong, regardless of this kind of calculus. It may be the case, nevertheless, that many of our moral intuitions about the pros and cons of various utilitarian decisions may rest on implicit appeals to the idea of the 'least inequitable' solution in cases where perfect equity is not possible.

CHAPTER 21

MODERN PHILOSOPHICAL VIEWS RECONSIDERED

If the preceding analysis is valid, and we have witnessed the fragmentation of the ancient desert centred schemes of justice, then if we look again at each of the modern theories of justice considered earlier in Part 2, we should expect to find distorted fragments not only of the original ancient schemes, but of those that followed. For example, perhaps the most ubiquitous and striking example of an idea taken out of context is Kant's categorical imperative. It will be remembered that, according to Kant, the categorical imperative was a device given by God, along with the gift of free-will in the noumenal world, to His children so that all would have the opportunity to work out the difference between virtue and vice and choose accordingly. God would then dispense reward and punishment according to desert 'with unerring precision' (though to a certain extent, particularly in regard to punishment, God's justice could partly be enacted in the earthly domain). Used outside of this context, however, not only is the categorical imperative incapable of specifying any rules of justice, but it is devoid of any theory that would justify its use. It is, therefore, little wonder that it can be adapted to more or less any political philosophy.

Nevertheless, if EAD remains the fundamental basis of what we mean by justice, then despite the appearance of such fragments we should also expect to find in modern theories the core features of EAD as a, if not the, primary force behind each theoretical perspective.

Rawls and deterministic egalitarianism

Rawls' theory is often described as 'contractarian'. However, as we have seen, historically, the idea of a 'social contract' was largely used by the political philosophers of the Enlightenment period to show why men should obey moral rules, without recourse to divine revelation or the authority of the church and monarchy. Hence, historical theories about the rules to which people ought or might consent or contract have inevitably turned out to be attempts to justify an already held conception of justice. Rawls clearly follows in this tradition; for more than anything else, his is a theory of desert.

According to EAD, the idea that more or less everything that could count as an input in a desert model is 'unchosen' or determined by forces outside our control, ultimately results in a philosophy of 'deterministic egalitarianism'. That is the view that, because our choices to engage in various types of input activity are virtually or entirely non-existent, no one can be judged more or less deserving than anyone else.; consequently, the most equitable, or least inequitable distributions of outcomes will always be equal. If we look closely again at Rawls theory, we find that this idea is not only contained in the theory; it is actually its whole driving force.

Rawls' 'veil of ignorance' derives directly from this logic. The assumption is that characteristics such as social status, levels of intelligence, physical strength and abilities, and other psychological attributes, are so determined by factors beyond our control, that there is basically no way any person can reasonably be termed more deserving than another on the basis of the exercise of any such attribute. Hence Rawls explicitly rejects the measurement of desert by 'effort' on the grounds that effort is influenced by natural abilities and skills for which a person can claim no credit; he says, 'the better endowed are more likely, other things equal, to strive conscientiously' (1971, pp. 310-312). He also rejects the idea that we can judge desert on the basis of character, for he says, 'character depends in large part upon fortunate family and social circumstances for which he can claim no credit' (p. 104).

The proposal that people do not deserve their natural abilities and skills is then used by Rawls to justify what he terms the 'tendency to equality' that is expressed in this theory. He argues that to treat people equally, and provide genuine equality of opportunity one must give more attention to those born with fewer native assets and born into less favourable social circumstances. Thus as people do not deserve their natural endowments and such as talent, character, physical advantages and the social environments into which they are born, they cannot acquire exclusive benefits from these advantages in ways that do not contribute to the welfare of others. Hence, he says 'undeserved inequalities call for redress .... in the direction of equality', and 'since inequalities of birth and natural endowment are undeserved, these inequalities are to be somehow compensated for (pp. 100-101). To this end, for example, the less intelligent might require greater resources spent on their education. He also says that people must neither gain nor lose from their 'arbitrary place in the distribution of natural assets or their initial position in society without giving and receiving compensating advantages in return' (p. 102). Those who end up on the top of the pile must compensate those at the bottom, because almost by definition, those at the top cannot deserve their superior position, and those at the bottom cannot deserve their inferior position.

The message is simple; as there is no basis for saying anyone is any more or less deserving than anyone else, all should receive the same, adjusted for need. But, having decided that all should receive the same, how do we implement this? The answer is to invent a hypothetical system in which a group of people come up with a set of rules that will generate a set of outcomes such that all receive equal shares, adjusted for their individualistic 'needs', regardless of their social status, assets, abilities, levels of intelligence, strengths, and other 'undeserved' attributes. In other words, 'the veil of ignorance' is a device invented so that equally deserving individuals can generate a set of truly equal outcomes.

Rawls' theory is thus not a piece of 'pure procedural justice'; it is a desert theory that assumes that, fundamentally, 'outcomes should be equal', taking into account that different individuals may require different sorts of outcomes to satisfy their own conception of what is 'good' for them. The 'procedures' that Rawls' devises are then the means of best realizing this end, given the different values that individuals may attach to the actual outcomes available.

Approximations to desert

However, although 'equal true outcomes' would seem to be the ideal goal of his system, Rawls actually ends up with a sort of hybrid system that in which mixes up equality in the various 'goods' to be distributed, with a concession to prudence or utility (the difference principle), that allows more to be given to the better off, if it is to the advantage of (is useful to) the less well off; thus he says the general conception of the difference principle is that 'All social primary goods - liberty and opportunity, income and wealth, and the bases of self-respect, are to be distributed equally unless unequal distribution of any or all of these goods is to the advantage of the least favoured (p. 303). As we have seen, however, the historical status of expedience or utility as a principle of justice has always been somewhat dubious, even amongst utilitarians. So it is not surprising that Rawls' 'utility' element has been criticized on the grounds that it is unjust (Dworkin, 1978b; Lucas, 1980). Rawls himself says that, 'undeserved inequalities call for redress .... in the direction of equality'. So whilst it might be prudent to help the poor who do not deserve their poverty by favouring the rich who do not deserve their wealth, by Rawls' own desert related criterion, if we want what is 'fair and equal', arguably this is no act of *justice*.

Nevertheless, we could argue, as I suggested in the last chapter, that an unequal distribution can be justified in terms of desert, if it is the *only* way of rescuing those at the bottom from 'undeserved poverty' that places them below the zero outcomes baseline for equity; for then such action may allow the 'least inequitable distribution', or the 'closest approximation to ideal desert' in a situation in which perfect EAD is not possible. In fact, arguably this is the main intuitive logic behind the appeal of the difference principle.

Just punishment

Rawls' treatment of 'rule-breakers' is also based on a clear, if somewhat inconsistent, appeal to desert. To reiterate, Rawls says that, in a just society, 'a propensity to commit criminal acts is a mark of bad character, and in a just society legal punishments will fall only upon those who display these faults' (p. 315). In Rawls view, it is an injustice to punish those who are not responsible for their actions. Nevertheless, he also argues that those behind the veil of ignorance might sometimes consider it legitimate to punish the innocent, for the 'greater good'; however, he adds 'All that can be done is to limit these *injustices* in the least unjust way' (p. 242, my emphasis). The obvious implication of this is that any decision to punish the innocent is an injustice, regardless of whether it derives from an original position ('just procedures'), because only the guilty deserve to suffer. In other words, we have yet more evidence that Rawls' theory is not primarily a contractarian theory of just procedures, it is a theory of desert.

However, it will also be remembered that, in defence of equality in distributive justice, Rawls also tells us that 'a person's character depends in large part upon fortunate family and social circumstances for which he can claim no credit' (p. 104). Thus apparently one is not entitled to advantages gained from good character, but one can be punished if one offends as the result of bad character. As I said previously, if responsibility is so important to Rawls, it is strange that punishments should fall only on those who largely, through no fault of their own, have a bad character. However, now we can see that difficulty does not arise from a clash between desert and equality, but rather a clash between two desert traditions. That is, the problem arises from an unhappy mix of a more modern piece of deterministic egalitarianism (all are equally deserving), with a piece of the older more animistic desert tradition in which character is seen as one's responsibility (people can be unequally deserving).

The practicability of desert

Despite the implicit appeals to desert in his theory, it is significant that Rawls claims to reject desert; and an important feature of his argument is that it is 'impracticable' to measure desert. His rationale is that if one bases desert on the principle of rewarding according to contribution, then in a competitive economy the extent or value of one's contribution will vary according to supply and demand, and a person's 'moral worth' should not vary according to the extent to which others happen to want the service that he or she provides. In the light of the analysis presented in this book, we can now see that this argument confounds two issues; the value of one's services to other people, and the degree of control one has over that value.

In its original sense, as used by the Greeks, one's 'moral worth' within a scheme of desert referred to one's ultimate worth or value in promoting what is assumed to be 'good' for men. In return, justice demanded that one should receive a reward in proportion to one's 'worth' in promoting the good of others. From this perspective, however, the ultimate rewards (*eudaimonia*, blessedness, or the highest quality of happiness) could only be achieved by performing certain activities or 'virtues' over which one had control; so the only sorts of contribution or measures of 'worth' that actually counted as deserving of reward were those that were both beneficial to others (including God) and in some sense 'chosen' (that is, unaffected by chance). However, the acts that comprised these virtues were not deemed to be invariant in terms of worth. To Aristotle, for example, bravery was a virtue; but it was not a virtuous act to be brave fighter when fighting was not demanded, as in defence of a tyrant, or whilst committing a crime; one's 'worth' was also dependent upon one's willingness and ability to adapt oneself to changing circumstances. To be most 'worthy' was to act in at the right time way, in the right way, for the right reason; not to act in the same way, all of the time, regardless of whether society welcomes your actions.

Moreover, justice was not limited simply to the distribution of the ultimate rewards. It could also apply to the distribution of more mundane social 'goods' such as income wealth and status. Hence, applying the same rationale to everyday economics, the scholastics later argued that it would be inappropriate for one's contributions to the welfare of others to vary unduly according to chance factors. Consequently, in the sort of economic systems envisaged by the scholastics, every effort must be made by the authorities to ensure that individuals' contributions do remained under their control. This involved, for example, preventing violent fluctuations in the market, paying workers a just wage according to capacity despite for temporary fluctuations in the market, and allowing workers to change jobs when the long term demand for a particular service drops. With regard to the latter, Fogarty notes, 'the scholastics' working assumption is normally that employees will be free to seek and employers to offer the jobs that suit them best' (1961, p. 290).

It follows, however, that should workers decide to ignore signs, and not avail themselves of opportunities to change the nature of their contributions in response to changing circumstances, then their 'worth' or 'desert' within the earthly system could quite legitimately be considered to vary according to certain fluctuations of supply and demand in the market place. For instance, in the Britain of 100 years ago, a man who worked hard walking the streets in all weathers lighting gas lamps would have been considered worthy of reward for his services. Today, however, a person attempting to do the same would probably considered in need of psychiatric help rather than worthy of reward. The essential point here is, although in a competitive economy it may indeed be difficult to find a measure of contribution that exactly accords with desert, the problem does not derive from the fact that desert based contributions must of necessity be independent of whether one's services are actually of any value or use to anyone else. Neither does it follow that one cannot intervene in the market to limit the effects of chance fluctuations on the value of one's contribution.

Nevertheless, the fact that Rawls claims that desert is impracticable is not to say that he dismisses desert *in principle*; in fact, far from it.

Equal worth and unequal desert

Rawls, of course is not alone in having problems with the treatment of criminals. The problem crops up for again for those egalitarian philosophers who attempt to base the case for an equal distribution on the premise that all human beings have 'equal worth' (which of course fits EAD; if all inputs are equal, then all outcomes should be equal).

Vlastos (1975), for example, argues that all human beings should receive equal shares (adjusted for need), 'Because the human worth of all persons is equal, however unequal may be their merit' (p. 143). By 'merit', Vlastos means all those valuable qualities or performances of which people can be graded, including moral merit or virtue. However, within the desert context from which these terms derived, the distinction between 'moral merit' and 'human worth' makes little sense. Perhaps the idea would make more sense if we were to argue, like Rawls, that, *if we disregard unchosen qualities that are irrelevant to desert*, then all are equally worthy, in the sense of equally deserving. But, in any case, Vlastos does not actually seem to believe his own statement, for he argues that criminals should be punished. But in what sense can we say that criminals should be punished because or even though they are of 'equal worth'? Punishment is supposed to result in negative and therefore very unequal outcomes for those on whom it is inflicted, and is thereby clearly at odds with the idea of 'equal outcomes' for 'equal worth'.

At the root of the problem may be a failure to distinguish between the idea of being worthy of the *means* to achieve one's desert, and the desert itself. As Campbell (1988) points out, one must not confuse the idea that people are to be accorded 'equal worth' in the Kantian sense that they are to be regarded as responsible agents, with the idea that people can possess 'unequal worthiness' on the basis of the ways they behave as responsible agents. Indeed, the ideas should be closely connected. According to EAD, everyone should be accorded equal worth in the sense of being given an equal opportunity to perform the inputs, and receive the rewards or punishments commensurate with those inputs. This might suggest, for example, that, in societies in which such provisions are available, all should receive at least the basic means for survival, including health care, equal educational opportunities and protection by the law, including the opportunity of a fair trial. Moreover, to protect these provisions, it may be necessary to allow all to have the political power to influence governmental decisions. It may, therefore, be the case that, because under some circumstances it looks as though people should be treated as 'equally worthy', regardless of their deserts, Vlastos has drawn the conclusion that people must always be 'equally worthy', regardless of anything they do. Consequently, when it comes to the situation in which desert may explicitly demand unequal outcomes on grounds of 'unworthiness' (as in the case of criminals), his 'equal worth' argument breaks down.

Significantly, therefore, the problem that arises in Vlastos' analysis derives not from a clash between desert and an egalitarian principle of justice, but a confusion between two aspects of the same desert principle.

Nozick, desert and utility

On first consideration, Nozick too seems to reject the notion of desert. However, examined more closely, his theory seems full of implicit references to desert. To understand the importance of desert in Nozick's theory, it is useful to stand the theory on its head. Let us assume that the primary aim of Nozick's approach is not to reflect how natural rights operate, but to attempt to justify a free-market economic system in which people are free to exchange and accumulate private property. How can we do this? An obvious way to proceed would be to adopt the approach of that most famous of supporters of property rights, John Locke. Unfortunately, however, taken out of its historical and religious context, John Locke's theory loses much of its coherence and force.

Nozick starts from the premise the premise that 'Individuals have rights, and there are things no person or group may do to them (without violating their rights)' (1980, p. ix). This is an obvious appeal to the Lockean notion of the natural 'right' in the 'state of nature' to pursue one's aims, and dispose of one's possessions, unhindered by others. However, the context of Locke's theory of property rights is entirely missing from Nozick's account. In Locke's account, the natural right to pursue one's aims, and dispose of one's possessions, unhindered by others derives from God, because we are all 'God's property', and to harm another person would be to damage the property of God. Moreover, God has provided people, in common, with a vast pool of resources to maintain themselves, such that everyone has a more or less equal opportunity (undeserved natural inequalities notwithstanding) to combine his or her labour with these resources, thus contributing to the public stock of available resources, and receiving his due rewards for industry and labour. Consequently, according to Locke, so long as all operate according to the 'just price' system, that treats equals equally, the God given laws of the free-market will make sure that justice is done. In contrast, Nozick's theory makes no reference to God or the 'just price'; Nozick's 'rights' 'appear from nowhere, out of nothing'. In fact, one is left with no more reason for adopting Nozick's conception of natural right than Hobbes' view that 'every man has a (natural) right to everything; even to one another's body' (p. 85).

The idea that all should have the opportunity to combine their labour with the a vast pool of resources that God has provided to maintain themselves, is also missing from Nozick's account, though the remains of this idea can be found in Nozick's reference to the ubiquitous 'Lockean proviso'. The proviso provides a sort of abstract version of a situation in which all are given the equal opportunity to combine their labour with the land, and to receive their just deserts in terms of the fruits of their labours. Basically the proviso states that you can grab an unequal share of resources and the opportunities they provide, so long as you can demonstrate I am no worse off by you doing this. However, if, having received my real or hypothetical share, a calamity accidentally befalls the resources allocated to me, that threatens my life (like my water supply dries up), and I am disadvantaged *through no fault of my own*, then you are obliged to give me some of your share. In other words, a) you can use the lion's share of resources to generate more outcomes so long as I still end up with what I would have deserved anyway, and b) if I suffer a loss of my share of resources undeservedly, you are obliged to help me out. Nozick's 'Lockean proviso' thus bares the hallmarks of Locke's theory of desert, but without an explicit appeal to the idea that through hard work and industry we serve God and improve to lot of others.

Implicit appeals to desert can also be found in the major examples of what Nozick presents as more or less self-evident expressions of his case for 'natural rights'. Consider the famous 'Wilt Chamberlain' example again. Suppose we start with a distribution of wealth that is equal. Wilt Chamberlain then signs a contract with a basket-ball team so that twenty-five cents from the price of each ticket of admission to each match goes to him. People then turn up and freely choose buy tickets because they want to see Wilt Chamberlain, and it is worth it to them to buy a ticket. At the end of the season Chamberlain winds up with 250,000 dollars, a much larger income than anyone else. Nozick argues, 'can anyone else complain on grounds of injustice?' (p. 161); everyone was entitled to the twenty-five cents they had before they freely chose to give it to Chamberlain, so how can the new distribution be unjust? Well, relative to what many others receive, some might complain that 250,000 dollars is rather excessive for playing a season of basket-ball. Nevertheless, it could be argued that at least Wilt Chamberlain '*earned*' some if not all of his money; he presumably gave pleasure to all his fans, and *deserved* some reward for the benefits that he bestowed on others as a result of his skills and all his years of training.

Take another example; Nozick argues that taxation of earnings inevitably involves the violation of people's rights. Thus he says, 'Taxation of earnings from labour is on a par with forced labour ... Seizing the results of someone's labour is equivalent to seizing hours from him and directing him to carry on various activities' (pp. 169-172). Again, this example, makes an intuitive appeal to desert; indeed, it looks very much like the demand of the 19th century socialists that workers receive the 'unlimited fruits of their labour'. If you work hard, and earn money, 'labouring' to provide things for exchange, your earnings are yours; you *deserve* them, and seizing part of your just deserts is exploitation. Nozick also goes on to imply that there is something wrong with an income tax system that taxes those who work, but not those who choose not to work. Again, the implication is that by taxing the hardworking, but not the lazy, there is an injustice; relative to the lazy, the hardworking are receiving less than they deserve.

Nozick also criticizes the concept of distributive justice because it treats production and distribution as two separate issues. He says that, in reality, 'In the non-manna-from-heaven world in which *things have to be made or produced or transformed by people*, there is no separate process of distribution for a theory of distribution to be a theory of' (p. 219, my emphasis), and 'Whoever makes something, having bought or contracted for all other resources for all other held resources used in the process .... , is entitled to it' (p. 160). Again the implication, in true Lockean tradition, is that what you produce through your own efforts, including those directed towards buying and selling materials and hiring workers, is yours; it is your just reward for your industry and initiative; you *deserve* it.

Similarly, Nozick criticizes what I have called Rawls' 'deterministic egalitarianism'; he says that Rawls attributes 'everything noteworthy about the person to certain sorts of "external factors". So denigrating a person's autonomy and prime responsibility for his actions'. Nozick also says that Rawls makes 'no mention at all of how persons have chosen to develop their natural assets' (p. 214). Again, the implication of Nozick's remarks is that a theory of justice should take account of the *choices* that people make in employing the assets they have, and the responsibility they bear for the outcomes for those choices; factors that are an integral part of the notion of desert.

When it comes to the punishment of criminals, Nozick follows a more or less traditional desert line. Hence, according to Nozick, one should be able to retaliate to defend oneself, but the degree of retaliation should be *proportional to the harm done or intended*, and one must not use more in self-defence than is necessary to repel an attack. And, although, in addition to this defensive retaliation, one is also allowed, for the purposes of deterrence, to punish the attacker further, *but only to the extent that the attacker deserves it*. The amount of deserved punishment is a function of both the harm intended or done, and the offenders degree of responsibility (pp. 62-63). Thus the more harm intended or done, and the greater the offenders responsibility for his or her actions, then the greater the punishment one is allowed to inflict. As we have seen, however, there is nothing whatsoever in Nozick's theory of natural rights that gives rise to the argument that punishment to be proportional to the harm intended and inflicted. This idea is simply borrowed from the proportional desert tradition.

And even when Nozick does claim to argue against desert, it is still not entirely clear that desert has been eliminated as a primary consideration in the argument. For example, he asks, rhetorically, *is* it unfair that a child in a home with a swimming pool can use it daily even though he is no more *deserving* than another child whose home is without one? And he adds, 'Should such a situation be prohibited' (p. 238). One is reminded here of Frederick Miller's claim that the idea that people are only entitled only to what they deserve is 'strikingly counter intuitive', thus Miller says, 'It is not at all necessary from the standpoint of commonsense to prove that I deserve my left kidney, in order to have a basis for claiming that it shouldn't be reallocated to contribute to the welfare of others' (1982 p. 278). To Nozick and Miller such examples supposedly speak for themselves.

However, others might indeed seem strikingly unfair and unjust for one spoilt child to have access to a pool whilst other destitute orphan children are prevented from having such access. It could even be argued quite reasonably that it is grossly unfair and unjust for a person to die of kidney failure whilst others have one more kidney than they need. But what if the owners of the pool have worked hard serving the community to earn their pool; would we really want the law to prohibit owners of pools from denying access to the local neighbourhood children, who might destroy the pool, and the well earned privacy of its owners? And would be really want to force people to undergo possibly life threatening surgery so that they can donate a kidney to someone who, at the moment needs it more than they do? What if, they themselves suffered kidney failure later? Within a theory of desert, it is indeed an injustice for some to have more than others when the inequality is undeserved; but the balance of desert is not necessarily best restored by dispossessing those who have gained their assets serving the community, or forcing a perfectly healthy person to undergo undeserved physical suffering. These are complex and delicate issues within a theory of desert, but they do not necessarily indicate a clash between desert and some other conception of justice.

What Nozick fails to do, however, is give the sort of counter example that emphasizes more clearly, the discrepancy between his property rights approach, and desert. Consider a rather different situation. Ned Smith is 30 and has never done an honest day's work in his life. He is on parole for crimes of rape and paedophilia. He has inherited a mansion and 10 million dollars from his father. He has played no part whatsoever in the production of the fortune he has inherited. Nelly Salmon is a 70 year old physically handicapped widow who has worked as a low paid nurse all her life. She is now left struggling to bring up five young grandchildren after their parents and her husband have been accidentally killed in a road accident. Nelly is finding it very hard to make ends meet; one of her grandchildren is dying and she cannot afford private health insurance. Ned Smith refuses to help, and there is no welfare system to help her out. Now ask the question again; can anyone complain on grounds of injustice?

Many libertarians apparently would have no complaint, but I guess to many readers the answer is not as obvious as in the examples that Nozick gives us.

'It will all come out in the wash' desert

Nozick does not present his theory primarily as a desert theory, and it admits of discrepancies between 'property rights and deserts'. Nevertheless, desert related language permeates Nozick's whole approach, sometimes very explicitly; for example, he says that he agrees with the socialist who 'holds on to the notions of earning, producing, entitlement, desert and so forth'; he also adds, 'historical principles of justice hold that past circumstances or actions of people can create differential *entitlements or differential deserts* to things', and it is an injustice to 'violate people's *entitlements or deserts*' (p. 155).

Indeed, it is perhaps because of this that his theory has had a popular appeal with those wanting to justify inequalities in wealth and opportunity. For those who do not follow Rawls' deterministic egalitarian line, and think that unequal desert is both possible and should be considered, at least Nozick *allows* unequal desert to operate to some extent, even if he does not actually legislate for it. Nozick says that 'No doubt people will not long accept a distribution they believe is *unjust*. People want their society to be and look just' (p. 158). In saying this, Nozick seems to be admitting that his historical principles could, in theory, give rise to distributions that people might believe are unjust. However, again in true Lockean fashion, he believes that in a free-market capitalist society people will so arrange things that it will 'look just'. So what 'looks just'? Although he allows for the possibility that people might wish to make bequests to children, and gifts to loved ones, like Locke, the society that Nozick ultimately seems to have in mind is one in which those who show industry and initiative keep their just rewards, the lazy (that is, those who exercise their preference for leisure) usually get nothing, and the bad are punished in proportion to their offences. However, Nozick does not see provision for the needy to be an principle of justice; instead charity to the needy is a 'non-arbitrary' component of the fabric of transfers in a capitalist society.

In summary, Nozick's theory amounts to a sort of 'it will all come out in wash' theory of desert. Give people their freedom, punish the guilty, and, notwithstanding a few hiccups, the rest will more or less receive the rewards they deserve. Ultimately then, it could be argued that the theories of Rawls and Nozick draw their main force from an appeal to the same EAD principle; except one is egalitarian in orientation, and the other inegalitarian. But to what extent is this true of the other philosophical theories we considered?

David Gauthier: desert by agreement?

David Gauthier's theory, like that of Rawls, is supposed to generate principles of justice from a sort of hypothetical contract; though Gauthier's contract derives from a bargaining position that takes no account of inequalities in the distribution of natural assets. Basically, however, Gauthier's approach ends up as an attempt to justify a situation in which all receive a) an outcome equivalent to that they would have received had they acted alone (without cooperation), plus b) an equal share of the remaining surplus. In other words, in a cooperative endeavour, all receive something akin to 'the unlimited fruits of their labour', plus an equal share of the surplus that can be attributed to the additional efforts of others. Interestingly, such a distribution accords exactly with that specified by Wagstaff and Perfect (1992) to deal with an equity situation in which one a) has to distribute outcomes exactly commensurate with one's inputs, and then b) has to distribute a set of outcomes for which one can claim no particular responsibility (see also, Wagstaff, Huggins and Perfect, 1996).

Ultimately, therefore, Gauthier's theory ultimately turns out to be a desert theory in which one is rewarded according to one's contribution to the sum of socially valuable goods to be distributed. And, according to Gauthier, this is achieved best through the competitive market; indeed, he states quite explicitly that, so long as there is no inheritance of wealth, the 'competitive market is the mechanism by which an optimal social surplus is produced and distributed in accordance with the contribution which each person makes' (1974, p. 22). In saying this, Gauthier, like Nozick, apparently adds his name to the list of other supporters of 'it will all come out in the wash' desert approach to the competitive free-market capitalist system. That is, the view that the distribution of wealth in a competitive free-market system will reflect, even if a little roughly, the productive contributions that people have made to the system, and their choices with regard to those contributions and the outcomes they have received (for other examples see, Green, 1987; Posner, 1981). It can also be noted that, in Gauthier's theory, desert is also maintained through his version of the Lockean proviso which, using the language of EAD, maintains that 'I can use my resources to increase my deserved outcomes so long as I do not stop you using yours to increase your deserved outcomes, and vice versa'.

As a theory of desert, Gauthier's approach is, of course, extremely primitive. In particular, there is very little attempt to control for the effects of 'dumb luck', over which people have little or no choice, whether they be accidents of birth or other chance happenings in the market. But that its main appeal is to a raw, contribution based principle of desert, seems difficult to deny.

Brian Barry: impartiality and equal desert

According to Brian Barry justice is fundamentally about impartiality; thus he argues that 'everybody's point of view must be taken into account', and accordingly, 'To say that a principle could not reasonably be rejected by anyone covered by it is, I suggest, a way of saying that it meets the test of impartiality' (p. 372). Unfortunately, as we have seen, it is impossible to derive a theory of justice from such a conception for impartiality can only act as part of a conception of justice. Impartiality is a procedural device for maintaining whatever conception of justice one has already decided upon. Though if Barry truly believes *everybody's* point of view (wishes, desires etc.) must be always taken into account (including the views and wishes of our usual range of antisocial characters) then presumably the approach must be fundamentally egalitarian, resting on the premise that no one is to be deemed any more or less deserving than anyone else, so outcomes should be, in some sense 'equal', in terms a distribution of the various things that each individual finds valuable.

Bruce Ackerman: neutrality and desert

Bruce Ackerman claims that his rules of justice would derive from a position of 'neutral dialogue'. However, once again, the idea of some sort of agreement as the basis for his rules turns out to be something of an irrelevance. His theory is ultimately a defence of what he calls the 'liberal democratic welfare state'. Included in this state are the conditions that a) no citizen genetically dominates another, in terms of cultivating inherited abilities; b) each citizen begins adult life under conditions of material equality; c) each citizen receives a liberal education, and d) each citizen can freely exchange his initial entitlements within a flexible transactional network.

The idea that we insist that everyone start of with equal resources (including some control over unequal genetically inherited abilities) and a liberal education, but then allow some to end up considerably better off than others, might puzzle some egalitarians. But to a desert theorist, who like Ackerman (1980), believes that ultimately the distribution of wealth in a free-market economy reflects how people have *'used* the transactional system' (p. 201, my emphasis), it should all make sense. EAD requires that each should have an equal opportunity to perform the inputs for which proportionate rewards are available. Hence each must start of with equal resources, (which include controls for gross differences in genetic capacities), and equal opportunities for education. From this more or less equal starting point, what people do with their resources determines their ultimate desert.

Ackerman thus appears to recognize something that other free-marketeers have found difficult to face. Without recourse to concepts such as transmigration of souls and differential inherited needs, inherited wealth is contrary to a principle of desert. For desert to prevail, people must start with more or less equal opportunities to perform the requisite inputs or contributions; and this means equal resources. From this baseline, within a free-market system, so Ackerman's argument goes, those who work hard and exchange their entitlements wisely (contributing to the good of others in the process) should end up rich; whilst those who are are lazy and squander their resources (contributing little to the welfare of others beyond the good they do simply by spending), should end up poor. Hence, says Ackerman, 'some will have used the transactional system to gain enormous wealth (whilst) others will die with nothing to their name'(p. 201). In other words, in the end, the rich will deserve to be rich, and the poor will deserve to be poor.

To followers of deterministic egalitarianism, and more sophisticated conceptions of desert, Ackerman's theory might still appear very primitive. It apparently ignores the way in which transactions in the market place may be influenced by chance events (see Campbell, 1988). Nevertheless, it is an advance on the theories of Nozick and Gauthier in that it attempts to control more systematically for certain inequalities in opportunities and the undeserved outcomes that might ensue. In it we see again the broad structure of EAD, and arguably, this is its most basic appeal.

Ronald Dworkin: equal opportunity, ambition and desert

Ronald Dworkin's theory is usually presented as a theory of 'rights' (Dworkin, 1978a, 1981, 1986). But as we have seen, one cannot develop a theory of 'justice as rights' unless one already has a conception of justice that those rights are designed to uphold. Neither can one evolve a set of justice principles from Kantian ideas such as the fundamental moral right 'to be treated with equal concern and respect', or economic concepts such as the 'envy-free' criterion for resource distribution. However, the rationale that Dworkin gives us for his theory of rights turns out to be far less significant than the actual principles that he claims to derive from these ideas.

Dworkin's first basic principle of justice is that all should start in a situation in which 'no one is antecedently entitled to any of the resources, but that they shall instead be dispersed equally among them', so there should be 'an equal share of resources available for each to consume or invest as he wishes' (1986, pp. 285 and 297). It is also necessary to control for chance or luck, such as the distribution of natural endowments, such as natural talents, and the effects of accidental misfortune. Thus Dworkin's scheme is allegedly 'endowment insensitive'; this being accomplished through his proposed insurance scheme whereby 'Insurance is provided against failing to have an opportunity to earn whatever level of income, within the projected structure, the policy holder names' (p. 101). Once again all looks very familiar, for using the language of EAD, Dworkin seems to be arguing that each must have the equal choice or opportunity to provide those inputs for which various levels of income are the commensurate return.

Having been provided with this equal opportunity, people in Dworkin's scheme then make choices and express their preferences through market transactions, as their 'ambition' dictates. In other words, those who are ambitious and want to increase their bundles of resources by providing services to others, and acting wisely and frugally with their original stock of resources and the extra they earn, may, should they desire, end up rich. And those who want to be lazy, and squander their resources, will end up poor. Criminals, however, who unjustifiably harm the good of others, and perform disservices, should be punished, if it is not too inexpedient. In other words, ultimately, if Dworkin's scheme goes to plan, everyone should, more or less, end up with what he or she *deserves*.

Michael Walzer: allocation preferences and desert

The obvious lesson to be learned from looking at these modern theories in this way is that their most fundamental problems seem to stem from a tendency take concepts that were originally construed as tools necessary to maintain grand schemes of desert (such as contract, equal opportunity, choice, impartiality, neutrality, and various 'rights'), and to elevate them to a status that is allegedly superior to the schemes they were originally designed to maintain. As a result, although claims are made that one can generate rules of justice from these concepts, in practice, these concepts tend to be used more as devices to rationalize or justify various versions of same original desert conception of justice from which they were derived.

However, we have yet to account for the Michael Walzer's (1983) 'multiprinciple' approach to justice. Walzer argues that there are, and should be, different principles for each 'distributive sphere', because different social goods have different social meanings, which, in turn, determine the reasons and procedures for different distributions. However, one can still see the basic structure of EAD pervading some of Walzer's analysis. For example, Walzer argues, as EAD would predict, that public honour should be distributed according to desert, and offenders should be punished according to desert. His idea that the provision of relief, work, and training is appropriate in relation to the needy, also makes sense with a theory of EAD, assuming the 'needy' are not simply squandering the resources given to them.

Nevertheless, some of Walzer's other principles fit less easily into the EAD framework. But are they actually principles of justice? As Campbell (1988) argues, the fact that there may be 'good reasons' for distributing resources in a certain way does not necessarily mean that those reasons coincide with the requirements of justice. For example, Walzer says that the principle of 'membership rights' is most appropriate for establishing associations or communities of men and women. However, it could be argued that 'membership rights' themselves can be constrained by the dictates of justice, and, in particular EAD. If membership of a club confers considerable privileges (positive outcomes) on its members, yet membership is limited by considerations (inputs) that are irrelevant to desert (such as sex), and cannot be justified in terms of differential need (men and women by nature of their genetic differences, 'need' different things), one might expect some to complain of injustice, as campaigners for sexual equality often do. One might also expect, according to EAD, that membership rights to be denied to 'unworthy members' (such as criminals), as they frequently are.

Similarly, the idea that free exchange, or 'the right to give and the right to receive' (p. 127), is the principle that, according to Walzer, should govern money and commodities, might seem 'just' if one follows the standard free-market 'it all comes out in the wash' desert model, but as we have seen, many object to the idea that some should be entitled to fortunes in 'undeserved' gifts whilst others receive nothing. Also, being 'open to talents' may be a *useful* principle to apply to public office. But is it just? If we assume that those with talent have achieved their abilities through their own efforts under conditions of equal opportunity, then the principle may be considered just. But if we take a Rawlsian line that 'talent' is something for which we can claim no credit, then arguably, awarding high public office to the talented may be 'useful', but not necessarily 'just'. Also Walzer's idea that hard work should be shared as equally as possible has a nice egalitarian ring to it, but some might object to the idea that, having worked as hard as everyone else, they are still denied public office because of a lack of 'talent'. And why should people allocate 'sexual love' solely on the basis of justice? We know from the psychological studies that feelings of being treated inequitably *can* affect those we chose as our sexual partners, and frequency of love making, but 'justice' is hardly the term that comes to mind as the main determinant of how often and to whom we make love.

It seems, therefore, Walzer has come across the main stumbling block of modern multiprinciple theories of justice. Having failed to present any unified, overriding conception of the meaning of 'justice', he leaves the door open for virtually any sort of allocation rule to be labelled 'a rule of justice'. Consequently, he is unable to specify the circumstances under which a particular rule might be considered 'just' or 'unjust', rather than simply 'expedient' in achieving some other aim.

However, perhaps this is to misrepresent Walzer to some extent, because he does actually a label to his overall scheme of rules; he calls the scheme one of 'complex equality'. This seems to imply that, despite the undoubted inequalities that many of his distributive principles might create, when all the spheres are put together a sort of 'it all comes out in the wash' *equality* emerges. The idea seems to be that, so long as the various spheres of justice are kept separate from each other, then things will sort of cancel themselves out, resulting in a rough and ready sort of equality, 'complex equality'. If we accept that it is this idea of 'equality' that essential captures Walzer's conception of justice, rather than a multitude of 'expedient' rules, then the picture that emerges takes on a certain familiarity; a familiarity that may help to make sense of some of Walzer's less obvious intuitions about particular rules.

For example, at first it might seem odd to insist that hard work should be shared 'equally', when some might be receiving more wealth than others, and some might achieve positions of higher public office, and receive more public honour than others. Besides, who decides the level of 'work'? If some want to be workaholics, do the rest have to work equally hard? But suppose we consider, as have many, that especially under conditions of unequal opportunity, the most appropriate input or measure of one's contribution in a desert equation is 'effort', 'labour', or 'hard work' in the service of others. If so, according to EAD, if all work equally hard, all inputs will be equal, and all should receive equal outcomes. This is significant, for Walzer implies, that, as long as the various justice spheres are kept separate, a sort of 'complex equality of outcomes' emerges. If Walzer's scheme goes to plan then, EAD is satisfied; for *all put in equal inputs, and all receive (approximately) equal outcomes*. Moreover, in that the provision of relief, work, and training is appropriate in relation to the needy, then the distribution will be adjusted for need. And, as the finishing touch, Walzer argues that for criminals (who contribute negative inputs), should be punished according to desert.

In other words, at a 'macrojustice' level, Walzer's theory is a theory that derives its broad appeal from EAD; it prescribes equal positive outcomes for equal inputs, adjusted for need, and negative outcomes in proportion to negative inputs.

Conclusion

The main conclusion that I would draw from all this is that virtually all of the theories I have examined so far make significant explicit and implicit appeals to the main structure of EAD; indeed, if we take away these appeals to desert, there is little argument of any force left to identify any of them as theories of 'justice'. Unfortunately, however, many modern theorists have found themselves so entangled in various fragments, taken, often out of context, from earlier historical schemes, that the most basic raw appeal of their arguments has been overlooked.

Also, in the theories of Rawls and Walzer, especially, we saw the problems that can arise when reasons of justice are not clearly separated from other reasons that people may have for adopting different allocation rules. Bearing this in mind, let us now look again at some of the main psychological approaches to justice and associated research. Can we find the core features of EAD in this literature too?

CHAPTER 22

THE PSYCHOLOGY OF JUSTICE RECONSIDERED

With regard to psychological approaches to justice, the first obvious point to make is that what is popularly known as 'equity theory' has an enormous contribution to make to our understanding of justice as desert. Also, there is a large volume of empirical research showing that, in a wide variety of situations, people want both themselves and others to get what they deserve on the basis of their positive and negative contributions or services.

Defining the equity formula

A fundamental problem for the traditional approach to equity, however, has been the failure to agree on a workable formula. But, hopefully, we now have one in Wagstaff and Perfect's equal ratio formula for 'perfect equity', $O_i = aI_i$ (see also Harris, 1983, 1993). In fact, studies conducted at Liverpool University have shown that, provided it is made clear to be subjects that, a) all participants in a relationship do not differ in terms of 'undeserved need', and b) all have more or less equal opportunity to perform the inputs or contributions, then allocations according to a strict equal ratio formula are preferred by an overwhelming majority of subjects (Wagstaff, 1994; Wagstaff and Perfect, 1992; Wagstaff and Worthington, 1997; Wagstaff, Chadwick, and Brunas-Wagstaff, 1996; Wagstaff and Preece, 1997; Wagstaff, Huggins and Perfect, 1996; Wagstaff et al., 1994).

Also, in accordance with EAD, our results on British samples show that allocations according to other formulae, such as Harris' linear formula, $O_i = aI_i + r_a$, are only made when, because of various circumstances, it is necessary to make an adjustment so that true equal proportional equity may obtain (such as when all start from a position where they have undeserved negative outcomes, or some of the outcomes to be distributed are undeserved). Though, even then out data indicate that many subjects seem very reluctant to abandon the basic equal ratio formulation (see again, Wagstaff 1993; Wagstaff and Perfect, 1992; Wagstaff and Worthington, 1997; Wagstaff, Chadwick, and Brunas-Wagstaff, 1996; Wagstaff, Huggins and Perfect, 1996; and Wagstaff et al., 1994). These clear trends have been found regardless, of sex, age, or occupation. Of course, our results do not rule out the possibility that subjects may have to recourse to other methods of allocation (involving equal shares or simple rankings of inputs and outcomes) when the calculations become very difficult, but it is difficult to dispute the conclusion that, when opportunities to perform the inputs are more or less equal, no adjustment for need is necessary, and judgements concern justice, then 'equal proportionality' is the preferred allocation rule.

Nevertheless, whilst the standard psychological approach to equity is useful in defining the proportionality element of desert, clearly traditional equity theory is incomplete as a theory of desert without a detailed consideration of the moderating effects of choice or moral responsibility. However, if apply the equal ratio equity formula in its modified guise, as EAD, perhaps we can clarify and even resolve many of the problems that have confronted psychologists working in this area.

Let us start with an approach that is often assumed to be contrary to the idea of equity, Lerner's theory of the 'Justice motive', and the 'Belief in a Just World'.

Lerner's 'Just World' reconsidered

According to Lerner, 'Individuals have a need to believe that they live in a world where people generally get what they deserve' (Lerner and Miller, 1978, p. 1030); and hence 'A Just World is one in which people "get what they deserve" ' (1980, p. 11). An important feature of Lerner's original view of desert is that we all need to believe in a world in which those whose attributes and actions are positive are rewarded, and those whose attributes and actions are negative are punished; moreover, argued Lerner, so committed are we to this view, that we tend to engage in a variety of cognitive strategies to manufacture and distort events such that all appear to receive the outcomes they deserve on the basis of their positive and negative attributes and actions. The obvious similarity between Lerner's original 'Just World Theory' view and Hatfield et al.'s idea of the psychological restoration of equity as already been commented on. The hypotheses that Lerner tested in his studies of fortuitous reward and victim derogation are also clearly derived from this classical conception of desert (see Lerner, 1965, 1971, 1980; Lerner and Matthews, 1967; Lerner and Simmons, 1966).

As Lerner's approach to justice in his original 'Just World' theory is clearly based on the traditional historical conception of desert in terms of 'reward for good', and 'punishment for bad', predictably his views about the development of the 'justice motive' bear some correspondence with how we might expect EAD to develop. For instance, it makes sense from the viewpoint of EAD that children should develop a system of particular desert preferences (or what Lerner calls, 'personal contracts') only when they perceive (and are capable of perceiving) that their environments are stable and controllable enough to sustain such a system. A child who is incapable of making an evaluative comparison, and/or is unwilling to 'delay gratification' is unlikely to support a system that rewards people in proportion to prolonged socially beneficial activity, or punishes them in proportion to their impulsive or reckless behaviour. Indeed, the empirical findings of Lerner and his colleagues on this issue could be considered highly supportive of EAD. They found that children did not respond to 'need' indiscriminately, rather help was provided most often when the need was accidental and the help was thereby 'deserved'; significantly, however, this distinction was made most consistently by those who are most able to delay gratification (Brabant and Lerner, 1975; Lerner, 1977; Long and Lerner, 1974).

It is also interesting to note here the finding by Reis (1984) that, in adults, impulsivity is associated with a preference for equality. Of course a person who is impulsive may prefer an equal distribution for pragmatic reasons that may be unrelated to justice, but this finding might also make sense in terms of EAD; a person who is impulsive may feel himself or herself less in control of his or her actions than someone who can delay gratification, and may therefore prefer to adopt a more deterministic egalitarian perspective.

Is the 'justice-motive' selfish?
One of the most important alleged differences between Lerner's position and that of the equity theory concerns the view held by equity theorists that justice is motivated by selfishness. Lerner argues strongly that justice is not based on selfishness, but but has he actually ruled out 'selfishness' as the main motive for justice? The position adopted by equity theorists such as Hatfield is that, even when we help deserving others, we are acting 'selfishly' in the sense that our behaviours are directed towards the reduction of our own distress (guilt, anxiety, empathy) on perceiving the victim's plight. The position that we help others for intrinsic 'psychological gain' in this way has been referred to as 'subtle cynicism', as opposed to 'vulgar cynicism' which assumes that we help others to gain more obvious extrinsic rewards, such as money, power or status (Sabini, 1995). However, from the perspective of 'subtle cynicism', it is difficult to see how attempts to restore the 'Just World' could be motivated by any thing other than 'selfishness'. According to Lerner's theory, violations of 'personal contracts' threaten the whole stability and framework of individuals' conceptions of the relationships between what they do and are, and what happens to them. So,

presumably violations are 'felt' in some way. They must, in some sense, be 'upsetting', 'distressing', or 'uncomfortable', otherwise it is difficult to see what could possibly be the motive for restoring the contract. And if this is so, then arguably, from the position of 'subtle cynicism', Lerner's justice motive must also be 'selfish'.

Interestingly some of the research conducted by Lerner and his colleagues, assumed by them to show that the 'justice motive' is not selfish, could easily be construed as showing the opposite. For example, their research shows that people apparently put their own deserving before that of others; thus people will not help others until they themselves have first received what they consider to be a just reward (Lerner, 1977, 1980; Miller, 1977). But, if it is assumed to be distressing in some way to receive more or less than one deserves, then the act of alleviating one's own distress before that of others could be construed as extremely 'selfish'. Accordingly, Hogan and Emler (1981) have actually categorised Lerner's theory with equity theory and argued that *both* approaches adopt 'self-interest' as the prime motive for maintaining justice.

Desert and the Just World Scale

The original conception of a 'Just World' adopted by Lerner and his colleagues is also represented in the items that constitute the 'Just World Scale'; these largely emphasize the relationship between good and bad actions and rewards and punishments (see, Rubin and Peplau, 1975). Moreover, this traditional conception of justice as desert is also implicit in virtually all of the research employing the Just World Scale (see, for example, Furnham and Procter, 1989; Rubin and Peplau, 1975; Wagstaff, 1984; Wagstaff and Quirk, 1983).

Nevertheless, despite the remarkable correspondence between Lerner's original approach to desert and EAD, like many other psychologists Lerner and his colleagues seem gradually to have switched their attention away from the more traditional desert orientation to one of multiple rules of 'entitlement', many of which, on first consideration, seem to bear no relationship at all to the traditional concept of desert (though Lerner and others still describe them as rules of 'deserving').

Multiple rules of justice

The philosophical literature warns us that, without some clear definition of what is meant by 'justice', virtually any social rule, convention, or preferred rule for treating others can be termed a rule of 'justice'. Unfortunately, having rejected equity, it now seems that many psychologists find themselves unable to distinguish, theoretically, between rules of justice, and general 'allocation preferences'; hence, as Folger, Sheppard and Blair (1995) comment, 'New principles of justice seem to spout like weeds in a garden' (p. 261). However, if justice is viewed from the perspective of EAD, perhaps it may be possible to impose a more coherent structure on some of the multiprinciple approaches to justice now favoured by many psychologists.

From the perspective of EAD, the ubiquitous equity, equality and need allocation principles are not three separate principles of justice that operate in different situations, rather they are variations on a single desert principle. Thus, 'equity' or (also known as 'contributions' and 'proportionality') in this context corresponds to unequal outcomes for unequal inputs, when choices or opportunities to perform inputs are present and approximately equal; 'equality', corresponds to equal outcomes for equal or effectively equal inputs, including situations in which choices to perform inputs opportunities are absent; and 'need' is an 'outcome adjustment', when some participants start with an outcome deficit, or the outcome units have different values for different participants, or an 'input moderator', as when choice is restricted by necessity.

Such an account explains why, when people are given information about contributions, need and responsibility, they do not adopt one of the above rules and drop the others, instead they tend to 'mix-up' these various components in accordance with the predictions of EAD (see, for example, Elliott and Meeker, 1986; Wagstaff, 1994). Of course it has been argued that the fact that people use of more than one allocation rule at a time is not necessarily contrary to the multiprinciple view, however, by taking into account attributions of responsibility, EAD makes further predictions that cannot be derived from the main multiprinciple theories of justice.

Making sense of 'equity', equality and need

According to the multiprinciple theorists, the 'equality' and 'need' principles ignore inputs. According to EAD, however, 'inputs' are of crucial importance to the operation of the equality and need components. Within the framework of EAD, people will only apply equality as a principle of justice when they consider inputs to be equal or neutral (as when opportunities to perform inputs are unequal), and they will only make an adjustment for need when they perceive that the need is deserved; and, indeed, there is much evidence from studies on both adults and children to support this perspective (see, for example, Brabant and Lerner, 1975; Lerner, 1977; Long and Lerner, 1974; Schmidt and Weiner, 1988; Wagstaff, 1994; Weiner 1980; 1985). As Lerner says, 'Undeserved suffering elicits compassion and help; but people react with indifference or satisfaction to deserved suffering, depending upon whether the suffering was caused by the victim's blameworthy act or was the "deserved" fate meted out to a villain by the agents of goodness and truth' (p. 1).

This is not to say, however, that people do not use the contributions, equality and need principles in the ways suggested by the multiprinciple theorists, only that most of reasons that psychologists have put forward to explain why people operate these principles probably have little or anything to do with people's intuitions about 'justice'. Consider the typical schema for describing the operation of the 'equity', equality and need principles; the popular assumptions are as follows (see, for example, Deutsch, 1975, 1985; Mikula, 1980; Schwinger, 1980; Leventhal Karuza and Fry, 1980; Folger, Sheppard and Buttram, 1995).

1) The 'equity' or contributions rule operates in relationships where there is little or no intimacy or affection (these are neutral), and although the relationship

still possesses a degree of cooperation, it is impersonal, and there is a greater sense of conflict and competition; and also, the goal of the interaction is to maximize economic productivity.

2) The equality rule, on the other hand, operates where there is more intimacy, and slightly less potential for conflict; an affective bond and attraction are present; the relationship is cooperative, and the group goal is one of group solidarity, harmony, and enjoyable social relations.

3) The need rule then operates in situations where there is intimacy, affection, empathy, attraction, an absence of conflict, and welfare is the shared goal.

These might be valid observations, but we are still left wondering what any of this has to do with 'justice'. Productivity maximization, the fostering of enjoyable social relations and the promotion of group welfare all look like reasons of *expediency*, a factor that has always had a very uneasy relationship with the idea of justice. And we still need to consider *why*, in any case, these allocations should have the various effects attributed to them. Why does a contributions or proportionality rule maximize productivity, an equality rule foster cooperation and group harmony, and a needs rule promote welfare?

Ironically, it may the case that it is precisely because there is only *one* core principle that people unique identify with justice, namely EAD, that these allocations can have the effects attributed to them. Indeed, the idea that people attempt to operate a single principle of justice may be able to provide a unique insight into what is going on when people apply different allocation rules, and may help to explain many of the empirical findings that seem to fit uneasily with the multiprinciple view.

Suppose for example, we want to maximize productivity. If we distribute proportionally according to 'raw' contribution, then so long as people feel that they have a more or less equal chance to contribute, rewarding those who work hardest will tend to motivate all or most workers, productivity will increase, and, in accordance with EAD, the situation should be considered by most people as 'fair'. Thus, other things being more or less equal, if individuals are told that the goal of the task is productivity, they will tend to prefer a contribution based scheme (Assmar and Rodriques, 1994; Deutsch, 1985). However, if workers feel that they have not had equal opportunities to contribute, they may find such a system of reward divisive, unjust, and resentment may be created. In the latter instance, productivity may still be maintained, but perhaps at the expense of group cohesion. This would help to explain why, when asked to make a fair allocation, people prefer to reward 'effort' or 'output', rather than 'ability' or 'capability' even though the latter might help more to maximize productivity (Stake, 1983). And if even 'effort' is not something that people can choose equally to contribute, they may go for an equality rule, even though they are not necessarily friends or intimately acquainted (Wagstaff, 1994).

Suppose now we want to foster a cooperative and enjoyable atmosphere. If we award shares equally, then as people want justice to obtain, and EAD to exist, they will tend to assume that all are 'pulling their weight', and inputs are equal. An equal shares allocation gives out the message that people can be trusted to do the best they can; thus fostering an enjoyable cooperative environment in which people trust each other, and do not feel they are in competition for rewards; they all 'deserve' equal. So, if individuals are told that the goal of the task is friendship formation or to work as members of a team, they may tend towards an equal outcomes rule (Assmar and Rodriques, 1994; Deutsch, 1985; Lerner, 1974). Problems will result, however, if some abuse this trust, clearly do not pull their weight, and a situation of unequal inputs becomes transparent. Under such circumstances productivity may be curtailed as those who have input more attempt to adjust their input/outcome ratios to suit the equal distribution, and resentment may again develop. This would then explain the findings that, even amongst friends, in situations where their were sizeable differences in performance, an equal distribution may generate conflict, hence subjects may consider that harmony is best preserved by applying an unequal distribution that takes contributions into account (Lamm and Kayser, 1978; see also, Leventhal, Karuza and Fry, 1980).

And, finally, suppose we want to maximize the welfare of the groups so that some individuals do not suffer. We are most likely to be sensitive to the needs of others when we know them and are familiar with them; if they are strangers we may not know their circumstances. Hence when we are intimate terms with others we will know best how to allocate the help that is needed. But more than this, if we see others being given shares of some good according to their 'needs', and we want 'justice', again we will be more likely to assume that those receiving the need are innocent victims, 'worthy' of help, and are legitimate objects of our compassion. Hence, distribution according to need, can itself, through our desire for 'justice' in terms of EAD, evoke feelings of compassion and empathy, promote trust that each is inputting as much as anyone else, and sensitize us to the welfare of the group. In line with research findings, however, EAD predicts that an adjustment according to need may still operate amongst strangers or competitors if needs are made salient. Also, allocation according to need may break down when it is made clear that those in need have placed themselves in a position of need through their own choices; either by lack of inputs (such as, laziness), or through unwise and impulsive outcome substitutions (such as, spending all their money on temporary pleasures) (Brabant and Lerner, 1975; Berkowitz, 1969; Lerner, 1977; Utne and Kidd, 1980; Thomas, Wagstaff and Brunas-Wagstaff, 1996; Schmidt and Weiner, 1988; Wagstaff, 1994; Weiner, 1980, 1985; Meyer and Mulherin, 1980).

Such considerations might also help to explain, for example, why, in intimate relationships, some partners react negatively to receiving requests for repayments for benefits received, and they do not like 'book keep' or keep track of individual inputs and outcomes (Clark, 1984; Clark and Mills, 1979; Clark, Mills and Corcoran, 1989). Apart from the effort involved, such behaviour would imply a lack of trust in the other partner; an assumption that the other partner is not pulling his or her weight in what should be a joint equal input endeavour. The idea that close relationships should rest on 'equal inputs', and 'equal outcomes adjusted for need', is also supported by Desmarais and Lerner's (1994) finding that dating partners preferred a conflict-resolution strategy based on reciprocity in respecting needs, and equal contributions to decisions, regardless of how they described their relationship in terms of Lerner's 'identity', 'unit' and 'non-unit' constructs. If equal distributions are associated with trust (because they give the message, 'I believe you will input equally'), this might also explain why some individuals allocate rewards more equally when they want to present themselves favourably to recipients (Austin, 1980; Leventhal, Michaels and Sanford, 1972; Reis and Gruzen, 1976; Von Grumbkow, Deen, Steensma and Wilke, 1976).

Macro and micro justice

According to EAD, subjects will show a preference for more egalitarian distributions when circumstances emphasize the unchosen nature of input decisions. As decisions made by large numbers of people tend to be interpreted as more situational in origin (refecting the 'consensus' rule in attributional judgements), another prediction from EAD is that when very large numbers of people are involved, there may be a tendency to show a preference for more egalitarian distributions. In line with this prediction, Brickman et al. (1981), found that at the level of individual cases, or 'microjustice', people seem to prefer distributions based on contributions, but when they look at the overall shape of the distributions of various benefits and burdens for society as a whole and between societies, at the level of 'macrojustice', their preferences appear to be more egalitarian.

Nevertheless, it should be emphasized that more recent research indicates that, even at a societal level, when individuals are specifically asked to allocate fairly, a contribution based scheme is prefered (Ordonez and Mellers, 1993). (See also, Himmelweit, Humphries, Jaeger and Katz 1981; Robinson and Bell, 1978; Swift, Marshall, Burgoyne and Routh, 1992).

Justice versus allocation preferences

It is important, however, not to overestimate the effect that justice considerations may have on allocation decisions. There may be other things in life besides 'justice'. For example, it is not really unexpected that some people are willing to tolerate some degree of inequity in their relationships, if they are satisfied with their overall level of rewards (Cate, Lloyd, Henton and Larson, 1982; Clark and Chrisman, 1994; Desmarais and Lerner, 1994; Martin, 1985; Reynolds, Remer and Johnson, 1995). Also, the fact that high contributors sometimes follow a 'politeness ritual' and distribute rewards more equally to co-recipients, probably says more about their views on 'beneficence', their social skills, and their desire to win favour, than justice (Major and Deaux, 1982; Schwinger, 1980). And as for the finding that some individuals may apply more equal allocations when they are unable or unwilling to perform the calculations necessary to operate a proportionality rule, this hardly leads one to invoke 'justice' as an explanatory principle (Harris and Joyce, 1980; Leventhal, 1976; Tornblöm, 1992).

When making allocations, therefore, there is presumably always a trade-off between the considerations of justice and other reasons for adopting a particular rule, and given this, it is also not surprising that people sometimes differ in the their attitudes to allocation rules. Hence people are who are high on what Buunk and VanYperen (1991) call 'exchange orientation' and feel uncomfortable when they receive favours they cannot reciprocate, might be considered more 'justice oriented' than people high on 'communal orientation'; who seem relatively unconcerned about whether they are disadvantaged, advantaged or treated equally. Alternatively, or additionally, perhaps those high on communal orientation are more trusting in relationships than the 'highs' (and assume that reciprocal desert will eventually obtain), which might explain perhaps why the 'lows' generally feel more satisfied with their relationships (Buunk and VanYperen, 1991).

If we adopt a perspective that makes a distinction between justice, as described in terms of EAD, and allocation preferences in general, we may also be able to make more sense of some other empirical findings. For instance, in Chapter 8, I noted various studies that showed that people allocate differently if asked specifically to allocate 'justly' or 'fairly' rather than in accordance with the various goals that psychologists have identified in relation to the 'equity' equality and need principles. Hence, in the study by Stake (1983), when asked to award bonuses and raises such as to maximize productivity, subjects awarded them according to capability, and when asked to maintain positive personal relationships, they tended to award more equally. However, when asked to allocate them *fairly*, subjects allocated them according to the actual inputs or contributions in terms of outputs. These results suggest that although 'productivity maximization', and 'maintaining harmonious relationships' might be construed as a useful allocation goals, subjects do indeed differentiate them from rules of 'fairness' or 'justice'. Similarly, Lamm and Schwinger (1983) found that, when inputs were equal, the level of attractiveness of the recipient affected allocations according to need, however, attractiveness was not considered when the allocators were specifically asked to allocate 'justly'. These results again suggest that, although we might wish to allocate more resources to those we hold dearest and would like to please most, these allocation goals must not be confused with conceptions of 'justice'.

Such an analysis might also help explain some of the findings regarding sex differences. As we have seen, although the stereotypical view is that women tend to allocate positive outcomes more equally, and less according to contributions, the evidence regarding this is complex and inconsistent (see, for example, Asdigan, Cohn and Blum, 1994; Benton, 1971; Kahn, Nelson and Gaeddert, 1980; Kidder, Bellettirie and Cohn, 1977; Stake, 1983). Rather the data suggest that sex differences, if and when they emerge, are specific to certain circumstances; for instance, when the allocator is a co-recipient women take less for themselves than men, and if their performance is superior to the other participants, women will tend to distribute resources more equally than men. When their performance is inferior, however, both men and women follow an equity rule (Major and Deaux, 1982). The reasons for these findings are unclear; they might result from sex differences in allocation goals, or attempts to live up to traditional sex roles under experimental conditions, or a greater tendency for women to follow a politeness ritual when making allocations. But, though interesting, perhaps these results should not concern us too much, for there is little evidence that men and women have different conceptions of *justice* (see Sabini, 1995). Indeed, in the numerous British samples we have studied at Liverpool, we have not found a consistent difference in the way men and women make judgements of 'fairness' (see also, Alves and Rossi, 1978).

However, perhaps most important illustration of the distinction between 'justice' and allocation preferences in general is the finding by Ordonez and Mellers (1993) that, when asked to judge what was a fair society, most people selected a society in which salaries were awarded in proportion to work or contribution; in contrast, when asked what sort of society they preferred, they chose one with high minimum salaries. In other words, if given the choice to make such a distinction, although people might *prefer* a society that protects those who earn least, they do not necessarily consider such a system *just* or *fair*; a fair society is one that rewards people in proportion to their deserts in terms of contributions.

Considered in this way, all the findings and interpretations reviewed here are very compatible with a conception of justice in terms of EAD; that is, one that integrates conceptions of contribution, equality, need and responsibility, and allows a distinction between 'just' allocations, and allocations made for other reasons.

Games, Sport and 'maximal difference' allocation rules

So far, like most other psychologists, I have concentrated on only three allocation rules, contributions, equality and need. But what of the other rules that have been suggested as alternatives to equity? If one examines the wide range of rules described by Desmarais and Lerner (1994) and Reis (1984), it seems that most, in one way or another, are related to or derived from the basic 'equity, equality and needs' framework. The obvious exceptions, however, are what Lerner calls 'utilitarian decisions', and rules based on self-interest and 'maximizing differences'. However, the problem remains that, without some clear conception of what is meant by the term 'justice', it is not at all obvious what any of these other rules, and the reasons proposed for applying them, have to do with justice.

I have already discussed some of the problems associated with labelling utilitarian rules of expediency as 'rules of justice', however, the idea that there may be a rule or set of rules relating to justified 'self-interest', or 'maximal difference' has been advocated by a number of other multiprinciple theorists (see, for example, Kayser, Schwinger and Cohen, 1984). The rules related to this concept are supposed to operate when there are no affective bonds and no desire for cooperation amongst participants; instead, conflict and competition abound, and the goal is maximize one's own individual outcomes.

According to Lerner, this sort of 'self-interested', 'grab as much as you can get' conception of justice can be split into components such as, formal contests, or what he terms 'parallel competition', 'fight' to maximize differential outcomes, and regulated conflict, to maximize legal outcomes (see Desmarais and Lerner, 1994). The first observation to make, however, is that a straight fight, without any rules, does not really seem to justify the term a rule of 'justice'. Rather, as Hobbes and Hume would argue, it seems more like a situation in which justice does not exist. In contrast, the idea of a contest within an established set of rules might seem more like a system in which justice might operate; but normally our conception of whether the outcome of a contest or conflict within a set of rules is considered fair or just depends very much on whether the rules are considered fair or just, and this assumes a theory of what 'just' rules should be. So what is a 'just' set of rules for a contest?

The idea of contests automatically brings to mind sporting contests and games. However, the connection between sport and justice may be somewhat misleading. The object of most sports and games is to provide stimulation and entertainment for participants and spectators; hence, many of the rules are geared solely to this end, not to dispense 'justice'. Nevertheless, there are many elements in games that show a interesting correspondence with EAD. For instance, the rules of most games are designed to create a situation of equal opportunity, so although a winning team might not be considered deserving in terms of the entertainment they provided, they might reasonably claim that they did 'deserve' to win on the grounds that, under conditions of equal opportunity, they geared their behaviour to produce optimum outcomes within the rules (they selected those activities that best produce the 'goals', 'baskets', ''runs', 'punches' etc. that are deemed to contribute most to the aims or 'good' of the game).

Nevertheless, it is also notable how, in sport, we frequently we applaud the favourite desert inputs of 'effort' and 'skill', and how often the rules are devised so that, in the long run, these contributions will be rewarded. So, for example, if athletes take drugs to increase their performance, or a referee continually and incorrectly penalizes one team, or one boxer is twice the size of another, we may deem such contests 'unfair' and the results 'unjust'; not simply because the contests cease to be entertaining, but because the opportunities to contribute the necessary effort and skill, and reap the appropriate rewards, are deemed unequal; in other words, they offend EAD. Interestingly also, often we do complain of injustice when a team wins within the rules, but does not 'deserve it' by more conventional criteria; consider the following quote from the journalist, Patrick Collins, after Argentina had lost a game of Rugby Football to England. 'As for Argentina, well you could have cried for them. Swift, resourceful and endlessly appealing; last night should have seen them celebrating the victory they deserved rather than cursing the luck which had denied them justice' (Mail on Sunday, Dec. 15, 1996, p. 64).

Of course, in pure desert terms, although many of the skills and capacities required to win a game might result from effort in the form of hard training, others might be considered genetically inherited, in which case the desert element in sports can only be a poor approximation to 'real desert'. Hence, the evidence suggests that when it comes to the business of allocating outcomes 'fairly', rather than to produce entertainment, people are more likely to allocate higher outcomes to those whose superior contributions are based on effort (something we might all be able to contribute), rather than inherited ability, or other 'chance' factors; and this is even true for competitions involving athletic prowess (see, for example, Cohen, 1974; Greenberg, 1980; Lamm, Kayser and Schanz, 1983; Leventhal, 1976; Leventhal and Michaels, 1971).

Other examples of alleged 'self-interested' justice can also readily be construed as 'approximations to desert'. Consider again Lerner's (1977) example of the study by Lerner and Lichtman (1968). In this experiment, students had to choose whether to let themselves, or their partner, take a dose of electric shock. Only one member of each pair was given the opportunity to choose, and the decision as to which student would be allowed to choose was determined by lot in the form of random number tables. The results showed that about 90 percent of the students who were selected by this procedure chose to assign their partner to receive the shocks, and seemed happy to do this. However, given these circumstances, this outcome is perhaps not unexpected. If the participants had no knowledge of each other's previous behaviours or personal situations, there were no 'inputs' or 'outcome deficits' to speak of that could be used as the basis for a proportional desert allocation. All inputs were effectively neutral. Furthermore, there was only one outcome to be allocated, and this had been determined, more or less, by random number tables. Viewed in this way, Lerner's example of so-called 'parallel competition' is a situation in which inputs are neutral, the outcome to be distributed is negative, but although the outcome is indivisible, it must be assigned. Under these circumstances, EAD predicts that the least inequitable solution is to *draw lots*; and, in effect, this was exactly what the subjects in this study did (it is interesting to note that both Plato and Hobbes saw 'lots' as an inferior rule of allocation, but as Hobbes pointed out, when an equality rule is operative, and the thing to be allocated is indivisible, the best we can do is to draw lots).

This example illustrates a general problem with attempts to argue that there exists a rule of justice, independent of proportional desert, that operates in 'bargaining games'. If the 'bargaining situation' is artificially set up, as it usually is, as a sort of game in which there are no existing inputs to speak of, and participants have no knowledge of each others situations or skills, then, in effect, participants start from a position of equal desert. From then on, if EAD operates, the result of the bargain should reflect a distribution of outcomes that, in some sense, is equal for both. In fact, as Hobbes and Adam Smith tell us, this was assumed to be the basis of bargaining in commutative justice. However, if the outcomes are indivisible, such that 'winner takes all', there is no 'perfectly just' solution. But given that it is *equally* unjust whoever wins, it should not really surprise us if participants decide to interpret such situations as games they can legitimately 'win'.

The true test of the 'maximal difference' rule, therefore, is how it operates when people are given explicit background knowledge about the 'starting positions' of the participants. A most obvious example of a 'winner takes all' game, is the UK National Lottery. Twice a week in the UK a single individual, or a small group of individuals, can win prizes that may sometimes amount to £10 million or more. The fact that a single individual can win £10 million pounds on a game of chance has been seen by some political commentators and Church leaders as unjust, if not disgusting and repulsive. From the perspective of EAD, this response is not unexpected; £10 million pounds hardly seems a reward commensurate with an 'input' that involves nothing more than purchasing a lottery ticket, and it is not really the case that we have an indivisible outcome to be divided amongst those of equal desert. But to those participating in the lottery, considerations of justice may seem secondary to the opportunity to live the rest of their lives in luxury; and, in any case, the lottery was not set up to dispense justice. Nevertheless, the lottery could still construed has having an element of EAD about it. All, in theory, have an equal chance (though not positive choice) of making the appropriate contribution (buying a winning ticket) that may result in the desired outcome, and if you do not buy a ticket (make an appropriate contribution) you do not 'deserve' a prize.

However, winners of the national lottery are normally anonymous creatures whose deserts are unknown. What if we knew of their previous actions and circumstances? As a pilot study to investigate this, we gave a sample of students at Liverpool details of the backgrounds of lottery winners. Our results showed that if the lottery winner was described as a man unworthy in terms of desert (he had criminal convictions and was suspected of other offences), the majority of subjects rated this win as less fair than when the character of the winner was not mentioned, or the winner someone was described as very worthy (because of his unpaid services to the community). Thus even judgements of the fairness of that epitome of 'winner takes all' games, the National Lottery, appear to be subject to the familiar influence of EAD. The 'quasi-equity' nature of the lottery is well illustrated by this comment from one subject in this study; this person rated the outcome as 'very fair' when the winner was the person for whom no background details were provided. 'If Mr Milner takes the time to buy a lottery ticket it is fair that he wins it. How just that one who person should have such a large amount of money when half the world is starving is another thing'. This comment implies that somehow the lottery win can be viewed as a return for the 'effort' involved in purchasing the ticket; though the problems created by such a return within the general scheme of things are also acknowledged![1]

Other research also supports the idea that people attempt to apply EAD rules to lottery type outcomes. Thus, a study by Allison (cited by Messick, 1993) showed that when given a chance to win in a set of 'winner-takes-all' situations, regardless of the situation, subjects who won did not take all of the outcome to which they were 'entitled' by the rules of the game. Moreover, they took least in a condition where their chance of winning was determined by their birth date. Referring to this result, Messick (1993) comments that, 'For reasons that are not yet clear, this procedure suppresses the winner-take-all (rule) more than any of the other procedures', but he suggests, 'Perhaps the reason stems from the obvious fact that people do not choose their birthdates and hence should not be penalized for them' (p. 24). If Messick is correct, and people tend to take outcomes to the extent that they feel they have some choice, or equal choice, over the criteria that are used to determine the outcome, then again there is an obvious overlap between the reasoning that subjects applied, and EAD.

The essential conclusion to be drawn from this brief analysis of the so-called 'maximal difference' rules that govern games and contests, is that they can exist to serve many purposes; however, when considerations of justice in terms of fairness are concerned, they seem to derive their main force through implicit references to EAD. In fact, take away these appeals to EAD, and arguably there is again really nothing of any substance left to relate them to justice. It is also worth emphasizing that, although games and contests can be entertaining and stimulating, according to most justice theorists, the main motive for employing rules of justice is supposedly to prevent life being like a game of chance, not to make it into one.

Allocation preferences and justice rationalizations

Once we define justice in terms of EAD, and differentiate considerations of justice from allocation preferences in general, many of the *rationalizations* that people tend to make for their allocation decisions also become more understandable. If people make allocation decisions for a variety of reasons besides those of justice, then it is inevitable that sometimes their allocation preferences will conflict with the dictates of justice. Accordingly we might expect people to try to rationalize, or quite literally, 'justify', their allocations by attempting to convince themselves and others that their allocations are, in fact, 'just' in terms of EAD.

Consider again the some of the other findings I referred to in Chapter 8. For instance, Harris and Joyce (1980) that some subjects may use an equality rule in allocating outcomes to individuals who have made unequal contributions, simply because an equitable allocation may be too difficult to calculate. Nevertheless, many subjects would attempt to justify giving equal shares on grounds that the recipients put in equal effort, or the unequal contributions 'weren't their fault' (p. 179). In other words, they attempted to argue that inputs were equal, or there was an unequal opportunity to perform the inputs. Reis and Gruzen (1976) also found that subjects tended to invoke effort factors to justify unequal as well as equal outcomes, even when these outcomes were clearly motivated by other concerns. Similarly, Mikula (1972) found that, although apparently in the interests of politeness, high contributors divided rewards equally between themselves and their lower input partners, they attempted to justify the equal distribution by saying that their greater contribution was accidental. Lower input partners, however, who used an equity or contributions rule, justified this by reference to differential effort and /or ability (see also, Feather and Simon, 1971). However, in competitive situations, when politeness is not an issue, lower contributors attributed performance differences to chance, and higher contributors attributed them to effort (Snyder, Stephan and Rosenfield, 1976).

All of these findings can clearly be interpreted as rationalizations or justifications in terms of EAD for allocation behaviours determined by other factors.

History, politics, allocation preferences and justice
Contrary to the views of some modern theorists, the concept of proportional desert is not simply a feature of modern capitalist ideology; its origins can be traced back to the dawn of Western civilization.

It is an obvious fact of history that different cultures at various times have adopted different allocation principles. At times, slavery has been tolerated and/or resources have concentrated in the hands of a few, whilst on other occasions, resources may have been more evenly distributed, and people have been more humanely treated. But this is not necessarily evidence that radically different conceptions of 'justice' pertained in these various societies. Of course, throughout history, those in positions of privilege have sought to impose inegalitarian rules on others, and many of those ill-treated have sought a more egalitarian society. But if we want to find out how *justice* was really construed in these societies, we need to concentrate less on the allocation rules themselves, and more on the *justifications* given by supporters of the various systems.

For example, according to the historical perspective I have presented in this book, one of the main reasons why the supporters of slavery and sex discrimination were able to justify their views, was not because they had a radically different conception of justice compared to the kind we hold today, but because they thought slaves and women were inferior beings with different genetically created 'needs', and we no longer accept these premises. Similarly, to supporters of educational privilege, one of the main reasons why it was deemed appropriate to give academic education only to the most able (whose ability did not necessarily arise from their own choices), was because the 'least able' were considered genetically deficient in some way and would not appreciate or benefit from such opportunities; they had different 'needs' (indeed, many still hold such views). Also, it might indeed have been the case that some of the early Christians adopted a communalist, egalitarian/needs orientation to social organization, because they wanted to foster a non-competitive humanitarian community spirit; but this must be seen within an ideological context that stressed that only an omnipotent and omniscient God was truly capable of dispensing justice, and that He would dispense rewards and punishments in heaven.

It also follows from EAD, that ideologies that wish to justify inequalities in outcomes will not only attempt to argue that people have unequal needs, but also that people have control over their behaviour; hence they will propose that people can choose whether to work or be lazy, whether to invest their earnings or outcomes, or squander them on temporary pleasures. In contrast, ideologies espousing a more equal distribution of resources, will be more likely to assume a position of 'deterministic egalitarianism'; they will contend that people are subject to forces beyond their control; they cannot equally choose the value of the contributions they make, or how they deal with their outcomes. Empirical research strongly supports these propositions; thus people of different political persuasions not only often hold different attitudes to poor and needy, but attempt to justify their attitudes to least well-off with corresponding assumptions about the causes of poverty.

For example, research from a number of countries has shown that political conservatism is associated with both support for inequality, and the endorsement of the view that behaviour is mainly internally or dispositionally caused. Thus members of right-wing organizations not only have more negative attitudes towards the poor and programmes directed towards helping the poor, but also tend to blame those who are poor for their plight, claiming that poverty arises from factors such as indolence and recklessness. On the other hand, supporters of centre and left wing political parties, whose views tend more towards egalitarianism, are likely to argue that the poor are largely if not entirely innocent victims who are made poor by circumstances beyond their control (see, for example, Furnham, 1982; Katz, 1981; Kluegel and Smith, 1986; Pandey et al., 1982; Wagstaff, 1994; Wagstaff, 1984; Wagstaff and Quirk, 1983; Williams, 1984). As Lane points out, 'At the roots of every ideology there are premises about the nature of causation, (and) the appropriate ways for explaining events' (1962, p. 318).

Given that inequalities can be justified in terms of differential need (including genetic need) as well as differential chosen inputs, particularly effort, it is particularly revealing when supporters of inequality attempt to apply both at once. For example, in some research conducted at Liverpool, we found that political rightists were more likely than left-wingers to endorse the idea that intelligence is inherited, and they also agreed with the view that 'intelligence is important in determining how successful a person will become'. However, at the same time, rightists were also more likely to endorse statements such as, 'people achieve the success they deserve', and 'almost anyone can be successful if he or she is prepared to work hard enough' (Wagstaff, 1983, 1984: Wagstaff and Quirk, 1983).

A similar combination of arguments based on contribution and need can be found in attempts to justify the unfettered free-market as an ethical system. Thus, not only do proponents of the free-market often assume that the market rewards people according to their contributions, but, at the same time, they assume that these contributions arise from free choices which reflect different values or needs. As Posner (1981) points out, in strict economic terms, the 'value' of something to someone is determined by that person's willingness *and* ability to pay for it (in the market place, a loaf of bread has no 'value' to a starving man if he is also destitute and no one wishes to lend him the money). But if we apply economic principles to model psychological processes, it is then an easy step to the argument that people who have no money place less value on things than people who have money. So, as the popular argument goes, if the poor really 'valued' or 'needed' educational opportunities as much as the rich, they would work to buy them, wouldn't they? And if the unemployed really 'valued' or 'needed' the rewards of work, they would find a job wouldn't they? (See, for example, Friedman, 1978.)

Such examples illustrate, rather graphically, that the differences in political ideologies that can give rise to such radically different perspectives on inequality and attitudes to the various sections of society, do not necessarily represent radically different perspectives on *justice*. On the contrary, perhaps it is the fact that these different ideologies share exactly the *same* principle of justice, EAD, that accounts for how they attempt to *justify* their positions.

The development of EAD

Another advantage of viewing justice in terms of EAD is that enables to make some sense of the psychological literature on the development of justice.

If we look at the developmental literature on justice as a whole, two major trends seem to emerge. The evidence suggests that children start with allocations according to pure self-interest, but over time for they eventually take on board other perspectives; first equality, then reciprocity or contribution; this is followed by need, and eventually they adopt a sort of proportionality principle based on contribution, with adjustments for need, depending on the situation. This is followed by a recognition of possible conflicts between these principles of desert (the combined rules of contribution and need) and the welfare of others (Damon, 1977, 1981; Hook and Cook, 1979; Keil and McClintock, 1983; Lerner, 1974; Morgan and Sawyer, 1967; Piaget, 1932/1965).

Accompanying this developmental trend, however, is another that reflects an understanding of the concept of personal or moral responsibility. Piaget (1932/1965), in particular, relates this to punishment. At first children seem to have no conception of personal responsibility; an act is judged right or wrong depending on its consequences, regardless of whether the action was intended or accidental. Children also tend to operate a very primitive attribution process, and assume that a misdeed will automatically be punished ('immanent justice'), and punishment by adults, and other authorities is, in itself, proof of wrongdoing. As children grow older, however, they are able to take intentions into account, and there is an understanding of reciprocity and cooperation; hence, older children are more likely to take into account moral responsibility when deciding whether punishment is justified, and argue that should relate to the crime. Finally, older children also consider other forms of punishment such as *restitutive* punishment, or compensating the victim.

If we superimpose the two developmental trends, then theories of 'moral development' seem to map well onto the development of an understanding of proportional desert. As children are able to make decisions involving increasing cognitive complexity, we see a developmental trend from pure self interest, through equality, simple reciprocity and need to 'complex reciprocity' or EAD; and this is accompanied by a growing sophistication in the understanding of the importance of choice, and personal or moral responsibility. Older children are thus more able to balance the elements of contribution, need, restitution and responsibility that go to make up EAD. They are also willing to balance individual desert with wider conceptions of welfare, such as the relative deserts of others.

However, although some of these trends are also to be found in Kohlberg's (1971, 1975, 1976) original theory, much of Kohlberg's analysis seems to be tied to more general considerations about whether people think the goodness and badness of acts are determined by internal principles, or conformity to external norms. Hence, according to Kohlberg, justice at the highest stage is assumed to exist when the child adopts reputedly Kantian ideals such as 'the equality of human rights and respect for the dignity of human beings as individual persons'. Thus Kohlberg's approach looks rather divorced from EAD; but is it?

Kohlberg reconsidered

Unfortunately, like others who have attempted to use Kant's categorical imperative as an ultimate principle of justice, Kohlberg inevitably fails to come up with any meaningful definition of the term 'justice' that will enable us to generate rules or principles. It is notable, for example, that Kohlberg argues that those who are at the highest stage of moral development adopt the dictum that 'life is more important than property'; but as we know, Kant's categorical imperative does not dictate any such thing.

More recently, however, Kohlberg and his colleagues have revised his theory to take on board the more familiar notions of distributive, corrective and commutative justice (see Colby and Kohlberg, 1987). Within this revised scheme, Colby and Kohlberg (1987) adopt a distinctly Rawlsian approach; hence they argue that at the highest stage of moral development, stage 6, people reject the reward of talent, merit or achievement as the basis of distributive justice. This is because at stage 6 there is an understanding that, 'these (characteristics) are largely seen as resulting from differences in genetic endowment or in educational and social opportunities, which are morally arbitrary'. However, Colby and Kohlberg go on to say that, 'equity does include the recognition of need, i.e. the obligation to consider the least advantaged'. They also say that when an unequal distribution of goods is unavoidable, the distribution should be by lot (p. 32). Also, at stage 6 corrective justice is no longer seen as retributive (because presumably criminals cannot 'help it'). Rather punishment is a seen as a way of protecting potential and actual victims of crime from further. And, finally, in terms of what Colby and Kohlberg term 'commutative justice' or justice in exchange, justice is, they say, is 'partly' regulated by contracts and promises, that can be broken in certain cases, such as when a third party is in urgent need.

In other words, Kohlberg's 'ideal justice structure' now seems to be a manifestation of the 'deterministic egalitarian' variant of EAD. The argument is that, as all the usual characteristics that would normally form the basis of unequal desert are now 'largely seen as resulting from differences in genetic endowment or in educational and social opportunities, which are morally arbitrary', it follows that outcomes and exchanges should result in strict equality of outcomes (adjusted for need), right down to the assignment of outcomes by lot when an unequal distribution of outcomes is unavoidable. Though of course, like most deterministic egalitarians, having rejected 'retribution', stage 6 reasoners are left struggling with a rather dubious utilitarian justification for punishment. This is important, because, if we now assume that Kohlberg's 'ideal justice' is simply a position of deterministic egalitarianism, then the rest of his stage theory can be used to describe a broad framework for the development of EAD, leading up to this position. Thus, incorporating some of the revisions described by Colby and Kohlberg (1987, pp. 25-32), we can come up with a more recognizable developmental justice scheme such as the following.

At stage 1, both rewards and punishment are based on the consequences of one's actions, or 'what happens to you', regardless of choice or responsibility. The attribution process is therefore primitive; you deserve 'what happens to you'; if bad things happen to you, you have been bad, if good things happen to you, you have been good. However, there is also a tendency positive outcomes are distributed according to strict equality, but as a simple heuristic or rule of thumb.

At stage 2, there is a consideration of both intention and real contribution or input in the distribution of both positive and negative outcomes, and some provision for need. The basic elements of EAD are present, but there is no reference to external norms; desert is based solely on individual needs and interests of those involved in the immediate relationship.

At stage 3, the concept of EAD continues to develop, but is modified by reference to external or shared norms about motives and what constitutes a 'good' or 'bad' input. If you do what others consider good, you deserve reward, and if you do what others consider bad, you deserve to be punished, and you respond to the needs of others because it is good to care for people. Choice and responsibility also receive weight as motives are considered more fully. An action that has bad consequences may not deserve punishment if the actor did not intend to do perform it.

At stage 4, 'inputs' in the EAD scheme are considered in the wider context of general merit or contributions to society; and one respects for property rights in as much as they are a deserved return for such investments or inputs. Also impartiality in the application of the principles governing desert is deemed important. Hence, in accordance with EAD, punishments should be administered impartially according to desert, so that the offender 'pays a debt to society'. Contracts and promises must be also kept. Moreover, all this is seen as necessary to promote the successful functioning, or 'good' of society and/or to obey natural or divine law.

In their discussion of stages 5 and 6 (the 'postconventional' levels), Colby and Kohlberg appear to leave the broad notions of contribution, equality, need, and responsibility and focus their analysis on ideas such as the 'universalizable values and rights that anyone would choose to build into a moral society' (p. 29). For reasons previously stated, this is probably the weakest and most confusing part of their analysis. 'Reading between the lines', however, they seem to be saying that, at stages 5 and 6, the integrated EAD rule becomes more abstract. At stage 5, it is applied impartially to all as humans; hence the effects of giving one person his or her proportional deserts must be considered in the context of the deserts of others; thus certain utility or group welfare considerations are taken into account, that may overrule individual desert. There is also a recognition that the rules of society are not absolute; they are social conventions brought about by common agreement, and may sometimes be considered unjust; hence a person who breaks a rule, even one generally agreed to, does not necessarily deserve punishment.

Eventually, however, some people come to stage 6. Although Colby and Kohlberg have commented that 'The exact nature and definition of Stage 6 are uncertain at this point' (p. 32), as noted previously, it appears to be a position of pure 'deterministic egalitarianism'. Thus, recognizing that most of the 'inputs' used to assess desert rest on criteria that are largely influenced by chance factors, people at this stage believe in 'equal rights' to the extent that no one actually deserves any more or less than anyone else, and punishment is only justified as a means of minimizing negative outcomes for all. There is also a full recognition that contracts and promises, and the conventions and rules of society, can be broken if they infringe this egalitarian ideal.

Considered as a framework to describe the development of EAD, therefore, Kohlberg's stage scheme can be interpreted in a way that fits in rather better with other more familiar conceptions of justice. Even Kohlberg's idea that 'life is more important than property' now has a basis. If life is considered to be the most precious resource (outcome) that anyone possesses, and all are ultimately equally deserving, it would obviously create more inequity to sacrifice what is normally considered one person's most valuable resource for another's less valuable resource.

Of course, whether further research will be able to corroborate these proposed trends remains to be seen. It must be born in mind that not all accept the view that there are clear developmental trends in the development of justice thinking (see, Moore, Hembree and Enright, 1993). Moreover, there is some evidence to suggest that a majority of 4-year olds will utilise information about work and need when distributing rewards (Anderson and Butzin, 1978; Nelson and Dweck, 1977), although according to both Kohlberg (1976) and Damon (1977), 4 years is somewhat young to be using these rules. Such results suggest that an understanding of the basic elements of EAD may be present even in very young children. Interestingly also, the empirical work reported by Colby and Kohlberg (1987) indicates that very few subjects use stage 6 reasoning; in fact, in the American samples they studied, 'moral decisions' tended to be dominated by stage 3 and stage 4 reasoning. Thus if Rawlsian 'deterministic egalitarianism' is presumed to the ideal, few people seem to display it.

Nevertheless, even the speculative scheme I have outlined here illustrates the advantages for theories of moral development that can accrue from identifying justice with its historical desert roots. If we adopt a more unitary conception of justice of this kind, at least we will all know that when we speak of justice, we are all talking about the same thing.

Justice, caring and morality

Another advantage of equating justice with EAD is that it may enable us to add some clarification to the psychological debate over whether the humanitarian norms of 'caring' and 'need' are rules of justice, or represent some other moral principle (for see, Furby, 1986; Gilligan, 1982). From the perspective of EAD, the extent to which one considers moral concepts such as 'caring', 'provision for need', and 'benevolence', to be acceptable as principles of justice, may depend very much on one's attitudes towards deterministic egalitarianism. If one considers that inputs can be unequal, and that outcome deficits can be chosen or 'blameworthy', then 'morality' and justice with regard to these issues can readily part company. But if one considers inputs always to be equal (because all humans are of 'equal worth'), and that ultimately humans have little or no choices over what they do with their outcomes, then benevolence and caring in response to need, in the direction of equality, become part of justice.

It should be emphasized, however, that even from the perspective of deterministic egalitarianism, if caring and provision for need actually offend equality of outcomes, then, once again, they become unjust; for example, benevolence towards a ruthless, wealthy drugs baron at the expense of the poor and homeless would be unjust as it would promote inequality.

Crude and complex equality

The possibility that a person operating at Kohlberg's post conventional level of morality might eventually employ an egalitarian conception of EAD, draws attention to another issue. There is some empirical evidence to suggest that children sometimes use an equality rule before adopting a simple equity or proportionality rule. Why?

It is likely that deterministic egalitarianism is a far more sophisticated conception of equality than the simple 'equal shares' heuristical device used by younger children. Indeed, it is very possible that when younger children adopt an 'equal shares' rule, this is not because they have developed some intuitive egalitarian conception of 'fairness', rather they are adopting the most simple allocation rule or simply imitating the way adults treat them. For example, according to EAD, one might expect adults to share things more equally amongst children than adults, because children are less responsible for their actions. To test this latter idea empirically, we gave adult subjects information about pairs of children of different ages who had behaved positively or negatively towards their parents. Subjects were asked to consider what, from the parents point of view, would be a fair allocation of gifts between the children. Our results fitted the above predictions. Subjects thought that parents should allocate the positive outcomes (gifts) equally to younger children, less equally to adolescents, and distinctly unequally to adult children, so in the latter cases, the 'good' child received most (see Wagstaff, 1997). (This study, along with others, also illustrates that when contributions are clearly unequal, the majority of subjects do not blankly apply an 'equality/needs' rule in family situations; see also, Wagstaff, Huggins and Perfect, 1993.)

The psychology of just punishment

Psychological theories of moral development thus illustrate well the confusion that is generated when fragments of various justice traditions are taken out of their historical context. If we separate justice into a diffuse array of components ('rights', moral imperatives, contributions, equality, need, intentionality, equal opportunity, contract, utility etc.) the result is chaotic. However, place them in the context of the desert tradition, and things take on a more coherent form. The fragmentation of concepts related to justice is also very apparent in psychological theories of justice and punishment, but, again, viewed from the perspective of EAD, perhaps we can now adopt a psychological approach to 'corrective justice' that makes rather more sense.

According to the view expressed in this book, probably the biggest mistake that psychologists have made in attempting to devise theories of corrective justice is to discard the one theory that had any real promise in this respect, equity theory. For contrary to what some would have us believe, there is no need on either theoretical or empirical grounds to adopt different formulae for positive and negative inputs, or to claim that 'equity' is about 'distributive justice' rather than 'retributive justice', or to argue that equity is 'comparative' whereas corrective justice is 'non-comparative'. Wagstaff and Perfect's (1992) equal ratio formula can accommodate both the reward of positive outcomes and the punishment of negative outcomes. Moreover, we have shown empirically that, regardless of whether positive or negative inputs are involved, subjects will follow the same equal ratio equity rule, and distribute 'deserved' and 'undeserved' negative outcomes amongst offenders in the same way as rewards amongst workers (that is, deserved positive and negative outcomes in proportion to positive and negative inputs, and undeserved outcomes equally). Moreover, as in the distribution of positive outcomes, subjects will adjust punishments or negative outcomes on the basis of 'need' such that an offender who will be left in an additional condition of 'need' following punishment, will be awarded a lesser punishment (Thomas et al., 1996; Wagstaff and Preece, 1997; Wagstaff, Chadwick et al., 1996).

Where, hopefully, EAD improves on basic equity theory, however, is by systematically incorporating the idea of culpability or responsibility; this enables us to account for the culpability/proportionality combination that is so prevalent in the theory and practise of punishment of offenders (Honderich, 1976; Raphael, 1981; Sadurski, 1985; Stephenson, 1992). People want punishment to fit the crime, but only when the criminal is guilty; EAD makes sense of this requirement and provides a description of how it operates. Thus, by incorporating attributions of responsibility, EAD can account for differences in attitudes to punishment. For instance, EAD predicts that if a position of deterministic egalitarianism is adopted (that is, offenders are deemed not to be responsible for their actions and do not deserve to be punished), then the treatment of offenders by rehabilitation will be preferred to punishment. This fits with the empirical finding that people who feel that criminals may be the 'accidental' victims of societal and economic pressures are more likely to favour rehabilitation than punishment (Carroll, Berkowitz, Lurigio, and Weaver, 1987).

The importance of the concept of psychological equity for the study of corrective justice has certainly yet to be fully realized. It is likely, for instance, that people may scale positive and negative outcomes differently; in particular, positive occurrences may decline in incremental value (the more you have, the less each successive increment means to you), whilst negative occurrences may increase dramatically in incremental value (the more negative increments you are subjected to, the worse each increment is experienced) (see Kahneman and Tversky, 1979; Lippa, 1994; Markovsky, 1991). It may be the case therefore that, so as long as they are not destitute, the negative feelings that people experience when they see someone 'undeservedly' materially better off than they are, may be considerably less distressing to them than the feelings experienced when they are harmed in some way. Unfortunately, the failure to perceive the common link the areas of so-called 'distributive' and 'corrective' justice has probably hampered research on these issues.

This this brings us to a more general point; how exactly is injustice experienced?

Justice as a cognitive evaluation process

There has been much discussion in the psychological and philosophical literature about the emotional reactions that are supposed to accompany various conceptions of justice (Adams, 1965; Hogan and Emler, 1981; Miller and Vidmar, 1981; Rawls, 1975; Walster and Walster, 1975; Walster, Walster and Berscheid, 1978). From the perspective of EAD, however, justice as desert is not in itself a 'sentiment' or emotion, it is a *cognitive evaluation process* that involves the application of a set of evaluative principles or algorithms. As such, (and as the equity theorists have always proposed) an awareness of inequity or injustice may have a variety of different emotional consequences depending on the individual and the situation.

For instance, having evaluated a particular situation in terms of EAD, those receiving fewer positive outcomes than they deserve may feel a variety of emotions, including anger, resentment, envy, low self-esteem, and humiliation; whilst those receiving more than they deserve, may experience emotions such as guilt, remorse, embarrassment and even fear of retaliation. Other reactions might include the experience of an unpleasant state of tension or 'dissonance' when situations are discrepant with our internal moral standards, perhaps because of cognitive incongruity or inconsistency involved (see, for example, Festinger, 1957), or as Lerner suggests, fear that the stability of our environment is threatened.

However, from this viewpoint, EAD can also be used to justify emotions motivated by other concerns; for instance, in response to the plight of another one may feel sadness, pity, or even repulsion. Similarly, our response to being threatened or harmed may be anger and a desire for vengeance. We may then seek to justify or rationalize such responses by an appeal to 'justice'; if we can believe that those we pity 'deserve' our help, our pity is justified; and if we believe that those who harm us 'deserve' our wrath, our anger is justified. Moreover, this desire to justify our emotions may then lead to more primitive attribution processes, in which personal responsibility is ignored or distorted; for instance, there is some evidence to suggest that 'harm done' seems to be more important than culpability in determining crime seriousness (Hoffman and Hardyman, 1986; Rossi, Simpson and Miller, 1985; Stephenson, 1992), and the more harm done (that is, severe the consequences), the more likely responsibility will be attributed to the offender (Miller and Vidmar, 1981). In other words, when people are made to suffer they want to blame someone, and the more they are harmed the more they will tend to do this; but they will also try to make this attribution 'just'.

In summary, if justice is defined in terms of EAD, there is no single emotion or group of emotions that uniquely atteaches to our 'sense of justice'; instead, in one way or another, justice may be at associated with virtually the full range of human emotions.

Procedural justice and deserved outcomes

Another issue that has been a bone of contention amongst both philosophers and psychologists is the status of 'procedural justice'. The problem relates to whether what is termed 'procedural justice' is a species of justice in its own right, or whether it is simply *part* of what we mean by justice.

From the perspective of EAD, procedural justice is not a species of justice that is separate from desert; rather 'just procedures' are those procedures that are most likely to secure 'deserved outcomes'. A number of research findings are supportive of this view. For example, research using Leventhal's (1980) procedural justice principles has shown that in evaluating the fairness of a procedure, consistency across people, or 'the similar treatment of equals', is the most important criterion when judging the fairness of a procedure, together with accuracy of information, the maintenance of ethical and moral standards, and bias suppression (Barrett-Howard and Tyler, 1986). These results are clearly compatible with the idea of justice as EAD; the idea of 'the similar treatment of equals' is an integral part of EAD, and it is difficult to see how anyone could be confident about obtaining their just deserts if the allocation procedures involve inaccurate information, the violation of ethical standards, and bias.

In comparison, although it figured much in the early literature on procedural justice, the idea of being able to voice one's case ('voice control' or 'representativeness') figured as relatively unimportant in this research (Barrett-Howard and Tyler, 1986). Other results also suggest that the opportunity to voice one's case may be less important than the probability that a procedure will produce a just outcome. For example, Wagstaff and Kelhar (1993) found that although subjects judged an adversarial procedure that enabled them the 'voice' their opinions as giving them more control, the fairness of the procedure was determined more by the ability to produce a correct decision or just outcome. In other words, when considerations of fairness are paramount, the probability that a procedure will produce a correct outcome seems to take precedence over perceived control. This presents the possibility that 'voice control' is chosen primarily as a means to end; to produce a just outcome. These results thus fit with others that show that procedural justice concerns are judged most important in situations in which outcome distributions depend crucially on the kinds of procedures adopted (see Barrett-Howard and Tyler, 1986).

Other results in 'procedural justice' research seem simply to emphasize the importance of personal responsibility in determining the relevant inputs for a set of outcomes. For example, Greenberg (1967) found that subjects who received a low share of a reward judged their share significantly less fair when the allocation was based on room allocation (a chance factor) rather than actual work performance. Such a finding is, of course, entirely predictable in terms of EAD.

However, perhaps most significantly, much of the problem in the 'just procedures' versus 'just outcomes' debate seems to have arisen from a failure to recognize that the many of features of 'just procedures' can be construed as outcomes in their own right. For instance, Tyler argues that the procedures used in making a decision can convey important messages about self-worth and self-esteem, particularly those that relate to neutral treatment, trustworthiness and respect and dignity (Tyler and Dawes, 1993; Tyler and Belliveau, 1995). This makes sense within the context of EAD, because any procedure that lowers a person's sense of self-worth or self-esteem could be seen as producing negative outcomes. Within EAD those who have done nothing wrong (have no negative inputs), or have yet to be found guilty of wrong, are entitled to impartial treatment and a degree of respect, trust and dignity; and any procedure that is negative in these respects is one that inflicts 'undeserved harm' and is 'unjust'. Moreover, if opportunities to voice one's arguments, and make procedural choices, are considered in themselves to be 'value expressive' positive outcomes, that convey information about status or worth, and should be available to all, then to deny someone who has done nothing wrong the opportunity to such opportunities, is once again, an 'undeserved harm', and an injustice. As Mill argued, 'it is a personal injustice to withhold from anyone, unless for the prevention of greater evils, the ordinary privilege of having his voice reckoned in the disposal of affairs in which he has the same interest as other people' (1861/1996, p. 302).

To summarize, there is no necessity to postulate a sort of justice, 'procedural justice', that exists separately from justice as desert. Instead, so-called 'just procedures' may labelled so either because they are a *means* to just outcomes, and/or they in themselves *are* just outcomes for those receiving them.

The currency of justice
These considerations further draw attention to the fact that the 'currency of fairness' may extend far beyond the standard issues of financial rewards for the

hardworking, and punishments for offenders. There are many other kinds of positive and negative outcomes that can operate in everyday social interaction. For instance, positive outcomes can include, the company or presence of others, attention, responsivity, sympathy, praise and affection, and negative outcomes can include, crowding, conspicuousness, overarousal, disrespect, criticism, and rejection (see Buss, 1983). The students tested by Messick, Bloom, Boldizar and Samuelson (1985) showed quite graphically that considerations of fairness are applied to a enormous range of actions and circumstances; these include, mistreating animals, apologising for clumsiness, listening to parental advice, showing independence, parking in handicapped zones, and having good study habits. Nevertheless, it is notable how virtually all of these behaviours can be described as 'unjust' or 'just' in terms of desert.

For instance, some students said that it is unfair to shoplift or charge prices that are too high. The scholastics would undoubtedly have agreed with the students on this one; in the language of desert, both of these behaviours would represent the gain of an undeserved positive outcome. Similarly, we could argue that to 'mistreat animals' is to harm innocent creatures who do not deserve to suffer;'to make everything for right-handed people' is to discriminate against people for reasons unrelated to their desert; 'to park in handicapped zones' is to gain an undeserved advantage and disadvantage those in need through no fault of their own; 'to work hard and make an effort to help others' is to pull your weight and put in the necessary inputs in a collective endeavour; to say 'excuse me' when bumping into someone is to compensate verbally for an undeserved social harm; to 'show good study habits' is to fulfil the desert requirement with regard to the opportunities that have been offered to you by parents and others; to 'listen to parental advice' is to give parents the respect they deserve for looking after you, supporting you through college and trying to help you; and to 'depend on no one' is to fail to enter into reciprocal relationships thus depriving others of the opportunities for favours when they are in need. Indeed, had they been alive today, one can imagine Plato and Aristotle and their successors endorsing many of these ideas. Within the historical philosophical literature, justice has traditionally concerned the whole of everyday human interaction, including ordinary reciprocal role obligations.

Desert versus utility

Although the relationship between justice and utility has long been controversial, only recently have psychologists begun to address this issue systematically. What evidence has been collected, however, seems to indicate, as Baron puts it, that 'people's intuitions often contradict utilitarian theory' (1993, p. 135), and often they behave in ways that cannot be explained in terms of utilitarianism. Hence people want the guilty punished even when deterrence is absent, and they are very reluctant to harm one innocent person to benefit another; moreover, they want more compensation or restitution when a person has been deliberately harmed by another than when the harm is an accident of nature, and they want more compensation when the harmdoer is the one providing the compensation (Baron, 1993; 1995). However, whilst such results might conflict with utilitarianism, as previously mentioned, all are compatible with, and are actually predicted by, the EAD model (for details see Chapter 14).

In this context, it is also worth noting that Bar-Hillel and Yaari (1993) have reported some intriguing data that suggest that, when inputs are equal, and subjects are required to 'justly' allocate resources that give individuals different amounts of pleasure, they tend to follow a utility principle and award more resources to the person who will derive most pleasure from them. However, other data collected by these researchers suggests that this result may have occurred because allocators work on the assumption that the person who derives less pleasure from the resources 'doesn't really care' whether he or she receives them or not, and is, therefore, pleased to give them, or allow them to be given, to the person who derives most pleasure. Consequently, when it is made clear that, despite the different amounts of pleasure they derive from the resources, both participants in the allocation want as much of the resources as they can get, the response of the majority of subjects is to allocate the resources equally.

Different rules for different resources

Another obvious implication of the present analysis is that EAD is not at all incompatible with the idea that people tend to use different allocation rules to distribute different kinds of resources. For example, Bar-Hillel and Yaari (1993) have argued that in the allocation of basic necessities, such as food or health services, compensation (or need) is the standard of justice; in the allocation of economic rewards, contribution is the standard of justice; in the allocation of political or legal rights, equality is the standard, and in the allocation of the means of production, efficiency or utility is the standard.

Obviously, some of the main motives for these different allocation rules, in as much as they are used in these ways, may have nothing to do with justice. For instance, people might want to distribute health care according to need out of a sense of compassion or pity, rather than because it is fair or just. Similarly, there may be sound economic reasons to distribute productive resources to those who can best make use of them; for presumably by doing so, everyone might benefit, regardless of the demands of justice. Moreover, to supporters of modern democracy, there are compelling reasons for allocating political power in a way that does not concentrate it in the hands of a minority. In oligarchies, tyrannies and monarchies, minority power can lead to consistent rule by the incompetent and decadent, in a way that is contrary to the welfare of the rest of society. Nevertheless, given the results of previous research in this area, when it comes to considerations of justice, we might also expect people to use EAD to justify their allocations. For instance, the distribution of economic rewards according to contribution speaks for itself. As regards health care, however, it might not go unnoticed, that most illnesses could be considered 'undeserved'; we rarely 'choose' to be ill under conditions of equal opportunity. And even those illnesses that might be considered indirectly to result sometimes from the reckless choices of the victim, such as lung cancer or heart disease, hardly seem to constitute 'commensurate outcomes' for the behaviours that may contribute to them. (Though apparently some doctors in Britain are seriously considering the idea of giving preference to non-smokers in the distribution of health care.)

But perhaps most important, within EAD, a supply of the basic necessities of life, such as food, shelter and health care, is essential the maintenance of the 'zero-outcomes baseline' in EAD. To deny a person the basic necessities of life is one of the most extreme negative outcomes one can impose; for by doing so one effectively reduces or eliminates the opportunity for that person to provide the relevant inputs in a system of desert (see also, Sadurski, 1985). This will also apply to criminals. In a system of corrective justice in which the courts already apportion punishment, it would be an injustice to allow those already receiving their deserts to endure the extra pain, suffering, and even death, that might accrue from the failure to provide basic health provision.

Also the allocation of the means of production to those most able to use them might still appear to be 'just' if such a distribution drastically reduces the incidence of 'undeserved' poverty and suffering; for then it may provide the 'least inequitable solution' in terms of overall desert (as with Rawls' 'difference principle'). But, even when this is not the case, such allocations do not have to conflict with desert. It does not follow that someone who can use resources best necessarily has to reap the most benefit from them. If A is a skilful lorry driver, and B is a lawyer, it may make more economic sense to give a £200,000 lorry to the lorry driver, and a £100 book on law to the lawyer. But this would not of itself imply that the former is necessarily entitled to, or has received greater rewards or positive outcomes than the latter (indeed, in practice the lawyer would probably be paid more); as the scholastics asserted, depending on their role, it is important than individuals should be provided with the appropriate means, including tools, to achieve a 'just' return for their efforts towards the social good.

Another reason why people might appear to adopt different allocation rules for different resources concerns 'divisions of labour'. In Western societies, for example, it is usually assumed that it is the job of the law courts to distribute punishments, of employers and the government to distribute financial rewards, of parents and aided by the social services to attend to the needs of children, of the health services to distribute health care, and of people in their day to day interactions to deal 'justly' with others in terms of the currency of social interaction (such as treating others with due courtesy and respect). Consequently, it may not be considered appropriate or feasible, to assign these all of tasks to different agencies. It is not seen as the job of the health services to punish offenders, or to reward economic contributions; or of the courts to administer health care, and they are not equipped to do so.

This last point calls attention to an important feature of the traditional notion of desert. According to this idea, which is implicit in EAD (and the operation of Wagstaff and Perfect's, 1992, formula), when people are awarded exactly what they deserve, there are no grounds left for treating them unequally in terms of outcomes. We can perhaps call this concept *'residual equality'*. One implication of this in practice is that, if all the agencies are doing their jobs appropriately, there should be no call to treat anyone unequally in other ways. Thus, if offenders are punished appropriately by the courts, there should be no call to treat them disrespectfully, or deprive them of health care.

Unfortunately, however, studies that attempt to examine the application of different allocation rules rarely attempt to examine them in combination; in other words, subjects are not asked to react to situations in which the task is to distribute one kind of resource to an individual when it is patently obvious that the same individual is undeserving with regard to other resources. If such disparities were made clearer, then the distributive principles that supposedly attach these different kinds of resource might show some modification. For example, in one study we found that when need was held constant, but differences in desert (inputs) were made salient, the distribution of resources to those in need was greatly modified. Thus people tended to give more money to a person who became homeless through accident (neutral inputs) than to someone who became homeless through attempts to extort money (negative inputs) (Wagstaff, 1994). Other studies we have conducted suggest that financial 'need' is taken into account in the assignment of penalties for motoring offences; those in need are assigned lower penalties than those not in need (Thomas, Wagstaff and Brunas-Wagstaff, 1996).

Conclusion

Much of this analysis of the psychological literature has necessarily been speculative, but hopefully, I have demonstrated how EAD may be able to provide a unifying theme in an otherwise confusing and fragmented area. This is important, because unless we can agree on the basic subject matter of justice we will never be able to ask, let alone answer, the most fundamental psychological question of all; why do humans want justice in the first place?

---

[1] The data were collected from 55 undergraduate students assigned to three conditions, one in which the character of the lottery winner was not described (n= 18); one in which he was described as of bad character (n= 18), and one of good character (n= 19). Subjects were asked to judge the fairness of the lottery win on a five point scale from 1 (very unfair), through 3 (Neutral) to 5 (very fair). The mean fairness ratings were 4.06 (SD= 0.80), 2.83 (SD= 1.42), and 4.26 (SD= 0.87), for the three conditions, respectively. The second condition (bad character) was rated as significantly less fair than the other two which did not differ significantly from each other (Mann-Whitney U-tests, $p < 0.05$).

CHAPTER 23

THE EVOLUTIONARY ORIGINS OF JUSTICE

If EAD, more than any other principle, resembles what most people intuitively feel is the basis of 'justice', it seems pertinent to ask why do humans attempt to operate this principle?

According to Barry, the assumption underlying many approaches to justice, both ancient and modern, is that 'Justice .... underwrites mutually advantageous cooperative arrangements, whether they arise from explicit agreement or not. (And) .... just terms of cooperation are those that would have been agreed upon by people trying to do the best for themselves (1989, p. 367). In other words, in situations where interests may conflict, 'just' rules are the rules that people *ought to adopt* to maximize their own selfish interests. As I have mentioned on a number of occasions, the idea of self-interest has been used by psychologists to underpin psychological equity theory (Walster et al., 1973, 1978). Given the popularity of self-interest as the origin of justice, it seems a reasonable to examine it as a possible basis for the evolution of EAD. So, is EAD a behavioural rule that has been evolved in humans as a particularly adaptive or advantageous way of regulating their conduct in conditions in which conflict is likely to occur'?

To answer this question, we need to explore rather more systematically the terms of cooperation that ought to be adopted by people trying to do the best for themselves. Here laboratory studies by game-theorists may be able to provide us with some clues.

Tit for tat (TFT)

Situations in which cooperation can be mutually advantageous are referred to by game-theorists as 'non-zero sum situations'; because the sum of one person's loss and another's gains need not be zero. A typical example of this type of situation is the 'prisoner's dilemma' game; so called because it was first applied to a scenario in which two prisoners had to make decisions about whether to confess or deny committing a crime. In this game, players can choose to cooperate or go for their own maximum outcome at the other's expense; that is, 'defect'. However, the contingencies are arranged such that the best outcome for an individual player 'X' occurs if 'X' is entirely selfish, and goes for his or her own most favourable outcome, but the other player 'Y' does not act entirely selfishly ('Y' cooperates, but 'X' does not). The next best outcome for 'X' is if they both cooperate. After this, the next best outcome for 'X' is if they both decide not to cooperate (both defect). However, the worst outcome for 'X', is if he or she cooperates, but 'Y' does not.

In one famous study, Axelrod invited psychologists, economists and other game theorists to submit strategies for a computer tournament involving this kind of dilemma. The object was to amass as many points as possible. Of the 14 entries submitted, the most effective strategy in amassing points was one submitted by Anatol Rapoport, known as 'tit for tat' (TFT), or simple reciprocity. This is basically a strategy of 'do unto others as is done unto you'. So if your partner cooperated on the previous move, you cooperate on the next move, and if he or she defected, you defect too. In a second round of the tournament, candidates were again invited to submit strategies, but were told that TFT had won the first time. A further 64 entries were submitted; but even though the others new they were up against TFT, TFT won again (Axelrod, 1980 ab; 1984). Other research also supports the view that TFT works far better as a strategy for inducing mutual cooperation than one of being consistently cooperative or uncooperative, and works particularly well if you announce that this is what you are doing (Lindskold, Han and Betz, 1986; Linskold, Walters and Koutsourais, 1983; Sermat and Gregovich, 1966; Oskamp, 1971).

However, although TFT works better than consistent cooperation or pacifism (which gets exploited), or consistent non-cooperation (which is returned in kind), if both partners play strict TFT, the effects of defecting in response to 'accidental' defections rebound on each, resulting in further unnecessary defections that reduce cooperation and are detrimental to both parties. Further research indicates, therefore, that TFT is even more effective if one cooperates on the first move and is then somewhat forgiving; that is, one allows one's partner to make a few mistakes or have some 'accidents' (say 80% cooperation over the last series of trials) (Bendor, Kramer and Stout, 1991; Molander, 1985). In other words, a particularly effective strategy for maximizing one's individual outcomes in non-zero sum situations is one in which one rewards helpful cooperative behaviours, returns non-cooperation with non-cooperation, but allows for some 'accidents' with regard to the latter.

The outcome of this research seems to support the idea that if justice does indeed derive from 'mutually advantageous cooperative arrangements', then the conception of justice that *should* 'be agreed upon by people trying to do the best for themselves' is one in which favours are returned with favours, and non-cooperation is returned with non-cooperation, but with some generosity in allowing for 'accidents', especially accidental non-cooperation. In fact, as Sabini (1995) has noted, a person using a tit for tat strategy in a prisoner's dilemma situation is seen, not only as strong and intelligent, but *fair* (McClintock and Liebrand, 1988). Already, this strategy looks rather familiar does it not? There is clearly a basis here for arguing that the rudimentary elements of EAD, favours for favours, and disfavours for disfavours, with an allowance for 'accidents', are not only judged as 'fair' but they might actually be, in Barry's terms, 'those (rules) that would have been agreed upon by people trying to do the best for themselves'. The similarity is made all the more significant by the fact that, according to many researchers, work on games such as these may provide us with a valuable insight into the evolutionary origins of social behaviours (see, for example, Maynard-Smith, 1982; Wright, 1995).

Reciprocal altruism: Cheats, grudgers and suckers

The picture often painted of so-called 'Darwinian justice' is a sort of 'no holds barred' free for all, in which the strongest take everything. Modern evolutionary psychologists and biologists, however, see things rather differently. In fact, Darwin recognized that one of the greatest puzzles of evolution is why, in a world in which each member of a particular species should presumably be attempting to maximize its own survival, some individuals appear to display 'altruism', and put others before themselves. According to Hamilton (1964), this happens because natural selection works at the level of the genes not the whole organizm. It is gene survival, or 'inclusive fitness', that really counts. Hence, people will tend to take considerable risks helping others to insure that those who share their genes survive; and the closer the relative, the more risks they will be prepared to take. But how can we account for the fact that people often help those who are not genetically related to them? Trivers (1971) has argued that there may be occasions when it is useful to help unrelated others, if it can be assumed that this will increase the probability of them helping you should the need arise in future. This strategy has been termed *reciprocal altruism*.

However, for reciprocal altruism to work, it is important that the costs and benefits are *proportional*; so, for example, it is not in your interests to take great risks to save another person's life, when all the other person is likely to return is a very small favour. Big favours demand relatively big favours in return. A major problem, therefore, for those engaging in reciprocal altruism, is *cheating*. If all members of a species possess an altruistic gene, and no one cheats, there is no problem. However, suppose some members of a species possess a genetic mutation that causes them not to return favours in proportion to those received, or, indeed, at all; whose genes would survive? According to Dawkins (1976), this situation represents a clash between *'cheats'*, who attempt to gain whilst incurring fewer or no costs to themselves, or attempt to gain at the expense of others, and *'suckers'*, who indiscriminately incur costs to benefit others, regardless of the benefits received in return. Computer simulations indicate that if cheats are pitted against suckers, then 'cheats prosper' and the 'suckers' are driven to extinction. To be a sucker amongst suckers works fine; but to be a sucker amongst cheats is not ultimately an evolutionary stable strategy (ESS).

But enter a third strategist, the *grudger*. Grudgers help those who have previously helped them; but they refuse to help cheats. In fact, they bear a grudge and play 'tit for tat', helping those who help them, but refusing to cooperate with those who defect. According to the simulations reported by Dawkins, initially grudgers do not do well as a small minority against cheats and suckers, because the suckers tend to sustain the cheats. In the short term, therefore, 'grudging' may not always look like the most adaptive strategy. Ultimately, however, over time, as the cheats gradually eliminate the suckers, the grudgers increase, until 'grudging' dominates as the most evolutionary stable strategy.

Negative reciprocity

But what should be the exact strategy of the grudger? Recent modelling studies suggest that a simple tit for tat strategy of 'cooperate with cooperators and do not cooperate with defectors', only works effectively with very small numbers of individuals. As group size evolves, however, the strategy of simply withholding cooperation from non-cooperators is less effective than a strategy of deliberate retaliation in some form. Boyd and Richerson (1991) term this reaction *retribution*. Indeed, according to Boyd and Richerson's analysis, in larger groups, more cooperation is produced when not only are non-cooperators punished, but those who fail to punish non-cooperation are punished! In other words, when cheats abound, suckers can be a liability for grudgers, so it makes sense to attempt to modify their behaviour. (One can note here, for example, that in

English law it is a criminal offence to harbour a criminal, even if one does not stand to benefit in any material way by doing so.)

Clutton-Brock and Parker (1995) have also argued that, although much consideration has been given to the concept of reciprocal altruism, or 'positive reciprocity', little attention has been given to 'negative reciprocity' or the punishment of those whose actions damage others. On the basis of both mathematical models and research on animals and humans, Clutton-Brock and Parker conclude that 'negative reciprocity' may serve a number of adaptive functions; these that include not only the maintenance of dominance relationships, but also the provision of a method for persuading reluctant individuals to cooperate and discouraging 'thieves, cheats, parasites, and even predators' (p. 215). In larger groups then, one might expect a joint strategy that combines both positive and negative reciprocity to be the most effective approach for the grudger. The grudger thus returns favours with favours, and returns non-cooperation and cheating with penalties.

Equity, cooperation and cheat detection

It is notable, however, that in human groups the reciprocity tends to go beyond simple 'direct' reciprocity, whereby returns are expected directly from the recipients of one's services or disservices; instead, what Alexander (1987) calls 'indirect reciprocity', or what Trivers (1971) refers to as 'generalized reciprocity', operates, whereby the return may come from any individual or collection of individuals in the group. As a result, says Alexander, 'everyone in a social group (is) continually being assessed and reassessed by interactants, past and potential, on the basis of their interactions with others' (p. 85).

The advantages of generalized reciprocity are fairly obvious. In the distribution of positive outcomes they allow for the division of labour, and stability of returns in an uncertain environment. It is also notable that, in larger groups, punishment tends to be institutionalized, such that serious offences are considered offences against the whole group and are carried out by community action, or delegates of the community (Clutton-Brock and Parker, 1995). Such institutions make it more costly for the offender to retaliate, spread the costs of punishment, and deter harmful acts against those other than the original victim.

However, in the light of these more complex social arrangements, humans would presumably also have found it necessary to evolve a number of characteristics, including mathematical abilities, to detect and avoid cheating. The idea that people have developed cognitive structures to guide social exchange and detect cheating has been developed by Cosmides and Tooby (1992), who argue that humans have developed a number of mathematical rules or algorithms for these purposes. These include algorithms for estimating costs and benefits of various actions and entities, estimating the probabilities of various actions and outcomes occurring, comparisons of these estimates, and detecting and punishing cheating.

EAD as a biological stratagem

The correspondence between all of this and EAD is very obvious. Positive and negative reciprocity are the hall marks of proportional desert; desert requires the return of favours in proportion to favours, and penalties in proportion to harms done. Seen from an evolutionary perspective, therefore, a system of proportional desert could be construed as a sophisticated group version of tit for tat; a set of biological algorithms designed to facilitate social exchange for the benefit of all, by encouraging cooperation, discouraging non-cooperation, and punishing cheating. Indeed, discussing positive and negative reciprocity, Wright (1995) says, 'The intuitively obvious idea of just deserts, the very core of the human sense of justice, is, in this view, a by-product of evolution, a simple genetic stratagem' (p. 205). Frans de Waal (1989) comes to a similar conclusion about the core nature of justice. Having closely observed some of our closest relatives in the animal kingdom, chimpanzees; he says, 'chimpanzee group life is like a market in power, sex, affection, support, intolerance and hostility. The two basic rules are, "one good turn deserves another" and "an eye for an eye, a tooth for a tooth" '. And de Waal adds that, 'reciprocity among chimpanzees is governed by the same sense of moral rightness and justice as it is amongst humans' (p. 207).

One of the most interesting implications of this research is that it may not be adaptive in an evolutionary sense for individuals to 'go it alone'; indeed, according to Boyd and Richerson (1991), it may actually adaptive to punish people who refuse to enter into cooperative arrangements. One is reminded here that, within the theory of desert I have outlined in this book, a man who works solely himself with no intention of benefitting others does not strictly 'deserve' the so-called 'fruits of his labour'. It is also worth remembering that the students studied by Messick et al. (1985) thought that it was unfair for a person to 'depend on no one'. If we accept the Boyd and Richerson's analysis, we can now see a good reason why people should feel this way. The man who 'goes it alone', 'feathers his own nest', and 'depends on no one' may, in evolutionary terms, be a social liability.

Responsibility and a cost/benefit calculus for equity

However, apart from the evidence that it may be useful to err on the side of leniency when trading favours and harms, we have yet to consider the evolutionary basis of the responsibility component of EAD. According to Huxley (1911), human society has evolved from one in which justice was first considered solely in terms of rewards and punishment for acts, to one of punishment according to 'desert' or 'motive'. From an evolutionary perspective then, we might hypothesize that a sense of 'moral responsibility', might have evolved in humans as a method of 'fine tuning' the TFT strategy. (Though Byrne, 1995 suggests that chimpanzees may also possess a capacity to distinguish accidental from non-accidental behaviours.)

To understand how responsibility might operate from an evolutionary perspective, it is useful to consider EAD within a cost/benefit framework. It will be remembered that the simple conceptualisation of equity as a model in which costs and benefits more or less cancel themselves out, seems unworkable. Apart from anything else, if we call the positive outcomes 'benefits', and positive inputs 'costs', and assume that outcomes must in some sense be equal to inputs, then it is difficult to see what possible motive an organizm could have for performing any inputs. It is an assumption of evolutionary psychology, as well as the concept of 'rational economic man', that for organizms to engage in any sort of motivated action in an adaptive manner, they must assume that their gains will outweigh their costs. There are, however, other ways we can interpret the cost-benefit calculations involved in equity.

According to some evolutionary psychologists, there is much more to reproductive fitness than keeping productive organizms alive. As Alexander says, 'control of resources is the most appropriate route to reproductive success' (1987, p. 26). Power, status, reputation and wealth enable their possessors to outcompete others in sexual and parental matters, thus producing more offspring who will survive and prosper (see also, Betzig, 1986). Any favour or service that we do for others, whether it be to enhance their health, wealth or status, could be construed as offering them a reproductive gain relative to us, at the cost of reproductive resources that we could have used for our own benefit. In contrast, anything we do that might adversely affect the health, wealth or status of others could be construed as enhancing our own reproductive gain relative to them. Given that most positive and negative outcomes could be classed one way or another as factors affecting 'health, wealth and status', then at a basic biological level, all positive inputs could be considered 'costs' to the extent that they serve to decrease the reproductive fitness of the donor relative to others. Similarly all negative inputs could be construed as 'gains', in the sense that they serve to increase the reproductive fitness of the harmdoer.

If we adopt this idea with respect to the allocation of rewards or positive outcomes, then 'positive inputs' in the EAD model can indeed, as Sadurski (1985) suggests, be seen as costs incurred as a direct result of contributing to the good of others. However, because all positive inputs may involve 'costs', it does not follow that 'unit cost' is best way to measure them.

Consider an example. Suppose that one of our hominid ancestors, known to her friends as 'Mog', regularly spends 30 minutes grooming another member of her species 'Og'; each time removing 'X' number of dangerous parasites from Og's body. Og cannot do this by herself, and requires mog's cooperation or she will become seriously ill. On the basis of previous experience, both Mog and Og estimate that 30 minutes of this sort of grooming activity tends to result in the removal of 'X' number of parasites. Translated into equity, Mog has therefore contributed 30 minutes of grooming, and Og has received outcomes consisting of the benefits that accrue from the removal of 'X' dangerous parasites. For equity to be fully restored, Og must now also input 30 minutes of grooming, and remove 'X' parasites from Mog. When this is accomplished, both will have received outcomes commensurate with their inputs. Moreover, if both have behaved adaptively, in terms of their *actual* cost-benefit ratios, both should have gained.

As just noted, it is an assumption of the concept of reciprocal altruism (as well as the concept of 'rational economic man'), that no organizm would adaptively engage in any helping activity (at least towards unrelated others) unless the costs associated with providing the service are more than compensated for by the benefits received. So, if we assume that individuals will only help others when their expected returns will outweigh their costs in providing the help, then it follows that Mog should only groom Og if it can be assumed that the costs to Mog of providing this contribution are less than the outcome benefits to Og. The logic being that, if Og is similarly motivated to return an equivalent favour to Mog, then both should end up with a net gain (for both, 30 minutes grooming effort is more than compensated for by the benefits of having the parasites removed).

Suppose, however, that Mog has spent 30 minutes grooming Og, and has removed 'X' parasites; but when it comes to Og's turn, Og has used her ingenuity, and has invented a grooming device, a comb (it took her 5 minutes to invent). As a result, Og can regularly remove 'X' parasites from Mog in 5 minutes. It will be noted that, according to the above logic, both will still gain from this arrangement; they both end up clear of dangerous parasites, an outcome that more than outweighs the grooming costs involved. And for a very primitive organizm this situation may be acceptable; but if Mog is intelligent and shrewd enough, she will realize that, over time, Og will gain a relative advantage; their cost/benefit ratios will be very unequal. Every time they groom each other, Mog will incur the extra costs associated with the extra 25 minutes it takes her to groom Og. Nevertheless, if Mog is operating an EAD 'equal opportunity' algorithm, the situation should not be necessarily construed as unfair to her as long as she is aware that she could have acquired, and still can acquire a comb as easily as Og, and thus increase her efficiency. Indeed, if this is the case, and Mog is behaving adaptively, she should learn from the experience, thank Og for inventing the comb, and use a comb in future. Consequently, both Mog and Og should to 'write-off' any cost-benefit ratio difference, and simply measure their contributions in terms of the fact that each has removed 'X' number of parasites from the other.

A problem might occur, however, if it is clear to Mog that she has been denied the opportunity to invent and use a comb. She will then feel she has lost out; she has used up far more reproductive effort helping Og, than Og has used up helping her. Feeling resentful, she can do a number of things suggested by the equity theorists; she can work less hard at grooming Og next time, leaving Og with some dangerous parasites on her body; she can withdraw her cooperation altogether, or even retaliate against Og who has gained a reproductive advantage over her. So if Og still wants Mog's cooperation, she will have to appease her by giving her some extra grooming, or another favour, by way of compensation, such as teaching her how to acquire and use a comb.

Now consider a third scenario; Og has spent 30 minutes grooming Mog, thus removing 'X' parasites from Mog. A week later, Og now requires the favour to be returned. Mog is temporarily not around; she has gone hunting (as they all have to do to survive). In the meantime, 'Grog' has arrived for a very rare visit. Og asks Grog to groom her; which she duly does. However, the day after, Mog then returns expecting to groom Og, only to find she's been beaten to it. This upsets Mog, because she has now acquired more parasites, needs Og's help again, yet is already in debt because of the chance arrival of Grog. Og, however, cannot rely on Grog to groom her, and will need Mog's help in the future. So, Og decides to take a chance. She will 'write-off' Mog's debt, ignore the fact that Mog has done nothing, accept that Mog's lack of input was 'accidental', and act as though Mog had actually groomed her.

These scenarios would, of course, parallel those I identified in Chapter 15 regarding the input measures used in the EAD model. Thus *output or productivity* (here the number of parasites removed) should be the appropriate measure of contribution when there is equal opportunity to choose between different types of input activity; *effort* (here the grooming time) should be the appropriate contribution when there are unequal opportunities to choose between different kinds of input activity, and *equal sharing of outcomes, or shares based on hypothetical inputs*, will dominate when there is no or minimal choice to perform the inputs. Significantly, from the viewpoint of maximizing reproductive fitness, this scheme, which combines simple reciprocity with considerations of causal responsibility, would obviously have considerable advantages in efficiency over one that simply bases the value of the inputs on actual costs. Contributors using this scheme will be encouraged to select those inputs that are efficient in providing mutual benefits. Whereas if inputs were always valued on the basis of actual costs, then individuals would have to invest huge resources attempting to compensate, and even emulate, incredibly inefficient members of the community who have chosen to spend hours of effort in wasteful, minimally effective activity; indeed, indiscriminate compensation for actual costs would operate to encourage such inefficient activity by clearly rewarding it. At the same time, however, a controlled 'equal opportunities' policy would tend to reduce conflicts between individuals arising from large disparities in their actual cost-benefit ratios, and through teaching and aid, increase the efficiency of the whole group.

Also, from an evolutionary perspective, the distribution of resources to individuals who have been denied an opportunity to provide inputs may be a risk worth taking to ensure future cooperation (and even survival); indeed, provision for those who accidentally, and contrary to equity, find themselves in need could also be construed as an insurance policy for all.

However, any scheme that makes allowances for 'accidents' must be sensitive to cheating; people who deliberately place themselves in need, or claim falsely they have been denied the opportunity to contribute, will be continually building up a reproductive advantage at minimum cost, continually consuming resources, and then having them replaced at no cost. An allocation scheme that also recognizes differences in the locus of causal responsibility for need might therefore also be adaptive in an evolutionary sense.

There is a remarkable overlap between these ideas and some observations made by Cosmides and Tooby (1992). As Cosmides and Tooby point out, the common characterization of primitive peoples leading a hunter-gatherer life is 'an orgy of indiscriminate, egalitarian cooperation and sharing' (p. 216). Archaeological and ethnographic records show, however, that hunter gathers have engaged in a number of different forms of social exchange (see, Cashdan, 1989; Roberts, 1979). Particularly interesting are decision rules that govern reciprocity on food sharing. For instance, amongst the Ache tribe of Paraguay, meat is a very 'high-variance' food item. Its availability varies from day to day, and whether a hunter finds any is very much a matter of luck. In contrast, collected plant foods are a very 'low-variance' item. Their availability depends primarily on the effort that is put in to collect them. It is notable, therefore that meat tends to be distributed equally throughout the band, whereas, plant foods are only shared within the nuclear family.

According to Cosmides and Tooby (1992), this makes good economic sense. If success in finding food is highly variable and based on luck, everyone might come across occasions in which he or she would starve. By pooling the risk, however, the variance decreases, and the food supply becomes more stable.

Moreover, to punish someone in such a situation for a failure to contribute is a high risk business. As Cosmides and Tooby state, 'If the charge is false, then not only will the ostracized person's survival be jeopardized, but each member of the band will have lost a valuable reciprocation partner' (p. 214). Amongst the Ache, therefore, it is significant that little consideration is given to the idea of punishing those who fail to 'pull their weight' when hunting for meat. In contrast, acrimonious arguments erupt over whether various individuals are doing their fair share of work in the garden. However, gardening provides a low-variance food source; an equal distribution would simply act to redistribute food from those who put in most work to those who do nothing. Moreover, punishment is less risky in terms of adverse effects on food supply. Cosmides and Tooby (1992) point to a number of other examples from Africa, such as the Kalahari San bands and the !Kung, that illustrate this same relationship between the variability of the food supply and the way it is distributed.

Not surprisingly, Cosmides and Tooby (1992) comment on the obvious correspondence between these observations and political debates over issues such as the homeless. Thus, those opposing help and sharing will stress the chosen or self-caused dimensions of the situation. The homeless are lazy and have 'brought it on themselves'. In contrast, those wishing to motivate sharing will, they say, 'emphasize the random, variance-driven dimensions of the situation. The potential recipient of aid is viewed as worthy because he or she is the unlucky victim of circumstances, such as unemployment, discrimination, or mental illness' (p. 219). It also follows that the former may be more reticent about punishing than the latter. Cosmides and Tooby conclude that these responses reflect the operation of adaptive psychological mechanisms that evolved originally as ways of dealing with variance in the availability of resources, and our capacities to obtain them.

If we accept this account, then the implications for our understanding of the origins of EAD may be considerable. EAD could be construed as a basic psychological model, or set of algorithms, common to all humanity, that has evolved to help us adapt to changing local conditions. Thus, by using the *same* model, with the same set of rationalizing principles, we can switch from allocations based on proportionality - culpability to others based on equality - nonculpability, depending on local circumstances, in a coherent and adaptive way.

Negative inputs as 'gains'

A meaningful cost/benefit analysis can also be applied to negative inputs and outcomes within the EAD model. Thus, in accordance with the intuitions of both Aristotle and Sadurski, negative inputs could indeed be construed as 'gains', or at least, 'attempts to gain'. However, they are not the abstract gains that accompany a loss of self-restraint, rather they are the actual gains received (or that one might be expected to receive) whilst, or as a direct result of, engaging in activity directed towards procuring social harms or costs'. However, for a cost/benefit calculus to work, we would need first to *disregard any costs that the offender has incurred as a direct result of his or her actions*. It would obviously be maladaptive to compensate harmdoers for the costs incurred whilst planning and committing their offences. If we ignore these latter costs, then in terms of a cost/benefit calculus, the proportional negative reciprocity principle should normally be adaptive. For example, if I gain a reproductive advantage by hitting you in your eye and blinding you, and you suffer an equivalent loss of reproductive fitness through my actions; then, equity will be restored if you are compensated and, in the process, I receive back the equivalent of the costs I imposed on you, plus any extra costs you incurred by having to punish me. In the event, I will have lost out in the cost/benefit stakes, because I end up in a situation in the which I not only receive back the costs I imposed on you, cancelling or more than cancelling out my relative gains in terms of reproductive advantage, but now to these I have to add the extra costs that I incurred whilst carrying out my actions. So, after paying my debts, I end up in debt; and presumably, if I have any sense, deterred. In fact, the greater the cost I am prepared to incur to harm you, the more I will lose out, and, if I have any sense, the more I should be deterred.

There are obvious advantages to adopting such a system of proportional negative reciprocity. Severe punishment not only can incite the recipient, and those related to or friendly with the recipient to retaliate in kind, but we run the risk of disabling or putting out of action a potentially useful member of society. It therefore makes sense to be cautious and match our punishments to the harms rendered; such that the more serious the harm, the greater the punishment. With minor offences, we can afford to take a few risks and punish lightly; with more serious crimes, however, the costs and risks attached to severe punishment may be worth incurring to prevent greater costs to those participating in a cooperative endeavour. In other words, the idea of a harm returned in exact proportion for a harm rendered, serves to provide a measured degree of deterrence at minimum cost. Such an analysis might also help to explain the empirical finding that, in cases of serious crime, 'overpunishment', that is, punishment greater than that prescribed by equity, is preferred to 'underpunishment', that is punishment less than that prescribed by equity (Wagstaff and Preece, 1997). If the whole point of punishment is to deter at minimum risk or cost, there is little point 'underpunishing' people for serious crimes, as this is unlikely to deter them.

This kind of analysis might also help to explain why, when more than one person conspires to commit a crime, the courts tend to treat each person as if he or she had committed the crime separately, rather than simply distributing the total harm rendered amongst the conspirators. Consider, for example, a murder of one individual by three others. According to evolutionary psychology, the reproductive gains that individuals receive from murdering someone might go far beyond the reproductive advantage of simply taking the victim out of the gene pool. They also involve gains in dominance and power over others. But there is no reason why these individual 'gains' should necessarily be diluted because a murder has been carried out by three people. Moreover, the costs of performing the murder will presumably have been shared amongst the three murderers.

Consequently, apart from the practical difficulties involved, if we distribute the costs suffered by the victim between the three murderers, any deterrence value will be drastically reduced, and may even disappear. It makes more sense, therefore, to simply treat each of the conspirators as though he or she had individually committed the crime.

In practice the obvious role that deterrence plays in sentencing policy is also evident in the way information on the past behaviour of defendants (their 'characteristic' ways of behaving) has fundamental influence on sentencing decisions. A 'hardened criminal' is considered worthy of more punishment than a first time offender (see, for example, Cohen, Fishman and Soroka, 1985; Konecni and Ebbeson, 1982; Stafford and Hill, 1987; von Hirsch and Jareborg, 1989).

But how does the concept of 'moral responsibility' map onto a cost/benefit analysis of negative reciprocity?

Punishment and responsibility

From an evolutionary perspective, it could also be argued that the introduction of the notion of 'moral responsibility' into the algorithms for negative reciprocity might have evolved as a method of fine tuning what would otherwise be a fairly primitive and inefficient instrument for discouraging cheating.

As the work on TFT suggests, punishing those who harm us by 'accident' can be costly, unnecessary, and have repercussions that prevent future cooperation. In all likelihood, the offender would not have offended again, and it may also cause resentment from others who may fear that 'they will be next', thus increasing acts of non-cooperation and preventative retaliation. On the other hand, punishing those who deliberately choose to offend may serve to discourage both them and others from repeating the same behaviour. At the same time, those so discouraged, or not inclined to offend, will know that 'they will not be next' on some arbitrary basis, and will have no inclination to withdraw their cooperation, and/or to retaliate on a preventative basis. By the same token, punishing 'negligence' according to the costs actually inflicted in a single case, when the outcomes were not actually intended, could be deemed an unnecessary punishment risk. If we punish instead in accordance with a more diluted estimate based on the expected costs to others of generally engaging in such activity, then when the costs imposed as a punishment are added to the costs to the offender of performing the activity, the offender should still 'lose out', but in a measured way.

According to Posner (1981), however, the extent to which responsibility is taken into account in a particular society may depend very much on costs involved in gathering the necessary information. Thus, whilst recognizing that it may be inefficient to punish those whose conduct is accidental or unavoidable, Posner also points out that in some societies it may not actually be possible or cost-effective to gather the necessary information, in which case 'strict liability' will tend to dominate (the degree of choice will be ignored entirely). In other words, strict liability could be considered the 'least inequitable solution' when gathering the necessary information for a fuller operation of EAD is not possible or cost-effective. Posner also suggests that in what he calls 'primitive societies', there may even be an economic basis to the idea of 'collective responsibility' in the assignment of punishment. Hence, in societies in which there is no public investigatory machinery, the threat of 'collective responsibility' will increase the probability that the kinsmen of an offender will 'turn him in'; by doing so they will remove the threat to themselves. Collective responsibility also enables society to set an adequate level of compensatory payment that might be impossible if it were left simply to offending individual. This gives the kinsmen of the victim an incentive other than costly revenge for seeking to punish the offender. From this perspective, concepts such as 'natural punishment', 'divine punishment' and 'pollution' may also serve to deter antisocial (uncooperative) activities, at minimum cost, by frightening people into thinking that, in accordance with desert, their evil deeds will automatically be punished, if not in this life, then in the next, or through harm to their descendants.

A cost/benefit analysis might lie behind the way those who are mentally ill are treated. On the one hand, the public will need potentially costly protection from a dangerous person, insane or not. However, the punishment of a man whose reason is defective is unlikely to deter him, so to punish such a person as a deterrent might be considered a potentially dangerous waste of time and effort. This might account for the fact that although, in practice, there is actually little distinction in the way the law treats 'sane' and 'insane' offenders (Norrie, 1993; Wright, 1994), we still consider it more appropriate to simply detain or rehabilitate mentally ill offenders, than 'punish' them.

In sum, from an evolutionary perspective, there may be obvious advantages to allowing for 'accidents', sometimes in a fairly sophisticated way, before dispensing punishment. However, the degree of sophistication, and the extent to which responsibility is individualised, may vary according to local conditions.

The problem of inherited wealth
So far then, EAD could be construed as a set of biologically based algorithms that have evolved to encourage cooperation, and deter non-cooperation and cheating, in an efficient way. Indeed, if a community operates an EAD rule it should positively encourage people to do favours for each other, and deter harms. But if this is the case, why do so many people, including writers on justice, cling so tenaciously to the institution of inherited wealth? Inherited wealth is clearly at variance with any conception of reciprocity, particularly a conception that assumes that one's outcomes should be related in a meaningful way to one's choices, and not based on 'dumb luck' or 'accidents of birth'. Again evolutionary psychology may be able to help us.

As we have seen, the justifications for inherited wealth have ranged from the ingenious to the laughable. At a biological level, however, the conflict seems inevitable. If positive and negative reciprocity constitute an adaptive strategy for the survival of one's genes, then so also does doing everything one possibly can for one's offspring; including passing on to them the benefits of one's endeavours. Indeed, recent surveys of population samples from Europe and the United States indicate that agreement with the idea that people should be entitled to pass their wealth onto their children is consistently associated with endorsement of the views that people who work hard, and take on responsibility, deserve to earn more than those who do not (Swift, Marshall, Burgoyne and Routh, 1995). For those who possess it, the passing on of wealth to one's offspring may therefore be considered 'parental investment' in future generations; though, not surprisingly, the attitudes towards the redistribution of wealth of those who possess little, are consistently more egalitarian (see, for example, Himmelweit, Humphreys, Jaeger and Katz, 1981; Robinson and Bell, 1978; Swift et al., 1995).

Inherited wealth as a parental investment would have been particularly important for our distant ancestors. As Mace (1996) comments, 'In agricultural and pastoralist societies heritable wealth is an important part of parental investment in children. In many cases, those heritable resources provide the seeds, or even the major part, of each child's future opportunities to generate income' (p. 264). This is significant, argues Mace, because research into pastoralist societies shows that fertility increases with household wealth. However, the possession of an 'unearned' surplus is also an inviting target to other members of society, anxious to detect cheats. Those who inherit great wealth, have an obvious head start in perpetuating their genes; relative to others they have received outcomes without actually contributing to the good of others; they can then do more favours for others, and thus receive more in return. Indeed, they look suspiciously like 'cheats'.

As a result, one might expect to see the emergence of various of strategies for dealing with the problem of inherired wealth; and, indeed, a number of strategies seem to have evolved in this respect. For instance, in some societies the possessions of the dead have been buried with them or destroyed (Posner, 1981). However, in most societies, two major strategies seem to have been favoured.

The first is to devise elaborate mythologies and intellectual abstractions to promulgate the views that inherited wealth and/or privilege are, more often than not, 'earned' or result from some sort of fundamental property right that supposedly applies 'equally' to all. The Platonic concept of reincarnation and the libertarian idea of the 'equal right to private property' typify this approach.

The second, perhaps now more popular view, is to adopt practical compromise measures such as, the reduction or elimination of hereditary privilege so that wealth can be passed down but not position or status (such as the elimination of hereditary peers in the British Parliament), the introduction of taxes such as 'death duties', and making education and health care, at some level, available for all.

From an evolutionary perspective, however, the aims of these strategies are the same; they are attempts to make the concept of inherited wealth compatible with the core algorithms of 'desert'.

Conclusion

And so we seem to have come full circle. If what the evolutionary psychologists and biologists have to tell us is valid, and we link their ideas to justice in the form of EAD, then most of the philosophical speculation about the origins of justice throughout the ages actually rings true. Justice, in the form of EAD, is indeed part of 'natural law' (and in accordance with the law of God, if one wishes to adopt a religious perspective); it really does derive from an instinct for 'self-preservation'; it really does create the circumstances for the common interest and self-interest to coincide, and it really is a sort of implicit contract between people designed for their mutual benefit.

Moreover, at the fundamental biological level, there really is no necessary conflict between justice and utility, for justice is nothing more than a supreme example of *rule utilitarianism*, with long-term (indeed, very long-term) benefits, though with a rather different *telos*, to the more familiar classical forms; that of maximal 'gene survival'. And, as such, the preference that people tend to exhibit for their 'moral intuitions' about desert over other utilitarian criteria, may actually be less arbitrary than many have assumed. From the viewpoint of evolutionary psychology, it is understandable that people attempt to follow apparently 'intuitive' rules of desert, evolved to maximize the very survival of their own genes, rather than rules designed to maximize the 'happiness' or 'pleasure', of society as a whole.

Of course, the idea that biological evolution may underlie our most basic core conception of justice is controversial, and, in any case, as many have argued, even if we are influenced by such biological predispositions, we do not necessarily have to act on them. Indeed, it may not be in our interests to do so; the algorithms that may have evolved as an evolutionary stable strategy for our hunter-gatherer ancestors, might be entirely inappropriate in modern technologically developed societies. However, if algorithms for desert do exist, and continue to have a profound influence on our behaviour, this may account for why many academics, lawyers and politicians so often find themselves out of step with public opinion. If, fundamentally, people want what they deserve, it is little wonder that the public tends to be suspicious of intellectual abstractions such as the 'natural right' to gain vast amounts of wealth with minimal effort, and to share it with no one; or the 'equal right' to an equal share of just about everything regardless of anything anyone does. Neither should we be shocked that people continue to want what they have always wanted, and what politicians always offer them at election time; opportunities to work; their efforts and skills rewarded when they do; the sick and needy provided for; those who live parasitically off them discouraged; those who deliberately seek to harm them, punished in strict proportion to the severity of their offences.

But even if we were to reject all of the assumptions of evolutionary psychology, I still think that my main conclusion would be valid. If we want to go beyond the rather vacuous idea that justice is 'anything to do with social rules', it makes a most sense to identify the term 'justice' primarily with a combination of the philosophical concept of desert, and the psychological concept of equity, such that *perfect justice exists when all receive exactly what they deserve.* And, if in making this statement I am doing no more than restating what philosophers and theologians have been telling us for thousands of years, then perhaps there is something in the idea!

BIBLIOGRAPHY

Ackerman, B.A. (1980). *Social justice in the liberal state.* New Haven: Yale University Press.
Acton, H.B. (1970). *Kant's moral philosophy.* London: Macmillan.
Adams, J.S. (1963). Toward an understanding of inequity. *Journal of Abnormal and Social Psychology,* 67, 422-436.
Adams, J.S. (1965). Inequity and social exchange. In L.Berkowitz (ed.), *Advances in experimental social psychology, Vol. 2.* New York: Academic Press.
Adams, J.S. and Freedman, S. (1976). Equity theory revisited: Comments and annotated bibliography. In L. Berkowitz and E. Walster (eds.), *Advances in experimental social Psychology, Vol. 9.* New York: Academic Press. 43-90.
Adams, J.S. and Jacobsen, P.R. (1964). Effects of wage inequities on work quality. *Journal of Abnormal and Social Psychology,* 69, 19-25.
Alexander, R.D. (1987). *The biology of moral systems.* New York: Aldine de Gruyter.
Alves, W. and Rossi, P. (1978). Who should get what? Fairness judgments in the distribution of earnings. *American Journal of Sociology,* 84, 3, 541-564.
Anderson, N.H. (1976). Equity judgments as information integration. *Journal of Personality and Social Psychology,* 33, 291-299.
Anderson, N.H. and Butzin, C.A. (1978). Integration theory applied to children's judgments of equity. *Developmental Psychology,* 14, 593-606.
Andrews, I.R. (1967). Wage inequity and job performance: An experimental study. *Journal of Applied Psychology,* 51, 39-45.
Aquinas, St. Thomas (1925). *Summa Theologica.* Trans. Fathers of the English Dominican Province. London: Burns, Oates and Washbourne.
Aquinas, St. Thomas (1988). *The philosophy of Thomas Aquinas: Introductory readings.* C. Martin (ed.). London: Routledge.
Aquinas, St. Thomas (1951). *Philosophical texts.* London: OUP.
Aristotle (1984). In B. J. Barnes (ed.), *The complete works of Aristotle.* Guilford: Princeton University. Press.
Arrow, K.J. (1973). Some ordinalist-utilitarian notes on Rawls' theory of justice. *Journal of Philosophy,* 70, 245-263.
Asdigan, N.L., Cohn, E.S., and Blum, M.H. (1994). Gender differences in distributive justice: The role of self-presentation revisited. *Sex-Roles,* 30, 303-318.

Assmar, E.M.L. and Rodriques, A. (1994). The value base of distributive justice: Testing Deutsch's hypotheses in a different culture. *Revista-Interamericana-Psicologia*, 28, 1-11.
Augustine, St. (1976). *The city of God*. Trans. H. Bettenson. Harmondsworth, Middx: Penguin.
Austin, W. (1980). Friendship and fairness: Effects of type of relationship and task performance on choice of distribution rules. *Personality and Social Psychology Bulletin*, 6, 402-407.
Austin, W. and Hatfield, E. (1980). Equity theory, power and social justice. In G. Mikula (ed.), *Justice and social interaction*. New York: Springer-Verlag. 25-61.
Austin, W. and Tobiasen, J.M. (1984). Legal justice and the psychology of conflict resolution. In R. Folger (ed.), *The sense of injustice: Social psychological perspectives*. New York: Plenum. 227-274.
Austin, W. and Walster, E. (1974). Reactions to confirmations and disconfirmations of expectancies of equity and inequity. *Journal of Personality and Social Psychology*, 30, 208-216.
Averill, J.R. (1994). Inner feelings, works of the flesh, the beast within, diseases of the mind, driving force, and putting on a show: Six metaphors of emotion and their theoretical extensions. In D.E. Leary (ed.), *Metaphors in the history of psychology*. Cambridge: Cambridge University Press. 104-132.
Ayensu, E.S. (ed.)(1980). *Jungles*. London: Book Club Associates.
Axelrod, R. (1980a). Effective choice in the prisoner's dilemma. *Journal of Conflict Resolution*, 24, 3-25.
Axelrod, R. (1980b) More effective choice in the prisoner's dilemma. *Journal of Conflict Resolution*, 24, 379-403.
Axelrod, R. (1984). *The evolution of cooperation*. New York: Basic Books.
Baier, K. (1958). *The moral point of view*. Ithaca: Cornell University Press.
Bar-Hillel, M. and Yaari, M. (1993). Judgments of distributive Justice. In B.A. Mellers, and J. Baron, J. (eds.) *Psychological perspectives on justice: Theory and applications*, Cambridge: Cambridge University Press. 55-84.
Baron, J. (1993). Heuristics and biases in equity judgments: A utilitarian approach. In Mellers, B.A. and J. Baron, (eds.) *Psychological perspectives on justice: Theory and applications*, Cambridge: Cambridge University Press. 109-137.
Barrett-Howard, E. and Tyler, T.R. (1986). Procedural justice as a criterion in allocation decisions. *Journal of Personality and Social Psychology*, 50, 296-304.
Barry, B. (1973). *The liberal theory of justice: A critical examination of the principal doctrines in 'A theory of justice' by John Rawls*. Oxford: Clarendon Press.
Barry, B. (1989). *Theories of justice*. Hemel Hempstead, Herts: Harvester-Wheatsheaf.
Bayley, J.E. (1981). Human nature and justice. In R.L. Braham (ed.), *Social Justice*. Boston: Martinus Nijhoff. 1-27.

Bell, J. (1992). Justice and the law. In K.R. Scherer (ed.), *Justice: Interdisciplinary perspectives*. Cambridge: Cambridge University Press. 114-142.
Bendor, J., Kramer, R.M. and Stout, S. (1991). When in doubt: Cooperation in a noisy prisoner's dilemma. *Journal of Conflict Resolution*, 35, 691-719.
Bentham, J. (1996). *An introduction to the principles of morals and legislation*. J. Henderson and H.L.A. Hart (eds.). Oxford: Clarendon Press. (First published 1789.)
Bentham, J. (1962). Introduction to the principles of morals and legislation. In M. Warnock)ed.), *Utilitarianism, On Liberty, Essay on Bentham*. Glasgow: Collins. (First published 1789.)
Bentham, J. (1972). Principles of legislation. In D.H. Munro (ed.). *A guide to the British moralists*. London: Collins, 204-209. (First published 1802.)
Benton, A. (1971). Productivity, distributive justice, and bargaining among children. *Journal of Personality and Social Psychology*, 18. 68-78.
Berg, N.E. and Mussen, P. (1975). The origins and development of concepts of justice. *Journal of Social Issues*, 31, 183-202.
Berger, F.R. (1984). *Happiness, justice and freedom: The moral and political philosophy of John Stuart Mill*. Berkeley: University of California Press.
Berger, J., Zelditch, M., Anderson, B. and Cohen, B.P. (1972). Structural aspects of distributive justice: a status value formulation. In J. Berger, M. Zelditch, and B. Anderson (eds.), *Sociological theories in progress, Vol. 2*. Boston: Houghton-Mifflin.
Berkowitz, L. (1969). Resistance to improper dependence relationships. Journal of Experimental Social Psychology, 5, 283-294.
Berkowitz, L., Fraser, C., Treasure, F.P, and Cochran, S. (1987). Pay, equity, job gratifications, and comparisons in pay satisfaction. *Journal of Applied Psychology*, 72, 544-551.
Berscheid, E. Boye, D. and Walster, E. (1968). Retaliation as a means of restoring equity. *Journal of Personality and Social Psychology*, 10, 370-376.
Berscheid, E. and Walster, E. (1978). *Interpersonal attraction (2nd ed.)*. Reading, MA: Addison-Wesley.
Blau, P. (1964). *Exchange and power in social life*. New York: Wiley.
Bodenheimer, E. (1962). *Jurisprudence: The philosophy and method of law*. Cambridge, Mass.: Harvard University Press.
Boyd, R. and Richerson, P.J. (1992). Punishment allows the evolution of cooperation (or anything else) in sizeable groups. *Ethology and Sociobiology*, 13, 171-195.
Brabant, J. and Lerner, M.J. (1975). 'A little time and effort'- Who deserves what from whom? *Personality and Social Psychology Bulletin*. 1, 177-181.
Bradley, F.H. (1927). *Ethical studies*. New York: Oxford University Press. (First published 1876.)
Brickman, P. (1975). Adaptation-level determinants of satisfaction with equal and unequal outcome distributions in skill and chance situations. *Journal of Personality and Social Psychology*, 32, 191-198.

Brickman, P., Folger, R., Goode, E. and Schul, Y. (1981). Microjustice and macrojustice. In M.J. Lerner and S.C. Lerner (ed.), *The justice motive in social behavior*. New York: Plenum. 173-202.
Brock, T.C. and Buss, A.H. (1962). Dissonance, aggression and evaluation of pain. *Journal of Abnormal and Social Psychology*, 65, 197-202.
Brock, T.C. and Buss, A.H. (1964). Effects of justification for aggression in communication with the victim on post -aggression dissonance. *Journal of Abnormal and Social Psychology*, 68, 403-412.
Buchanan, A. (1982). *Marx and justice: The radical critique of liberalism*. London: Methuen.
Buchanan, A. and Mathieu, D. (1986) Philosophy and justice. In R.L. Cohen (ed.), *Justice: Views from the social sciences*. New York: Plenum. 11-45.
Buchanan, J. (1986). *Liberty, market and state*. Brighton: Wheatsheaf.
Buss, A.H. (1983). Social rewards and personality. *Journal of Personality and Social Psychology*, 44, 553-563.
Buunk, B.P. and VanYperen, N.W. (1991). Referential comparisons, relational comparisons and exchange orientation: Their relation to marital satisfaction. *Personality and Social Psychology Bulletin*, 17, 710-718.
Camerer, C.F. and Loewenstein, G. (1993). Information, fairness, and efficiency in bargaining. In Mellers, B.A. and J. Baron, (eds.) *Psychological perspectives on justice: Theory and applications*. Cambridge: Cambridge University Press. 155-182.
Campbell, T. (1988). *Justice: Issues in political theory* . Basingstoke: Macmillan.
Carroll, J.S., Berkowitz, W.T., Lurigio, A.J. and Weaver, F.M. (1987). Sentencing goals, causal attributions, ideology and personality. *Journal of Personality and Social Psychology*, 52, 107-118.
Cashdan, E. (1989). Hunters and gatherers: Economic behavior in bands. In S. Plattner (ed.), *Economic anthropology*. Stanford: Stanford University Press.31-48.
Casson, L. (1969). *Ancient Egypt*. Amsterdam: Time-Life International.
Cate, R.M., Lloyd, S.A., Henton, J.M. and Larson, J. (1982). Fairness and reward level as predictors of relationship satisfaction. *Social Psychology Quarterly*, 45, 177-181.
Cicero, M.T. (1991). On Stoic good and evil. Trans. M.R. Wright. Warminster, Wilts.: Aris and Phillips.
Clark, M.S. (1984). Record keeping in two types of relationship. *Journal of Personality and Social Psychology*, 47, 549-557.
Clark, M.S. and Chrisman, K. (1994). Resource allocation in intimate relationships: Making sense of a confusing literature. In M.J. Lerner and G. Mikula (eds.), *Entitlement and the affectional bond: Justice in close relationships*. New York: Plenum Press. 43-63.
Clark, M.S. and Mills, J. (1979). Interpersonal attraction in exchange and communal relationships. *Journal of Personality and Social Psychology*, 37, 12-24.

Clark, M.S. and Mills, J. (1989). Keeping track of needs and inputs of friends and strangers. *Personality and Social Psychology Bulletin*, 15, 533-542.
Clarkson, U. (1989). Aggression as equity restoration. *Journal of Research in Personality*, 23, 398-409.
Clutton-Brock, T.H. and Parker, G.A. (1995). Punishment in animal societies. *Nature*, 373, 209-216.
Cohen, B-Z, Fishman, G. and Soroka, J. (1985). Judicial discretion and sentencing disparity in adult felony courts in Israel. *Journal of Criminal Justice*, 13, 99-115.
Cohen, R.L. (1974). Mastery and justice in laboratory dyads: A revision and extension of equity theory. *Journal of Personality and Social Psychology*, 29, 464-474.
Cohen, R.L. (1982). Perceiving justice: An attributional perspective. In J. Greenberg and R.L. Cohen (eds.), *Equity and justice in social behavior*. New York: Academic Press. 119-160.
Cohen, R.L. and Greenberg, J. (1982). The justice concept in social psychology. In J. Greenberg, and R.L. Cohen (eds.), *Equity and justice in social behavior*. New York: Academic Press. 1-41.
Colby, A. and Kohlberg, L. (1987). *The measurement of moral judgment - Volume 1 - Theoretical foundations and research validation*. London: Cambridge University Press.
Cooter, R. (1987). Justice at the confluence of law and economics. *Social Justice Research*, 1, 67-81.
Copp, D. (1991). Contractarianism and moral skepticism. In P. Vallentyne (ed.), *Contractarianism and rational choice: Essays on David Gauthier's morals by agreement*. New York: Cambridge University Press. 196-228.
Cosmides, L. and Tooby, J. (1992). Cognitive adaptations for social exchange. In J.H. Barlow, L. Cosmides and J. Tooby (eds.), *The adapted mind: Evolutionary psychology and the generation of culture*. New York: Oxford University Press. 163-228.
Coulton, G.C. (1993). *Chaucer and his England*. London: Bracken. (First published 1908.)
Craig, K.M., O'Neal, E.C., Taylor, S., Levi, S. and Yost, E.A. (1993). Equity and derogation of those against whom we have aggressed. *Aggressive Behavior*, 19, 355-360.
Cropanzano, R. and Folger, R. (1989). Referent cognitions and task decision autonomy: Beyond equity theory. *Journal of Applied Psychology*, 74, 293-299.
Cross, R., Jones, P.A. and Card, R. (1988). *Introduction to Criminal Law*. London: Butterworths.
Cullen, B. (1992). Philosophical theories of justice. In K.R. Scherer (ed.), *Justice: Interdisciplinary perspectives*. Cambridge: Cambridge University Press. 15-64.
Curzon, L.B. (1980). *Criminal Law*. Plymouth: Macdonald and Evans.

Curzon, L.B. (1989). *Dictionary of law (3rd ed.)*. London: Pitman.
Damon, W. (1977). *The social world of the child*. San Francisco: Jossey-Bass.
Damon, W. (1981). The development of justice and self-interest during childhood. In M.J. Lerner and S.C. Lerner (eds.), *The justice motive in social behavior*. New York: Plenum. 57-72.
Daniels, N. (1975). *Reading Rawls: Critical studies of A Theory of Justice*. New York: Basic Books.
Dawkins, R. (1976). *The selfish gene*. London: Oxford University Press.
de Waal, F. (1989). *Chimpanzee politics: Power and sex among apes*. Baltimore/London: John Hopkins Press.
Demore, S.W., Fisher, J.D. and Baron, R.M. (1988). The equity-control model as a predictor of vandalism among college students. *Journal of Applied Psychology*, 18, 80-91.
Desmarais, S. and Lerner, M.J. (1994). Entitlement in close relationships: A justice-motive analysis. In M.J. Lerner and G. Mikula (eds.) *Entitlement and the affectional bond: Justice in close relationships*. New York: Plenum Press. 43-63.
Deutsch, M. (1975). Equity, equality and need: What determines which value will be used as the basis of distributive justice? *Journal of Social Issues*, 31, 137-149.
Deutsch, M. (1983). Current social psychological perspectives on justice. *European Journal of Social Psychology*, 13, 305-319.
Deutsch, M. (1985). *Distributive justice: A social psychological perspective*. New Haven, CT: Yale University Press.
Donnerstein, E. and Hatfield, E. (1982). Aggression and inequity. In J. Greenberg, and R.L. Cohen, (eds.) *Equity and justice in social behavior*. New York: academic Press. 309-336.
Dunbar, R.I.M., Clark, A. and Hurst, N.L. (1995). Conflict and cooperation among the Vikings: Contingent behavioral decisions. *Ethology and Sociobiology*, 16, 233-246.
Dunn, J. (1968). Justice and Locke's political theory. *Political Studies*, 16, 68-87.
Dworkin, R. (1978a). *Taking rights seriously*. London: Gerald Duckworth.
Dworkin, R. (1978b). *Conversation with B. Magee in Men of Ideas*. London: BBC. 240-260.
Dworkin, R. (1981). What is equality? Part 1: Equality of welfare; Part 2 equality of resources. *Philosophy and Public Affairs*, 10, 185-246 and 283-345.
Dworkin, R. (1986). *Law's Empire*. London: Fontana.
Edgeworth, F.Y. (1973). The pure theory of progressive taxation. In S. Phelps (ed.), *Economic justice*. Harmondsworth, Middx: Penguin. 371-385.
Elliott, G.C. and Meeker, B.F. (1986). Achieving fairness in the face of competing concerns: The different effects of individual and group characteristics. *Journal of Personality and Social Psychology*, 50, 754-760.
Evans, C. (1981). Justice as desert. In R.L. Braham (ed.)., *Social justice*. Boston: Martinus Nijhoff. 45-54.

Eysenck, H.J. (1977). *Crime and Personality*. St. Albans, Herts: Paladin.
Farkus, A.J., and Anderson, N.H. (1976). Multidimensional input in equity theory. *Journal of Personality and Social Psychology*, 37, 879-896.
Feather, N.T. and Simon, G.S. (1971). Attribution of responsibility and valence of outcome in relation to initial confidence and success and failure of self and others. *Journal of Personality and Social Psychology*, 18, 173-188.
Feinberg, J. (1970). *Doing and deserving*, Princeton, NJ: Princeton University Press.
Feinberg, J. (1973). *Social philosophy*. Englewood Cliffs: Prentice-Hall.
Festinger, L. (1957). *A theory of cognitive dissonance*. Evanston, Ill.: Row, Peterson.
Fincham, F.D. and Jaspers, J.M. (1980). Attribution of responsibility: From man the scientist to man as lawyer. *Advances in Experimental Social Psychology*, 13, 81-138.
Finley, M.I. (1977). Aristotle and economic Analysis. In J. Barnes, M. Schofield, and R. Sorabji (eds.), *Articles on Aristotle*. London: Duckworth. 142-152.
Finnis, J. (1980). *Natural law and natural rights*. Oxford: Clarendon.
Flew, A. (ed.) (1979). *A dictionary of philosophy*. London: Pan.
Flew, A. (1982). Libertarians versus egalitarians. In T.R. Machan (ed.), *The libertarian reader*. New Jersey: Rowman and Littlefield. 252-263.
Fogerty, M. (1961). *The just wage*. London: Geoffrey Chapman.
Folger, R., Sheppard, B.H. and Buttram, R.T. (1995). Equity, equality and need: Three faces of social justice. In B.B. Bunker, and J.Z. Rubin (eds.), *Conflict, cooperation and justice: Essays inspired by the work of Morton Deutsch*. San Francisco: Jossey-Bass. 261-289.
Folger, R., Rosenfield, D., Hays, R.P. and Grove, R. (1978). Justice versus justification effects on productivity: Reconciling equity and dissonance findings. *Organizational Behavior and Human Performance*, 22, 465-478.
Frankena, W. (1962). The concept of social justice. In R.B. Brandt (ed.), *Social justice*. Englewood Cliffs, NJ: Prentice-Hall. 1-29.
Franklin, R.L. (1968). *Freewill and determinism*. London: Routledge and Paul.
Friedman, D. (1978). *The machinery of freedom: Guide to radical capitalism*. New York: Arlington House.
Friedman, M. and Friedman, R. (1981). *Free to choose*. Harmondsworth: Penguin.
Furby, L. (1986). Psychology and justice. In R.L. Cohen (ed.), *Justice: Views from the social sciences*. New York: Plenum. 154-203.
Furnham, A. (1982). Why are the poor always with us? Explanations for poverty in Britain. *British Journal of Social Psychology*, 21, 311-322.
Furnham, A. and Procter, E. (1989). Belief in a just world: Review and critique of the individual difference literature. *British Journal of Social Psychology*, 28, 365-384.
Gauthier, D. (1974). Justice and natural endowment: Toward a critique of Rawls' ideological framework. *Social Theory and Practice*, 3, 3-26.
Gauthier, D. (1986). *Morals by agreement*. Oxford: Oxford University Press.

Gauthier, D. (1991). Why contractarianism? Rational Constraint: Some last words. In P. Vallentyne, (ed.), *Contractarianism and rational choice: Essays on David Gauthier's morals by agreement*. New York: Cambridge University Press. 15-30, 323-330.
Gay, P. (1966). *Age of Enlightenment*. Amsterdam: Time Life Inc.
Garcia, J.L.A. (1986). Two concepts of desert. *Law and Philosophy*, 5, 219-235.
Gebotys, R.J. and Roberts, J.V. (1987). Public views of sentencing: The role of offender characteristics. *Canadian Journal of Behavioral Science*, 19, 479-488.
Gergen, K.J. (1969). *The psychology of behavior exchange*. Reading, MA: Addison-Wesley.
Gergen, K. J., Morse, S.J. and Bode, K. (1974). Overpaid or overworked? Cognitive and behavioral reactions to inequitable rewards. *Journal of Applied Social Psychology*, 4, 259-274.
Gilligan, C. (1982). *In a different voice*. Cambridge, Mass: Harvard University Press.
Glass, D.C. (1964). Changes in liking as a means of reducing cognitive discrepancies between self-esteem and aggression. *Journal of Personality*, 32, 520-549.
Gordon, S. (1973). John Rawl's difference principle, utilitarianism and the optimum degree of inequality. *Journal of Philosophy*, 70, 275-280.
Green, D.G. (1987). *The new right*. Brighton: Harvester.
Greenberg, J. (1980). Attentional focus and locus of performance causality as clues to the relationship between exchange participants. *European Journal of Social Psychology*, 38, 579-585.
Greenberg, J. (1983). Equity and equality as clues to the realtionship between exchange participants. *European Journal of Social Psychology*, 13, 195-196.
Greenberg, J. (1987). Reactions to procedural injustice in payment distributions: Do the means justify the ends? *Journal of Applied Psychology*, 72, 55-61.
Greenberg, J. (1988). Equity and workplace status: A field experiment. *Journal of Applied Psychology*, 73, 606-613.
Greenberg, J. (1989). Cognitive reevaluation of outcomes in response to underepayment inequity. *Academy of Management Journal*, 32, 174-184.
Greenberg, J. (1990). Employees theft as a reaction to underpayment inequity: The hidden cost of pay cuts. *Journal of Applied Psychology*, 75, 561-568.
Greenberg, J. and Cohen, R.L. (eds.) (1982a). *Equity and justice in social behavior*. New York: Academic Press.
Greenberg, J. and Cohen, R.L. (1982b). Why justice? Normative and instrumental interpretations. In J. Greenberg, and R.L. Cohen (eds.), E*quity and justice in social behavior*. New York: Academic Press. 437-469.
Griffith, R., Vecchio, R.P. and Logan, J.W. (1989). Equity theory and interpersonal attraction. *Journalof Applied Psychology*, 74, 394-401.
Hamilton, W.D. (1964). The genetical theory of social behaviour (1 and 2). *Journal of Theoretical Biology*, 7, 1-16, 17-32.

Hamilton, V.L. and Retina, S. (1980). Social consensus on norms of justice: Should the punishment fit the crime? *American Journal of Sociology*, 85, 1117-1144.
Harder, J.W. (1992). Play for pay: Effects of inequity in a pay for performance context. *Administrative Science Quarterly*, 37, 321-335.
Hardin, G. (1968). The tragedy of the commons. *Science*, 162, 1243-1248.
Hardin, R. (1987). Social justice in the large and small. *Social Justice Research*, 1, 83-105.
Hare, R.M. (1981). *Moral thinking: Its levels, method and point*. Oxford: Clarendon Press.
Harman, G. (1982). Libertariansim and morality. In T.P. Machan (ed.), *The liberatarian reader*. New Jersey: Rowman and Littlefield. 226-234.
Harper, D.J., Wagstaff, G.F., Newton, J.T. and Harrison, K.R. (1990). Lay causal perceptions of third world poverty and the Just World theory. *Social Behavior and Personality*, 235-238.
Harris, R.J. (1976). Handling negative inputs: On the plausible equity formulae. *Journal of Experimental Social Psychology*, 12, 194-209.
Harris, R.J. (1980). Equity judgments in hypothetical four-person partnerships. *Journal of Experimental Social Psychology*, 16, 95-115.
Harris, R.J. (1983). Pinning down the equity formula. In D.M. Messick and K.S. Cook (eds.), *Equity theory: Psychological and sociological perspectives*. New York: Praeger. 207-242.
Harris, R.J. (1993). Two insights occasioned by attempts to pin down the equity formula. In B.A. Mellers and J. Baron (eds.), *Psychological perspectives on justice: Theory and applications*. Cambridge: Cambridge University Press. 32-54.
Harris, R.J. and Joyce, M.A. (1980). 'What's fair?' It depends on how you phrase the question. *Journal of Personality and Social Psychology*, 38, 165-179.
Harris, R.J., Messick, D.M. and Sentis, K.P. (1981). Proportionality, linearity, and parameter constancy: Messick and Sentis reconsidered. *Journal of Experimental Social Psychology*, 17, 210-225.
Hart, H.L.A. (1961). *The concept of law*. Oxford: Clarendon Press.
Hart, H.L.A. (1968). *Punishment and responsibility*. Oxford: Clarendon.
Hassebrauck, M. (1986). Ratings of distress as a function of degree and kind of inequity. *Journal of Social Psychology*, 126, 269-270.
Hatfield, E., Walster, G.W. and Traupman, J. (1979). Equity and extramarital sex. In M. Cook and G. Wilson (eds.) *Love and attraction*. New York: Pergamon.
Hayek, F.A. (1976a). *Law, legislation and liberty*. London: Routledge and Kegan Paul.
Hayek, F.A. (1976b). *The mirage of justice*. London: Routledge and Kegan Paul.
Hegel, G.W.F. (1942). *Philosophy of right*. Oxford: Clarendon. (First published 1864.)
Heider, F. (1985). *The psychology of interpersonal relations*. New York: Wiley.

Heilbrun, A. and Georges, M. (1990). The measurement of principled morality by the Kohlberg Moral Dilemma Questionnaire. *Journal of Personality Assessment*, 55, 183-194.

Hermstein, R.J. (1973). *I.Q. in the meritocracy*. London: Allen Lane.

Hertz, J.H. (1956). *The Pentateuch and Haftorahs*. London: Soncino Press.

Himmelweit, H.T., Humphries, P., Jaeger, M. and Katz, M. (1981). *How voters decide: A longitudinal study of political attitudes and voting extending over fifteen years*. London: Academic Press.

Hobbes, T. (1960). *Leviathan*. Oxford: Basil Blackwell. (First published 1651.)

Hochschild, J. (1981). *Whats fair? American beliefs about distributive justice*. Cambridge, MA: Harvard University Press.

Hoffman, L.R. and Maier, N.R.F. (1959). The use of group decision to resolve the problem of fairness. *Personnel Psychology*, 12, 545-559.

Hogan, R. and Emler, N.P. (1981). Retributive justice. In M.J. Lerner and S.C. Lerner (eds.), *The justice motive in social behavior*. New York: Plenum. 125-143.

Homans, G.C. (1982). Foreward. In J. Greenberg and R.L. Cohen (eds.), *Equity and justice in social behavior*. New York: Academic Press.

Homans, G.C. (1974). *Social behaviour: Its elementary forms*. New York: Harcourt Brace Jovanovich.

Hook, J.G. and Cook, T.D. (1979). Equity theory and cognitive ability of children. *Psychological Bulletin*, 86, 429-445.

Honderich, T. (1976). *Punishment: The alleged justifications*. Harmondsworth: Penguin.

Hospers, J. (1961). *Human Conduct: An Introduction to the problems of ethics*. New York: Harcourt Brace and World.

Houlihan, M.M., Jackson, J. and Rogers, T.R. (1990). Decision making of satisfied and dissatisfied married couples. *Journal of Social Psychology*, 130, 89-102.

Hume, D. (1962). *Enquiries: Concerning the human understanding and concerning the principles of morals (2nd ed)*. Oxford: Clarendon Press. (First published 1777.)

Huppertz, J.W. (1978). On the possibility of the existence and measurement of negative inputs in social exchange. *Personality and Social Psychology Bulletin*, 4, 469-472.

Huxley, T.H. (1911). *Evolution and ethics and other essays*. London: MacMillan.

Irani, K.D. (1981). Values and rights underlying social justice. In R.L. Braham (ed.). *Social justice*, 29-44.

Jasso, G. (1978). On the justice of earnings: A new specification of the justice function. *American Journal of Sociology*, 83, 1398-1419.

Jasso, G. (1983). Social consequences of the sense of distributive justice: Small group applications. In D.M. Messick and K.S. Cook (eds.), *Equity theory: Psychological and sociological perspectives*. New York: Praeger. 243-295.

Jecker, J. and Landy, D. (1969). Liking a person as a function of doing him a favor. *Human Relations*, 22, 371-378.

Jenyns, S. (1972). A free inquiry into the nature and origin of evil. In D.H. Munro (ed.), *A guide to the British moralists*. London: Collins. 227-230. (First published 1758.)

Johnson, S. (1984). *Journey through the Western Isles of Scotland.* Harmondsworth, Middx. Penguin. (First published 1775.)

Kahneman, D. and Tversky, A. (1979). Prospect theory: An analysis of decision under risk. *Econometrica*, 47, 263-291.

Kamin, L.J. (1974).*The science and politics of IQ*. Harmondsworth, Middx: Penguin.

Kant, I. (1949). *Critique of Practical Reason.* Translated by T.K. Abbott, and L.W. Beck. Chicago. (First published 1781.)

Kant, I. (1963). *Lectures on Ethics.* Translated by L. Infield. New York: Harper (Written 1775-1780.)

Kant, I. (1965). *Fundamental principles of the metaphysic of ethics.* Translated by T.K. Abbott. London: Longmans. (First published 1785.)

Kant, I. (1970). *Metaphysical elements of justice* Translated by A. Ladd. Indianapolis: Bobbs-Merrill. (First published 1797.)

Kant, I. (1973). Two essays on right. In S. Phelps (ed.), *Economic justice.* Harmondsworth, Middx: Penguin. (First published 1793-1797.)

Karniol, R. and Miller, D.T. (1981). Morality and the development of conceptions of justice. In M.J. Lerner, and S.C. Lerner (eds.), *The justice motive in social behavior*. New York: Plenum.

Katz, M.B. (1989). *The undeserving poor*. New York: Pantheon.

Kayser, E.T., Schwinger, T. and Cohen, R.L. (1984). Layperson's conceptions of social relationships: A test of contract theory. *Journal of Social and Personal Relationships*, 1, 433-548.

Kelley (1967). Attribution theory in social psychology. In D. Levine (ed.), *Nebraska Symposium on Motivation, Vol. 15.* Lincoln, NE: University of Nebraska Press. 192-241.

Kelsen, H. (1973). What is justice? In O. Weinberger (ed.), *Hans Kelsen: Essays in legal and moral philosophy*. Dortrecht: Reidel.

Kemp, J. (1968). *The philosophy of Kant*. London: Oxford University Press.

Kessler, J.J., and Wiener, Y. (1972). Self-consistency and inequity dissonance as factors in undercompensation. *Organizational Behavior and Human Performance*, 8, 456-466.

Kleinig, J. (1971). The concept of desert. *American Philosophical Quarterly*, 8, 71-78.

Kluegel, J.R. and Smith, E.R. (1986). *Beliefs about inequality*. New York: Aldine.

Kohlberg, L. (1971). From is to ought: How to commit the naturalistic fallacy and get away with it in the study of moral development. In T. Mischel (ed.), *Cognitive development and epistomology*. New York: Academic Press. 151-235.

Kohlberg, L. (1976). Moral stages and moralization: The cognitive-developmental approach. In T. Lickona (ed.), *Moral development and behavior: Theory research and social issues*. New York: Holt Rinehart and Winston. 31-53.
Komorita, S.S. and Kravitz, D.A. (1979). The effects of alternatives on bargaining. *Journal of Experimental Social Psychology*, 15, 147-157.
Konecni, V.J. and Ebbeson, E.B. (1979). External validity of research in legal psychology. *Law and Human Behavior*, 3, 389-390.
Kramer, S.N. (1969). *Cradle of civilization*. Amsterdam: Time-Life International.
Lamm, H.E. and Kayser, E. (1978). The allocation of monetary gain and loss following dyadic performance. The weight given to effort and ability under conditions of low and high intra-dyadic attraction. *European Journal of Social Psychology*, 8, 275-278.
Lamm, H., and Schwinger, T. (1983). Need consideration in allocation decisions: Is it just? *Journal of Social Psychology*, 119, 205-209.
Lamm, H.E., Kayser, E., and Schanz, V. (1983). An attributional analysis of interpersonal justice: Ability and effort as inputs in the allocation of gain and loss. *Journal of Social Psychology*, 119, 205-209.
Lane, R. (1962). *Political ideology: Why the American common man believes what he does*. New York: MacMillan.
Lansberg, I. (1984). Hierarchy as a mediator of fairness: A contingency approach to distributive justice in organizations. *Journal of Applied Psychology*, 14, 124-135.
Laurence, J-R. and Perry, C. (1988). *Hypnosis, will and memory*. New York: Guilford.
Lee, D. (1987). Translator's introduction. *Plato: The Republic*. Harmondsworth, Middx: Penguin.
Lee, J.R. (1981). The arrest and punishment of criminals: Justification and limitations. In T.R. Machan (ed.), *The Libertarian Reader*. Totowa, NJ: Rowman and Littlefield. 87-97.
LeGrand, J. (1991). *Equity and choice: An essay in economics and applied philosophy*. London: Harper/Collins.
Legant, P. and Mettee, D.R. (1973). Turning the other cheek versus getting even: Vengeance, equity and attraction. *Journal of Personality and Social Psychology*, 25, 243-253.
Lenin, V. (1939). The teachings of Karl Marx, and class, society and the state. In M. Oakeshott (ed.), *The social and political doctrines of contemporary Europe*. Cambridge: Cambridge University Press. 101-151.
Leo XIII, Pope (1939). Rerum Novarum. In M. Oakeshott (ed.), *The social and political doctrines of contemporary Europe*. Cambridge: Cambridge University Press. 45-77. (First published 1891.)
Lerner, M.J. (1965). Evaluation of performance as a function of performer's reward and attractiveness. *Journal of Personality and Social Psychology*, 1, 355-360.

Lerner, M.J. (1971). Observer's evaluation of a victim: justice, guilt and veridical perception. *Journal of Personality and Social Psychology*, 20, 127-135.

Lerner, M.J. (1974). The justice motive: 'Equity' and 'parity' among children. *Journal of Personality and Social Psychology*, 29, 538-550.

Lerner, M.J. (1975). The justice motive in social behavior: Introduction. *Journal of Social Issues*, 31, 1-20.

Lerner, M.J. (1977). The justice motive: Some hypotheses as to its origin and forms. *Journal of Personality*, 45, 1-52.

Lerner, M.J. (1980). *The belief in a just world: A fundamental delusion.* New York: Plenum.

Lerner, M.J. (1981). The justice motive in human relations: Some thoughts about what we need to know about justice. In M.J. Lerner and S.C. Lerner (1981). *The justice motive in social behavior.* New York: Plenum. 11-40.

Lerner, M.J. (1991). Integrating societal and psychological rules of entitlement: The basic task of each social actor and a fundamental problem for the social sciences. In R. Vermunt and H. Steensma (eds.), *Social justice in human relations, Volume 1: Societal and psychological origins of justice.* New York: Plenum. 13-32.

Lerner, M.J. and Matthews, G. (1967). Reactions to suffering of others under conditions of indirect responsibility. *Journal of Personality and Social Psychology*, 5, 319-325.

Lerner, M.J. and Miller, D. T. (1978). Just World research and the attribution process: Looking back and ahead. *Psychological Bulletin*, 85, 1030-1051.

Lerner, M.J., Miller, D. T. and Holmes, R. (1976). Deserving and the emergence of forms of justice. In L. Berkowitz and E. Walster (eds.), *Advances in experimental social psychology, Vol. 9.* New York: Academic Press. 133-162.

Lerner, M.J. and Simmons, C.H. (1966). Observer's reaction to the innocent victim: Compassion or rejection? *Journal of Personality and Social Psychology*, 4, 203-210.

Leventhal, G.S. (1976). Fairness in social relationships. In J.W. Thibaut, J.T. Spence, and R.C. Carson (eds.), *Contemporary topics in social psychology*, Morriston, NJ: General Learning Press. 211-239.

Leventhal, G.S. (1980). What should be done with equity theory? In K.J. Gergen, M.S. Greenberg, and R.H. Weiss (eds.), *Social exchange: Advances in theory and research.* New York: Plenum. 27-55.

Leventhal, G.S., and Lane, D.W. (1970). Sex, age and equity behavior. *Journal of Personality and Social Psychology*, 15, 312-235.

Leventhal, G.S. and Michaels, J.W. (1971). Locus of cause and equity motivation as determinants of reward allocation. *Journal of Personality and Social Psychology*, 17, 229-235.

Leventhal, G.S., Allen, J. and Kemelgour, B. (1969). Reducing inequity by reallocating rewards. *Psychonomic Sciences*, 14, 295-296.

Leventhal, G.S., Karuza, J. and Fry, W.R. (1980). Beyond fairness: A theory of allocation preferences. In G. Mikula (ed.), *Justice and Social Interaction.* New York: Springer-Verlag. 167-218.
Leventhal, G.S., Michaels, J.W. and Sanford, C. (1972). Inequity and interpersonal conflict: Reward allocation and secrecy about reward as methods of preventing conflict. *Journal of Personality and Social Psychology*, 23, 88-102.
Levin, M. (1981). Equality of opportunity. In R.L. Braham (ed.), *Social justice.* Boston: Martinus Nijhoff. 55-77
Lickona, T. (1976). Research on Piaget's theory of moral development. In T. Lickona (ed.), *Moral development and behavior: Theory research and social issues*, New York: Holt Rinehart and Winston. 219-240.
Lippa, R.A. (1994). *Introduction to social psychology.* Pacific Grove, Calif.: Brooks/Cole.
Lind, E.A. and Tyler, T.R. (1988). *Social Psychology of procedural justice.* New York: Plenum.
Lind, E.A., Kanfer, R. and Earley, P.C. (1990). Voice, control and procedural justice: Instrumental and noninstrumental concerns in fairness judgements. *Journal of Personality and Social Psychology*, 59, 952-959.
Lind, E.A., Kurtz, S., Musante, L. Walker, L., and Thibaut, J.W. (1980). Procedure and outcome effects on reactions to adjudicated resolution conflicts of interest. *Journal of Personality and Social Psychology*, 39, 643-653.
Lindskold, S., Han, G. and Betz, B. (1986). The essential elements of communication in GRIT strategy. *Personality and Social Psychology Bulletin,* 12, 179-186.
Linskold, S., Walters, P.S. and Koutsourais, H. (1983). Cooperators, competitors, and response to GRIT. *Journal of Conflict Resolution*, 27, 521-532.
Lissak, R.I. and Sheppard, B.H. (1983). Beyond fairness: The criterion problem in research on dispute intervention. *Journal of Applied Psychology*, 13, 45-65.
Locke, J. (1988). *Two treatises of government.* P. Laslett (ed.). Cambridge: Cambridge University Press. (First published 1690.)
Long, G.T. and Lerner, M.J. (1974). Deserving, the 'personal contract' and altruistic behavior by children. *Journal of Personality and Social Psychology*, 29, 551-556.
Lord, R.G. and Hohenfield, J.A. (1979). Longitudinal assessment of equity effects on the performance of major league baseball players. *Journal of Applied Psychology*, 64, 19-26.
Lucas, J.R. (1980). *On justice.* Oxford: Clarendon Press.
Luce, R.D. and Raiffa, H.(1957). *Games and decisions.* New York: Wiley.
Lukes, S. (1982). Marxism, morality and justice. In G.H.R. Parkinson (ed.), *Marx and Marxisms.* Cambridge: Cambridge University Press. 177-205.
Lukes, S. (1985). *Marxism and morality.* Oxford: Oxford University Press.

Mace, R. (1996). When to have another baby: A dynamic model of reproductive decision making and evidence from Gabbra pastoralists. *Ethology and Sociobiology*, 263-273.
Machan, T.R. (1982) (ed.), *The libertarian reader*. New Jersey: Rowman and Littlefield.
MacIntyre, A. (1982). *After virtue: A study in moral theory*. London: Duckworth.
MacIntyre, A. (1988). *Whose justice? Which rationality?* London: Duckworth.
MacPherson, C.B. (1962). *The political theory of possessive individualism: Hobbes to Locke*. Oxford: Clarendon.
Major, B. and Deaux, K. (1982). Individual differences in justice behavior. In J. Greenberg, and R.L. Cohen (eds.), *Equity and justice in social behavior*. New York: academic Press. 43-76.
Mark, M.M. and Greenberg, J. (1987). Evening the score. *Psychology Today*, Jan., 44-50.
Markovsky, B. (1991). Prospects for a cognitive-structural justice theory. In R. Vermunt and H. Steensma (eds.), *Social justice in human relations: volume 1: Societal and psychological origins of justice*. New York: Plenum Press. 33-58.
Martin, M.W. (1985). Satisfaction with intimate exchange: Gender role differences and the impact of equity, equality and rewards. *Sex-Roles*, 13, 597-605.
Marwell, G., Ratcliff, K. and Schmitt, D.R. (1969). Minimizing differences in a maximizing difference game. *Journal of Social Psychology*, 12, 158-163.
Marx, K.H. (with changes by F. Engels) (1965). *Capital: A critique of political economy*. London: Lawrence and Wishart. (First published in English in 1887.)
Marx, K.H. (1976). *Capital: A critique of political economy, Vol.1*. Harmondsworth, Middx.: Penguin. (First published in English in 1887.)
Marx, K.H. (1978). *Capital: A critique of political economy, Vol.2*. Harmondsworth, Middx.:Penguin. (First published in English in 1887.)
Marx, K.H. (1986). Critique of the Gotha Programme. In J. Elster (ed.), *Karl Marx: A Reader*. Cambridge: Cambridge University Press. 162-167. (First published 1875.)
Marx, K.H. (1986). Comments on James Mill. In J. Elster (ed.), *Karl Marx: A Reader*Cambridge: Cambridge University Press. 31-35. (Written 1844, first published 1932).
Maynard Smith, J. (1982). *Evolution and the theory of games*. New York: Cambridge University Press.
McClintock, C.G. and Liebrand, W.B.G. (1988). Role of interdependence structure, individual value orientation, and another's strategy in social decision making: A transformational analysis. *Journal of Personality and Social Psychology*, 55, 396-409.
Mellers, B.A. (1982). Equity judgment: A revision of Aristotelian views. *Journal of Experimental Psychology: General*, 111, 242-270.

Mellers, B.A. (1986). 'Fair' allocations of salaries and taxes. *Journal of Experimental Psychology: Human Perception and Performance*, 12, 80-91.
Mellers, B.A. and Baron, J. (eds.) (1993). *Psychological perspectives on justice: Theory and applications*. Cambridge: Cambridge University Press.
Mellers, B. and Hartka, E. (1989). Test of a subtractive theory of fair allocations. *Journal of Personality and Social Psychology*, 56, 691-697.
Messick, D.M. (1993). Equality as a decision heuristic. In B.A. Mellers, and J. Baron, (eds.) *Psychological perspectives on justice: Theory and applications*, Cambridge: Cambridge University Press. 11-31.
Messick, D.M. and Cook, K.S. (eds.)(1983). *Equity theory: Psychological and sociological perspectives*. New York: Praeger.
Messick, D.M., Bloom, S., Boldizar, J.P. and Samuelson, C.D. (1985). Why we are fairer than others? *Journal of Experimental Social Psychology*, 21, 480-500.
Meyer, J.P. and Mulherin, A. (1980). From attribution to helping: An analysis of the mediating effects of affect and expectancy. *Journal of Personality and Social Psychology*, 39, 201-210.
Mikula, G. (1972). Gewinnaufteilungsverhalten in gleichgeschlechtlichen dyaden: Eine vergleichsstudie an osterreichischen und amerikanischen studenten. *Psychologie und Praxis,*16, 97-106. (Cited by Schwinger, 1980.)
Mikula, G. (1980). On the role of justice in allocation decisions. In G. Mikula (ed.), *Justice and social interaction*. New York: Springer-Verlag. 127-165.
Mill, J.S. (1960). *Autobiography*. J. Jacob (ed.). New York: Columbia University Press. (First published 1873.)
Mill, J.S. (1970). The subjection of women. In A.S. Ross (ed.), *Essays on sex equality*. Chicago: University of Chicago Press. (First published 1869.)
Mill, J.S. (1993) Utilitarianism. In G. Williams (ed.), *Utilitarianism. On Liberty. Considerations on representative government. Remarks on Bentham's philosophy*. London: Everyman (First published 1861; On Liberty, 1859.)
Miller, F.D. (1982). The natural right to private property. In T.R. Machan (ed.), *The libertarian reader*. New Jersey: Rowman and Littlefield. 275-278.
Miller, D.T. (1976). *Social justice*. Oxford: Clarendon Press.
Miller, D.T. (1977). Personal deserving versus justice for others: An exploration of the justice motive. *Journal of Experimental Social Psychology*, 13, 1-13.
Miller, D.T. and Vidmar, N. (1981). The social psychology of punishment reactions. In M.J. Lerner and S.C. Lerner (1981). *The justice motive in social behavior*. New York: Plenum. 145-172.
Molander, P. (1985). The optimal level of generosity in a selfish, uncertain environment. *Journal of Conflict Resolution*, 29, 611-618.
Moore, C.F., Hembree, S.E. and Enright, R.D. (1993). The unfolding of justice: A developmental perspective on reward allocation. In B.A. Mellers, and J. Baron, (eds.), *Psychological perspectives on justice: Theory and applications*, Cambridge: Cambridge University Press. 183-204.
Moore, L.M. and Baron, R.M. (1973). Effects of wage inequities on work attitudes and performance. *Journal of Experimental Social Psychology*, 9, 1-16.

Montada, L. (1980). Developmental changes in concepts of justice. In G. Mikula (ed.), *Justice and social interaction*. New York: Springer-Verlag.
Montague, P. (1980). Comparative and non-comparative justice. *Philosophical Quarterly*, 30, 132.
Morgan, W.R. and Sawyer, J. (1967). Bargaining, expectations, and preference for equality over equity. *Journal of Personality and Social Psychology*, 6, 139-149.
Moschetti, G.J. (1979). Calculating equity: Ordinal and ratio criteria. *Social Psychology Quarterly*, 42, 172-175.
Murphy, J.G. (1970). *Kant: The philosophy of right*. London: Macmillan.
Murphy, C.F. (1972). Distributive justice, its modern significance. *The American Journal of Jurisprudence*, 17, 153-165.
Nelson, S.A. and Dweck, C.S. (1977). Motivation and competence as determinants of young children's reward allocation. *Developmental Psychology*, 13, 192-197.
Nielsen, K. (1979). Radical egalitarian justice: Justice as equality. *Social Theory and Practice*, 5, 209-226.
Norrie, A. (1993). *Crime, reason and history: A critical introduction to criminal law*. London: Weidenfield and Nicolson.
Nozick, R. (1980). *Anarchy, state and utopia*, Bristol: Arrowsmith.
Ordonez, L.D. and Mellers, B.A. (1993). Trade-offs in fairness and preference judgments. In B.A. Mellers, and J. Baron, *Psychological perspectives on justice: Theory and applications*. 138-154.
Orpen, C. and Bonnici, J. (1990). The causes and consequences of pay satisfaction: A test of Lawler's model. *Psychology: A Journal of Human Behavior*, 27, 27-29.
Oskamp, S. (1971). Effects of programmed strategies on cooperation in the prisoner's dilemma and other mixed-motive games. *Journal of Conflict Resolution*, 15, 225-259.
Pandy, J., Sinha, Y., Prakesh, A., and Tripathi, R.C. (1982). Right-Left political ideologies and attribution of the causes of poverty. *European Journal of Social Psychology*, 12, 327-331.
Peterson, C. (1987). Need, equity and equality in the adult family. *Journal of Social Psychology*, 127, 543-544.
Pietras, M. (1992). Between doing harm and breaking the law: A social psychological perspective. In F. Losel, D. Bender, and T. Bliesener (eds). *Psychology and law: International perspectives*. Berlin: Walter de Gruyter.
Pius XI, Pope (1939). Papal letter to the Church in Germany, and Encyclical Quadragesimo Anno. In M. Oakeshott (ed.), *The social and political doctrines of contemporary Europe*. Cambridge: Cambridge University Press. 45-77.
Plato (1960). *The laws*. Translated by A. E. Taylor. London: Dent.
Plato (1976). *Gorgias*. Translated by W. Hamilton. Harmondsworth, Middx.: Penguin.

Plato (1987) *The Republic*. Translated by D. Lee. Harmondsworth, Middx.: Penguin.
Posner, R.A. (1981). *The economics of justice*. Cambridge, MA: Harvard University Press.
Pritchard, R.D. (1969). Equity theory: A review and critique. *Organizational Behavior and Human Performance*, 4, 176-211.
Pritchard, R.D., Dunnette, M.D. and Jorgenson, D.O. (1972). Effects of perceptions of equity and inequity on worker performance and satisfaction. *Journal of Applied Psychology* Monograph, 56, 75-94.
Raphael, D.D. (1981). *Moral philosophy*. Oxford: Oxford University Press.
Rasmussen, D. (1982). Essentialism, valus and rights: The objectivist case for a free society. In T.R. Machan (ed.), *The libertarian reader*. New Jersey: Rowman and Littlefield. 37-52.
Rawls, J. (1972). *A theory of justice*. Oxford: Clarendon.
Rawls, J. (1973). Distributive justice. In S. Phelps (ed.), *Economic justice*. Harmondsworth: Penguin. 319-361.
Rawls, J. (1975). The sense of justice. In J. Feinberg (ed.), *Moral concepts*, Oxford: Oxford Uiversity Press. 120-140.
Rescher, N. (1972). *Welfare: The social issue in philosophical perspective*. Pittsburgh: University of Pittsburgh Press.
Reis, H.T. (1984). The multidimensionality of justice. In R. Folger (ed.), *The sense of injustice: Social psychological perspectives*. New York: Plenum. 25-61.
Reis, H.T. and Gruzen, J. (1976). On mediating equity, equality, and self-interest: The role of self-presentation in social exchange. *Journal of Experimental Social Psychology*, 12, 487-503.
Reynolds, W.A., Remer, R. and Johnson, M. (1995). Marital satisfaction in later life: An examination of equity, equality and reward theories. *International Journal of Aging and Human Development*, 40, 155-173.
Roberts, S. (1979). *Order and dispute: An introduction to legal anthropology*. Harmondsworth, Middx: Penguin.
Robinson, J. (1964). *Economic philosophy*. Harmondsworth, Middx: Penguin.
Robinson, J. and Spitze, G. (1992). Whistle while you work? The effect of household task performance on women's and men's well-being. *Social Science Quarterly*, 73, 844-861.
Robinson, R.V. and Bell, W. (1978). Equality, success, and social justice in England and the United States. *American Sociological Review*, 48, 125-143.
Roemer, J. (1985). Equality of talent. *Economics and philosophy*, 1, 151-187.
Romer, D. (1977) Limitations in the equity theory approach: Toward a resolution of the 'negative inputs' controversy. *Personality and Social Psychology Bulletin*, 3, 228-231.
Rook, K.S. (1987). Reciprocity on social exchange satisfaction among older women. *Journal of Personality and Social Psychology*, 145-154.
Ross, W.D. (1937). *Aristotle*. London: Methuen.
Ross, M. and DiTecco (1975). An attributional analysis of moral judgments. *Journal of Social Issues*, 31, 91-109.

Rossi, P.H., Simpson, J.E. and Miller, J.L. (1985). Beyond crime seriousness: Fitting the punishment to the crime. *Journal of Quantitative Criminology*, 1, 59-60.
Rousseau, J.J. (1988). *Rousseau's political writings: Discourse on inequality: Discourse on political economy: On social contract.* A. Ritter and J. Bondanella (eds.). New York: Norton. (First published 1755.)
Rousseau, J.J. (1968). *The social contract.* Harmondsworth, Middx: Penguin. (First published 1755.)
Rubin, Z. and Peplau, L.A. (1975). Who believes in a just world? *Journal of Social Issues*, 29, 73-93.
Russell, B. (1979). *A history of western philosophy.* London: Unwin.
Ryan, W. (1971). *Blaming the victim.* New York: Vintage.
Sabini, J. (1995). *Social psychology (2nd ed.).* New York: W.W. Norton.
Sadurski, W. (1985). *Giving desert its due: Social justice and legal theory.* Dordrecht: Reidel.
Sampson, E.E. (1971). *Social psychology and contemporary society.* New York: Wiley.
Sampson, E.E. (1975). On justice as equality. *Journal of Social Issues*, 31, 45-64.
Samuel, W. (1975). Contemporary social psychology: An introduction. Englewood-Cliffs, N.J. : Prentice-Hall.
Samuel, W. (1978). Toward a simple but useful equity theory: A comment on the Romer article. *Personality and Social Psychology Bulletin*, 4, 135-138.
Schafer, R.B. and Keith, P.M. (1980). Equity and depression among married couples. *Social Psychology Quarterly*, 43, 430-435.
Scherer, K.R. (1992). Issues in the study of justice. In K.R. Scherer (ed.), *Justice: Interdisciplinary perspectives.* Cambridge: Cambridge University Press. 1-14.
Schmidt, G. and Weiner, B. (1988). An attribution-affect-action theory of behavior: Replications of judgments of help-giving. *Personality and Social Psychology Bulletin*, 14, 610-621.
Schokkaert, E. (1992). The economics of distributive justice, welfare and freedom. In K.R. Scherer (ed.), *Justice: Interdisciplinary perspectives.* Cambridge: Cambridge University Press. 65-113.
Schwartz, S. (1975). The justice of need and the activation of humanitarian norms. *Journal of Social Issues*, 31, 111-136.
Schwinger, T. (1980). Just allocations of goods: Decisions among three principles. In G. Mikula (ed.), *Justice and social interaction.* New york: Springer-Verlag. 95-125.
Semmel, B. (1984). *John Stuart Mill and the pursuit of virtue.* New Haven: Yale University Press.
Sermat, V. and Gregovich, R.P. (1966). The effect of experimental manipulation on cooperative behaviour in a chicken game. *Psychonomic Science*, 4, 435-436.
Sen, (1985). *Commodities and capabilities.* Amsterdam: North-Holland.
Shaver, K.G. (1985). *The attribution of blame: Causality, responsibility, and blameworthiness.* Cambridge, MA: Springer-Verlag.

Shaver, K.G. and Drown, D. (1986). On causality, responsibility and self-blame: A theoretical note. *Journal of Personality and Social Psychology*, 4, 697-702.
Sher, G. (1981). The historical dimension of justice. In R.L. Braham (ed.) *Social justice*, Boston: Martinus Nijhoff. 17-27.
Sidgwick, H. (1907). *The method of ethics (7th ed.)*. London: Macmillan. (First published 1874.)
Silver, M. (1981). Men, monkeys and morals: A property rights theory of social justice. In R.L. Braham (ed.), *Social justice*, Boston: Martinus Nijhoff.
Simon, E. (1966). *The Reformation*. Amsterdam: Time Life International.
Slote, M.A. (1973). Desert, consent and justice. *Philosophy and Public Affairs*, 2, 323-347.
Smith, A. (1986). *The wealth of nations: Books 1-3*. Harmondsworth, Middx: Penguin.
Snarey, J.R. (1985). Cross-cultural universality of social-moral development: A critical review of Kohlbergian research. *Psychological Bulletin*, 97, 202-232.
Spinoza, B. (1986). *Ethics and the correction of understanding*. London: Dent. (First published 1677.)
Stafford, E. and Hill, J. (1987). The tariff, social inquiry reports and the sentencing of juveniles. *British Journal of Criminology*, 27, 411-420.
Stake, J.E. (1983). Factors in reward distribution: Allocator motive, gender and protestant ethic. *Journal of Personality and Social Psychology*, 44, 410-418.
Stephenson, G.M. (1992). *The psychology of criminal justice*. Oxford: Blackwell.
Summers, T.P. and DeNisi, A.S. (1990). In search of Adam's other: Reexamination of referents used in the evaluation of pay. *Human Relations*, 43, 497-511.
Sweeney, P.D. (1990). Distributive justice and pay satisfaction: A field test of an equity theory prediction. *Journal of Business and Psychology*, 4, 329-341.
Swift, A., Marshall, G., Burgoyne, C. and Routh, D. (1995). Distributive justice: Does it matter what people think? In J.R. Kluegel, D.S. Mason, and B. Wegener (eds.), *Social justice and political change: Public opinion in capitalist and post-communist states*. New York: Aldine de Gruyter.
Symonds, M. (1975). Victims of violence: Psychological effects and aftereffects. *The American Journal of Psychoanalysis*, 35, 19-26.
Tawney, R.H. (1929). *Religion and the rise of capitalism*. London: Murray.
Thibaut, J.W. (1950). An experimental study of the cohesiveness of underprivileged groups. *Human Relations*, 3, 251-278.
Thibaut, J.W. and Kelley, H.H. (1959). *The social psychology of groups*. New York: Wiley.
Thibaut, J.W. and Walker, L. (1975). *Procedural justice: A psychological analysis*. Hillsdale, N.J. : Erlbaum.
Thibaut, J.W. and Walker, L. (1978). A theory of procedure. *California Law Review*, 66, 541-666.
Thomas, S., Wagstaff, G.F., and Brunas-Wagstaff, J. (1996). The influence of responsibility and need on the assignment of penalties for traffic violations. *Proceedings of the British Psychological Society*, 4, 54.

Topitsch, E. (1971). *Sozialphilosophie zwischen ideologie und wissenschaft.* Neuwied: Luchterhand. (Cited by Schwinger, 1980.)
Törnblöm, K.Y. (1992). The social psychology of distributive justice. In K.R. Scherer (ed.), *Justice: Interdisciplinary perspectives.* Cambridge: Cambridge University Press. 177-236.
Törnblöm, K.Y. Muhlhausen, S.M. and Jonsson, D.R. (1991). The allocation of positive and negative outcomes: When is the equality principle fair for both? In R. Vermunt and H.Steensma (eds.), *Social justice in human relations, Volume 1: Societal and psychological origins of justice.* New York: Plenum. 59-100.
Trivers, R.L. (1971). The evolution of reciprocal altruism. *Quarterly Review of Biology,* 46, 35-57.
Trusted, J. (1984). *Freewill and responsibility.* Oxford: Oxford University Press.
Tyler, T.R. (1987a). Procedural justice research. *Social Justice Research,* 1, 41-65.
Tyler, T.R. (1987b). Conditions leading to value-expressive effects in judgments of procedural justice: A test of four models. *Journal of Personality and Social Psychology,* 52, 333-344.
Tyler, T.R. and Belliveau, M.A. (1995). Tradeoffs in justice principles: Definitions of fairness. In B.B. Bunker, and J.Z. Rubin (eds.), *Conflict, cooperation and justice: Essays inspired by the work of Morton Deutsch.* San Francisco: Jossey-Bass. 291-314.
Tyler, T.R. and Dawes, R.M. (1993). Fairness in groups: Comparing the self-interest and social identity perspectives. In B.A. Mellers and J. Baron (eds.). *Psychological perspectives on justice: Theory and applications.* Cambridge: Cambridge University Press. 88-108.
Utne, M.K. and Kidd, R.F. (1980). Equity and attribution. In G. Mikula (ed.), *Justice and social interaction.* New York: Springer-Verlag.
Valenzi, E.R. and Andrews, I.R. (1971). Effect of hourly overpay and underpay inequity when tested with a new induction procedure. *Journal of Applied Psychology,* 55, 22-27.
Vallentyne, P. (ed.) (1991). *Contractarianism and rational choice: Essays on David Gauthier's morals by agreement.* New York: Cambridge University Press.
Van Yperen, N.W. and Buunk, B.P. (1990). A longitudinal study of equity and satisfaction in intimate relationships. *European Journal of Social Psychology,* 20, 287-309.
Vaughn, K.I. (1980). *John Locke: Economist and social scientist.* London: Athlone.
Vickrey, W.S. (1973). Risk, utility and social policy. In S. Phelps (ed.), *Economic justice.* Harmondsworth, Middx: Penguin. 286-297.
Vlastos, G. (1975). Human worth, merit and equality. In J. Feinberg (ed.), *Moral concepts.* Oxford: Oxford University Press.
Von Grumbkow, J., Deen, E., Steensma, H. and Wilke, H. (1976). The effect of future interaction on the distribution of rewards. *European Journal of Social Psychology,* 6, 119-123.

von Hirsch, A. (1985). *Past or future crimes: Deservedness and dangerousness in the sentencing of criminals.* Manchester: Manchester University Press.
von Hirsch, A. and Jareborg, N. (1989). Sweden's sentencing statute enacted. *Criminal Law Review*, 275-281.
Wagstaff, G.F. (1982). Attitudes to rape: The just world strikes again? *Bulletin of the British Psychological Society*, 35, 277-279.
Wagstaff, G.F. (1983a). Attitudes to poverty, the Protestant Ethic, and political affiliation: A preliminary investigation. *Social Behavior and Personality*, 11, 45-47.
Wagstaff, G.F. (1983b). Correlates of the just world in Britain. *Journal of Social Psychology*, 121, 145-146.
Wagstaff, G.F. (1983c). Attitudes to sex-roles, political conservatism and belief in a Just World. *Psychological Reports*, 52, 813-814.
Wagstaff, G.F. (1984). Political ideology, intelligence, heredity and social justice: Is there a paradox? *Psychological Reports*, 54, 286.
Wagstaff, G.F. (1994). Equity, equality and need: three principles of justice or one? *Current Psychology: Research and Reviews*, 13, 138-152.
Wagstaff, G.F. (1997). Equity, equality and allocations to adults and children. *Journal of Social Psychology,* 137, 445-448.
Wagstaff, G.F. (1998). Equity, justice and altruism. *Current Psychology: Developmental, Learning, Personality and Social*, 17, 111-134.
Wagstaff, G.F. and Kelhar, S. (1993). On the roles of control and outcomes in procedural justice. *Psychological Reports*, 73, 121-122.
Wagstaff, G.F. and Perfect, T.J. (1992). On the definition of perfect equity and the prediction of inequity. *British Journal of Social Psychology*, 31, 69-77.
Wagstaff, G.F. and Preece, D. (1997). Is overpunishment fairer than underpunishment? Perceptions of deviations from equity. *Law and Psychology*.
Wagstaff, G.F. and Quirk, M.A. (1983). Attitudes to sex roles, political conservatism, and belief in a just world. *Psychological Reports*, 2, 813-814.
Wagstaff, G.F. and Worthington, J. (1997). Equity, relative need, and allocations to zero input workers. *Journal of Social Psychology.*
Wagstaff, G.F., Chadwick, D. and Brunas-Wagstaff (1996). *Equity and the distribution of undeserved outcomes.* Unpublished manuscript, Department of Psychology, University of Liverpool.
Wagstaff, G.F., Huggins, J.P. and Perfect, T.J. (1993). Equity, equality and need in the adult family. *Journal of Social Psychology*, 133, 439-444.
Wagstaff, G.F., Huggins, J. and Perfect, T.J. (1996). Equal ratio equity, general linear equity and framing effects in judgments of allocation divisions. *European Journal of Social Psychology*, 26, 29-41.
Wagstaff, G.F., Bowles, R.J., Hughes, D., Rogers, B., Turner, S. and Perfect, T.J. (1994). Judgments concerning zero inputs in equity situations. *Journal of Social Psychology*, 134, 649-654.

Walker, L., LaTour, S., Lind, E.A. and Thibaut, J. (1974). Reactions of participants and observers to modes of adjudication. *Journal of Applied Social Psychology*, 4, 295-310.

Walster, E. and Prestholdt, P. (1966). The effect of misjudging another: Overcompensation or dissonance reduction? *Journal of Experimental Social Psychology*, 2, 85-97.

Walster, E and Walster, G.W. (1975). Equity and social justice. *Journal of Social Issues*, 31, 21-43.

Walster, E., Berscheid, E. and Walster, G.W. (1973) New directions in equity research. *Journal of Personality and Social Psychology*, 25, 151-176.

Walster, E., Walster, G.W. and Berscheid, E. (1978) *Equity: Theory and Research*. London: Allyn and Bacon.

Walster, E., Walster, G.W. and Traupman, J. (1978). Equity and premarital sex. *Journal of Personality*, 36, 82-92.

Walvin, J. (1992). *Black ivory: A history of British slavery*. London: Fontana.

Walzer, M. (1983). *Spheres of justice: A defence of pluralism and equality*. Oxford: Martin Robertson.

Weick, K.E. (1964). Reduction of cognitive dissonance through task enhancement and effort expenditure. *Journal of Abnormal and Social Psychology*, 66, 533-539.

Weiner, B. (1980). A cognitive (attribution)-emotion-action model of motivated behavior: An analysis of judgments of help-giving. *Journal of Personality and Social Psychology*, 39, 186-200.

Weiner, B. (1985). An attributional theory of achievement motivation and emotion. *Psychological Review*, 92, 548-573.

Weinreb, L.L. (1987). *Natural law and justice*. London: Harvard University Press.

Williams, S. (1984). Left-Right ideological differences in blaming victims. *Political Psychology*, 5, 573-581.

Williams, B. (1975). The idea of equality. In J. Feinberg (ed.), *Moral concepts*. Oxford: Oxford University Press. 153-171.

Wright, M.R. (1991). *Commentary on De Finibus III. In Cicero: On Stoic good and evil*. Warminster, Wilts.: Aris and Phillips.

Wright, R. (1995). *The moral animal: Evolutionary psychology and everyday life*. Boston: Little-Brown.

AUTHOR INDEX

Ackerman, B.A., 19, 51, 52, 57, 384, 385
Acton, H.B., 323
Adams, J.S., 77, 78, 79, 80, 81, 82, 83, 84, 85, 88, 90, 91, 93, 94, 129, 131, 155, 194, 206, 211, 213, 424
Alexander, R.D., 440, 443
Allen, J., 86
Anderson, B., 85
Anderson, N.H., 88, 92, 93, 94, 129, 420
Andrews, I.R., 86
Aquinas, St. Thomas, 4, 287, 288, 289, 290, 299, 344
Aristotle, 10, 13, 169, 171, 183-211, 227, 233, 235, 236, 237, 238, 239, 241, 242, 245, 246, 273, 274, 280, 281, 282, 288, 289, 294, 299, 306, 309, 325, 327, 328, 331, 344, 354, 355, 357, 359, 372, 428, 449
Asdigan, N.L., 114, 403
Augustine, St., 285, 286, 288
Austin, W., 77, 82, 84, 85, 114, 145, 401
Axelrod, R., 436
Ayensu, E.S., 237

Baier, K., 223
Bar-Hillel, M., 429, 430
Barnes, B.J., 185
Baron, J., 89, 133, 137, 155, 156, 230, 429
Barrett-Howard, E., 141, 426
Barry, B., 19, 32, 49, 50, 51, 52, 57, 72, 224, 383, 435, 437
Bayley, J.E., 6, 20, 72
Bell, J., 7
Bentham, J., 14, 328, 330, 331, 359
Benton, A., 114, 403
Berger, J., 85, 158, 334, 335
Berkowitz, L., 88, 118, 120, 400
Berkowitz, W.T., 133, 423
Berscheid, E., 82, 85, 87, 90, 107, 424
Betz, B., 437
Blau, P., 77
Bloom, S., 147, 428
Blum, M.H., 114, 403
Bode, K., 86
Bodenheimer, E., 4, 20, 72, 167, 169, 184, 281
Boldizar, J.P., 147, 428
Bonnici, J., 88
Boyd, R., 439, 442
Boye, D., 87
Brabant, J., 99, 394, 397, 400
Bradley, F.H., 22, 24, 25, 59, 232
Brickman, P., 138, 139, 401
Brock, T.C., 86, 87
Brunas-Wagstaff, J. 216, 219, 222, 271, 391, 392, 400, 433
Buchanan, A., 6, 9, 10, 32, 33, 37, 73, 91, 340, 348, 350
Burgoyne, C., 139, 401, 454
Buss, A.H., 86, 87, 428
Butzin, C.A., 420
Buunk, B.P., 111, 402

Campbell, T., 6, 15, 32, 52, 55, 59, 68, 71, 156, 340, 374, 385, 387
Card, R., 64, 120, 130, 223, 240, 242, 245, 246, 247, 248, 251, 270
Carroll, J.S., 133, 423
Cashdan, E., 447
Casson, L., 167
Cate, R.M., 112, 402
Chrisman, K., 110, 112, 115, 402
Cicero, M.T., 281, 282
Clark, A., 230
Clark, M.S., 110, 111, 112, 115, 400, 402

Clarkson, U., 89
Clutton-Brock, T.H., 440, 441
Cochran, S., 88
Cohen, B.Z., 451
Cohen, R.L., 85, 88, 106, 117, 118, 121, 144, 150, 255, 405, 407
Colby, A., 126, 416, 417, 418, 419, 420
Cook, T.D., 88, 121, 123, 415
Cooter, R., 155
Copp, D., 49
Cosmides, L., 441, 447, 448
Coulton, G.C., 230
Cross, R., 64, 120, 130, 223, 240, 242, 245, 246, 247, 248, 251, 270
Cullen, B., 32, 73, 340
Curzon, L.B., 21, 64, 77, 120, 223, 240, 241, 242, 246

Damon, W., 122, 415, 420
Daniels, N., 32
Dawes, R.M., 140, 141, 427
Dawkins, R., 439
de Waal, F., 441
Deaux, K., 114, 402, 404
Deen, E., 114, 145, 401
Demore, S.W., 89
DeNisi, A.S., 88
Desmarais, S., 100, 102, 110, 111, 112, 401, 402, 404, 405
Deutsch, M., 11, 18, 105, 106, 109, 117, 138, 150, 397, 399
Donnerstein, E., 131, 134
Dunbar, R.I.M., 230, 260
Dunn, J., 311
Dunnette, M.D., 85, 86
Dweck, C.S., 420
Dworkin, R., 4, 5, 7, 10, 15, 16, 33, 37, 38, 52, 53, 54, 55, 56, 57, 139, 370, 385, 386

Ebbeson, E.B., 451
Edgeworth, F.Y., 330, 363
Elliott, G.C., 112, 396
Emler, N.P., 130, 131, 132, 133, 196, 395, 424
Enright, R.D., 123
Evans, C., 5, 8, 9, 13, 23, 59, 60, 62, 63, 64, 65, 67, 69, 233, 236
Eysenck. H.J., 24

Feather, N.T., 149, 411

Feinberg, J., 11, 13, 59, 60, 61, 62, 63, 66, 67, 69, 207, 209, 218, 235, 236, 249, 265, 266, 268
Fincham, F.D., 120
Finley, J., 183, 197
Fisher, J.D., 89
Flew, A., 4, 9, 12, 17, 25, 38, 64, 232
Fogerty, M., 9
Folger, R., 109, 138, 142, 143, 151, 396, 397
Frankena, W., 6, 9, 11
Franklin, R.L., 59, 60, 64, 65, 233
Fraser, C., 88
Freedman, S., 77
Friedman, D.,414
Friedman, M., 276
Friedman, R., 276
Fry, W.R., 109, 113, 144, 145, 397, 400
Furby, L., 5, 6, 128, 420
Furnham, A., 97, 395, 413

Gauthier, D., 47, 48, 49, 50, 52, 57, 138, 382, 383, 385
Gay, P., 300
Gergen, K.J., 80, 86
Gilligan, C., 127, 420
Glass, D.C., 87
Goode, E., 138
Gordon, S., 32
Green, D.G., 383
Greenberg, J., 88, 89, 106, 110, 118, 143, 144, 145, 151, 255, 407, 426
Gregovich, R.P., 437
Griffith, R., 88

Hamilton, V.L, 132
Hamilton, W.D., 438
Han, G., 437
Harder, R., 89
Hardin, G., 5, 47, 156
Harper, D.J., 97
Harris, R.J., 88, 92, 93, 94, 112, 114, 145, 149, 211, 391, 392, 402, 410
Hart, H.L.A., 245
Hartka, E., 88
Hassebrauck, M., 88
Hatfield, E., xvi, 82, 83, 84, 85, 86, 89, 90, 107, 117, 131, 134, 155, 393, 394
Hayek, F.A., 73
Hegel, F., 22, 45
Heider, F., 118, 120, 260

Henton, J.M., 112, 402
Herrnstein, R.J., 272
Hertz, J.H., 166, 260
Hill, J., 451
Himmelweit, H.T., 139, 401, 454
Hobbes, T., 3, 4, 9, 18, 23, 302, 303, 304, 305, 306, 307, 309, 310, 311, 320, 328, 331, 361, 376, 405, 407, 408
Hoffman, L.R., 112, 133, 425
Hogan, R., 130, 131, 132, 133, 196, 395, 424
Hohenfield, J.A., 89
Homans, G.C., 5, 77, 78, 79, 80, 81, 82, 83, 85, 88, 94
Honderich, T., 22, 23, 24, 65, 133, 423
Hook, J.G., 121, 123, 415
Hospers, J., 3, 4, 7, 16, 17, 18, 22, 59, 60, 64, 65, 156, 190, 233, 236, 243, 319
Houlihan, M.M., 90
Hume, D., 14, 301, 328, 329, 363, 364, 405
Humphries, P., 139, 401
Huppertz, J.W., 92
Hurst, N.L., 230
Huxley, T.H., 260, 442

Irani, K.D., 11

Jackson, J., 90
Jacobsen, P.R., 77, 80, 86
Jaeger, M., 139, 401, 454
Jaspers, J.M., 120
Jasso, G., 92
Jecker, J., 87
Johnson, M., 90, 112, 402
Johnson, S., 275
Jones, P.A., 64, 120, 130, 223, 240, 242, 245, 246, 247, 248, 251, 270
Jonsson, D.R., 128
Jorgenson, D.O., 86
Joyce, M.A., 112, 114, 145, 149, 213, 402, 410

Kahneman, D., 423
Kamin, L.J., 272, 273
Kanfer, R., 140
Kant, I., 16, 17, 19, 22, 30, 33, 127, 154, 318, 319, 320, 321, 322, 323, 324, 325, 331, 339, 357, 361, 362, 364, 367, 416

Karniol, R., 6
Karuza, J, 109, 113, 144, 145, 397, 400
Katz, M., 18, 139, 401, 413, 454
Kayser, E., 106, 114, 118, 255, 400, 405, 407
Kayser, E.T., 106, 114, 118, 255, 400, 405, 407
Kelley, H.H., 77, 246
Kelsen, H., 4
Kemp, J., 158, 319
Kleinig, J., 46, 59, 60, 61, 62, 63, 65, 67, 218, 236, 265
Kluegel, J.R., 413
Kohlberg, L., 6, 7, 123, 125, 126, 127, 128, 154, 416, 417, 418, 419, 420, 421
Komorita, S.S., 94, 137, 218
Konecni, V.J., 451
Kramer, R.M., 165, 166, 437
Kramer, S.N., 165, 166, 437
Kravitz, D.A., 94, 137, 218
Kurtz, S., 140

Lamm, H., 112, 114, 118, 148, 255, 400, 403, 407
Landy, D., 87
Lane, R., 413
Lansberg, I., 5, 88
Larson, J., 112, 402
Laurence, J-R., 123, 125, 237
Lee, D., 22, 43, 167, 170, 172
Legant, P., 87
Lenin, V., 345, 348, 349
Leo XIII, Pope, 292, 308
Lerner, M.J., 10, 13, 87, 95, 96, 97, 98, 99, 100, 101, 102, 103, 104, 109, 110, 111, 112, 117, 119, 121, 130, 140, 222, 260, 392, 393, 394, 395, 397, 399, 400, 401, 402, 404, 405, 407, 415, 424
Leventhal, G.S., 86, 109, 112, 113, 114, 118, 139, 140, 144, 145, 147, 255, 397, 400, 401, 402, 407, 425
Levi, S., 89
Levin, M., 12
Lickona, T., 126
Liebrand, W.B.G., 437
Lind, E.A., 10, 140
Lindskold, S., 437
Lippa, R.A., 423
Lloyd, S.A., 112, 402

Locke, J., 34, 36, 42, 311, 312, 313, 314, 315, 316, 317, 339, 342, 359, 376, 377, 381
Lord, R.G., 89
Lucas, J.R., 6, 10, 11, 13, 32, 41, 59, 60, 61, 63, 131, 236, 370
Luce, R.D., 137
Lukes, S., 340
Lurigio, A.J., 133, 423

Mace, R., 454
Machan, T.R., 12
MacIntyre, A., 8, 13, 17, 37, 38, 44, 45, 72, 159, 174, 224, 236, 280, 281, 299, 300, 327, 353
MacPherson, C.B., 317
Maier, N.R.F., 112
Major, B., 114, 402, 404
Mark, M.M., 89
Markovsky, B., 72, 423
Marshall, G., 139, 401, 454
Martin, M.W., 112, 286, 402
Marwell, G., 86
Marx, K.H., 73, 265, 317, 335, 336, 340, 341, 342, 343, 344, 345, 346, 347, 348, 349, 350, 359
Matthews, G., 87, 96, 393
McClintock, C.G., 123, 415, 437
Meeker, B.F., 112, 396
Mellers, B.A., 88, 93, 137, 149, 155, 401, 404
Messick, D.M., 88, 93, 147, 148, 409, 428, 442
Mettee, D.R., 87
Meyer, J.P., 120, 400
Michaels, J.W., 114, 118, 145, 255, 401, 407
Mikula, G., 109, 144, 149, 397, 411
Mill, J.S., 328
Miller, D.T., 6, 12, 37, 59, 67, 70, 95, 96, 100, 132,133 134, 159, 393, 395, 424, 425
Miller, F.D., 379
Miller, J.L., 133, 425
Mills, J., 110, 111, 400
Molander, P., 437
Montada, L., 6
Montague, P., 13
Moore L.M., 86
Moore, C.F., 86, 122, 419
Morgan, W.R., 415
Morse, S.J., 86

Moschetti, G.J., 92
Muhlhausen, S.M., 128
Mulherin, A., 120, 400
Murphy, C.F., 25, 38, 42, 232
Musante, L., 140
Mussen, P., 123, 126

Nelson, S.A., 114, 403, 420
Nielsen, K., 32
Norrie, A., 240, 246, 247, 453
Nozick, R., xi, 7, 8, 9, 12, 13, 19, 20, 29, 33, 34, 35, 36, 37, 38, 39, 42, 43, 44, 45, 46, 47, 51, 52, 56, 57, 159, 375, 376, 377, 378, 379, 380, 381, 382, 383, 385

Ordonez, L.D., 149, 401, 404
Orpen, C., 88
Orpheus, 167
Oskamp, S., 437

Parker, G.A., 440, 441
Peplau, L.A., 97, 395
Perry, C., 237
Peterson, C., 110
Pietras, M., 206
Pius XI, Pope, 291, 293, 362
Plato, 169, 170, 171, 173, 174, 175, 176, 177, 178, 179, 180, 181, 182, 183, 184, 185, 191, 192, 194, 200, 201, 202, 203, 205, 207, 231, 236, 237, 244, 261, 274, 280, 281, 288, 307, 331, 354, 364, 407, 428
Posner, R.A., 7, 15, 17, 156, 315, 365, 383, 414, 452, 454
Pritchard, R.D., 85, 86
Procter, E., 97, 395

Raiffa, H., 137
Rasmussen, D., 20, 44
Rawls, J., 5, 7, 8, 9, 10, 13, 19, 21, 25, 29, 30, 31, 32, 33, 37, 38, 39, 40, 41, 42, 44, 45, 46, 47, 48, 52, 57, 66, 156, 159, 232, 265, 368, 369, 370, 371, 372, 374, 378, 381, 382, 390, 424, 431
Rescher, N., 11
Reynolds, W.A., 90, 112, 402
Roberts, J.V., 132
Roberts, S., 221
Robinson, J., 90
Robinson, R.V., 139, 401, 454

Rodriques, A., 110, 399
Roemer, J., 55
Romer, D., 93
Rook, K.S. 90
Rosenfield, D., 150, 411
Ross, W.D., 73, 190, 191, 198
Rousseau, J.J., 335, 336, 337, 338, 339, 361, 364
Routh, D., 139, 401, 454
Rubin, Z., 97, 105, 395
Russell, B., 165, 166, 167, 168, 174, 176, 260, 282, 284, 300, 337
Ryan, W., 18, 97

Sabini, J., 98, 137, 394, 404, 437
Sadurski, W., 4, 6, 9, 10, 13, 59, 60, 62, 63, 64, 65, 66, 67, 68, 69, 131, 133, 139, 191, 196, 206, 207, 208, 209, 219, 233, 236, 239, 245, 255, 265, 267, 269, 294, 308, 309, 357, 423, 431, 443, 449
Sampson, E.E., 11, 18, 105, 119, 137, 158, 244, 280
Samuel, W., 92, 98, 275
Samuelson, C.D., 147, 428
Sanford, C., 114, 145, 401
Sawyer, J., 415
Schanz, V., 118, 255, 407
Scherer, K.R., xi
Schmitt, D.R., 86
Schokkaert, E., 21, 54, 55, 153, 155, 156
Schwinger, T., 106, 107, 109, 112, 114, 118, 144, 148, 149, 255, 397, 402, 403, 405
Semmel, B., 332, 334
Sentis, K.P., 93, 148
Shaver, K.G., 120, 121, 238, 246, 248
Sheppard, B.H., 109, 144, 151, 396, 397
Sher, G., 6
Sidgwick, H., 6
Silver, M., 8, 12, 13
Simmons C.H., 87, 96, 393
Simon, E., 149, 300, 411
Simon, G.S., 149, 300, 411
Simpson, J.E., 133, 425
Slote, M.A., 59, 68, 209
Smith, A., 307, 313, 314 408
Smith, E.R., 413
Snarey, J.R., 126
Spinoza, B., 254
Stafford, E., 451
Stake, J.E., 109, 148, 399, 403

Steensma, H., 114, 145, 401
Stephenson, G.M., 128, 133, 423, 425
Stout, S., 437
Sweeney, P.D., 88
Swift, A., 139, 401, 406, 454
Symonds, M., 97

Tawney, R.H., 344
Thibaut, J.W., 77, 139, 141
Tobiasen, J.M., 77
Tooby, J., 441, 447, 448
Topitsch, E., 108
Traupman, J., 90
Treasure, F.P., 88
Trivers, R.L., 438, 440
Trusted, J., 174, 237, 301
Tversky, A., 423
Tyler, T.R., 10, 140, 141, 144, 145, 426, 427

Valenzi, E.R., 86
VanYperen, N.W., 111, 402
Vaughn, K.I., 311, 312, 313, 315, 317
Vickrey, W.S., 14
Vidmar, N., 132, 133, 134, 424, 425
Vlastos, G., 11, 12, 265, 347, 374, 375
Von Grumbkow, J., 114, 145, 401

Wagstaff, G.F., 88, 93, 97, 211, 212, 215, 216, 219, 222, 244, 252, 271, 365, 366, 382, 391, 392, 395, 396, 397, 399, 400, 413, 421, 422, 426, 432, 433, 450
Walker, L., 139, 141
Walster, E., 82, 83, 84, 85, 87, 90, 91, 92, 93, 94, 107, 117, 118, 129, 131, 194, 424, 435
Walster, G.W., 82, 84, 85, 90, 92, 93, 107, 424
Weaver, F.M., 133, 423
Wiener, Y., 86
Wilke, H., 114, 145, 401

Yaari, M., 429, 430
Yost, E.A., 89

Zelditch, M., 85

SUBJECT INDEX

Abstract labour, 342
Adversarial procedures, 140, 426
Agathon, 171
Agreement, 47
Allocation preferences, 145, 147, 150, 386, 396, 402, 404, 410, 411
Altruism, 438
   reciprocal, 438, 440, 444
Arete, 171, 186
Arithmetic proportion, 205, 208, 209, 240
Attractiveness, 79, 148, 403
Attributions, 117, 118, 120, 121, 126, 144, 149, 150, 200, 397, 423
Autonomous morality, 124
Axia, 193

Bargaining, 48, 50, 52, 137, 138, 307, 314, 382, 408
Behaviour control, 132
Blame, 59, 60, 64, 103, 120, 121, 144, 165, 188, 190, 201, 230, 239, 242, 243, 245, 246, 329, 413, 425

Capitalism, 158, 203, 340, 341, 344, 349, 350
Caring, 128, 420, 421
Categorical imperative, 16, 17, 19, 127, 154, 319, 323, 324, 325, 367, 416
Catholic Church, 300
Cheating, 170, 438, 440, 441, 447, 451, 453
Choice, 14, 30, 66, 120, 149, 178, 179, 186, 188, 189, 192, 200, 201, 230, 233, 239, 241-253, 258, 260-271, 264, 265, 266, 268, 270, 271, 281, 285, 286, 289, 293, 300, 339, 354, 360, 383, 386, 387, 392, 396, 404, 408, 410, 415, 417, 446, 452
Christianity, 108, 283, 288, 289

Collective responsibility, 260, 452
Commensurateness of inputs and outcomes, 216, 219, 223, 244, 257, 295
Communal orientation, 111, 159, 402
Communism, 283, 345, 348, 350
Complex equality, 71, 72, 389, 421
Consensus principle, 246
Consent, 16, 17, 18, 35, 158, 194, 306, 309, 315, 328, 356, 360, 361, 363, 368
Contract, 21, 37, 41, 99, 101, 103, 104, 291, 296, 303, 306, 307, 308, 312, 315, 320, 337, 343, 356, 360, 361, 363, 368, 377, 382, 387, 395, 422, 455
Contractarianism, 48, 172, 368, 371
Conventional morality, 125
Corrective justice, 21
Covenant, 18, 306, 307
Culpability, 56, 103, 133, 134, 360, 423, 425, 449

Darwinian justice, 109, 438
Desert, 13, 24, 31, 37, 44-71, 102, 103, 159-164, 169, 180, 182, 183, 184, 192, 200-220, 224, 231-236, 238, 240, 243, 244, 245, 248, 255, 256, 259, 260, 261, 263, 264-267, 269, 271-276, 279, 280, 283, 286, 287, 288, 294, 296, 299-311, 314, 316-318, 321, 325, 328, 329, 334, 335, 343, 348, 350, 353, 354, 355, 358-409, 411, 415, 417-425, 427, 428, 431, 432, 441, 442, 452, 455, 456
   entitlement and, 9, 13, 21, 35, 37, 45, 62, 63, 95, 99, 102, 103, 159, 223, 269, 314, 358, 363, 381, 395
   game theory and, 137

merit and, 11, 13, 19, 31, 61, 63, 122, 160, 164, 223, 245, 260, 286, 287, 289, 306, 307, 323, 325, 328, 333, 334, 337, 338, 374, 416, 418
philosophy of, 59-74
responsibility and, 64
virtue and, 66, 130, 186, 187, 189, 191, 192, 200, 201, 237, 247, 280, 281, 282, 285, 289, 290, 300, 301, 312, 322, 323, 324, 325, 328, 331, 332, 334, 337, 338, 353, 354, 357, 360, 362, 367, 372, 374
Determinism, 300, 301, 302, 309, 318, 332
Deterministic egalitarianism, 302, 349, 368, 371, 378, 385, 412, 417, 419, 420, 421, 423
Deterrence, 22
Development of justice, 121, 122, 414, 419
Difference principle, 31, 127, 370, 371, 431
Dikaiosune, 168, 170, 173, 174, 183, 282
Dike, 168, 170, 174, 176, 180, 183, 191, 202, 354
Distributive justice, 39, 131, 337
Divine justice, 284, 322
Duress, 245, 246, 247, 248, 249, 270, 306, 308

EAD (Equity as Desert) principle, 244, 252, 260, 263, 264, 268, 273, 276, 279, 282, 283, 284, 289-296, 304, 309, 310, 312, 317, 321, 328, 330, 333, 338, 342, 343, 346, 347, 364, 365, 367, 368, 371, 374, 375, 382, 383-412, 414- 427, 429, 430-437, 441, 442, 443, 445, 446, 448, 449, 452, 453, 455
Efficiency, 65, 67, 137, 155, 156, 430, 445, 446
Effort, 32, 60, 62, 65, 66, 68, 69, 78, 79, 101, 114, 118, 133, 148, 149, 150, 164, 182, 207, 208, 209, 219, 220, 229, 236, 255, 256, 257, 258, 259, 293, 294, 296, 324, 346, 347, 348, 368, 373, 389, 399, 400, 406, 409, 411, 413, 428, 444, 445, 446, 447, 453, 456
Egalitarianism, 33, 52, 53, 139, 157, 159, 264, 272, 281, 304, 305, 310, 330, 337, 374, 375, 381, 382, 384, 388, 394, 401, 412, 417, 419, 421, 447, 454
deterministic, 302, 349, 368, 371, 378, 385, 412, 417, 419, 420, 421, 423
Enlightenment, Age of, 299, 327, 360, 368
Equal opportunity, 244
Equal pay, 291
Equality, 105, 109, 146, 264, 333, 336
complex, 71, 72, 389, 421
geometrical, 183, 193, 194, 195, 198, 202, 206, 208, 211, 235, 244, 280, 325, 337, 355, 357
pay and, 291
residual, 432
Equity, 9, 54, 77-150, 155, 156, 158, 160, 163, 164, 191, 194, 199-240, 250, 254, 259, 263, 265, 266, 267, 276, 282, 304, 305, 306, 324, 325, 329, 338, 355, 364, 365, 371, 382, 391, 392, 393, 394, 395, 396, 397, 403, 404, 411, 416, 421, 422, 423, 424, 435, 442- 449, 450, 457
desert as, 243, 244, 247, 249, 250, 256, 263, 264, 266, 267, 268, 270, 279, 304, 323, 335, 348, 350
game theory and, 137
inputs in, 79-106, 110, 114, 118, 129, 143, 150, 194, 199, 207, 208, 211-219, 222-275, 283, 284, 289, 291-296, 308, 312, 321, 323, 324, 339, 342, 344, 346, 347, 349, 357, 366, 374, 375, 382-392, 396-422, 426, 428, 429, 431, 432, 443, 444, 446, 447, 449
negative inputs in, 83, 87, 92, 93, 98, 210, 211, 213, 216, 223, 228, 231, 263, 264, 265, 323, 365, 389, 390, 422, 427, 433, 443, 449
outcomes in, 10, 12, 53, 79, 80, 81, 82, 83-95, 98, 101-112, 118-120, 129, 131, 139, 140, 144, 146, 149, 181, 194, 199, 207-225, 228, 230, 231, 238-244, 249-259, 263- 271, 273, 274, 283, 284, 291-5, 296, 301, 308, 309, 314, 316, 317, 323, 339, 342, 345, 346, 347, 349, 356, 358, 359, 365- 371, 374, 375, 377, 379, 382-, 396, 399-412, 417- 428, 431, 432, 437, 440, 441, 443, 444, 446, 449, 452, 453, 454
theory, 77-94, 95-135, 137-151, 392-395, 422, 423, 435

491

Fairness 5, 8, 13, 29, 30, 40, 53, 54, 56, 77, 125, 127, 139, 140, 142, 143, 144, 145, 147, 149, 155, 163, 183, 202, 235, 306, 355, 360, 403, 404, 409, 410, 421, 425, 426, 427, 433

Inequity, 78
Inheritance, 293, 316, 322, 382
Inherited wealth, 293, 317, 339, 354, 364, 384, 453, 455
Input moderators, 270, 271, 396,382-392, 396-400, 403, 406-408, 411, 413, 418-422, 426, 428, 429, 431, 432, 443, 444, 446, 447, 449
Intelligence, 30, 61, 62, 65, 66, 79, 164, 235, 255, 272, 273, 275, 281, 368, 369, 413

Jus aequitatis, 325
Just price, 290, 291, 296, 307, 313, 314, 315, 316, 376
Just wages, 71, 176, 216, 291, 292, 294, 295, 341, 343, 345
Just World theory, 97, 98, 222
Justice
  adversarial, 140, 426
  allocation preferences and, 145, 147, 150, 386, 396, 402, 404, 410, 411
  Ancient Greece and, 165, 167, 169, 185, 309, 354
  attributions and, 117, 118, 120, 121, 126, 144, 149, 150, 200, 397, 423
  benevolence and, 4, 6, 17, 282, 288, 319, 320, 324, 327, 420, 421
  cognitive evaluation and, 424
  commutative, 9, 290, 294, 306, 307, 309, 355, 360, 408, 416
  comparative, 13, 129, 243, 271, 422
  consent and, 16, 17, 18, 35, 158, 194, 306, 309, 315, 328, 356, 360, 361, 363, 368
  contract and, 21, 37, 41, 99, 101, 103, 104, 291, 296, 303, 306, 307, 308, 312, 315, 320, 337, 343, 356, 360, 361, 363, 368, 377, 382, 387, 395, 422, 455
  corrective, 7, 8, 21, 194, 206, 207, 355, 416, 422, 423, 431
  covenants and, 18, 306, 307
  Darwinian, 109, 438
  desert and, 13, 24, 31, 37, 44, 45- 71, 102, 103, 159, 160, 163, 164, 169, 180-184, 192, 200-211, 214, 218, 219, 220, 224, 231-240, 243, 244, 245, 248, 255, 256, 259, 260-273, 276, 279, 280, 283, 286, 287, 288, 294, 296, 299, 300, 302, 305-311, 314, 316-318, 321, 325, 328, 329, 334, 335, 343, 348, 350, 353, 354, 355, 358, 359-396, 402, 406-409, 411, 415, 417-422, 424-428, 431, 432, 441, 442, 452, 455, 456
  development of, 103, 105, 110, 121, 122, 123, 125, 126, 166, 284, 300, 312, 393, 414, 415, 417, 419
  distributive, 8, 9, 11, 21, 31, 35, 38, 39, 40, 42, 45, 70, 71, 105, 122, 123, 129, 130, 131, 139, 141, 142, 145, 191, 194, 195, 220, 227, 233, 280, 290, 304, 306, 330, 333, 371, 378, 387, 389, 416, 422, 424, 432
  divine, 284, 322
  economic, 9, 11, 14, 15, 31, 33, 62, 65, 105, 109, 110, 112, 113, 133, 147, 148, 153, 154, 155, 156, 157, 158, 197, 290, 294, 299, 312, 314, 316, 344, 348, 362, 373, 375, 385, 398, 414, 423, 430, 431, 432, 443, 444, 447, 452
  efficiency and, 65, 67, 137, 155, 156, 430, 445, 446
  entitlement and, 9, 13, 21, 35, 37, 45, 62, 63, 95, 99, 102, 103, 159, 223, 269, 314, 358, 363, 381, 395
  equal treatment and, 10
  equality and, 12, 13, 19, 30, 31, 32, 37, 38, 40, 41, 52, 53, 54, 55, 67, 68, 73, 78, 79, 101, 103, 104, 105, 106, 107, 108, 109-113, 119-128, 134, 143, 145, 146, 147, 149, 150, 158, 178, 182, 183, 193- 203, 206- 210, 250, 264, 265, 273, 276, 280- 283, 299, 304, 306, 308, 310, 321, 328, 330, 335,-339, 347, 348, 349, 358, 360, 369, 370, 371, 384, 388, 389, 394, 396-399, 403, 404, 407, 410, 414-421, 422, 430, 449
  evolutionary theory and, 438, 439, 441, 442, 443, 447, 450, 451, 453, 455, 456
  expediency and, 15, 40, 146, 147, 333, 398, 405
  fairness and, 5, 8, 13, 29, 30, 40, 53, 54, 56, 77, 125, 127, 139, 140, 142,

143, 144, 145, 147, 149, 155, 163,
183, 202, 235, 306, 355, 360, 403,
404, 409, 410, 421, 425, 426, 427,
433
impartiality and, 16, 19, 48, 50, 51,
153, 333, 356, 360, 383, 387, 418
law and, 3, 4, 5, 7, 8, 16, 17, 20, 21,
23, 31, 44, 46, 56, 64, 68, 77, 108,
120, 125, 130, 163, 165, 166, 167,
168, 171, 183, 188, 191, 193, 194,
200-209, 222, 223, 227- 232, 239,
241- 251, 254, 270, 275, 281, 282,
283, 289, 291, 299, 302-306, 308,
309, 310, 313, 316, 319, 320, 324,
336, 337- 340, 349, 355, 356, 360,
361, 363, 375, 380, 418, 431, 432,
440, 453, 455
liberty and, 19, 20, 29, 31, 33, 34, 39,
41, 42, 44, 53, 56, 125, 269, 303,
304, 339, 370
macro and micro, 138, 139, 290, 390,
401
Mesopotamian, 165, 166, 167, 168
moral development and, 123, 124, 125,
126, 144, 415, 416, 420, 422
morality and, 4, 5, 6, 8, 16, 24, 38,
44, 47, 72, 123, 125, 127, 128, 154,
170, 191, 236, 318, 320, 322, 323,
325, 327, 334, 353, 362, 363, 420,
421
motive, 98, 99, 101, 102, 103, 117,
119, 121, 130, 141, 154, 393, 395
multiprinciple approach to, 70, 100,
103, 105, 107, 108, 110, 112, 113,
115, 119, 123, 143, 144, 146, 147,
150, 155, 387, 388, 396, 397, 398,
405
natural, 292, 308, 364
need and, 10, 12, 18, 19, 24, 37, 45,
64, 67, 70, 73, 80, 84, 91, 94, 96,
98, 99, 100-122, 127, 128, 137,
144, 146, 147, 148, 159, 163, 165,
186, 196-200, 209, 210, 214, 216,
219, 236, 252, 255, 257, 264-276,
286, 293, 294, 296, 300, 304, 307,
311, 313, 314, 317, 325, 336, 339,
341, 344, 347-350, 359, 364, 365,
369, 373, 374, 380, 387-398, 400-
404, 412-, 428, 430, 432, 435, 436,
438, 446, 447, 449, 453
neutrality and, 51, 154, 384, 387

procedural, 8, 10, 53, 139, 140, 141,
142, 143, 144, 145, 154, 157, 370,
383, 425, 426, 427
property and, 7, 11, 14, 19, 20, 21, 31,
36, 38, 40, 42, 52, 86, 89, 127,
153, 176, 222, 264, 280, 281, 293,
305, 311, 312, 316, 317, 319, 321,
329, 336, 337, 339, 340, 341, 342,
345, 348, 350, 359, 363, 364, 375,
376, 380, 381, 416, 418, 419, 455
punishment and, 22, 23, 24, 39, 41,
42, 43, 56, 59, 60, 64, 65, 69, 95,
103, 124, 126, 128-133, 157, 158,
165, 167, 168, 172, 175, 177, 180,
192, 196, 201, 205- 210, 213, 214,
218, 220, 228- 232, 240, 245, 247,
249, 251, 252, 267, 270, 284, 286,
288, 289, 301, 305, 306, 317, 321,
325, 330, 334, 338, 348, 349, 358,
360, 361, 367, 371, 379, 393, 415,
417, 418, 419, 422, 423, 431, 440,
442, 448, 450, 451, 452, 453
rationality and, 14, 16, 17, 30, 33, 42,
45, 47, 48, 49, 50, 52, 72, 73, 137,
173, 186, 289, 315, 318, 319, 323,
325, 443, 444
reciprocity and, 79, 101, 105, 111,
122, 124, 125, 191, 196, 197, 201,
223- 225, 227, 229, 233, 307, 355,
360, 401, 414, 415, 436, 439, 440,
441, 446, 447, 449, 450, 451, 453
rectificatory, 191, 194, 195, 196, 227,
233, 309
responsibility and, 40, 43, 46, 55, 60,
62- 65, 66, 69, 103, 106, 117, 118,
119, 120, 121, 124, 126, 133, 140,
144, 149, 150, 178, 179, 180, 187,
188, 189, 192, 196, 199, 200, 209,
219, 220, 233, 236, 238, 239, 242,
243, 247, 248, 249, 255, 259, 260,
261, 263, 266, 271, 272, 289, 301,
325, 354, 358, 364, 371, 378, 379,
382, 392, 396, 404, 415, 417, 418,
423, 425, 426, 442, 446, 447, 451,
452, 453, 454
retribution and, 22, 23, 43, 44, 59,
130, 132, 133, 134, 180, 331, 417,
439
retributive, 43, 130, 131, 132, 133,
417, 422
rights and, 5, 7, 8, 11, 12, 13, 20, 21,
22, 34, 36, 37, 38, 42, 43, 44, 45,

52, 53, 70, 108, 125, 127, 153, 300,
317, 321, 325, 329, 330, 333, 348,
357, 358, 360, 376, 377, 385, 387,
416, 418, 419, 422, 430
sport and, 89, 405, 406
universal, 190, 191, 192, 193
utility and, 11, 14, 15, 19, 29, 122,
155, 156, 157, 274, 276, 321, 328,
329, 330, 331, 334, 339, 360, 362,
363, 366, 370, 375, 419, 422, 429,
430, 455

Kantianism, 16, 17, 365

Labour abstract, 342
Labour surplus, 343
Labour theory of value, 313, 314, 343,
344, 345, 359
Law, 3, 4, 5, 7, 8, 16, 17, 20, 21, 23, 31,
44, 46, 56, 64, 68, 77, 108, 120,
125, 130, 163, 165, 166, 167, 168,
171, 183, 188, 191, 193, 194, 200,
202, 205, 206, 209, 222, 223, 227,
229, 230, 232, 239, 241, 242, 245,
246, 247, 248, 249, 251, 254, 270,
275, 281, 282, 283, 289, 291, 299,
302, 304, 305, 306, 308, 309, 310,
313, 316, 319, 320, 324, 336, 337,
338, 339, 340, 349, 355, 356, 360,
361, 363, 375, 380, 418, 431, 432,
440, 453, 455
Law of nature, 4, 23, 281, 299, 305, 355
Least inequitable solution, 212, 213, 218,
220, 230, 240, 251, 365, 407, 431,
452
Lex talionis, 166, 196, 227, 229, 230, 283
Libertarianism, 231
Liberty, 31, 38, 268
Lot, allocation by, 407
Lottery, 97, 217, 244, 408, 409, 433

Maat, 167, 168, 180, 183
Macrojustice, 138, 139, 290, 390, 401
Market price, 295, 314, 315
Maximal difference rule, 106, 404, 405,
408, 410
Me, 165, 166, 167, 168, 180, 183
Microjustice, 138, 139, 290, 401
Moral development, 123, 124, 125, 126,
144, 415, 416, 420, 422
Morality, 4, 5, 6, 8, 16, 24, 38, 44, 47,
72, 123, 125, 127, 128, 154, 170,

191, 236, 318, 320, 322, 323, 325,
327, 334, 353, 362, 363, 420, 421
conventional, 125
heteronomous, 123
Multiprinciple approach to justice, 70, 100,
103, 105, 107, 108, 110, 112, 113,
115, 119, 123, 143, 144, 146, 147,
150, 155, 387, 388, 396, 397, 398,
405

Natural rights, 34, 55, 300, 375, 377, 379
Necessity, 18, 52, 233, 245, 247, 256,
270, 301, 308, 315, 325, 332, 373,
396, 427
Need, 109, 265, 270, 272
Negative inputs, 83, 87, 92, 93, 98, 210,
211, 213, 216, 223, 228, 231, 263,
264, 265, 323, 365, 389, 390, 422,
427, 433, 443, 449

Original sin, 260, 285, 286
Outcome adjustment, 265, 268, 275, 293,
396

Parallel competition, 101, 102, 405, 407
Pareto-optimality, 155, 157, 158, 231, 362
Perfect equity, 211, 212, 213, 214, 215,
216, 217, 218, 222, 224, 227, 230,
231, 232, 238, 240, 244, 250, 263,
266, 358, 365, 366, 391
Plato's Republic, 169, 170, 175, 179, 231,
307
Positive evaluation, 145
Post conventional morality, 127
Procedural choice, 143, 144, 427
Procedural justice, 141, 142, 425
Productivity, 105, 109, 112, 113, 129,
141, 146, 147, 148, 312, 398, 399,
403, 446
Promises, 174, 309, 319, 356, 417, 418,
419
Property, 7, 11, 14, 19, 20, 21, 31, 36,
38, 40, 42, 52, 86, 89, 127, 153,
176, 222, 264, 280, 281, 293, 305,
311, 312, 316, 317, 319, 321, 329,
336, 337, 339, 340, 341, 342, 345,
348, 350, 359, 363, 364, 375, 376,
380, 381, 416, 418, 419, 455
Property rights, 19, 36, 52, 127, 153, 264,
311, 329, 364, 376, 380, 381, 418
Protestantism, 300
Punishment, 22, 132, 374, 451

deterrence and, 22, 23, 43, 56, 69, 132, 133, 158, 379, 429, 450, 451
expiatory, 124
rehabilitation and, 133, 423

Rationalizations, 149, 150, 410, 411
Reciprocal altruism, 438, 440, 444
Reciprocal proportion, 197, 198, 206, 208, 210, 294
Reciprocity, 79, 101, 105, 111, 122, 124, 125, 191, 196, 197, 201, 223, 224, 225, 227, 229, 233, 307, 355, 360, 401, 414, 415, 436, 439, 440, 441, 446, 447, 449, 450, 451, 453
Rectificatory justice, 191, 194, 195, 196, 227, 233, 309
Rehabilitation, 133, 423
Reparation, 168, 229
Residual equality, 432
Responsibility, 120, 239, 266, 325, 442
Rewards, 201, 338

Scholastics, 290, 291, 292, 293, 296, 299, 306, 307, 308, 313, 314, 315, 316, 318, 344
Self-restraint, 206, 207, 449
Slavery, 15, 18, 180, 197, 249, 275, 358, 411, 412
Social contract, 30, 33, 41, 153, 337, 368
Social value, 154, 291, 295, 314, 316
Socialism, 337, 345, 350
Sport, 404

State of nature, 34, 42, 303, 309, 311, 320, 336, 337, 376
Stoicism, 281, 282
Suckers, 438, 439
Summum bonum, 280, 289, 362
Surplus labour, 343

Tit for tat, 436, 437, 439, 441

Universal justice, 190, 191, 192, 193
Utilitarianism, 154, 155, 331
Utility, 11, 14, 15, 19, 29, 122, 155, 156, 157, 274, 276, 321, 328, 329, 330, 331, 334, 339, 360, 362, 363, 366, 370, 375, 419, 422, 429, 430, 455

Veil of ignorance, 30, 33, 45, 50, 368, 370, 371
Virtue, 66, 130, 186, 187, 189, 191, 192, 200, 201, 237, 247, 280, 281, 282, 285, 289, 290, 300, 301, 312, 322, 323, 324, 325, 328, 331, 332, 334, 337, 338, 353, 354, 357, 360, 362, 367, 372, 374
Voluntariness, 179, 187, 188, 189, 192, 194, 195, 196, 233, 239, 242, 245, 246, 267, 280, 309

Winner takes all, 128, 137, 143, 408, 409

Zero inputs, 91, 92, 216, 222, 223, 254, 366

PROBLEMS IN CONTEMPORARY PHILOSOPHY

1. Petra von Morstein, **On Understanding Works of Art: An Essay in Philosophical Aesthetics**
2. David Basinger and Randall Basinger, **Philosophy and Miracle: The Contemporary Debate**
3. Francisco Peccorini Letona, **Selfhood as Thinking Thought in the Work of Gabriel Marcel: A New Interpretation**
4. Corbin Fowler, **The Logic of U.S. Nuclear Weapons Policy: A Philosophical Analysis**
5. Marcus P. Ford (ed.), **A Process Theory of Medicine: Interdisciplinary Essays**
6. Lars Aagaard-Morgensen (ed.), **The Idea of the Museum: Philosophical, Artistic, and Political Questions**
7. Kerry S. Walters, **The Sane Society in Modern Utopianism**
8. Steven William Laycock, **Foundations for a Phenomenological Theology**
9. John R. Jacobson and Robert Lloyd Mitchell (eds.), **Existence of God: Essays** from *The Basic Issues Forum*
10. Richard J. Connell, **The Empirical Intelligence - The Human Empirical Mode: Philosophy As Originating in Experience**
11. Sander H. Lee (ed.), **Inquiries into Values: The Inaugural Session of the International Society for Value Inquiry**
12. Tobias Chapman, **In Defense of Mystical Ideas: Support for Mystical Beliefs from a Purely Theoretical Viewpoint**
13. Donald Stewart (ed.), **Entities and Individuation: Studies in Ontology and Language in Honour of Neil Wilson**
14. Peter Preuss, **Reincarnation: A Philosophical and Practical Analysis**
15. Tibor R. Machan, **The Moral Case for the Free Market Economy: A Philosophical Argument**
16. George Frederick Schueler, **The Idea of a Reason for Acting: A Philosophical Argument**
17a. William Lovitt and Harriet Brundage Lovitt, **Modern Technology in the Heideggerian Perspective, Volume I**
17b. William Lovitt and Harriet Brundage Lovitt, **Modern Technology in the Heideggerian Perspective, Volume II**
18. William Cooney (ed.), **Reflections on Gabriel Marcel: A Collection of Essays**
19. Mari Sorri and Jerry Gill, **A Post-Modern Epistemology: Language, Truth, and Body**
20. Adolf Portmann, **Essays in Philosophical Zoology by Adolf Portmann:** *The Living Form and The Seeing Eye*, Richard B. Carter (trans.)

21. George Englebretson, **Essays on the Philosophy of Fred Sommers: In Logical Terms**
22. Kevin Doran, **What is a Person: The Concept and the Implications for Ethics**
23. Ronald Roblin (ed.), **The Aesthetics of the Critical Theorists: Studies on Benjamin, Adorno, Marcuse, and Habermas**
24. William Lane Craig and Mark S. McLeod (eds.), **The Logic of Rational Theism: Exploratory Essays**
25. Barrie A. Wilson, **Hermeneutical Studies: Dilthey, Sophocles, and Plato**
26. John D. Jones, **Poverty and the Human Condition: A Philosophical Inquiry**
27. Fred Seddon, **An Introduction to the Philosophical Works of F.S.C. Northup**
28. Henry Benedict Tam, **A Philosophical Study of the Criteria for Responsibility Ascriptions: Responsibility and Personal Interaction**
29. Loretta Dornisch, **Faith and Philosophy in the Writings of Paul Ricoeur**
30. Charles Goossens, **Toward a Theory of Relativity of Truth in Morality and Religion**
31. Gerald Rochelle (ed.), **Time and Duration: A Philosophical Study by S.V. Keeling**
32. A.P. Martinich and Michael J. White, **Certainty and Surface in Epistemology and Philosophical Method: Essays in Honor of Avrum Stroll**
33. Albert B. Randall, **The Mystery of Hope in the Philosophy of Gabriel Marcel, 1888-1973: Hope and** *Homo Viator*
34. Jolana Poláková, **The Possibility of Transcendence: Human Destructiveness and the Universality of Constructive Relations,** translation from the Czech by Jan Valeska
35. Aidan Donalson, **The Thought of Lucien Goldmann: A Critical Study**
36. Aldo Trione, **The Aesthetics of the Mind–After Mallarmé,** translated by Gordon Poole, edited by Sergio Sorrentino
37. Daniel Rothbart, **Explaining the Growth of Scientific Knowledge: Metaphors, Models and Meanings**
38. Albert W.J. Harper, **The Philosophy of Time**
39. J. Fang, **Kant and Mathematics Today: Between Epistemology and Exact Sciences**
40. George Englebretsen, **Line Diagrams for Logic: Drawing Conclusions**
41. Garrett Barden, **Essays on a Philosophical Interpretation of Justice: The Virtue of Justice**
42. Jolana Poláková, **Searching for the Divine in Contemporary Philosophy: Tensions Between the Immanent and the Transcendent,** translated from Czech by Jan Valeška
43. Albert W.J. Harper, **The Philosophy of Self**

44. Anna Makolkin, **The Genealogy of Our Present Moral Disarray: An Essay in Comarative Philosophy**
45. Daniel Shaw, **A Study of the Complex and Disputed Philosophical Questions Surrounding Human Action**
46. Paul Bishop, **Synchronicity and Intellectual Intuition in Kant, Swedenborg, and Jung**
47. Keith A. Robinson, **Michel Foucault and the Freedom of Thought**
48. Adrian J. Reimers, **An Analysis of the Concepts of Self-Fulfillment and Self-Realization in the Thought of Karol Wojtyla, Pope John II**
49. Tchafu Mwamba, **Michael Polanyi's Philosophy of Science**
50. Graham F. Wagstaff, **An Integrated Psychological and Philosophical Approach to Justice: Equity and Desert**

B
105
.J87
W34
2001